THE PRACTICE OF HUMAN DEVELOPMENT AND DIGNITY

THE PRACTICE OF HUMAN DEVELOPMENT AND DIGNITY

EDITED BY
PAOLO G. CAROZZA
AND CLEMENS SEDMAK

University of Notre Dame Press
Notre Dame, Indiana

Library of Congress Control Number: 2020947033

ISBN: 978-0-268-10869-4 (Hardback)
ISBN: 978-0-268-10872-4 (WebPDF)
ISBN: 978-0-268-10871-7 (Epub)

CONTENTS

FIGURES AND TABLES

FIGURES

TABLES

ACKNOWLEDGMENTS

Special recognition is due above all to Elizabeth Hlabse for all her work in coordinating this project; without her help it is unlikely that the book would have come to fruition. We also thank Paula Mulherr for her support, along with the many outstanding staff persons at the Kellogg Institute for International Studies who contributed to the three successful international gatherings on dignity and development, in Rome and in South Bend, Indiana, that led to this volume. We are grateful for all the discussions with colleagues at the Kellogg Institute and the Center for Social Concerns, which helped clarify and develop the ideas explored in this book. Among them we would like to acknowledge especially Fr. Robert Dowd, CSC, and the Ford Family Program in Human Development Studies and Solidarity for providing a platform from which to engage in dignity-based development work and research.

We dedicate this volume to our families, through whom we have learned far more about the enactment of human dignity in practice than we could ever learn from books.

Human Dignity and the Practice of Human Development

Paolo G. Carozza and Clemens Sedmak

In the process of drawing up and adopting the Sustainable Development Goals (SDGs) in 2015, the United Nations secretary general's synthesis report endorsed human dignity as one of the six essential elements for delivering on the SDGs and appealed even in its title to the central ideal of dignity in the new development agenda.[1] But what exactly does human dignity have to do with, for example, the first SDG and its ambition to "eliminate poverty in all of its forms everywhere"? In fact, it is possible to reduce poverty in ways that simultaneously violate people's dignity—for instance, by allowing the grave abuse of human rights. Resettlement strategies that displace thousands of people and destroy rural communities come to mind. Efficiency in the production and distribution of material resources is not enough.

In his well-known radio talk "Education after Auschwitz," Jewish philosopher Theodor Adorno talks about the role of efficiency in the postwar world. He characterizes "the manipulative character" as a person who "makes a cult of action, activity, of so-called *efficiency* as such which reappears in the advertising image of the active person." And he continues by saying: "If I had to reduce this type of manipulative character to a formula—perhaps one should not do it, but it could also contribute to understanding—then I would call it the type of *reified consciousness*. People of such a nature have, as it were, assimilated themselves to things."[2] Adorno's remarks from April 1966 warn against a prevalence of a paradigm of agency that places efficiency at the center and encourages the development and employment of persons eager and able to enact this value. Enacting efficiency calls for a manipulative character who concentrates on fixing and transforming the world of things.

Obviously, transforming the world of things is a much-needed aspect of development work. We need wells and roads and communication tools and proper systems of production. But this is clearly not enough. Broadening the material things of development beyond economic growth to more human dimensions—say, through the Human Development Index or concepts of multidimensional poverty—can serve to remind us that a person does not live by bread alone. Even realizing the multitude of quantifiable aspects (e.g., employment rates, literacy rates, mortality rates) will not automatically lead to a more humane society.

What is missing in practices that accelerate economic performance and realize strategies of efficiency but cause people to lose their homes and treasured forms of life? One could argue that development work that is primarily focused on the efficiency of systems without attention to the human person suffers from "blindness to the human aspect," as Avishai Margalit called it.[3] It suffers from a distorted way of thinking that reduces human beings to objects. And then, what is missing is respect for, understanding of, and sensitivity to *human dignity*.

Development work done without sensitivity to human dignity is blind, and an understanding of human dignity without attention to human experiences and practices is empty. This is to say that development work can be "blind to the human aspect" and treat people as if they were objects, without a proper understanding of their dignity. The concept of dignity, in turn, can be abstracted from concrete life situations and experiences and can thus lose credibility and impact. We need to work toward a sincere dialogue between the experience of people and the concept of human dignity in development work. Dignity opens development to an awareness of those often-unidentified factors that are at play within development but make for the sustainability or unsustainability of the efforts. Dignity is a lens to a more integrated way of understanding and pursuing development. These are the fundamental concerns of this book.

ASPECTS OF THE CURRENT DEBATE

"Integral human development" is a concept that refers to the development of the whole person and to the development of all persons; this concept, referring to a variation of personalism,[4] pays special attention to practices of respecting human dignity. There have been significant developments in this area in recent years. In his foreword to the UN's 2015 *Millennium Development Goals Report*, then–Secretary General Ban Ki-Moon ended with this remark: "Reflecting on the MDGs and looking ahead to the next fifteen years, there is no question that we can deliver on our shared responsibility to put an end to poverty, leave no one behind and create a world of dignity for all."[5]

"A world of dignity for all"—this is a call to integral human development. Development theory and practice reflect a broad consensus that mere attention to aggregate economic growth is insufficient to advance people's well-being. Contemporary approaches to development seek ways to broaden its effective impact on a wide variety of conditions related to human flourishing. The growing recognition that development involves more than economic growth is reflected in the remarkable upsurge in international efforts to devise indices of well-being, referred to as part of the "beyond GDP" movement, which includes, *inter alia*, the Better Life Index, launched by the Organisation for Economic Co-operation and Development (OECD) in 2011; the establishment of the Stiglitz-Sen-Fitoussi Commission on economic performance and social progress in 2008 by the French government to investigate more comprehensive metrics for social progress; the Human Development Index, launched in 1990 by the United Nations Development Programme (UNDP); and national efforts to measure well-being in more than a dozen countries, including Bhutan, China, France, Germany, and the United Kingdom.

One clear expression of this desire for a more comprehensive or integral understanding of the ends of development can be found in the pervasive presence of appeals to human dignity in the work of development actors today. Paul Perrin's contribution to this volume provides a remarkable collection of invocations of dignity in the mission statements of international development and humanitarian relief organizations from all different parts of the world and diverse ethical and religious traditions.

Even so, it is far from clear exactly where and how human dignity fits into the development agenda. Notwithstanding the UN secretary general's reports referred to above, the term "human dignity" did not enter into the language of the formal UN resolution adopting the SDGs in 2015.[6] And even if present implicitly, what should we understand human dignity to actually mean in practice, and what does human dignity imply as to how we structure our efforts to achieve sustainable progress?

In fields such as bioethics and human rights, the meaning of human dignity and the exploration of its implications have been the subjects of intense discussion in recent years. In the development studies literature, however, there is at present a lacuna of rigorous or systematic scholarship relating the content and implications of human dignity for international development theory, policy, and practice.

THE CONCEPT OF HUMAN DIGNITY

While human dignity persists as a salient concept in the international context, particularly insofar as it undergirds the modern-day human rights framework, it remains a deeply contested concept. Human dignity has been presented as an imperative, as freedom, as autonomous status, as mutual recognition. The idea has been challenged by bioethical questions, especially with beginning and end-of-life issues and the possibilities offered by new biotechnological developments, for example, in the field of genetics. The concept has also had to confront a deeper understanding and recognition of pluralism and the increasingly controversial role of human rights in political discourse. There are voices that consider the concept of dignity redundant (as long as there is a proper understanding of autonomy) or misleading and suspect for use in establishing and preserving power constellations or even an empty placeholder for concepts and commitments that always come from elsewhere. Some would warn against the loftiness of the concept: it has been called a reminder of the "mystery" of the human person as well as a "conversation stopper" in public discourse.[7]

One key challenge of the concept has been the question of operationalization or enactment. How can dignity be "done"—how do we judge when it is being violated, and what is required in order to honor it? There are those who suggest that we do not need a general understanding of human dignity and that we will recognize violations of human dignity when we see them. There are philosophers like Avishai Margalit who would identify "humiliation" as the key criterion by which to judge violations of human dignity.[8]

In short, dignity is contested in terms of its status (inherent, conferred?), its foundation and justification (nature, reason, and conscience, or religious grounds?), and its enactment (what actions and practices does it constrain or require?). Does the idea of human dignity need a foundation at all? Is it a circular concept, as Joel Feinberg would see it, or a concept that does not require deeper anchoring, as anti-foundationalists (like Richard Rorty) might claim?[9]

Irrespective of its contested nature, the concept of dignity shapes the designs of programs as well as the self-understandings of nongovernmental organizations (NGOs). Most development actors today will make use of and reference the concept of human dignity. Indeed, human dignity has become a buzzword in development discourse; and buzzwords, as Paul Perrin reminds us in his contribution to this volume referring to development deconstructivist Andrea Cornwall, "gain their purchase and power through their vague and euphemistic qualities, their capacity to embrace a multitude of possible meanings, and their normative resonance."[10] This is certainly the case for the concept of dignity. It is vague, sounds beautiful, is semantically multifarious, and makes claims on people's behavior. It can be used to justify different types of arguments as well as different positions—so much so that both proponents and opponents of certain practices (abortion and assisted suicide obviously come to mind) invoke human dignity.

Is the invocation of dignity anything more than a compromise? Eleanor Roosevelt, who chaired the committee that approved the Universal

Declaration of Human Rights, noted: "Perhaps one of the things that some of us learned was that in international documents you must try to find words that can be accepted by the greatest number of people. Not the words you would choose as the perfect words, but the words that most people can say and that will accomplish the ends you will desire, and will be acceptable to practically everyone sitting around the table, no matter what their background, no matter what their beliefs might be."[11] Are "human dignity" such words? They clearly have the potential to keep antagonists in conversation as long as there is a commitment to dignity. They clearly have the potential to create common ground, so much so that conflicting parties can justify their conflicting claims by simultaneously making reference to the concept of dignity.

The Dutch philosopher Antoon de Baets has compared the role of philosophers when discussing the concept of human dignity with the pillow-bearer of the late Ethiopian emperor Haile Selassie; the pillow-bearer had to slide a pillow under the emperor's feet as soon as His Majesty had sat down to prevent his short legs from hanging in the air: "Dignity is a majestic term with short legs that needs to be supported from time to time when it appears in public."[12] The concept of dignity, as de Baets intimates, needs legs; these legs can be proper metaphysical foundations.

There is, however, not much hope that metaphysics is able to provide a basis that persons from different ideological backgrounds can agree upon. These legs, then, can also be "roots in practice." Ludwig Wittgenstein uses this image in a prominent place when he talks about the importance of being able to walk in practice: "We want to walk: so we need *friction*. Back to the rough ground!"[13]

THE EXPERIENCE AND PRACTICE OF HUMAN DIGNITY

We need exposure to and the contact with this rough ground. Many "legs" for the concept of dignity are on offer. Nonetheless, the extensive debate over human dignity, particularly as evidenced in the human rights context, has proven that theoretical or philosophical reflections, while important, are limited in their ability to generate shared understandings. What is their connection to experiences and practices? Taking human dignity seriously will lead to a specific culture of dignity, a particular way of life. Swiss philosopher Peter Bieri has argued that the concept of human dignity constitutes a form of life, a way of perceiving the world, and a way of living one's life. The main pillars of this form of life, according to Bieri, would be autonomy, encounter, respect for intimacy, truthfulness, self-respect, moral integrity, a sense of what matters, and acceptance of finitude.[14] Respecting human dignity would lead to a particular way of life built upon these pillars.

Conversely, development practice can benefit from more sustained systematic reflection in order to grasp the role of dignity beyond its inclusion in an organization's mission statement. Elaborating a conceptualization of dignity so as to produce both theoretical substance and practical import for development thus requires uniting rigorous normative reflection with contextually rich ethnographic data into a genuine *experience* of dignity in the context of human development.[15]

This volume, *The Practice of Human Development and Dignity*, gives emphasis to human experience, endeavoring to conceptualize human dignity in light of development *practice*. The book addresses what has been called the challenge of "doing dignity" in development work—what does it mean, in action, to take the dignity of the human person seriously? What does it mean to design programs and projects that are based on a fundamental respect for human dignity? What does it mean to practice and experience human dignity?

By asking these questions, the book follows an inductive approach; it refers to people's experiences, and it considers dialogue and encounter as important ways of doing justice to human dignity in practice. It emphasizes "dignity-enacting practices" such as listening and accompaniment. The various contributors to the book look at real people (rather than epistemic objects, that is, types of people who have been removed from concrete circumstances) and concrete contexts.

In so doing, the book follows upon a cascade of paradigm shifts in the development field. Des Gasper and Thanh-Dam Truong summarized the first three as a move from economism to human development and from human development to human security.[16] They describe the transition in the 1990s away from a singular emphasis on GDP to include other aspects of human development, taking into account the capability approach. While the human security approach never gained traction, more recently it could be said that the newest paradigm represented by the SDGs, following the influential work of the Brundtland Commission,[17] has added ecology and climate change to the human development agenda.

In this book, we do not propose a new "human dignity paradigm" to follow and replace its predecessors. Rather, we suggest that the implicit ideal behind all of these paradigms, and also behind the overall movement toward ever-broader understandings of those aspects of human flourishing that ought to be central to development work, is the recognition of human dignity. We find it worthwhile, therefore, to reflect on the role of human dignity in development work and development practices as the unifying key across varying ideas of development and the larger horizon within which ideas and practices of development evolve.

The volume is methodologically distinctive in bringing normative discourse regarding the ontological status of dignity into dynamic conversation with qualitative and quantitative insights related to the experience of dignity in development. Engaging the social sciences, philosophy, and legal and development theory, the volume undertakes a dialectical and systematic examination of human dignity, generating dialogue across the present impasse between theory and practice. The result is a rich multidisciplinary narrative argument relating how human dignity might serve as a point of synthesis across diverse development approaches by bringing clarity to development outcomes as well as to which interventions most effectively promote such outcomes.

CENTRAL CLAIMS AND CONCERNS

This volume, with its various contributions, has four overarching thematic areas of concern within which it makes its principal claims. First, the book argues for the *central importance of human experience and human practices*. We need to pay attention to the roles of encounter and accompaniment. An illustration of the real possibility and moral plausibility for this attention in the practice of development work has been offered by Steve Reifenberg and Elizabeth Hlabse, who discuss in this volume the role of community-based health workers who cultivate listening skills and honor local knowledge, that is, the experiential knowledge of people.

This respect for local knowledge is an expression of the attempt to over-come "epistemic injustice," as Miranda Fricker has called the fact that certain types of knowledge and certain persons as knowledge subjects are discounted.[18] A patient has, in many respects, a better understanding of her body and her health condition than a health professional who sees her for the first time during a brief consultation. Doctors and health workers trained in a relational paradigm are trained to think about the patients' needs as they understand them within their families and communities. They take the experience of the person in her social and cultural setting seriously. They need to understand their patients' lives and family contexts; they try to be "in the patients' shoes." Maria Sophia Aguirre and Martha Cruz-Zuniga convincingly argue on the basis of recent social network research that the relevance of relations for understanding health outcomes can hardly be overestimated. Relations provide a context, and a context provides "a sense of the given." Ilaria Schnyder von Wartensee talks about "tacit knowledge" as the kind of knowledge that is taken for granted on an experiential level.

The person with her experience is at the center of any sound narrative of development. One way of understanding the lived experience of dignity is the connection between identity and dignity via the concept of a narrative life story. Narrative identities refer to concrete and deep experiences that are at the same time socially embedded. Authenticity is the result of a life that allows a person to express her coherent and complex self, as Matt Bloom and Deirdre Guthrie argue in this volume. We must develop proper instruments to help us pay attention to human experiences. There are significant problems, Robert Dowd, CSC, reminds us in his chapter, with an approach to assessing awareness of human dignity in a manner not informed by the experience of people. There is a need to integrate behavioral and attitudinal variables—in other words, a focus on what can be observed externally is not enough for a proper understanding of human experience. This understanding requires a reappraisal of listening and a rethinking of the category of "passivity" as "the practice of enjoying things as they are" (Dominic Burbidge). This allows us to understand development work not so much as transforming the world of things but as identifying and respecting vocations. The term "vocation" points to a commitment to honoring the uniqueness of the person and her experience.

Paying attention to human experiences will make us enter "the messy world" that challenges some of the language and categories used in human rights and human dignity discourses. Catherine Bolten's case study on the mixed effects of the implementation of human rights policy in Sierra Leone is a telling example of practices that challenge discourses and experiences that challenge categories. How are we to respond to Bolten's claim that "the focus on autonomy in universalist human rights doctrine threatens the basis of Sierra Leonean understandings of personhood, as being 'for others' is replaced with being 'for myself'"? Questions like these reflect the price of taking experience seriously; as Bolten writes: "Though rights in the abstract have the potential to enhance people's life chances by affirming their dignity as autonomous, unique beings, the experience of rights in Sierra Leone has diverged from this expectation." This leads to a question about the context-sensitive operationalization of the dignity concept: What is the relationship between human rights and dignity, and how can a cross-cultural examination of human rights assist us in the quest to understand human dignity?

A second systematic claim of the book is the need for *the proper consideration of the nonmaterial (including spiritual) aspects of human life*, particularly the importance of taking "soft aspects" of human practices seriously. We cannot understand integral human development, this book's authors claim, without thick descriptions of agents and their experiences. A thick description will allow the understanding of soft factors beyond the observable surface level. In many cases, we can easily understand the object of agency that would allow for an answer to the question What is X doing? But there is yet more to human agency. With reference to the agency in development work, we could distinguish three dimensions: the "what" dimension (together with the who, when, and where: dealing with content and matter), the "why" dimension (concerned with motivations, desires, values, and reasons), and the "how" dimension (referring to style and form). One central claim of this book is that the "why" and the "how" dimensions are of key importance in practices that seek to honor and promote human dignity. A caretaker in a Catholic nursing home once said: "If you wash a person in the way you would wash a car, you have not washed the person." This points to this very idea of what really matters beyond the content and the observable and maybe measurable aspects of actions and projects. How do we do what we do? And why? Human dignity cannot be understood as an "outcome" to be achieved, as one achieves a certain level of literacy or per capita income. It is something that pervades the manner and form of development work; it is a path to follow rather than an end state to be attained.

This reminder of the "why" and "how" is at once a reminder of the central role of the nonmaterial and the intangible. By underlining the key role of a deep reading of human lives in their richness, this book also suggests taking the intangible infrastructure of institutions and practices seriously—their knowledge, values, desires, reasons, and style. Structures are based on agency, and agency is based on a sense of the good life. Dominic Burbidge exemplifies this point with a remark about privileges: "The important point is not changing the distribution of material privileges but changing the perception . . . of what privilege is." Bruce Wydick, Robert Dowd, and Travis Lybbert have explored the importance of one nonmaterial aspect of people's lives, namely, hope. They have shown that hope, translated into goals, agency, and pathways, matters for lives that intensify the sense of human dignity. Clearly, human development cannot be reduced to increased wealth—even though that which is beyond the material is hard to measure and to monitor. This is one of the challenges this book tries to address, e.g. in Robert Dowd's and Paul Perrin's contributions.

One important aspect of the nonmaterial is the spiritual, that is, a person's attitude toward life as such and to the world as a whole. Spiritual values count in community building and in creating a sense of belonging. As Tania Groppi's example of L'Arche shows, dignity-consonant development work calls for a new religious "musicality" in development work, as some other recent discussions have also shown.[19] Martin Schlag's contribution makes similar claims from a different perspective, arguing that human development requires religion and religious freedom in order to be truly integral; where there is religious freedom, there is more space for human dignity. Schlag not only reminds us of the importance of the nonmaterial aspects of development such as values; he also makes the more substantial claim that within the landscape of nonmaterial aspects, the spiritual has an indispensable role: "Values without spiritual foundations . . . wither away like cut flowers in a vase." Dignity-sensitive discourses and practices need to make a double move, from the technological to the ethical and from the ethical to the spiritual—a double move we can observe in Pope Francis's encyclical *Laudato si*, perhaps best summarized in this statement: "The external deserts in the world are growing, because the internal deserts have become so vast."[20]

A third key area that this book explores is the *central role of community and relationality*. The human person is a relational and social being, a "political animal." Relationships shape our experience of dignity and give insight into how people experience dignity; key categories are once again "accompaniment" and "encounter." As Simona Beretta has emphasized here, our constitutive need for others makes us extremely vulnerable. The concept of vulnerability is an important element in the thick discourse on human dignity. This aspect can be translated into policy endeavors. Small decisions on certain levels have huge impacts on the real lives of people. This is a lesson in connectedness and interdependence, but also in power relations. Poverty reduction without taking the real lives of real people into consideration cannot claim to be dignity-sensitive. Equally, planning development work as if we are dealing with "rational fools," to use Sen's famous essay title, will not do justice to the relational nature of the person. We are involved in decision-making processes not as self-utility maximizers but as social persons, beings in relationships. Human dignity broadens our conception of human motivation as also involving gratuitousness, self-gift, and shared vulnerability. One could see the entire approach of L'Arche as an exemplification of this respect for the relationality of the person; Tania Groppi's skeptical remarks in this volume about individualism, medicalization, bureaucratization, and the replacement of communities through networks can be understood as warning signs of the fragile character of dignity-sensitive development work.

As relational beings we can experience our vulnerability as a strength rather than a weakness. Understanding the human person means understanding a person in relationships and in community. Several contributors to this book suggest "personalist readings" of situations; Séverine Deneulin even portrays Amartya Sen as an ethical personalist expressing the assumption that to be a human being is to interact with others and that this interaction is constitutive of what a person values being and doing. It is not surprising, then, that dignity-sensitive practices will pay special attention to patterns of recognition, be they material, social, intimate, legal, or symbolic. Human agency needs to be supported, and one indispensable aspect of support is sincere recognition. In a deeper reading of our relationality, accompaniment emerges as a key concept; accompaniment, as Steve Reifenberg and Elizabeth Hlabse write in their contribution, is about human relationships, about empathy and mutuality, about listening and walking together. Ilaria Schnyder von Wartensee provides not only illustrations but also tangible reasons as to why accompaniment matters in projects with a mentoring component and why mentoring is a promising feature of development work if based on encouragement and mutual care. The encouragement provided by a mentor is an invitation to recognize one's value and thus to have a deeper sense of one's own dignity. By its emphasis on the social nature of the person, this volume underlines the central role of mutuality and reciprocity in development work, a point that Luigino Bruni expands to the point of making it one of the core dynamics of the market in the civil economy. Accompaniment is one concrete aspect of what others have termed "being with" rather than "working for." It is a kind of relationship that sustains people so that they have "the heart to continue," as Ilaria Schnyder von Wartensee writes. The dignity of the human person is only truly honored when the person is seen in her uniqueness. This is, by the way, one of the paradoxical aspects of the concept of human dignity: It can be used to justify the equality of all persons and the uniqueness of each person at the same time.

The fourth and final systematic claim of the book is that *the concept of dignity, as informed by experience, can be translated into a language of projects and programs and into institutional practices.* Dignity is a contested concept, but it is possible to make use of the concept in planning efforts to operationalize the concept and to assess the extent to which human dignity is respected. Paul Perrin provides a concrete example of using the concept of dignity in monitoring efforts. The case studies from Mexico (Reifenberg and Hlabse and Wydick, Dowd, and Lybbert), Guatemala (Aguirre and Cruz-Zuniga), Uganda (Dowd), and Kenya (Schnyder von Wartensee) make this point in different ways but with the same claim: even though we may not be able to agree on the foundation of human dignity, by seriously reflecting on experience and practice and by bringing into dialogue the empirical and the theoretical, we can arrive at a sufficiently articulated understanding of human dignity that allows it to be translated into an array of development practices in different contexts.

Those contexts include some of the most pervasively important institutionalized forms of social life. Schlag and Bruni illustrate the role of dignity in the healthy operation of economic forces in market systems, while Schlag's emphasis on religious freedom also links it to the protections of the rule of law. Violini and Ragone address dignity in legal rules and structures even more explicitly in their analysis of EU conditionality clauses, suggesting that dignity is the "dark matter" that can be only detected indirectly but that makes coherent sense of the system as a whole. Dignity also gets translated into institutionalized practice in designing policy. In all of these ways, human dignity is more than a discourse; it is rather a principle that informs and shapes practices—and a concept, the meaning of which depends on these practices.

Based on these four central claims (the role of the soft factors of agency, the role of community and relationality, the role of experiences and practices, the possibility for enacting the dignity concept) we see one overarching key conclusion emerge: *the future of development work stands and falls with the proper consideration of human dignity in practice.* Read together, the following contributions intend to show the plausibility of this claim.

STRUCTURE AND CONTENTS OF THIS VOLUME

The book is structured in five parts, including the introduction, then part I, consisting of four chapters on conceptualizing dignity through practice (by Clemens Sedmak, Séverine Deneulin, Simona Beretta, and Dominic Burbidge). After that, dignity, well-being, and flourishing are discussed in their subjective and objective dimensions (in part II, with three chapters by Matt Bloom and Deirdre Guthrie, Robert Dowd, and Bruce Wydick with co-authors Robert Dowd and Travis Lybbert). The third part is dedicated to dignity and institutionalized practices (in four chapters authored by Paul Perrin, Martin Schlag, Luigino Bruni, and Lorenza Violini together with Giada Ragone). The last part introduces five case studies (by Steve Reifenberg and Elizabeth Hlabse on Compañeros en Salud [in English, "Partners in Health"] in the Sierra Madres of Mexico, Catherine Bolten on children's rights discourse in Sierra Leone, Ilaria Schnyder von Wartensee on mentorship in Kenya, Tania

Groppi on "L'Arche," and Maria Sophia Aguirre and Martha Cruz-Zuniga on field experiments conducted with cooperation and initiative). In this way, the book, with its focus on "practicing dignity in development," moves from the conceptual to the field of application, thereby connecting dignity to flourishing and institutions.

Let us take a closer look at the individual chapters. In chapter 1 of part I, Clemens Sedmak discusses the question of the enactment and application of concepts and principles in general and of the concept of human dignity in particular. An application is never a simple transfer from one fixed entity to another sphere; rather, it involves the work of interpretation and appropriation. A proper enactment of human dignity is particularly important in situations that involve people with increased levels of vulnerability. It is through particular experiences that the concept of human dignity is nourished and enriched; there is a need for particularly nurturing practices that can then serve as "testimonial practices." The concept of dignity is ultimately based on experiences of encounter. The experiences providing depth and strength to the concept of dignity are especially powerful when dignity is upheld and defended under adverse circumstances—in a "deep practice of human dignity." The realities of poverty and disease leave no moral alternative to that of a deep practice of human dignity that will then inform details and facets of development work.

In the second chapter Séverine Deneulin works with the capability approach. She takes up the idea of the enacting of dignity as a relational process. Based on this volume's experiential and relational approximation of human dignity, Deneulin explores the kind of human agency implied in dignity practices (and discourse). In dialogue with Amartya Sen's capability approach (and its emphasis on development as freedom), she establishes a link between dignity and freedom and reconstructs relational features of Sen's approach, which has sometimes been called "ethically individualistic." This allows for a link between dignity and agency, which Deneulin presents by making use of Axel Honneth's theory of recognition. She then exemplifies this agency-related understanding of dignity (and this concept of intersubjective agency) by dignity-enacting practices in a marginalized urban context in Buenos Aires; she observes the regaining of self-trust through processes of recognition in mutual listening circles. The reality of an encounter nourishes a sense of dignity, which nonetheless can be fostered through institutionalized practices.

In chapter 3 Simona Beretta explores the nonmaterial drivers of development (especially meaningful relations) and offers thick descriptions of human freedom and agency as experienced in action. Complex interactions shape (the use of) resources, technology, institutions, and preferences. Beretta is particularly concerned with the inner dynamism of freedom, which cannot be properly understood from a set of conditions for agency. Actual agency occurs, as Beretta writes, "in the 'here and now' of contingent situations, yet it can transcend them on the basis of reasonable expectations that something new is possible. Dynamic freedom and agency, thus, respond to a broader, more well-rounded notion of rationality." A person is doubly "nonisolated" as a relational being and as a being in action. This provides grounds for developing a "we rationality." In order to properly understand the idea of integral human development Beretta invokes the notion of a "transcendent humanism" from Pope Paul VI's encyclical on development, *Populorum progressio*. A view of development emerges that sees development, micro and macro, "as a process driven by human freedom and agency, according to the human heart's deepest needs and evidences."

The last chapter of part I is authored by Dominic Burbidge, who sets out to offer a new reading of agency-dominated discourses in development, focusing on agency and the corresponding power dynamics. Burbidge suggests that we consider the category of "passivity." He begins the chapter by examining the challenges of Kenyan local governance with the insight that it is important to grow "in the virtue of passivity," in the virtue of listening and presence. He writes, "Instead of exploring what it means to listen, in development studies we have tended to listen to the voice of the underprivileged." Burbidge challenges the dominant "agency paradigm" and offers an "agency passivity framework" with the concept of passivity as "the practice of enjoying things as they are." The exercise of this kind of passivity enhances development because of its potential for mutuality, a sense of vocation, and self-transformation. Burbidge develops this core idea in conversation with Sen. As in previous chapters, the central message regards encounter: "Listening well to the practices and realities of those different from oneself is an encounter that threatens to change one's definitional aims."

The second part of the volume approaches aspects of well-being and flourishing in connection with dignity, which involves a sense of a dignified and decent life—a life in accordance with human dignity. Matt Bloom and Deirdre Guthrie (chapter 5) approach dignity from a psychological perspective, which has not always played a prominent role in such considerations. They endeavor to understand "what people think, feel, and do when they experience themselves as having or not having dignity and also what causes people to experience that their dignity has been honored or impugned." Having investigated the experience of dignity among international humanitarian and global health professionals—persons for whom dignity is a major concern in their work—the authors consider correlations between identity and dignity, including the insight that a person's sense of self is shaped by relationship and interaction, once again emphasizing the relational model treated in this volume. Their research confirms the hypothesis that "the process of how we come to know who we are is inseparable from our lived experience of dignity." A person's identity is at the center of psychological experiences of dignity. A related key element that emerges is how a sense of mission, service, and accompaniment leads to experiences that mutually strengthen the experience of dignity.

In chapter 6 Robert Dowd takes a rich notion of "human development" as his starting point, defining development as "sustained improvements in the quality of life people enjoy;" he suggests that these improvements typically begin "with a growing awareness of human dignity, an appreciation for the inherent value of oneself and others." The spark of human development is a (new, deep, deeper, renewed) sense of the dignity of one's self and others in the community. Dowd illustrates this point by referring to the work done through the University of Notre Dame's Ford Program in Human Development Studies and Solidarity in Uganda, with its special emphasis on participatory practices. Failure to work in an inclusive manner will also hamper human development. Human dignity, understood by Dowd as "the value or worth that every human being has in equal measure by virtue of his or her existence," cannot be easily "produced" in benefactor-beneficiaries relationships. A model of respectful encounter is the basis for dignity-sensitive human development. From a researcher's perspective, there remains the vexing question of how to "measure" an awareness of dignity or its increase.

Reports from a research project in Ugandan villages show that both change in the sense of one's own capabilities and change in observable features, like agricultural production, could be observed. The latter reflects Dowd's point that "what people do" is a more reliable indicator of awareness of human dignity than "what people say."

The final contribution of part II (chapter 7) takes us from Uganda to Mexico as Bruce Wydick, Robert Dowd, and Travis Lybbert consider an experiment among indigenous microfinance borrowers in Oaxaca, Mexico, and the question of how religious beliefs influence a person's capacity to aspire, to conceptualize pathways out of poverty, and to grasp the role of personal agency. The experiment included a "hope intervention" that led to significant results, especially in the case of evangelical Protestant women (in terms of levels of aspirations and agency) and also in the case of Catholic women (in terms of impact). The chapter is based on the well-justified idea that dignity and hope are connected. The authors sketch the idea of hope as it developed in the Jewish and Christian traditions and the role of hope in the experience of poverty, as studied in a major participatory World Bank study. The success of the intervention described bears hope for the "hope effects" of development work, and it can be safely stated that "developing hope and its components represents a fundamental process in the cultivation of human dignity."

Part III takes a closer look at institutionalized practices and the role of dignity in politics, economics, and law. In chapter 8 Paul Perrin discusses the "measurability" of dignity in the context of monitoring and evaluating; he states that "dignity" has become a buzzword in the practice of international development, and he provides an impressive list of its usages to make this point. He reasons that dignity as a term "is virtually omnipresent in international development and humanitarian settings." But the challenge of operationalizing dignity has not been met. Dignity can gain meaning only through the respect accorded to it (through what has been called "dignity-enacting practice" in this volume). Through a series of examples, Perrin shows how dignity can become a central feature of humanitarian practices, including monitoring and evaluation efforts. Inviting narratives of stakeholders is an important aspect of attending to dignity through monitoring and evaluation. Perrin introduces a pilot project of a particular software, "Sense-Maker," that has been tested by Catholic Relief Services. He describes promising experiences in enacting dignity in development work while conveying the potential for a paradigm shift if we were to perceive international development and humanitarian assistance through a "dignity assurance" lens.

Chapter 9, authored by Martin Schlag, argues for a full understanding of "integral human development," which requires "religion and religious freedom in order to be truly integral." Schlag engages Catholic social teaching and its tradition of developing a notion of "integral human development." Faith is of undeniable weight in its life-shaping and identity-conferring character. Dignity and religious freedom cannot be separated; religion adds something significant to dignity. The role human dignity plays in opening up space for religion in modern liberal democracy and in promoting (political and economic) development cannot be denied, but it is expressed differently in the U.S.–American and the European traditions. Schlag explores both traditions. He is clear about the difference between "values" and "faith." He explains: "Values without spiritual foundations, however, wither away like cut flowers in a vase." And further: "Religious moral messages are cultural factors worth taking into account both in politics and in business, also by mere standards of well-understood self-interest: after the collapse of the great ideologies, the only remaining creators of culture are the big world religions." Schlag also discusses the invitations to rethink public life and religion in the light of migration dynamics, in dialogue with Rowan Williams's widely discussed suggestion that the concept of human dignity be used for a "transformative accommodation" of Sharia law in the English legal system. He then moves from law and politics to business to discuss the important input of Catholic social teaching, especially as regards the notion of the common good. Human dignity can thus be linked to work and agency, to initiative and responsibility. A "preferential option for the poor" gains important momentum through an understanding of human dignity based on the *imago Dei* tradition (a momentum that the Roman *dignitas* cannot give). Schlag concludes: "We can consider Christianity as a propulsive force in the 'expanding circle narrative' regarding the idea of human dignity: formerly a quality confined to social elites, it expanded out and down until it referred to all humans. And thus the circle of religious freedom, human dignity, and integral development closes conceptually but remains an open challenge for our actions."

Luigino Bruni, in chapter 10, deals with a new dignity-sensitive way of doing business and understanding economics: the economy of communion, based on cooperation and trust. Bruni reconstructs the civil economy tradition in Italy and thereby gains reference points for discussing the role of sociality and relationality in economics with a special emphasis on trust and trust experiments. A perception emerges of relationships between individuals as both mutually advantageous exchanges and also genuine social interactions. A new understanding of the market and market transactions thus takes shape: Bruni makes the claim that market interactions (or "contracts") "can be understood and represented as that which makes the parties into a collective agent with reference to the particular joint action that is the object of the contract." A view of the market as a domain of interactions offers a view of economics and economic agency that is much more person-centered and dignity-aware. Hence, it is unsurprising that Bruni can evoke "the forgotten principle of modernity," namely "fraternity," at the conclusion of his text.

The authors of the final chapter (chapter 11) of part III, Lorenza Violini and Giada Ragone, write from the legal perspective. They pose the question of whether human dignity is a principle that can influence policy makers when they are dealing with problems related to development. In the chapter they develop an affirmative answer. Violini and Ragone consistently argue, against the background of a historical and philosophical understanding of human dignity, for the special role and place of dignity in the understanding of development policies; dignity is taken to be a foundational aspect of all rights. The discourse on dignity cannot be separated from the discourse on humanity and the question of what it means to be human and to live a human life. These metaconsiderations will inevitably enter specific policies as well, as dignity is translated into coherent political practices. The case in point is the conditionality policy of the European Union. It becomes clear that the "cooperation and development policies are not only a matter of material economic aid but must also be functional toward the enhancement of a whole series of values." Among these values, the flourishing of human dignity is of paramount importance.

Part IV moves us to case studies and explorations of dignity in practice. Steve Reifenberg and Elizabeth Hlabse present in their chapter 12 an integrated healthcare model based on accompaniment. They describe the work model of the organization Compañeros en Salud in Mexico with its relational and person-centered approach of accompaniment. This model is not only one of healthcare but also, more broadly, a model of development with elements of material assistance, service, mentorship, exchange, and encounter. Empathy and listening are key elements in the daily work of these healthcare providers. Accompaniment as a way of "walking with" and "being with" people can also be rooted in Latin American liberation theology with its emphasis on the dignity of the poor. Reifenberg and Hlabse describe the accompaniment-based model that supports the realization of people's rights as "a pathway for dignified healthcare." A particular challenge of the model is the question of scaling and systemic change. How can this be done with the same attention to the dignity of the person?

Catherine Bolten, in chapter 13, takes us to Sierra Leone; an anthropologist, she grapples with the fascinating and rarely asked question of whether the institution of human rights legislation can actually damage human dignity. She works with two vignettes from Sierra Leone, both of which illustrate a shift in perception of dignity and rights due to the introduction of the discourse on children's rights. The introduction of an individualistic interpretation of rights and personhood challenges traditional ways of understanding a person; Bolten shows that there are culturally delicate "opportunity costs" when introducing a new language and set of categories such as child rights. The enactment of the Child's Right Act in Sierra Leone has changed the relational landscape, the way adults and children interact with each other. Even interfamily relations have been affected. Bolten's text is a reminder that the perception of dignity is embedded in cultural practices and ideas. Culture means complexity, and complexity means that the question of unintended and undesired consequences of human rights discourse is relevant and justified.

Chapter 14, authored by Ilaria Schnyder von Wartensee, describes Dandora, an eastern suburb of Nairobi, Kenya, which was the site of a research project carried out by the Ford Program of the University of Notre Dame. The project showed that young female entrepreneurs who were mentored benefited more in the year following the conclusion of the experiment than both young female entrepreneurs who received standard business training and their counterparts in a control group. Schnyder von Wartensee collected qualitative data to explore these findings in greater depth, looking especially into the question of why mentors and mentees continued to meet following the experiment. She reconstructs "encouragement" and "mutual care" as key elements of sustainable mentoring relationships. The key to a dignity-focused way of interacting is a culture of encounter. Mentoring relationships in this setting have the potential to generate experiences of human (and economic) empowerment based on a sense of a person and her dignity.

Tania Groppi, in chapter 15, describes the work of L'Arche, an international movement of residential communities of people with disabilities and their companions founded by the late Jean Vanier. Groppi describes the dignity-centered approach of Vanier and his communities with core values such as mutual relationships and trust in God. A key aspect is the recognition of people's unique value: "We celebrate the unique value of every person and recognize our need of one another." There is the recognition of a common humanity and of the needs for relationship and community for growth. As a result, L'Arche is less an institution and more a community, a way of life. It provides a place for transformation; Jean Vanier, as Groppi describes, had been transformed by the initial experience of sharing his life with two men affected by intellectual disabilities. Relationships are at the center of L'Arche. Groppi describes the signs and symbols and the faith life of the movement—all of which contribute to a deep sense of the mystery of each human person.

The final chapter, chapter 16, authored by Maria Sophia Aguirre and Martha Cruz-Zuniga, describes a nutritional intervention within the framework of an integral economic approach in Guatemala. The authors recount the work of Asociación Puente, a Guatemalan nonprofit organization that "seeks to reduce extreme poverty and prevent malnutrition through the development of skills by women living in extremely poor rural communities." The organization pursues a dignity-focused approach. Both the research and the program that was evaluated focus not on individuals but on relationships and persons as relational beings. Decisions are made by social beings, not isolated individuals. Deriving a relational vision of "human development," Aguirre and Cruz-Zuniga suggest that development interventions should take a person in her relationality and commitment structure seriously. Their research design has carefully followed this approach and included participatory elements. This chapter, thus, exemplies that the concept of human dignity can inform even the fundamental research methodology and approach of development economics.

Each of these sixteen chapters stands on its own, but the framing as well as the dialogue between authors and the intertextuality of the chapters adds value to the contributions, which can thus be read as a whole (however incomplete). It is through the diversity of approaches and voices that the multifariousness of dignity in development practices emerges. In this sense, this book is a beginning, not an end product.

NOTES

1. United Nations, General Assembly, *The Road to Dignity by 2030: Ending Poverty, Transforming All Lives and Protecting the Planet*, Report of the Secretary General, A/69/700 (December 4, 2014), https://sustainabledevelopment .un.org/index.php?page=view&type=111&nr=6179&menu=35.

2. Theodor W. Adorno, "Education after Auschwitz," in *Critical Models: Interventions and Catchwords*, trans. Henry W. Pickford (New York: Columbia University Press, 2005), 191–204.

3. Avishai Margalit, *The Decent Society* (Cambridge, MA: Harvard University Press, 1996), 96–103.

4. See Jacques Maritain, *L'humanisme integral* (Paris: Aubier, 1936); trans. as *True Humanism* (New York: Charles Scribner's Sons, 1938). This work is cited in footnote 44 of Pope Paul VI's encyclical *Populorum Progressio* (March 26, 1967), which develops the concept of integral human development (in the English translation, the term used is "complete development"). See http://w2.vatican.va/content/paul-vi/en/encyclicals/documents/hf_p-vi_enc _26031967_populorum.html, secs. 5–6.

5. Ban Ki-Moon, "Foreword," in *Millennium Development Goals Report* (New York: United Nations, 2013), https://www.un.org/millenniumgoals/pdf /report-2013/mdg-report-2013-english.pdf.

6. See United Nations, General Assembly, *Transforming Our World: The 2030 Agenda for Sustainable Development*, Resolution A/7/L.1 (September 25, 2015), https://sustainabledevelopment.un.org/post2015/transformingour world.

7. See also the introduction and chapters of Christopher McCrudden, ed., *Understanding Human Dignity* (Oxford: Oxford University Press, 2013).

8. Avishai Margalit, *The Decent Society* (Cambridge, MA: Harvard University Press, 1996).

9. Joel Feinberg, *Social Philosophy* (Englewood Cliffs, NJ: Prentice-Hall, 1973), 88–94.

10. Andrea Cornwall, "Buzzwords and Fuzzwords: Deconstructing Development Discourse," *Development in Practice* 17, nos. 4–5 (2007): 472, https://doi.org/10.1080/09614520701469302.

11. Quoted by Hanna-Mari Kivistö, "The Concept of 'Human Dignity' in the Post-War Human Rights Debates," *Res Publica: Revista de Filosofía Política* 27 (2012): 99–110, at 102.

12. Antoon de Baets, "A Successful Utopia: The Doctrine of Human Dignity," *Historein* 7 (2007): 71–85, at 71.

13. Ludwig Wittgenstein, *Philosophical Investigations* (Oxford: Blackwell, 1967), 107.

14. Peter Bieri, *Human Dignity: A Way of Living* (Cambridge: Polity Press, 2016).

15. See Paolo Carozza, "Human Rights, Human Dignity, and Human Experience," in McCrudden, *Understanding Human Dignity*, 615–30.

16. Des Gasper and Thanh-Dam Truong, "Deepening Development Ethics: From Economism to Human Development to Human Security," *European Journal of Development Research* 17, no. 3 (September 2005): 372–84.

17. Also known as the World Commission on Environment and Development, the Brundtland Commission was created by the secretary general of the United Nations in 1983 with the aim of uniting countries in the pursuit of sustainable development.

18. Miranda Fricker, *Epistemic Injustice: Power and the Ethics of Knowing* (Oxford: Oxford University Press, 2007).

19. Cf., 4. Séverine Deneulin and Augusto Zampini Davies, "Engaging Development and Religion: Methodological Groundings," *World Development* 99 (2017): 110–21.

20. Pope Francis, *Laudato Si'* (May 24, 2015), http://w2.vatican.va/content/francesco/en/encyclicals/documents/papa-francesco_20150524_enciclica-laudato-si.html, sec. 217; the quotation is actually taken from a speech by Pope Benedict XVI.

PART I

Conceptualizing Dignity through Practice

ONE

Enacting Human Dignity

Clemens Sedmak

One of the more curious incidents in the history of translation is W. H. Auden's "translation" of Dag Hammarskjöld's *Markings* from Swedish to English. Auden knew no Swedish and had a collaborator, Leif Sjöberg, provide a literal translation, which he worked into a text with his own "freer" version of the book. He had done the same with Goethe's *Italienische Reise* in collaboration with Elizabeth Mayer. In both cases he merged "translating" with "editing," expressing his concerns, for instance, that "as an editor, Goethe did not do a very good job."[1] Obviously, getting rid of some passages in Goethe's source text (elements that Auden deemed "repetitious," "unintelligible," or even "verbose rubbish")[2] carries the risk of provoking the suspicion of unfaithfulness. Those concerns were explicitly raised with reference to Auden's translation of Hammarskjöld's original Swedish text. In this case, however, the linguistic situation was even more challenging since Auden, whose German was reasonably good, admitted openly: "It is no secret that I do not know a single word of Swedish."[3] Nobody could blame a person wondering about the feasibility of such a "translation project." The *Times Literary Supplement* featured a critical article in 1999, and the *New York Times* reported on a major dispute about the accuracy of the translation in May 2005.[4] Auden worked with "literal raw material" that he "refined" following his own preferences and moral desires. He saw his translation projects very much as redemptive projects, redeeming texts from flaws; in his understanding, "every text reaches toward a pre-Babelian unity and oneness; in order to get there it must rid itself of all elements reminiscent of the Fall."[5]

In an attempt to reconstruct the epistemological aspects of Auden's methodology of translation we are able to identify two main elements: (A) he had strong beliefs (1) about his own linguistic capacities, (2) about the flaws of texts, (3) about the moral justifiability (or even moral necessity) to work on identifiable textual deficits, (4) about the possibility to engage in "redemptive linguistic labor" working with an almost unknown source language, and (B) he appointed a "linguistic ambassador" who could serve as a "bridge person" between the source and the target language, but primarily as a representative of the source language: Elizabeth Mayer (1884–1970) was a German-born American translator who came to the United States only after the Nazis had come to power; Leif Sjöberg (1925–2000) was a noted Swedish literary scholar who taught in the United States for many years.

Strong beliefs about the ethics of linguistics and collaboration with a linguistic ambassador enabled Auden to bridge a gap between a known and an unknown or less known language—with all the risks and epistemic vulnerabilities involved. One can see the plausibility of supporting Auden's case for hermeneutics in more general terms since the art of understanding has been presented (by Gadamer, for instance) as an exercise in translating (moving from a familiar to a less familiar context). In order to make sense of a text, a work of art, or anything for that matter, the interpretation process requires bridges to avoid "painfully untraveled roads."

TRANSLATING PRINCIPLES AND CONCEPTS INTO PRACTICES

Human dignity has been placed at the center of many development endeavors; many agencies are committed, at least in official statements, to respecting human dignity, the dignity of the human person. This may pose certain challenges, such as the development of general programs versus [those addressing] the uniqueness of the human person, efficiency versus slowness in the personal appropriation of changes, and social change and the creation of new entry points for humiliation (for example, introducing levels of computer literacy may create new mechanisms of social exclusion, and new medical cultures may offer new ways of objectifying the human person). The challenge is quite often one and the same: how to translate a concept or principle (like "human dignity") into practices or even programs.

Auden's example may also be relevant to this question on a more subtle level: development work, with its in-built bias toward elitism (so clearly described by Robert Chambers in his numerous publications), is creating a discourse on human dignity owned by privileged people with decreased levels of vulnerability. But it is especially people with increased levels of vulnerability—that is, those with high risks and fragile mechanisms to cope with these risks—who have a lot to say about what constitutes a dignified life, what threatens human dignity, and what nourishes a sense of self-respect.

Magnus MacFarlane-Barrow, founder of Mary's Meals, which aims to provide chronically hungry children with one meal every school day, was inspired by the words of Edward, a boy from Malawi; Magnus had met a lady called Emma while providing famine relief in Malawi. She was dying of AIDS on the floor of her hut, surrounded by her young children. Magnus asked her eldest son, Edward, what he hoped for in life. The simple reply: "I want to have enough food to eat and to go to school one day."[6] This is a clear and concise definition of the very idea of a "dignified life," a life corresponding to the demands of human dignity, as expressed in the Vatican Council II document *Gaudium et spes*: "There is a growing awareness of the exalted dignity proper to the human person. . . . and his rights and duties are universal and inviolable. Therefore, there must be made available to all men everything necessary for leading a life truly human, such as food, clothing, and shelter . . . the right to education, to employment, to a good reputation, to respect."[7] The vision "Every child deserves an education and enough to eat" is a translation of "human dignity," and this vision is translated into practices and programs such as having school feeding programs owned and run by community volunteers; establishing school feeding committees made up of parents, teachers, and volunteers; and using locally produced food wherever possible.

Auden's project was the translation of a text from one language into another; this was a challenge for Leif Sjöberg and Elizabeth Mayer, too, since translations are done "after Babel." Translating concepts from one language to another poses its own challenges (such as the irreducible moment of intranslatability and transmission loss), but translating concepts into practices is an even more puzzling undertaking; development work faces this challenge in a daily as well as on a programmatic basis. How does "human dignity" translate into practices "on the ground"?

We can identify with Auden's challenge of translating from a less familiar context of language into a more familiar context of practical ethics. This practice is sometimes called "applied ethics," suggesting that theoretical insights into moral questions (or, for that matter, "principles" and "rules") can be "folded into" ("translated into") practical contexts. According to this image, any set of principles or rules is carried over into a setting of human agency. This image creates the impression that a general principle as a stable normative unit can be "unfrozen" in a particular context and "translated" into specific practices. We may be tempted to think that a stable and firm principle such as human dignity can be translated into practices in a simple process that takes the principle from one place to another. In the United Kingdom Eglantyne Jebb and her sister Dorothy Buxton founded *Save the Children* in 1919 based on Jebb's knowledge of the plight of children on the continent. This first charity specifically established for nondomicile children, and the first to be founded by women, set out to respond to the challenges to human dignity identified in *Gaudium et spes* 26. But there was no simple procedure for translating human dignity into practices. The organization had to deal with complex logistical and legal questions as well as the difference between working with adults and working with children. There is no simple way to "translate" human dignity.

Translating is a creative act; it is not simply an exercise in "unfreezing," "removing," or "displacing," and linguistic principles of translation cannot be applied in transferring matter, such as boulders. In March 2012, a 340-ton boulder had to be transported from a quarry in Riverside County to the County Museum of Art in Los Angeles, where it would be used as the centerpiece of Michael Heizer's environmental sculpture *Levitated Mass*. The sculpture had been worked out and designed according to experiential knowledge. We know, for instance, that Heizer's 1968 sketch of a gigantic boulder seemingly hanging in midair (*Levitated Mass*) would take forty-two years to become a reality. The search to find the right rock was seemingly endless, and the first attempt to transport the 340-ton boulder to its destination was a failure. There was nothing wrong with the actual rock itself, but we could argue that the artist's quest for quarried "rock" or "a rock" was directed by a particular mode of perception; he was looking not for "rock" but for a suitable medium for his sculpture. Accordingly, one could argue that it was not a boulder but the essence of an art project that had to be transported 105 miles to Los Angeles.

There seems to have been much more epistemic agency involved (including concern-based imagination, experiential knowledge, appropriate planning, or structured perception) than the simple "selection of a rock" reading of the situation could suggest. A general ethical principle such as "Do not torture a human being" needs a proper definition of key terms and explications of the implications—both of which are to be found in the 1987 UN Convention against Torture and Other Cruel, Inhuman or Degrading Treatment or Punishment. The same can be said about general ethical principles as spelled out in the Ten Commandments (which have evoked many a casuistic investigation) or the Hippocratic oath with, for example, its obligation of anyone having recited the oath to help the sick according to their ability and judgment, but never with a view to injury and wrong-doing (which is constantly being fiercely debated in the context of cosmetic surgery and advanced medical machinery); these general principles require substantial epistemic labor, including experiential knowledge and a structured perception. One cannot take the concept of human dignity and "apply" it in the same way one would take ointment and apply it to a wound.

General principles have histories, and in this sense each has a "memory": general principles are based on particular experiences in the field of human praxis; at the same time, these principles change the perception of a particular concept. The story about "the stable universal" and "the dynamic particular," well known from the history of Christian mission, with its negotiation of "constants in context" and the question of faithfulness to the gospel and respect for local cultures at the same time, is much more complicated than a clear-cut distinction between "the universal principle" and "the particular situation" is able to capture. The encounter with universal principles takes place within a particular context; the place to encounter a concept with a universal claim such as human dignity or a principle such as the absolute prohibition of torture is communicative and reflective practice. Furthermore, a general principle or concept serves as an ordering mechanism that organizes the description of a situation (not unlike Kant's concept of intellect with regard to sense data).

The ethical principle "Respect the dignity of the human person!" is based on particular experiences, especially the experience of the denial of human dignity, and this principle also operates like an ordering lens that can organize local data in a particular way and set new standards to distinguish between relevant and irrelevant information. Kathleen Galvin and Les Todres have identified the concept of human dignity and its role in shaping human perception as the centrally important reason for human existence:

> It opens up a lived perception of a deep common humanity in which we participate in both vulnerability as well as honourable kinship. The philosophical grounding of this perception has a very practical normative possibility in that it points to the meaningful source of the ability to care, to respect, and to grant autonomy and beneficence to others. In other words, it provides the possibility of a living basic intuition or perception that is deeper, that "gives juice" or lived authenticity to respectful caring behaviours which could otherwise easily become instrumental without such perceptual-intuitive sustenance.[8]

"Translating" ethical principles is not like transferring an oversized rock from A to B, especially if A was "abstract territory" and B "concrete territory." There are differences between semantics and pragmatics, for sure, but not to the extent that a landscape can be easily and neatly divided into pragmatic "concepts" and "practices," "principles," and "examples." We could further envisage Michael Heizer's 340-ton boulder being moved from the Los Angeles museum to a museum in

San Francisco, but they would still be comparable types of contexts that could "meet" and "interact." Translating universal ethical claims such as the absolute prohibition of torture into particular contexts can also lead to processes of mutual interaction, processes that have been described in terms of "reflective equilibrium." The term suggests a "dialogue," with its emphasis on reciprocity and mutuality.

We have to face the challenge of translation in any context, not only in those of language and rocks but also in the sense that a particular reading or perception of human dignity depends on the particular reading of a situation. An understanding of human dignity in a post-Apartheid situation in South Africa will be significantly different from an understanding of human dignity in contemporary Germany or Austria, which are faced with neo-Nazi activities and agents. We could usefully put forward different readings of human dignity in order to broaden and "thicken" the possibilities for understanding the term and in doing so design and build new bridges between concepts and human practices. It becomes clear yet again that we are dealing here with the complex issue of translation. And in addition to that we face the challenge of finding appropriate translators.

NURTURING PRACTICES: HUMAN DIGNITY
AND HUMAN VULNERABILITY

Can privileged experts "translate" the concept of human dignity into practices? The minimum would be strong beliefs and the ability to dialogue, learn, and listen. Auden did not translate Swedish into English, but he did transport and transfer meaning on the basis of his own strong beliefs with the help of a linguistic and cultural ambassador. He created a linguistic practice on the basis of a "raw" translation, which he "cooked" (to use Lévi-Strauss's terminology). By doing this he opened a new (not uncontested) pathway to the project of translation. This novel cooking process—to continue the metaphor—could be applied to other ingredients, other contexts: human dignity is both concept and normative principle in a general (raw) sense, but it needs to be "enacted."

The litmus test for respecting human dignity is not the word, but the practice, and not the isolated practice, but the habitual practice, and not even the habitual practice, but the habitual practice in the face of adversities. Respecting human dignity in times of terrorist threats or in times of transitional justice is hard. Pope Francis's famous image of the Church as a "field hospital" comes to mind.[9] It is challenging to enact human dignity in the context of a field hospital; at the same time, one can say that the very point of the field hospital is the enactment of human dignity; it is an expression of a commitment to respecting dignity under adverse circumstances. The same can be said about a number of development projects (and most relief efforts): building "field hospitals" where they are needed is a tangible translation of the principle of human dignity into practices.

Enacting concepts is the art of translating a concept into stable practices, of creating "testimonial practices," that is, practices that give testimony to the depth and richness of a concept with its many semantic layers. In the Christian tradition, for instance, we face the challenge of enacting the concept of "love of God" in meaningful ways; there is a debate about whether the visible "love of neighbor" can serve (in accordance with 1 John 4:20) as a testimonial practice for the concept "love of God."[10] Enacting concepts suggests that there is an agent bridging concept and practice, bridging semantics and pragmatics, linguistics and extra-linguistic practices; both types of practice (linguistic as well as extra-linguistic) are relevant to our question of how to bridge the gap between a concept and human practice. The agent ensures that we cannot justify the idea of there being a clear line between a concept on the one hand and human practices on the other; concepts are embedded in expressions of practice as much as practices are shaped by conceptual kaleidoscopes that influence perceptions and appraisals.

Auden served as the agent who appropriated the draft translation and made it his own by weaving into it his own beliefs and practices at both the semantic and the pragmatic level. There is an element of judgment at play here that is indispensable; this judgment reflects the commitment and authority of the agent to apply an initial concept. There is epistemic agency involved here above and beyond "taking a concept and applying it." And the types and outcomes of agency can vary. In fact, the concept of "human dignity" can be compared to a toy lying in the grass of a children's playground; anybody can pick it up, appropriate it, and play with it. This multidimensional context of context and place means that different practices emerge that blur and confuse the clear meaning of the concept; any attempts to control the use of human judgment or human dignity, in the sense of safeguarding a standard, as in the way the 1889 *mètre des archives* was protected and kept in Paris, would invariably lead to a sterile meaning of the term coupled with ongoing issues about the power of definition. There is no one defining practice of human dignity, but in order for the concept to retain "cash value" in not only evaluating but also shaping human practice we need to find some creative ways to bridge the gap between a concept and human practice.

In the light of these observations on the contextual *embeddedness* of the term "human dignity" and in the light of the prominent role of the agent, outlined above, I suggest building a bridge to overcome the gap between concept and human practices—a pragmatic and dialogical theory of meaning. The meaning of the concept of human dignity, I suggest, should be approached by exploring uses of the concept whereby a second-person perspective with significant interlocutors determines the relevance of the contexts of usage. A pragmatic theory of meaning would suggest that concepts are not *about* practices but are indeed *embedded* in practices. A pragmatic theory of meaning operates on the basis of a "context principle"[11] that acknowledges the embeddedness of linguistic devices in linguistic and extra-linguistic activities. There is no context-free reading of the concept of human dignity; consequently, the term "contextual determination" has been used to explore "the features that dignity assumes when it is related to practice."[12] The question is this: Which practices make use of the concept of human dignity? A pragmatic theory of meaning is interested in a careful analysis of relevant contexts of usage; if the concept of human dignity is not to suffer the fate of certain general principles that "remain mere generalities which challenge no one,"[13] it has to have "friction."[14]

Which types of practices, however, are the ones to turn to? The question is puzzling since we are faced with the problem of multiple conflicting practices referring to the same principle—that is, the principle "respecting a person's dignity" is used by proponents of competing positions regarding end-of-life questions. The same concept will often be used to justify or establish different and even contradictory practices; diffuse semantics can lead to mutually exclusive practices; because of its semantic openness, the concept of human dignity is "essentially contested."[15] This implies that competing interpretations of the concept hold equally justifiable versions of the core and thus lead to equally justifiable practices based on the reading of the core of the concept. Which types of practice, then, should be considered?

Auden's strategy in realizing his ambitious translation projects was to seek advice from "ambassadors" (or "bridge builders"), persons representing the unknown context, like Elizabeth Mayer and Leif Sjöberg; if we were to choose appropriate ambassadors in appropriate situations or contexts we could identify relevant practices. Let us take another look at Mary's Meals. Magnus MacFarlane-Barrow could not have built the organization without ambassadors, without bridge builders. In 2002 the media reported about a terrible famine in southern Africa, especially in Malawi. Magnus's family remembered Gay Russell, a pilot who had been in touch with them in the early 1980s requesting information about Medjugorje after having read an article about the teenagers' experience in the village. While pondering how to get in touch with Gay Russell again, they met by chance a British businessman, Tony Smith, who knew Russell quite well (after a conversion experience in Medjugorje had motivated him to build a replica of the Medjugorje cross in Malawi); he established the connection with Gay, who, with her husband, was involved in famine relief work. Magnus also made connections with other people carrying out emergency work in Malawi, including an anthropologist from St. Andrews University. They issued an appeal to help the starving people in Malawi and prepared for the first trip of Scottish International Relief to the country in the fall of 2002. In Malawi, Magnus obtained firsthand knowledge of the situation, and three months later he returned to the country, accompanied by two journalists. This time he explored the issue of structures of aid: "I had realized by now that most effective emergency food-distribution projects were often being delivered by the churches, which had the advantage of a permanent structure that could be mobilized to create networks of community volunteers. On this visit I spent time with several groups of nuns and priests who were carrying out incredible work on a large scale. None seemed particularly shocked by this famine, and all had tried-and-tested systems they had been relying on and developing over many years."[16]

It is evident that there are "bridge experiences" (experiences like the encounter with Edward, who asked for food and education), "bridge persons" (persons like Gay Russell or Tony Smith, who are able to bridge different contexts and to enhance a person's bridging social capital), and "bridge structures" (such as the parish structures, which enable stable connections to be made between individual agency and collective practices). Connections were brokered on these three levels; bridges were built through these three means. It was especially the encounter with fourteen-year-old Edward that was a teaching moment; Edward's statement reminded Magnus of a previous conversation with Tony Smith, who had—while staying at Gay Russell's house—turned on the television and found himself watching American senator George McGovern's speech "in which he stated, with some passion, that if America decided to fund the provision of one daily meal in a place of education for every child in the world's poorest countries it would act like a 'Marshall Plan' that would lift the developing world out of poverty. . . . Tony said when he heard this speech he was inspired with the thought that if someone took the concept, gave it to Mary, the mother of Jesus, and called it Mary's Meals, then it would actually happen."[17] The vision of Mary's Meals was thus created: "for every child to receive a daily meal in their place of education."[18]

Edward, struggling with the prospect of having to fight for education, for food, for a place in life as an orphan, served as an important ambassador for human dignity. He taught Magnus an important lesson about enacting human dignity; he could teach this simple and profound lesson because of his experience and "knowledge by acquaintance" of the depth of *Gaudium et spes* 26. Enacting human dignity can benefit tremendously from the expertise of those who have "suffered through" knowledge of dignity as a fragile good. I would like to suggest that Pope Francis's invitation to see poor persons as teachers[19] can be of tremendous importance in responding to the question of how to translate the concept of human dignity into practices, of how to enact dignity on the ground.

Human dignity is a concept that has been developed as normative according to morally challenging social situations. It is a concept based on the practice of encounter, inimical or respectful. This is the matter of a "second-person perspective," that is, of the idea that dialogical situations change the way we deal with epistemological and normative claims. "Second-person accounts" generate specific responsibilities and moral demands. The presence of another person changes my personal moral situation.[20] Gerald Cohen developed what he called the "interpersonal test" asking "whether the argument could serve as a justification of a mooted policy when uttered by any member of society to any other member."[21] This test is undeniably relevant to the concept of human dignity. The meaning of dignity changes "in the face" of another person, or "face to face" with a second or third party. In telling his story, Diogo Mainardi recounts a key moment with his son Tito, who suffered brain damage during birth. "Up until that moment, I had always thought that if my son were to fall into a vegetative state, I would prefer him to die. . . . After that first contact with Tito in the corridor of the cloister of Venice Hospital, everything changed. All I wanted was for him to survive, because I would always love him and help him in whatever way I could."[22] Perspective changes the semantics of "person" or "dignity." So we could ask: Which statement made in a "third-person context" would still be acceptable in a "second-person situation"?

This is an important question in development contexts with their challenges of planned programs designed and owned by well-educated, well-connected, and well-travelled elites. The modern understanding of human dignity was created against the background of the experience of human vulnerability; without that experience we would not have a deep discourse on human dignity because it would be taken for granted. Our modern history of the concept of human dignity cannot be separated from an understanding of human vulnerability and the experience of wounding and being wounded. A normative force of the concept has emerged against a background of practices that denied the acknowledgment of personhood. Hence, one might argue, ambassadors representing especially relevant practice are especially vulnerable persons. Human dignity is a concept that has been translated into an ethical principle against the background of a morally painful history of slavery, genocide, and war. Significant practices to be closely analyzed for the purposes of developing a pragmatic theory of the meaning of "human dignity" are practices involving vulnerable persons such as children (practices surrounding the role of introductory or teaching situations), persons with disabilities, or persons living in (extreme) poverty.

These decisions about relevant practices are clearly based on normative commitments entered into prior to the decision. This was Auden's project: he had clear normative commitments regarding the framing of the translation projects (i.e., the ethics of linguistic work), and on that basis and within this framework he used ambassadors. On the basis of clear commitments regarding the link between human dignity and vulnerability (a link established through a particular reading of the "memory" of the concept of human dignity), I would go as far as to suggest that especially vulnerable persons can serve as especially important ambassadors to represent those contexts maybe less familiar to philosophers, lawyers, policy makers, and diplomats.

THE DEEP PRACTICE OF HUMAN DIGNITY

The concept of human dignity needs to be nurtured by appropriate practices of *doing* dignity. In reflecting on memory, Milan Kundera observed that memories have to be watered just like plants to be kept alive and thrive; and we water our memories by sharing and talking about them;[23] in other words, concepts need to be part of communicative memory and current practices in order to be kept semantically alive. Concepts need to be "culturally anchored." If they are not anchored and nurtured by human practices, concepts will ultimately lose their vitality and color, or die. Some concepts die by being defined, such as official terms that are replaced by others (examples from the European Union: "Commission Delegation" was replaced by "Union delegation" and "European Monetary Institute" was replaced by "European Central Bank"). Other concepts die because the parameters of their usage have changed; Naomi Oreskes and Erik Conway have identified concepts that will be obsolete after a catastrophic climate change, such as "environment," "external costs," "fugitive emissions," or "human adaptive optimism."[24] Concepts are vulnerable. We do not want the concept of human dignity to become obsolete or to die the death of a thousand qualifications (which would make it untranslatable into practices) because the concept of human dignity offers the foundation for a form of life, a specific way of perceiving a person, of experiencing situations, of dealing with intimacy, fragility, and the challenges of moral integrity.[25] If concepts or principles are meant to protect against the exploitation of human vulnerability, the vulnerability of the concepts has to be curbed. And here is, paradoxically maybe, a special and important place for especially vulnerable persons.

I suggest using practices involving vulnerable people as "preferentially relevant" practices to serve as bridges to translate the concept of human dignity into practices. In development work, especially in the face of scarce resources, achievement pressures, or situations with a sense of urgency, respecting human dignity has to happen not infrequently under adverse circumstances. It is tough to respect a person's dignity in the context of a refugee camp, in a field hospital, in a postdisaster context, but also in the context of slow processes of social transformation. It is tough to understand and accept the uniqueness of a person if you are driven by or under the pressure of maximization strategies (maximizing outcomes, maximizing profits). Jacqueline Novogratz, who had given up her high-profile career as a banker at the Chase Manhattan Bank on Wall Street to become involved in development projects in Africa, expressed her frustration with cultural obstacles to what she believed to be "development." She wanted to transform a bakery into a flourishing business ("the blue bakery") but had to accept that the women running the bakery could not work full time or flat out at the bakery since they had so many other social and family obligations to fulfill.[26]

It is tough to practice the art of listening in Haiti after the earthquake of 2010; it takes time and it is costly, financially but also in terms of sacrificing plans and programs. I would like to introduce the concept of *deep practice* here; Dan Coyle coined the term in his observations on high achievements.[27] He wondered about the remarkable soccer talent in Brazil and considered that training under adverse circumstances (e.g., playing rug ball in an uneven favela lot) would constitute a "deep" way of appropriating a practice; if you have mastered the art of playing soccer with a rug ball on a landfill site, how much easier would it be for you to excel in soccer on a real soccer field using a real soccer ball? "Adverse conditions" and "deep commitments" are characteristic of deep practices.

Working with especially vulnerable persons is challenging—very challenging; there are adverse conditions, including the challenge of learning *how* to respect a person who is especially vulnerable. Sheila Barton described her experience of loving her autistic child: she had to learn not to hug her son when he was banging his head against a wall.[28] Raising a child with autism makes families vulnerable; raising a child with autism means raising a particularly vulnerable person. These are challenges that require deep commitments in order for vulnerable persons to endure, to grow. In other words, raising a child with autism is a deep practice of living with a person. In some instances, development work calls for deep practices of human dignity; accepting the responsibility of accompaniment is costly in terms of opportunity costs and responsibility. Martin Kaempchen has described his "way of life" of accompaniment, living in a village in North India and "living with" the villagers rather than "working for" them; he describes his model of development work as "friendship-based accompaniment" and as the kind of approach that honors the dignity of the person.[29] He describes the simplicity of life it takes to be a companion in this setting, the patience, the humility to be guided, and the frustration in the face of persistent and self-sabotaging traditions. Kaempchen's approach may not be adopted as the main paradigm in development work, but it points to the challenge of respecting the dignity of the human person in her mystery and in her uniqueness; this challenge comes with substantial costs. This is a deep practice of human dignity by those prepared to make sacrifices, prepared to hold on to the value even when confronted with adverse conditions. It is especially deep practice if the people involved find themselves transformed.

One could suggest three consequences of the deep practice of human dignity: (1) there is no standard account of dignity; (2) any understanding of human dignity is constantly being challenged and faced with disruption; and (3) deep practice can transform persons and can change other practices. These are challenges to planned development efforts, especially on a large scale. Large projects will require a deep practice of human dignity that is sensitive to the "how" and not only to the "what" to implement. However, enacting human dignity in deep practices will change our social perspective, our outlook, of the world; "if we focus on caring relationships and the relationships between power and caring practices, such as bringing up children and caring for the sick, a radically different set of social arrangements will ensue."[30] There will be new arrangements, and there will be new ways of seeing the world.

Deep practices of human dignity can be identified by looking at "especially vulnerable persons" and by looking at "fundamental human acts" (actions connected to food, the human metabolism, hygiene). I would like to move away from such extreme cases in human dignity discourse (dwarf-tossing, torture, locked-in syndrome, and assisted suicide issues) and instead focus on difficult moments of a person's everyday life. Issues of "body" and "power" point in the direction of deep practices at which I suggest we start looking.[31] Showing respect for a person under adverse circumstances is an expression of a deep practice of human dignity; not reducing a person to a means for an end, even if it is difficult, constitutes a deep practice of human dignity. Reductionisms of all kind (reducing persons to numbers, to expenses, to achievements, to problems, to illnesses, etc.) undermine the possibility for deep practices of human dignity. Real encounters with real persons make it more difficult to engage in reductionist approaches. Ian Brown describes his life with his severely disabled son; he describes his being present in a demanding situation to one needing constant attention, and he describes in beautiful words his own transformation because of his son, the results of a "second-person encounter."[32] He is an ambassador of a deep practice of human dignity. We need these ambassadors—such as Edward, who brought both insight and inspiration to Magnus MacFarlane-Barrow—ambassadors who can help us translate concepts into practices. There is a special need for these ambassadors—that is, especially vulnerable people—in enacting human dignity in development work contexts, since this is ultimately the point of all the development efforts: making sure that each and every person can live a dignified life, as described in *Gaudium et spes* 26. Those who are particularly vulnerable have "deep stories" to tell about human dignity, and these stories invite deep practices of human dignity. Deep practices of dignity also have a prophetic dimension, announcing a world to come. Deep practices of dignity carry not only a memory but also a future.

Principles and concepts have to be nourished; they have to be nurtured by deep practices. These practices are testimonial practices in the sense that they give witness to the possibility of living a culture of dignity even under adverse circumstances. Some of the practices described in this book are testimonies to the possibility of deep enactments of human dignity. As Auden's example has shown, it takes strong beliefs and the ability to dialogue with, listen to, and learn from important ambassadors. The concept of human dignity can best be enacted by looking at practices that show firm commitments to the dignity of the human person in his uniqueness and vulnerability, even under adverse circumstances.

The persons involved in these practices can serve as ambassadors to help us understand the concept of dignity. Deep practices of enacting dignity and learning from these deep practices will lead—and should lead—to a transformation of the person, as Kimberley Brownlee has argued.[33] Vulnerable people and those living with them can be ambassadors of deep practices of human dignity.

If we have firm ethical commitments to the role of deep practices and if we turn to ambassadors of deep practices of human dignity, we can enact the concept in a way similar to the way that W. H. Auden enacted his project of translating from unknown Swedish into familiar English. It is, then, not a matter of translating the concept into separate practices but a matter of enacting human dignity.

NOTES

1. W. H. Auden and Elizabeth Mayer, introduction to *Italian Journey*, by Johann Wolfgang von Goethe, trans. Auden and Mayer (New York: Pantheon Books, 1962), xxiv.

2. Ibid., xxv.

3. W. H. Auden, introduction to *Markings*, by Dag Hammarskjöld, trans. W. H. Auden and Leif Sjöberg (New York: Knopf, 1964), xxii.

4. Kai Falkman, "Signposts in the Wrong Direction: W. H. Auden's Misinterpretation of Dag Hammarsjköld's *Markings*," *Times Literary Supplement*, September 10, 1999, 14–15; Warren Hoge, "Swedes Dispute Translation of a U.N. Legend's Book," *New York Times*, May 22, 2005.

5. Nirmal Dass, *Rebuilding Babel: The Translations of W. H. Auden* (Amsterdam: Rodopi, 1993), 54.

6. Magnus MacFarlane-Barrow, *The Shed That Fed a Million Children: The Extraordinary Story of Mary's Meals* (London: William Collins, 2015), 137.

7. Second Vatican Council, Pastoral Constitution on the Church in the Modern World: *Gaudium et spes*, December 7, 1965, http://www.vatican.va/archive/hist_councils/ii_vatican_council/documents/vat-ii_const_19651207_gaudium-et-spes_en.html, sec. 26.

8. Kathleen Galvin and Les Todres, "Dignity as Honour-Wound: An Experiential and Relational View," *Journal of Evaluation in Clinical Practice* 21 (2015): 410–18.

9. Cf. William T. Cavanaugh, *Field Hospital: The Church's Engagement with a Wounded World* (Grand Rapids, MI: Eerdmans, 2016).

10. Cf. Qingping Liu, "On a Paradox of Christian Love," *Journal of Religious Ethics* 35, no. 4 (2007): 681–94.

11. Cf. Joachim Schulte, *Chor und Gesetz* (Frankfurt am Main: Suhrkamp, 1990).

12. M. Edlund et al., "Concept Determination of Human Dignity," *Nursing Ethics* 20, no. 8 (December 2013): 852, https://doi.org/10.1177/096973 3013487193.

13. Francis, *Evangelii gaudium*, Vatican website, November 24, 2013, http://w2.vatican.va/content/francesco/en/apost_exhortations/documents /papa-francesco_esortazione-ap_20131124_evangelii-gaudium.html, sec. 182.

14. Ludwig Wittgenstein, *Philosophical Investigations*, trans. G.E.M. Anscombe, P.M.S. Hacker, and Joachim Schulte (Oxford: Wiley-Blackwell, 2009), 107.

15. Philippe-André Rodriguez, "Human Dignity as an Essentially Contested Concept," *Cambridge Review of International Affairs* 28, no. 4 (2015): 743–56.

16. MacFarlane-Barrow, *The Shed That Fed A Million Children*, 133. These observations echo the findings of research into the advantages of faith-based organizations (FBOs) in development work; cf. Gerard Clarke, "Faith-Based Organizations and International Development: An Overview," in *Development, Civil Society, and Faith-Based Organizations*, ed. Gerard Clarke, Michael Jennings, and T. Shaw (New York: Palgrave MacMillan, 2007); Dan Heist and Ram A. Cnaan, "Faith-Based International Development Work: A Review," *Religions* 7, no. 19 (2016): 1–17.

17. MacFarlane-Barrow, *The Shed That Fed A Million Children*, 138.

18. Ibid., 142.

19. "I want a Church which is poor and for the poor. They have much to teach us. Not only do they share in the *sensus fidei*, but in their difficulties they know the suffering Christ. We need to let ourselves be evangelized by them." Pope Francis, *Evangelii gaudium*, apostolic exhortation (November 24, 2013), 198.

20. Stephen Darwall, *The Second-Person Standpoint* (Cambridge, MA: Harvard University Press, 2006).

21. Gerald Cohen, *Rescuing Justice and Equality* (Cambridge, MA: Harvard University Press, 2008), 42.

22. Diogo Mainardi, *The Fall: A Father's Memoir in 424 Steps*, trans. Margaret Jull Costa (New York: Other Press, 2014), 25–26.

23. Milan Kundera, *Identity*, trans. Linda Asher (New York: Harper Collins, 1999).

24. Naomi Oreskes and Erik Conway, *The Collapse of Western Civilization: A View from the Future* (New York: Columbia University Press, 2014).

25. Cf. Peter Bieri, *Human Dignity: A Way of Living* (Cambridge: Polity Press, 2017).

26. Jacqueline Novogratz, *The Blue Sweater: Bridging the Gap between Rich and Poor in an Interconnected World* (New York: Rodale, 2009).

27. Dan Coyle, *The Talent Code* (New York: Bantam Books, 2009).

28. Sheila Barton, *Living with Jonathan* (London: Watkins, 2012).

29. Martin Kaempchen, *Leben ohne Armut: Wie Hilfe wirklich helfen kann* (Freiburg im Breisgau: Herder, 2012).

30. Steven D. Edwards, "Three Versions of the Ethics of Care," *Nursing Philosophy* 10, no. 4 (October 2009): 233, https://doi.org/10.1111/j.1466-769X.2009.00415.x.

31. As David J. Mattson and Susan G. Clark explain, "Power is a particularly important value in shaping dignity outcomes. More than wealth, dispositions of power have perhaps the greatest impacts of any value dimension on dignity-relevant dynamics." See their "Human Dignity in Concept and Practice," *Policy Sciences* 44, no. 4 (2011): 315, https://doi.org/10.1007/s11077-010-9124-0.

32. Ian Brown, *The Boy in the Moon: A Father's Journey to Understand His Extraordinary Son* (New York: St. Martin's Press, 2009).

33. Kimberley Brownlee, "Normative Principles and Practical Ethics: A Response to O'Neill," *Journal of Applied Philosophy* 26, no. 3 (2009): 231–37.

TWO

Human Dignity—Does It Imply a Certain Kind of Agency?

A Viewpoint from Sen's Capability Approach to Development

Séverine Deneulin

References to human dignity permeate the discourses of development organizations. From international to local agencies, from secular to faith organizations, all use the concept of human dignity to underpin and justify their work (see Paul Perrin in this volume). Yet the ubiquitous presence of human dignity in development discourses equally matches the conspicuous absence of discussions of what human dignity is. One reason advanced for this lack of conceptualization of human dignity is that concepts are best apprehended not in the abstract but when enacted into concrete practices (see Clemens Sedmak in this volume).

Consider the following two pairs of situations: prisoners crammed in a small prison cell with little ventilation and inadequate water and sanitation facilities versus men severely affected by HIV/AIDS cared for as unique persons in appropriate medical facilities; a man losing his employment because he refused to wear short hair to comply with internal employment guidelines versus a farmer deprived of means of subsistence because the land he lived on was taken by force by another party.[1] Experiencing the contrast within each pair is easier than speculating abstractly about what human dignity is. In the first comparative pair, in one case certain practices have been *enacted* to enhance physical and emotional health, but not in the other. In the second comparative pair, in one case certain practices have been *enacted* to deprive a person of the means of his subsistence, but not in the other.

A central argument of this volume is that the enacting (or nonenacting) of human dignity is a fully relational process. Because human beings are persons in relation (see Simona Beretta in this volume), what one is able to do and be as a human being—for example, be in good health or have decent work—is intrinsically interconnected to what others do or are. To refer to the first comparison, the HIV/AIDS sufferer is able to keep in good emotional health and live in decent material conditions because of other people's actions; the farmer is not able to keep his land and access means of subsistence because of other people's actions. This relational approximation of human dignity does not, however, imply the conclusion that what one is able to be and do is at the mercy of the actions of others and that one's life is a mere consequence of other people's actions. As I argue in this chapter, agency, or being an author of one's life and co-creator with others of one's living conditions, is a core aspect of human dignity.

The aim of this chapter is to examine whether this volume's experiential and relational approximation of human dignity implies a certain kind of human agency. It situates its discussion within the conceptual framework of Amartya Sen's capability approach to development. It is divided as follows. Part II discusses some of the reasons for which the capability approach is particularly suited to examining the kind of agency implied by human dignity. Part III outlines what kind of agency is implied by the anthropology of the capability approach and argues that it is a kind of agency that takes the form of dignity-enacting practices. Part IV illustrates its argument in the context of urban marginality in Argentina. Part V concludes by linking the discussion to the global development architecture.

HUMAN DIGNITY AND FREEDOM

There is no single definition of what the capability approach is.[2] Originally it was conceived as "a moral approach that sees persons from two
different perspectives: well-being and agency."[3] It is not a social theory
or a theory of justice but an approach to evaluating states of affairs from
the perspective of human freedom in its opportunity and process aspects
(well-being and agency, respectively).[4] A person's well-being is constituted by her opportunities to be and do what she has reason to value,
or her "capabilities." A capability is "a person's ability to do valuable acts
or reach valuable states of being,"[5] such as being adequately nourished,
being healthy, reading and writing, and expressing oneself, among others.
A person's agency is "the pursuit of whatever goals or values he or she
regards as important."[6]

The capability approach is particularly suited to exploring the implications of human dignity for agency in the context of development
practice. First, it is the framework that underpins the conception of
development adopted by many development institutions and known as
"human development." As the United Nations Development Programme
defines it in the twentieth-anniversary edition of its *Human Development
Report*, human development is "the expansion of people's freedoms to
live long, healthy and creative lives [the *well-being aspect of freedom*]; to
advance other goals they have reason to value; and to engage actively in
shaping development equitably and sustainably on a shared planet [the
agency aspect of freedom]."[7]

Second, the capability approach proposes an inductive methodology
for development that starts from human experience and not abstract
principles. This is particularly reflected in Sen's conceptualization of justice from the perspective of comparative assessments of the kinds of
lives people are able to live in given situations.[8] As he has recently put it:
"The basic argument for a realization-focused understanding, for which
I would argue, is that justice cannot be divorced from the actual world
that emerges."[9] In discussing the demands of justice, "Should we not,"
Sen asks, "also have to examine what does emerge in the society, including the kind of lives that people can actually lead, given the institutions
and rules and also other influences?"[10]

In contrast to Amartya Sen, Martha Nussbaum has proposed a version of the capability approach that includes an explicit conceptualization

of human dignity as the starting point for remedial action. She establishes a list of ten central human capabilities that we have to secure so that each person has the means to pursue her conception of the good life. Among Nussbaum's central capabilities are being able to move freely, to be free of violence, to express herself, to live a life of normal length, to form a life plan, and to associate freely with others.[11] Initially based on Aristotelian internal essentialism about what constitutes "good human functioning" and what perfects human nature or makes human life a good one, Nussbaum's list of capabilities is now framed within Rawlsian political liberalism. She appeals to human dignity as an intuitive idea to justify the list and what deserves to be respected and guaranteed at the constitutional level.[12] For the purpose of this chapter—to examine what kind of agency is implied by the capability approach and to shed light on what counts as dignity-enacting practices—the discussion will concentrate on Sen's capability approach, and not Nussbaum's version, because of its greater focus on agency.[13]

Freedom is a central aspect of what it is to be human in Sen's capability approach. Respecting one's humanity involves respecting one's freedom in its opportunity and agency aspects. A person who works fourteen hours a day at a wage that does not allow her and her family to be adequately nourished or sheltered—and who has no channel to voice concerns about her working conditions—has not had her freedom as a human being respected.

Freedom, or well-being and agency, is not, however, the only feature of human life in Sen's capability approach. In a box featured in the *Human Development Report* 2013 and titled "What is it like to be a human being?," Sen adds to the "richness of human life" the ability "to speak," "to enter in dialogue with others," and "to reason." He uses the analogy of a person wearing an ill-fitting shoe to illustrate his anthropology: "Only the wearer may know where the shoe pinches, but pinch-avoiding arrangements cannot be effectively undertaken without giving voice to the people and giving them extensive opportunities for discussion."[14] As he has put it more recently, "To be able to speak to each other, to hear one another, cannot but be a central capability that we human beings have great reason to value."[15]

A critical feature of the dialogue Sen highlights for promoting freedom is the ability to put oneself in the position of another person: "When we try to assess . . . which kind of societies should be understood to be patently unjust, we have reason to listen and pay some attention to the views and suggestions of others, which might or might not lead us to revise some of our own conclusions."[16] He sees "the ability to sympathize and to reason" as core human faculties.[17] Speaking about the importance of reasoning and sympathy in the context of famines, he writes: "The political compulsion in a democracy to eliminate famines depends critically on the power of public reasoning in making nonvictims take on the need to eradicate famines as their *own* commitment. Democratic institutions can be effective only if different sections of the population appreciate what is happening to others, and if the political process reflects a broader social understanding of deprivation."[18] Sen's capability approach has often been portrayed as "ethically individualistic" in the sense that it advocates that states of affairs be evaluated in terms of what each person is able to do or be and not some "being or doing" that pertains to a group or collectivity as a whole.[19] Beyond its surface, however, the approach contains a fundamental relational anthropology. It is *how* one relates to others, whether one listens, enters into another person's life, or takes the removal of a person's inability to be adequately nourished as one's own commitment, which provides the foundation for Sen's capability approach to development. "We are socially interactive creatures,"[20] he affirms, and even what counts as a "valuable" or "basic" doing or being of human beings is the result of an interactive process of public discussion.[21] As he put it in his *Idea of Justice*, "In valuing a person's ability to take part in the life of the society, there is an implicit valuation of the life of the society itself."[22] To avoid misunderstandings and mistakenly considering the capability approach as too "individualistic," Ingrid Robeyns proposes the principle of "each person as an end"— or each human being having equal moral worth—as an alternative to the philosophical jargon of ethical individualism, which sociologists and philosophers interpret differently (with the former tending to conflate ethical with ontological and methodological individualism).[23]

To be a human being is to interact with others, and this interaction is constitutive of what a person values being and doing. The ability to express oneself freely, to communicate, to be listened to and to act—in other words, to engage in social and political participation—"can be central to our creativity as well as our *dignity*."[24] The next part of the chapter expands this relational anthropology to outline some features of the kind of human agency implied by it.

AGENCY AND RELATIONALITY

The World Bank has defined agency as the "ability to make decisions about one's own life and act on them to achieve a desired outcome, free of violence, retribution and fear."[25] Sen's approximation of agency also takes this ability to make decisions and act freely as its key feature but proposes a more intersubjective, and intertemporal, perspective on agency. Agency is closely related to public reasoning, which is the result of interaction with others over time. Even the pursuit of goals or values a person regards as important (cf. Sen's own definition of agency, above), is the result of an interactive valuation process about what counts as important or not.[26]

In this respect, critical theory can offer a useful complement to Sen's intersubjective account of agency because it highlights that it is through processes of intersubjective recognition that one becomes an agent.[27] Linking Sen's freedom-based account of justice with Axel Honneth's recognition-based account of justice—that is, linking an account of justice based on "what you have" [capabilities] with one based on "how you are treated"[28]—Uruguayan philosopher Gustavo Pereira argues that there are three domains in which people need to be recognized by others in order to become agents à la Sen: (1) the domain of intimate and close relationships in which people acquire self-trust (people need to be recognized for who they are to be able to understand their own needs); (2) the domain of legal relationships in which people acquire self-respect (people need to be recognized as equal subjects of rights to be able to understand themselves as deserving equal treatment); and (3) the domain of social relationships in which people acquire self-esteem (people need to be recognized for their achievements to be able to understand themselves as having talents and as contributing to the life of society). When these intimate, legal, and social relationships are not functioning well, Pereira argues, people lose the conditions for being agents—that is, they are not able to engage in public reasoning processes, argue a position on the ground of reasons, make claims, or disagree with others.[29]

To illustrate his argument, Pereira tells the story of three fictional characters, Andrès, Luis, and Ana, each being a prototype of the millions of Latin Americans who live at the urban peripheries.[30] Andrès makes a living out of recycling the city's rubbish. He lives on a day-to-day basis and is not able to plan for the future. He would like to move out of the neighborhood because of the violence and lack of access to basic services there, but he cannot afford to live elsewhere. Luis lives in the same area. His father opened a carpentry workshop, and he has learned the craft of making furniture. Thanks to some vocational training given by a civil society organization, he has been able to obtain a technical secondary education and has expanded his workshop, hiring a few young people and training them in woodcraft. His business is profitable enough, and he has started saving so he can move his business and have better access to other areas of the city. Ana is another neighbor, who has been working in a factory since a very young age. When her factory closed, she mobilized with her co-workers to reclaim the factory and restart its activities under cooperative ownership. Through the many meetings she participated in, she was able to understand the economic policies that led to the factory's closure and her unemployment. She has joined a political organization that is pressing for policy change.

Each of these three characters illustrates how different modes of interaction with others have shaped their agency. Andrès has very little access to relations that would build his self-trust, self-respect, and self-esteem. Growing up in a context of public and domestic violence, he and his needs have not been recognized by his close relationships, nor has he learned how to express his needs due to fear. He is not recognized as equal to his neighbors in his worthiness of rights, as he does not receive the same treatment by state authorities as other citizens in the city. He has little self-esteem, for he is not recognized as contributing to society because his job as rubbish recycler is not socially valued. In contrast, Luis has gained self-trust and self-esteem, even if he does not enjoy the same access to basic rights as other citizens in the city. Although violence has sometimes characterized his family environment, the support he has received from the vocational school opened in the neighborhood has given him the space to express himself. His job in furniture making and the satisfaction of his customers have given him a sense of contributing to the lives of others. While doing a repetitive job with little sense of contributing to society, Ana has, however, through her relations with co-workers, been able to recognize her own needs and engage in critical reflection on how to act to maintain her employment after the factory closure.

Given this relational or intersubjective feature of agency in Sen's capability approach, it is not surprising that Sen has closely associated agency with responsibility. Concern for other people's lives is a constitutive element of one's reasoning about what actions to take.[31] As he explained in his first full exposition of the novel moral approach he was introducing in the social sciences: "The importance of the agency aspect, in general, relates to the view of persons as responsible agents."[32] The next section of this chapter illustrates this theoretical discussion of agency and human dignity in the context of marginal neighborhoods in the city of Buenos Aires and considers anew the fictional stories of Andrès, Luis, and Ana through real-life characters.

DIGNITY-ENACTING PRACTICES IN A MARGINALIZED URBAN CONTEXT

Sergio is a waste picker in the federal capital city of Buenos Aires.[33] He started searching for waste to recycle in the early 1990s after losing his job. In 2002, he met a group of students who had set up a soup kitchen in response to the December 2001 Argentine economic crisis. They progressively came to know each other and started a process of listening to the problems waste pickers faced—the exploitation of intermediaries, the bribes they had to pay, the dangerous work conditions, child labor, and economic insecurity, among others.[34] As the meetings on the streets continued, they formed an organization, the Movement of Excluded Workers, as an institutional platform for waste pickers to use to express themselves in the public domain. As Sergio puts it, "Before, every *cartonero* looked after him/herself only, but we had to speak with one voice. I was lucky to have had good teachers who taught me I had rights and had to fight for them."[35] Today, Sergio works as an urban recycler in a cooperative directly contracted by the city government.

This improvement in his life has been the result not of state beneficence but of exercising the agency of the workers themselves and of the processes of recognition that facilitated their participation in public reasoning. In the case of Sergio, there was a reconstruction of his relation to himself, which enabled him to voice his lived experience. It was through the relations he developed with the people at the soup kitchen and his friendship with Jorge Bergoglio, whom he met in 2007, that he learned to articulate his needs.

The formation of a political organization played a key role in amplifying the voices of the waste pickers in the public sphere. Thanks to their collective organizing, in 2002 they succeeded in repealing a municipal law that had proscribed waste picking. The abolition of the law contributed considerably to a positive appreciation of the work of waste pickers and their contribution to society as urban recyclers. It also led to the elimination of exploitation by intermediaries, as the workers could deal with companies directly through cooperatives to negotiate fair prices for their products. The organization also negotiated a public contract with the city government to collect the city's waste. This transformed waste pickers into public employees with secure incomes, health and social insurance, and safer labor conditions.

Sergio's life reflects the stories of the three fictional characters in the previous section. His relationship with the student activists and Bergoglio gave him a space in which he could articulate and express his needs (developing self-trust). The forming of a political organization provided the conditions for Sergio's legal and safe employment, with a stable income, health security, and labor guarantees (contributing to his self-respect), and for the recognition of his work as a service to society (contributing to his self-esteem).

Three persons who also bring to life the fictional characters of the previous section are Vicky, Delia, and Marta, women in their fifties who live in a marginalized neighborhood of Greater Buenos Aires.[36] At a young age, Vicky migrated with her family to the city in search of a better life. Her father was alcoholic and lost the family's money to gambling. She suffered from domestic violence as a child and, when a teenager, lost her mother, who had long suffered from depression. Vicky completed secondary education while working, but further education was made impossible by pregnancy and the lack of public transportation. Today she teaches in a school for adults in the neighborhood where she lives.

Delia is another rural migrant. The elder females in her family migrated first to the city to take on domestic work, leaving Delia alone to look after her father, older brothers, and younger siblings. She left school at age ten due to her domestic duties and, within a few years, moved to the city to work in domestic service. Delia completed secondary education as an adult. She now works as a secretary in her parish and in a community health center.

Marta lost her mother when she was nine. She never went to school and considers herself illiterate. Her father was alcoholic and violent. Having worked in domestic service and waste collection to survive, Marta is now the coordinator of a parish communal kitchen where she receives especially at-risk youth with drug addictions. Three of Marta's nine children are drug addicts, and one committed suicide.

As in the case of Sergio, the transformation in the lives of Delia, Vicky, and Marta is the result not merely of policy change but of their agency, fostered through relationships and intersubjective reasoning processes. A major difference between the case of Sergio and their cases, however, is that "dignity-enacting practices" were not mediated by collective organizing and direct engagement with state institutions. Delia, Vicky, and Martha joined a women's group centered on "mutual listening" that Irish nuns facilitated in the neighborhood.

This listening space helped them to articulate their pain and needs and to generate a healing process. In Delia's words: "I like it, and it did me a lot of good because I got out all the things from when I was a child. . . . Today I tell this as a story . . . because I have processed it. . . . Before, each time I tried to talk about it . . . I cried and cried and cried: Why did this happen to me? . . . And with time the wounds healed, and in fact, I now facilitate this mutual listening for other women. . . . I am helping other women so that they can live."[37] Vicky says: "I have learned a lot from my father . . . because I believe that one of the biggest graces I have is having learned to forgive. This is why I have been able to forgive my father, a lot of things I was able to forgive him. . . . And when one is able to forgive, one starts to understand and see the person from another place, and I could understand why my father was the way he was."[38]

This regaining of self-trust through processes of recognition in mutual listening circles has been a stepping stone for other actions. Through the mediation of three Irish nuns who had lived in the neighborhood since the early 1980s, the women became protagonists of a series of other "dignity-enhancing practices." A communal kitchen was opened following the first economic crisis in Argentina in 1989, and it is now a community hub, with Marta at its center. One user of the kitchen reported: "There are many children who come and eat, many mothers, many elderly people, and thanks to the strength of Marta, we keep going, in health or without health, in rain or no rain. Marta does not make black and white distinctions; she receives us like we are. . . . I was in crisis and she opened the door, and thanks to her I am better."[39]

In response to the 2001 economic crisis, the nuns opened a women's health center, in which Delia now works, and thanks to which many women have been able to exit situations of domestic violence. It is also through her relationship with the nuns that Delia found the confidence to complete her secondary education and to initiate a school for adults, for which Vicky is the coordinator.[40]

Contributing to the life of society through their work, Vicky, Delia, and Marta acquired greater self-esteem. They also developed greater self-respect as their efforts expanded the valuable capabilities of which they had been deprived, such as the capabilities to be adequately nourished, to complete secondary education, and to access basic healthcare.

Since 2015, the United Nations' Sustainable Development Goals (SDGs) have been at the forefront of development discourses and policies. They have been the object of many public discussions and catalysts for many social mobilizations demanding that governments be accountable to the targets. Framed as constituting a "road to dignity,"[41] many of the SDGs— decent work, social protection, women's education, freedom from domestic violence, recycling, healthcare, child labor, and others—touch the lives of the people in the above-mentioned narratives.

There is a danger, however, that human dignity–enacting practices— or, as Clemens Sedmak calls them in this volume, practices of "doing dignity"—may be reduced to achieving a set of statistical goals, losing sight of the lives of the women and men who make up the statistics. An experiential and relational perspective on human dignity does not eliminate the need for goal pursuit and data collection, but it highlights the equal centrality of the relational context in which actions toward these goals are framed, as the authors of other chapters in this volume point out (e.g., Ilaria Schnyder von Wartensee, and Steve Reifenberg and Elizabeth Hlabse). In the cases of Sergio, Delia, Vicky, and Marta, it was a socially interactive context, characterized by listening and dialogue, that made actions to improve labor standards, health and educational achievements, and violence reduction possible.

At the conference on which this volume is based, the organizers gave participants a glassed postcard of a sculpture that portrays a biblical narrative of an encounter of two pregnant women, with these words of Pope Francis on the back of the card: "This ability to see yourselves in the faces of others, this daily proximity to their share of troubles—because they exist and we all have them—and their little acts of heroism: this is what enables you to practice the commandment of love, not on the basis of ideas or concepts, but rather on the basis of genuine personal encounter. We need to build up this culture of encounter." By using Amartya Sen's capability approach to development, in this chapter I have sought to explore some social transformations that can be born from such "genuine personal encounters." Whether these transformations are best generated through engagement with the state (as in Sergio's narrative) or outside it (as in Delia, Vicky, and Marta's narratives) is a matter for "public reasoning" to settle in each context.

NOTES

1. These examples are taken from Paolo Carozza, "Human Rights, Human Dignity, and Human Experience," in *Understanding Human Dignity*, ed. Christopher McCrudden (Oxford: Oxford University Press, 2013), 615–30.

2. Ingrid Robeyns has attempted to present what she calls a "cartwheel" definition of the capability approach. See "Capabilitarianism," *Journal of Human Development and Capabilities* 17, no 3. (2016): 397–414, which she later revised as a modular account of the capability approach. See *Wellbeing, Freedom and Social Justice: The Capability Approach Re-examined* (Cambridge: Open Book Publishers, 2017). This lack of a definitional canon can be seen as one strength of the approach, as it can be associated with different theories and used in many contexts, but it can also be open to misinterpretation. See Elise Klein, "The Curious Case of Using the Capability Approach in Australian Indigenous Policy," *Journal of Human Development and Capabilities* 17, no. 2 (2016): 345–59.

3. Amartya Sen, "Well-Being, Agency, and Freedom: The Dewey Lectures 1984," *Journal of Philosophy* 82, no. 4 (1985): 169.

4. Ibid.; Sen, *Inequality Re-examined* (Oxford: Clarendon Press, 1992); *Development as Freedom* (Oxford: Oxford University Press, 1999); *Rationality and Freedom* (Cambridge, MA: Harvard University Press, 2002).

5. Amartya Sen, "Capability and Well-Being," in *The Quality of Life*, ed. Martha Nussbaum and Amartya Sen (Oxford: Clarendon Press, 1993), 30.

6. Sen, "Well-Being, Agency, and Freedom," 203.

7. United Nations Development Programme, *Human Development Report 2010: The Real Wealth of Nations*, November 2010, http://hdr.undp.org /en/content/human-development-report-2010.

8. Amartya Sen, *The Idea of Justice* (London: Allen Lane, 2009). For a more extended discussion of human suffering as a starting point for thinking about justice, see Amartya Sen, "The Contemporary Relevance of Buddha," *Ethics and International Affairs* 28, no. 1 (2014): 15–27.

9. Amartya Sen, *The Country of First Boys and Other Essays* (New Delhi: Oxford University Press, 2015), 182.

10. Ibid.

11. See, among others, Martha Nussbaum, "Poverty and Human Functioning: Capability as Fundamental Entitlements," in *Poverty and Inequality*, ed. David B. Grusky and Ravi Kanbur (Stanford: Stanford University Press, 2006): 47–75; *Women and Human Development* (Cambridge: Cambridge University Press, 2000); and *Creating Capabilities* (Cambridge, MA: Harvard University Press, 2011).

12. For a discussion of Nussbaum's appeal to human dignity, see Rutger Claassen, "Human Dignity and the Capability Approach," in *The Cambridge Handbook of Human Dignity*, ed. Marcus Düwell, Jens Braarvig, Roger Brownsword, and Dietmar Mieth (Cambridge: Cambridge University Press, 2014), 240–49; Paola Bernardini, "Human Dignity and Human Capabilities in Martha C. Nussbaum," *Iustum Aequum Salutare* 6, no. 4 (2010): 45–51. For a discussion of Nussbaum's move from Aristotelian internal essentialism to Rawlsian political liberalism, see Séverine Deneulin, "Recovering Nussbaum's Aristotelian Roots," *International Journal of Social Economics* 40, no. 7 (2013): 624–32.

13. See Muriel Gilardone and Antoinette Baujard, "Sen Is Not a Capability Theorist," *Journal of Economic Methodology* 24, no. 1 (2015): 1–19. Examining why Sen is so vehemently opposed to being labelled a capability theorist by his commentators, they argue that concerns for agency and public reasoning are central to his capability approach.

14. Amartya Sen, "What Is It Like to Be a Human Being?," in United Nations Development Programme, *Human Development Report 2013: The Rise of the South; Human Progress in a Diverse World*, 2013, http://hdr.undp.org/en /content/what-it-be-human-being, 24.

15. Sen, *Country of First Boys*, 88.

16. Sen, *Idea of Justice*, 88.

17. Ibid., 414–15.

18. Sen, *Country of First Boys*, xxxvii; italics mine.

19. Ingrid Robeyns, "Sen's Capability Approach and Feminist Concerns," in *The Capability Approach: Concepts, Measures and Applications*, ed. Sabina Alkire, Mozaffar Qizilbash, and Flavio Comim (Cambridge: Cambridge University Press, 2008), 82–104. See also Robeyns, "Capabilitarianism." For critiques that ethical individualism has to be a core feature of the approach, see Solava Ibrahim, "Collective Capabilities: What Are They and Why Are They Important?," in *Maitreyee, E-bulletin of the Human Development and Capability Association*, June 2013, https://hd-ca.org/publications/maitreyee-june-2013-collectivity-in-the-ca; Séverine Deneulin, "Beyond Individual Freedom and Agency: Structures of Living Together in Sen's Capability Approach to Development," in *The Capability Approach*, ed. Sabina Alkire, Mozaffar Qizilbash, and Flavio Comim, 105–24.

20. Sen, *Country of First Boys*, 81.

21. Ibid., 89.

22. Sen, *The Idea of Justice*, 246.

23. Robeyns, *Wellbeing, Freedom and Social Justice*, 57–59.

24. Amartya Sen, "Economic Development and Capability Expansion in Historical Perspective," *Pacific Economic Review* 6, no. 2 (2001): 188; italics mine.

25. World Bank, *Voice and Agency* (Washington, DC: World Bank, 2014). See also Sarah Gammage, Naila Kabeer, and Yana van der Meulen-Rodgers, "Voice and Agency: Where Are We Now?," *Feminist Economics* 22, no. 1 (2016): 1–29.

26. Sen, *Idea of Justice*, 244–47. For a discussion of agency as a "temporally embedded process of social engagement," see Mustafa Emirbayer and Ann Mische, "What Is Agency?," *American Journal of Sociology* 103, no. 4 (1998): 962–1023.

27. For the links between the capability approach and critical theory, see Gustavo Pereira, *Elements of a Critical Theory of Justice* (New York: Palgrave, 2013), and Rainer Forst, "Two Pictures of Justice," *Justice, Democracy and the Right to Justification*, ed. Rainer Forst, (London: Bloomsbury Academic, 2014), 3–26.

28. Forst, "Two Pictures of Justice," 6.

29. Pereira, *Elements of a Critical Theory*, 65. It is beyond the scope of this chapter to engage with the vast body of literature on critical theory and Honneth's work. See, among others, Nancy Fraser and Axel Honneth,

Redistribution or Recognition? A Political-Philosophical Exchange (New York: Verso, 2003), and Christopher F. Zurn, "Recognition, Redistribution, and Democracy: Dilemmas of Honneth's Critical Social Theory," *European Journal of Philosophy* 13, no. 1 (2005): 89–126.

30. Pereira, *Elements of a Critical Theory*, 114–17. The characters have been slightly modified from the original.

31. Sen, *Country of First Boys*, xxxvii, and *Idea of Justice*, 414–15.

32. Sen, "Well-Being, Agency, and Freedom," 204.

33. For a short story on his life as he tells it, see http://hosting.soundslides .com/tcfcz. For a similar story, see the life of Nohra Padilla, an urban recycler from Bogota, narrated in United Nations Development Programme, *Human Development Report 2015: Work for Human Development*, 2015, http://hdr.undp .org/en/2015-report,138.

34. Rafael Chamky, personal communication, December 3, 2014.

35. Sergio Sánchez, personal communication, December 4, 2014. A *cartonero* is a waste picker in Argentina.

36. Their stories are narrated in Ana Lourdes Suárez and Gabriela Zengarini, "Gracias a Que Caminamos con Ellas: Prácticas de Mujeres en Barrios Marginales desde una Mística de Ojos Abiertos," in *Ciudad Vivida: Prácticas de Espiritualidad en Buenos Aires*, ed. Virginia Azcuy (Buenos Aires: Editorial Guadalupe, 2014), 73–115. Also available at http:// www.catholicwomenspeak.com/wp-content/uploads/2015/08/Suarez-and -Zengarini_una-mística-de-ojos-abiertos1.pdf.

37. Delia, cited in Suárez and Zengarini, "Gracias a Que Caminamos," 95.

38. Vicky, cited in ibid., 96.

39. A user of the kitchen, cited in Suárez and Zengarini, "Gracias a Que Caminamos," 103.

40. When Delia expressed her desire to complete school but had no idea how to go about doing so, one of the nuns told her: "Well, look for five other women and I shall find you a teacher and we can start a school in this house." In this way, a program of secondary education for adults in the neighborhood developed. See Suárez and Zengarini, "Gracias a Que Caminamos," 95.

41. United Nations, *The Road to Dignity by 2030: Ending Poverty, Transforming All Lives and Protecting the Planet* (New York: United Nations, 2014), http://www.un.org/disabilities/documents/reports/SG_Synthesis_Report _Road_to_Dignity_by_2030.pdf.

THREE

Freedom and Agency

The Importance of Time and Relations for Development

Simona Beretta

In this chapter I would like to contribute to the dialogue on human dignity and development by exploring human freedom and agency as experienced in action, as real-time processes within factual constraints, uncertainties, and ambivalences, and in relation, embedded in a story of relations with things, with others, and with inner drivers of human decisions and choices (needs, evidence, aspirations, and motivations) that encompass and transcend material conditions. Inner drivers, however hard to define, are easy to recognize in practice; development itself is hard to encapsulate in a definition yet easy to recognize with reference to elemental human experience.

THE NONMATERIAL DRIVERS OF MATERIAL DEVELOPMENT

Development remains an enigmatic process: Despite insightful *ex post* narratives on the rise and the decline of nations, we still seem to lack the capacity to "produce" inclusive, sustainable development and even to spur economic growth. Lack of political commitment, inadequate financing, technical limitations, inadequacies in economic forecasting, and related reasons partly explain the limited success of development policies and practices; however, the roots of development processes run deeper and fundamentally concern symbolic transcendent motivations and meanings of human actions, which drive the determination to explore new possibilities beyond necessary routine behavior.

When Adam Smith wrote *An Inquiry into the Nature and Causes of the Wealth of Nations*, he connected the material dimensions of economic dynamism (the division of labor and extension of the market) with its human and social roots. Beyond writings of Smith that can be read as stereotypes underlining the material interests of the "brewer" and the "butcher,"[1] in other writings Smith actually frames the division of labor in a thorough discussion of the human "propensity to truck, barter, and exchange one thing for another" and connects this propensity to "the faculties of reason and speech,"[2] distinctive dimensions of the experience of being a person in relation.[3] Also, in discussing the extension of the market, Smith sets the process of wealth creation in a framework encompassing many nonmaterial, relational, and institutional conditions. We can summarize thus, using contemporary language: Accessing trustful and reliable networks of personal, social, and institutional relations makes it reasonable to work for others and with others (dividing labor) and to access economies of scale by specialization and trade (extending the market). Unfortunately, Smith's precious intuitions on the centrality of human work, social attitudes, and institutions in economic development—well beyond the metaphor of the "invisible hand"—got lost in the sequel: Economics became the dismal science of scarcity, in which atomistic agents are described to operate predictably "as if led by an invisible hand" within impersonal institutional mechanisms.[4]

Scarcity, means/ends, and trade-offs continue to underpin the common economic narratives and summarize the general public's perception of what economics is about. No wonder development theory, policies, and practices are often framed in terms of means and ends, focusing on prioritizing development aims (ends) or on expanding financial resources to scale up interventions (means). Inner motivations and aspirations of development-friendly actions, however, make the difference. When closely inspected, even the typical textbook drivers of growth (resources, technology, institutions, and preferences—which are ordered differently depending on the approach) exist only as the results of a previous "thick" history of human agency, embedded in meaningful personal and social relations.

Take *natural resources*: what we count as resources today are the fruits of a long story of human relations with material reality driven by a mix of wonder and control. Human agency is required to imagine how to transform raw matter into valuable economic resources; once resources are recognized as such, their use—or abuse—again reflects human decisions about who is entitled to access them and who is responsible for their sound use, with significant consequences for the quality and sustainability of economic growth. *Science and technology*, again, develop through actual people engaging reason and passion in learning and sharing among trusting relations and in receiving and transmitting discoveries and inventions across space and time. When wonder fades into technocratic ideology, the quality of material progress itself is endangered.

Similarly, *human resources* are not simply there: A story of personal, meaningful relations accompanies the transition from birth to creativity;[5] to be creative, one must have first been a curious and unquiet adolescent, a funny child, a tireless toddler, and a defenseless infant in need of care. As to *institutions*, their reappearance in mainstream macro studies of growth is a welcome sign of reconsidering the power relations and power structures driving historical processes toward development or decay; institutions' design and performance depend largely on the inner drivers of the people involved and on the quality of their interpersonal and social relations. Appropriation and accumulation are powerful instruments of command over material things, but the growth they temporarily spur is likely to contribute to the (slower or faster) decay of material wealth itself. Narratives of "why nations fail," in fact, identify "extractive," as opposed to "inclusive," institutions as the roots of failure.[6]

Last but not least, *preferences* matter for development; for example, intertemporal preferences—that is, how we relate with something so immaterial as the future—shape savings and investment decisions and, thus, material growth. Traditional economic approaches generally assume preferences to be exogenous and stable so as to identify causal connections between changes in opportunity sets and decisions and eventually to apply this learning to development policy. Behavioral economics focuses on the mental processes behind actual decision making, highlighting the potential impact of "priming" and "framing" actions and using the results to devise alternative development tools: People may in fact be "nudged" into behaving in ways conducive to better development outcomes.[7] The instrumental use of nudging techniques for development purposes raises sensitive ethical issues, which obviously need to be assessed case by case; however, this approach is innovative in its recognition that individual agency reflects preference structures that can be modified within social relations; in particular, "exposure to a given social context shapes who people are."[8]

In sum: All basic drivers of development—resources, technology, institutions, and preferences—are not simply exogenous, or exogenously manageable, conditions; they depend on complex interactions among individual decisions made in real time and within concrete relations. This perspective makes it possible to answer questions such as how and why agents undertake the sort of innovative, improbable, and occasionally gratuitous actions that contribute to development. Why might someone in a position of power choose to exploit resources to the point of depletion in order to pursue particular interests (be they individual, familial, tribal, ethnic, or related to special groups), while others, in similar circumstances, might strive to benefit the community? Agents need good reasons to take the risk of development actions, to dare the unthought-of, to trust others to work together instead of relying on one's own resources and routines.

THE IMPORTANCE OF TIME AND RELATIONS: THE DYNAMISM OF HUMAN FREEDOM AND AGENCY

There are important "achievement" dimensions of freedom and agency that correspondingly imply the duty to uphold universal, inviolable, inalienable, and indivisible human rights;[9] fortunately, there is broad consensus regarding the need to reinforce the external sociopolitical and economic conditions that are conducive to expanded and sustained individual agency. However, the inner-dynamic dimension of personal freedom and agency in sustaining socioeconomic development remains insufficiently explored and deserves attention within a dynamic relational perspective. Development is indeed about freedom.[10] Here I especially focus on the inner élan of freedom that encompasses and transcends a person's set of material endowments, functionings, and capabilities (similar to what Sen names "agency freedom as procedural control").[11]

A *static* view of freedom highlights the actual possibility of selecting the preferred option out of the available set of alternatives; in this case, freedom extends when the set of desirable options expands. Opportunity freedom is relevant to the perspective of well-being achievements; however, the static view of freedom also appeals to a consumerist mentality in which decision makers are in fact passive "adapters" (optimizers are actually smart adapters). The consumerist mentality is both attractive and easy to grasp: hence, it is diffuse and pervasive;[12] but it is inherently conservative, and it does not match with becoming a protagonist of development. The static view of freedom, in sum, represents human decisions and behavior when circumstances are taken as given and the effects of one's choices can be easily predicted; that is, static freedom involves routines and a narrow procedural reason.

However, whenever ignorance and "strong," or "radical,"[13] uncertainty prevail—which is the case in most of life's circumstances—the relevant notions of human reason, freedom, and agency need to be broadened. A *dynamic* view of freedom concerns why and how it is reasonable to engage one's energy for something valuable and desirable yet uncertain and even unlikely. This perspective takes into account the dynamic, relational nature of human experience: agency occurs in the "here and now" of contingent situations, yet it can transcend them on the basis of reasonable expectations that something new is possible. Dynamic freedom and agency, thus, respond to a broader, more well-rounded notion of rationality in which past and present interpersonal and social relationships matter.[14]

The static and dynamic representations of economic agency can be exemplified with reference to human work—the efficient cause of wealth creation and development. Economic "doing" (*homo faber*) and economic "acting" (*homo agens*) provide very different perspectives:

The process of doing inserts the *res* . . . in a logical sequence of physical and mental operations, conceived as a closed and autarchic system. Such operations can be analyzed in the categories of means and ends, causes and consequences, inputs and outputs; . . . *Homo faber* is lonely, individualist and autarchic. . . . His freedom coincides with his power of control over means, and it is constantly threatened by the antagonistic power of others. Hence, *homo faber* does not create personal identity, history or *polis*; he is rather structurally inclined to give up his freedom in exchange for security. . . .

While the process of doing can be expressed as a finite "monological" process, acting takes the form of an open "dia-logical" relation. Acting for another person is both doing something for her but also with her. . . . The point of view of *homo agens* is "im-perfect" by definition: in order to face the new, unpredictable things, it is necessary to continuously and freely dare, to try, to experiment. *Homo agens* has to be interested in others, since his action is mandated by others and he himself demands from others.[15]

Transcending the conservative means-ends rationality of *homo faber*, driven by necessary cause-consequence relations, one can creatively explore the space of possibility and—after prudent assessment—take the risk of innovative actions. Exposure to a concrete history of meaningful relations with reality, with other persons, and with one's inner needs and aspirations can make it reasonable to innovate; reasonable, in the sense that one can provide a sound narrative about why a given action should be taken, a narrative that does not contradict hard evidence, can be communicated to other persons, and is based on the common sense of prudence.[16]

Exposure to lasting relationships, whereby a person gains insight into what is true, good, and beautiful, is key for the maturation of an individual's personality, especially those domains of personality—cultural, spiritual, and moral—that favor creativity and innovation. Different nonmaterial dimensions appear to correlate with development outcomes: aspirations, self-control, and hope play a significant role in breaking the cycle of poverty.[17] Aspirational hope, in particular, involves several key components, among them goals, actual and perceived agency (or self-efficacy), and pathways (including the removal of actual or perceived constraints). Conversely, lack of hope can contribute to poverty and deprivation traps.[18]

Despite this evidence, shortcuts in policy design and practice are frequent. Personal action is reduced to predictable behavior—reaction to external incentives (of the "old" and "new" types: material incentives as well as framing, priming, and nudging) as if historical, biological, or sociopsychological conditions could determine human actions.

TAKING ELEMENTAL EXPERIENCE SERIOUSLY: THE PERSON IN ACTION IS PERSON IN RELATION

Intentionality, rationality, and consciousness are dynamic experiences that exceed the purely cognitive dimension. As Karol Wojtyła wrote: "Since Descartes, knowledge about man and his world has been identified with the cognitive function.... And yet, in reality, does man reveal himself in thinking or, rather, in the actual enacting of his existence? ... Action reveals the person, and we look at the person through his action.... Action gives us the best insight into the inherent essence of the person and allows us to understand the person more fully."[19] It is unlikely that one can grasp the essence of human reason and agency by abstractly *thinking* about it. Observing the person in action is an easier, more appropriate method for learning about the unified integral experience of deciding and acting within the vast multiform reality in which we live. Human reason is indeed about relations; literally, reason— *ratio*—is relation.[20]

When I observe my actions as if from outside, I find myself at the crossroads of my own material, bodily being, with nonmaterial dimensions that are equally vivid and real: sentiments, memories, desires, and evidence that shape the existential certainties I need to assess whether risky decisions are reasonable. Different cultural traditions provide different names for this elemental, universal experience: *who I am* cannot be entirely located in either the material or the nonmaterial dimensions of my being human. Whenever a person says "I," she implies the "dual unity" of her being human, which transcends mere materiality.[21]

The person in action, in short, discovers herself as a person in relation: with herself,[22] with others, and with reality—which always hints at realities beyond. She can tell who she is by referring to the narrative of her personal history of contingent multifaceted encounters: from birth (her genealogy) through all subsequent encounters (with things and people), up to the "here and now" of her present identity.

Thus, human identity is not static: it changes with experiencing the (fascinating and frightening) otherness of reality. Experiencing reality is more than simply perceiving things and people to be "out there": I really experience reality when I become aware of it and consciously compare it with the nucleus of my innermost evidence and needs. This nucleus, our "heart," is the primordial locus of human freedom and the spark for human action.[23]

Learning about human freedom and agency from elemental experiences, in action and in relation, permits the recovery of simplicity beyond complexity.[24] All persons—including the illiterate and the marginalized—live by relating with reality on the basis of their existential evidences and needs. Naming heart as the locus where freedom and agency originate can be naïve, but it is close to the language of the poor, who know the material hardships of life. They recognize in their "heart" the source of strength to endure a daily struggle to better their conditions (see Ilaria Schnyder von Wartensee in this volume). They also recognize this heart in the sense of lacking when hope fades. In simple, yet humanly dense, language, they make it clear that the heart is rekindled in friendship, trust, and accompaniment. Everyone's heart is indeed a heart in relation.[25]

When evidence and the needs of one's heart are set aside as if irrelevant or irrational, freedom and agency are impaired: people passively adapt to prevailing customs and conform to what is socially expected from them given the situations in which they live. When passive attitudes become the new normal, people end up living fragmented lives, wearing a guise, and playing according to the "rules of the game" depending on their circumstances. As the vivid experience of *who I am* fades into passive adaptation, personal creativity also fades; the breadth of inner freedom shrinks, and one ends up "freely" choosing only among those alternatives provided by social conventions.

If one generalizes the above representation of a passive, distracted attitude toward the social environment, one finds the recipe for social, economic, institutional, and cultural stagnation or decline. Disregarding ultimate human needs in favor of conformism does not leave society unchanged: passivity shapes reality no less than activity by reinforcing existing structures of power and objectively hindering innovation and development.

FREEDOM AND AGENCY: "WE," ACTING TOGETHER

Individual creativity (the person in action) embedded in a story of meaningful relations (the person in relation) can transform reality. Lasting relationships are especially important for individual agents, acting as a "we" (creative minorities, community agencies, development partnerships, cooperatives, etc.), to generate sustained social innovation from the local to the global level, to engage in conflict management and peace building, and to care for one's immediate environment and for global ecological sustainability.[26]

As a matter of fact, people tend to cooperate, both in real life and in experimental settings; they manage to coordinate with each other and tend to be quite successful in pursuing common interests. This occurs more frequently than predicted by theoretical models based on individual rationality. That is, individuals often appear to reason as one "we" rather than as individual "I's" and to undertake common action. The importance of interpersonal relations for achieving common goals is widely acknowledged in different strands of contemporary economic literature.[27] Among these strands, we-rationality models (such as team reasoning and cooperative game theory coalitions) explore alternative forms of agency. Team reasoning models,[28] for example, depart from the standard methodological individualism, which is typical of game theoretical settings, in order to study interdependent actions. While standard models are based on agents who maximize their individual utility, team reasoning allows for the possibility of groups acting "as one," asking themselves "What should we do?" rather than "What shall I do?"

Team reasoning and team action, thus, provide an alternative way to approach the dilemmas of public goods, which require cooperation and collaboration not typical of agents following an I rationality.[29] If we were to compare the decisions and outcomes of a we rationality or team rationality with the alternative I-rationality mindset, we would find that in a situation in which each I-rational agent selects her optimal strategy,[30] a situation results that is worse for all involved—in comparison to the situation that could have been achieved through collaboration. As we see in the prisoners' dilemma, for example, I rationality in one-shot games is well known not to deliver the best accessible outcomes for the agents involved, whereas repetition may enable cooperation (provided there are credible threats of punishment for noncooperating agents).[31] Thus, most applications of we rationality provide a rationale for cooperative actions that would appear to be at odds with individualistic rationality: they need not be regarded as irrational; rather, they possess a rationality of their own.[32]

However, these models tend to become especially complex when trying to simultaneously deal with time and interdependence; that is, the elemental experience of acting when time and relations matter seems not to fit (yet?) into the team-reasoning literature.[33] In other words, we-rationality models struggle to provide clear answers to simple, unavoidable questions such as the following: When, how, and why is the we mindset freely adopted?[34] Could the individual "I" end up being dissolved into the "we" so that common agency supersedes (temporarily? and for how long?) personal freedom?

These questions are analytically intractable in the we-reasoning framework because of their complexity; as an alternative, we can again take the route of simplicity, observing the elemental agency of the person in action and in relation. When we act, facing uncertainty and ignorance, we realize that our actions are embedded in preexisting relations that have shaped our personal history and inform our present identity. Relations are vividly present in the "here and now" of most decisions, surely of the important ones. It is unlikely that we will observe, in action, individual agency as a two-stage process, as if actions were taken after the *a priori* choice of adopting either an I-rationality or a we-rationality mindset. Further, acting may not be framed as if I decisions were conflicting with we decisions; the deeper the importance of a specific "we" for one's personal experience, the more the "I" and the "we" are inextricably linked in dialogue.

In addition, in the time and space of real life, each person is deeply related to different "we's" at the same time (whether family, friends, business partners, neighbors, or co-citizens, including even the broader awareness of humankind). Some of the "we's" that heavily condition one's opportunities and achievements are inevitably given—parents, for example. Other "we's," such as friends and partners, can instead be chosen; these choices require the active engagement of human freedom and entail sustained material and symbolic investment. Do these we relationships limit personal freedom? Yes and no. In a static vision of freedom, where actions depend on mutable contingencies, personal bonds may be perceived as a restriction of freedom of choice: fewer personal bonds, fewer constraints, and more (static) freedom. From a dynamic perspective, however, freedom entails acting and interacting, working with and for others; from this perspective, the we dimension can express—not necessarily diminish—personal freedom.[35] Elemental personal experience confirms that the dynamic freedom one experiences in stable, loving relations is qualitatively different, and broader, than the ability to choose among contingent options.

The I–you and I–we relations are constitutive of our inner identity and experience. Unsurprisingly, one's personality develops within relations, from fetal experiences through the arc of human maturity. Our personal uniqueness feeds on relations; there is no "I" outside of a relation with some "you." We are structurally open to others (we are not self-sufficient and accomplished in ourselves); we need to encounter others, on the ground of our common experience of being human, in order to become "more" human.

Encountering the plural forms of otherness in our neighbors and recognizing the universal human experience in which we share is key to all of us living together on the earth, our common home.[36] We have in common what we "are"—nothing less. In fact, we are able to recognize the multifaceted yet universal experience of being human across different ages, latitudes, and longitudes.[37] Living together on this earth builds on the recognition that the hearts of all of us long for fulfillment, for our lives to be "more human."

Abstract ideals can ideologically unite people; they can develop superficial forms of acting together, driven by temporary and potentially mutable interests and by sharing common procedural and contractual ties. But building on what we "have" in common does not experientially join people in a community, which rather entails "sharing in the humaneness of every person."[38]

The relationship of the individual to a community can also be troubled: our constitutive need for others makes us vulnerable. Human interactions may be the space for encounter or confrontation, for trade or robbery, for respect or abuse, for inclusion or marginalization. Human relationships may treasure one's otherness or take advantage of power asymmetries to the point of violence (possession, control, or exploitation). Human interactions exhibit the same kinds of ambivalence we observe in ourselves: we are attracted by living a "more human" life while we are also constantly tempted by cheaper forms of satisfaction; we can responsibly relate with material reality or we can follow the logic of power, appropriation, and technocratic control.

FREEDOM, AGENCY, AND DEVELOPMENT

The inevitable fragility and ambivalence of human actions and interactions makes development both personal and societal, nonmechanistic and unpredictable. An early statement of the Catholic magisterium articulates a vision of development as the possibility for each and every person to "do more, know more and have more in order to be more,"[39] with "transcendent humanism"[40] as the highest aim of human fulfillment, the apex and root of a development-friendly path. Development is indeed a process driven by freedom and agency, a path shaped over time by ambivalent actions and relations, a path that is inevitably twisted but oriented toward a "more accomplished" experience of human fulfillment. Along this path, each step matters: *how* we pursue a development goal is at least as important as *what* is achieved; and knowing *why* a given step has been taken is necessary to assess its immediate and durable outcomes.

Consider providing anti-retroviral drugs to HIV-infected persons: their physical well-being directly improves by receiving the treatment; however, their condition likely reflects a complex set of needs, including not only health, sanitation, and housing but also recognition, dignity, and appreciation within their community. Sustaining their health improvement over time requires more than drug provision and generally entails significant relational investment. As the scarcity of resources requires prioritizing interventions, *how* priorities are set is important: efficient technocratic rules are likely to result in different priorities than those that would emerge from dealing with persons from the dialogical, imperfect, open, nonmechanistic perspective of *homo agens*.[41]

Development requires intelligent love and durable care, accompaniment, and a sound understanding of the proximate and systemic causes of deprivation. At the end of the day, from a material point of view, the observable actions may be the same (providing treatment, for example); but the *how* and the *why* make the difference. Observable actions do not represent the end of the story, as would be the case in a technocratic intervention; if one invests her "whole" self in a material deed, a story of relations can begin; the other person ceases to be an anonymous terminal for a donor's individual agency, as would happen even in the best-managed comprehensive, developed project designed and executed along technocratic lines.

The relevance of *how* and *why* agency is expressed makes the dynamic process of development—and, by analogy, the process of recognizing and expressing human dignity—both terribly simple and terribly demanding. Development and dignity concern the whole person. Integral, "whole" agency does not amount to implementing an extensive set of pre-defined responses, as if delivering a multi-item package (meeting all needs would, in any case, be impossible). Integral development is a method with a different origin: encountering the "whole" of the other person and entering into a personalized, lasting relationship with her. Defining "integral" development, thus, cannot be a matter of top-down negotiations (where relative bargaining power may override human dialogue) or of the bottom-up aggregation of nonprioritized goals and targets.

The relevant criteria for common actions toward the goal of integral development in a composite, inherently plural society (our cities included) can emerge only from within the nucleus of elemental human experience; in practice, we cannot avoid engaging a serious dialogue about the elemental need for love and truth (for life "eternal," not immortal, to use Hannah Arendt's expression).[42] Love and truth are difficult to define but easy to recognize in daily life: they are "simple" human experiences, and children's hearts seem to have a special sense for recognizing them. The words "love" and "truth" can at times be brandished against humanity: many crimes against persons and peoples have been performed in the name of (misconceived notions of) truth and love. However, it would be unreasonable to deny that we can attain reasonable certainties about love and truth (at the very least, people can distinguish suffering from mistreatment and falsehoods). Time works as a sieve for truth: reality does not cheat, and falsity becomes evident in due time;[43] time works as a sieve for love as well: expressing personalized, lasting care for someone is possibly the best observable proxy of love as robust concern.[44]

Far from being abstract and sentimental, historical facts and personal experience show that it is reasonable to trust the transformative power of love, truth, and beauty as drivers of freedom and agency. There are episodes in which the heroic agency of single persons has changed history, enhancing human dignity and development. Heroism often takes apparently inconspicuous forms: every day and everywhere obscure agents make a difference, acting for the dignity and development of their families and neighbors and for peaceful living within and despite conflict. Their agency reflects a common thread, for through their actions they bear witness to the possibility of experiencing love and beauty, justice, truth, and forgiveness.

Famous heroes who have made a difference in various places and at various times come to mind; here I would like to mention the paradoxical, transformative power of powerless creative minorities when they "live within the truth," as seen in the greengrocer's tale by Václav Havel, a Czechoslovak hero of Charta 77.[45] Havel wrote in October 1978:

> Just imagine . . . that one day something in our greengrocer snaps and he stops putting up the slogans . . . merely to ingratiate himself. He stops voting in elections he knows are a farce. He begins to say what he really thinks at political meetings. And he even finds the strength in himself to express solidarity with those whom his conscience commands him to support. In this revolt the greengrocer steps out of living within the lie. He rejects the ritual and breaks the rules of the game. He discovers once more his suppressed identity and dignity. He gives his freedom a concrete significance. His revolt is an attempt to live within the truth.[46]

Though external realities can heavily condition us, they never fully determine how and why human beings express their freedom and agency. Personal élans of freedom can always be renewed; within meaningful relations, social creativity and development can begin again.[47]

This transformative process can be observed and measured, rein-forcing narratives and anecdotal evidence. With a small research team, we decided to empirically measure whether and how vulnerable persons' attitudes change when they are exposed to a significant experience of durable care and support in a love-based community where they are welcomed and accompanied through a restorative process. The anthropological premise for our research was that people learn to love, over time, by being loved; they learn to trust by being trusted, and so on. This simple premise is general enough to be applied to different kinds of love-based community "treatment" in various countries.[48]

In a lab-in-the-field experiment with a longitudinal design spanning ten months, we studied Guiding Rage into Power (GRIP), an offender accountability program for inmates in two Californian State Prisons sentenced to long terms. GRIP aims at providing inmates with the skills to undo and prevent violent behavior so as to become "people with skills to defuse conflicts around them."[49] We tested whether GRIP also changed inmates' pro-social attitudes (trust and altruism); differences-in-differences estimation shows that trust significantly increased in GRIP participants compared to the control group.[50]

The decision to create and sustain personalized, friendly relations with poor, oppressed, vulnerable, "unlikely" people can change much more than their material living conditions: their dignity can be restored, their hope and creativity rekindled. The humanity of all those involved is transformed in the process; this personal transformation may be so profound as to spur human freedom into generating new stories of development.

The practical implication of thinking of development, micro and macro, as a process driven by human freedom and agency, according to the human heart's deepest needs and evidences, is huge—and simple. In this regard, Pope Francis's candid statement before the United Nations Assembly in 2015, speaking of the SDGs, reads:

> The number and complexity of the problems require that we possess technical instruments of verification. But this involves two risks. We can rest content with the bureaucratic exercise of drawing up long lists of good proposals—goals, objectives and statistics—or we can think that a single theoretical and aprioristic solution will provide an answer to all the challenges. . . . Above and beyond our plans and

programmes, we are dealing with real men and women who live, struggle and suffer, and are often forced to live in great poverty, deprived of all rights. To enable these real men and women to escape from extreme poverty, we must allow them to be dignified agents of their own destiny.[51]

Enabling vulnerable people to become protagonists—dignified agents of their own destiny—is the only path to sustainable development.

NOTES

1. Smith wrote: "It is not from the benevolence of the butcher, the brewer, or the baker, that we expect our dinner, but from their regard to their own interest." See his *An Inquiry into the Nature and Causes of the Wealth of Nations*, ed. R. H. Campbell, A. S. Skinner, and W. B. Todd (Oxford: Clarendon Press, 1976), I.ii.2.

2. "Whether this propensity be one of those original principles in human nature, of which no further account can be given, or whether, as seems more probable, it be the necessary consequence of the faculties of reason and speech, it belongs not to our present subject to inquire. It is common to all men, and to be found in no other race of animals, which seem to know neither this nor any other species of contracts." Smith, *An Inquiry*, I.ii.2.

3. For this reading of Smith, see Angelo Scola, "The Good Reasons for a Broader Reason," *Rivista Internazionale di Scienze Sociali* 3 (2012): 263–68.

4. Smith, *An Inquiry*, IV.ii.9.

5. Human development requires more than the food, shelter, and practical training sufficient for social animals. Being human requires meaningful relations through which the quest for beauty, for understanding, and for communication can be pursued. This quest ultimately drives responsibility and creativity, innovation, and development.

6. Daron Acemoglu and James A. Robinson, *Why Nations Fail: The Origins of Power, Prosperity, and Poverty* (New York: Crown Business, 2013).

7. World Bank, *World Development Report 2015: Mind, Society, and Behavior* (Washington, DC: World Bank, 2015).

8. Karla Hoff and Joseph E. Stiglitz, "Striving for Balance in Economics: Towards a Theory of the Social Determination of Behavior," *Journal of Economic Behavior and Organization* 126 (2016): 26.

9. Pontifical Council for Justice and Peace, *Compendium of the Social Doctrine of the Church* (Vatican City: Libreria Editrice Vaticana, 2004), 153–54.

10. Amartya Sen, *Development as Freedom* (Oxford: Oxford University Press, 1999).

11. Amartya Sen, "Well-Being, Agency, and Freedom: The Dewey Lectures 1984," *Journal of Philosophy* 82, no. 4 (April 1985). Measuring human development relies on indicators that typically measure opportunity freedom (the wider set of choices available to people), while process freedom (that is, participation and agency) is more difficult to identify and to measure.

12. Pope Francis explains: "The techno-economic paradigm . . . leads people to believe that they are free as long as they have the supposed freedom to consume. But those really free are the minority who wield economic and financial power. Amid this confusion, postmodern humanity has not yet achieved a new self-awareness capable of offering guidance and direction, and this lack of identity is a source of anxiety. We have too many means and only a few insubstantial ends." See Pope Francis, *Laudato si': On Care for Our Common Home*, encyclical letter (May 24, 2015), http://w2.vatican.va/content/francesco/en/encyclicals/documents/papa-francesco_20150524_enciclica-laudato-si.html, sec. 203.

13. A *static* vision of rationality can deal with risk (*alea*), not with uncertainty. "Strong," or "radical," uncertainty, in particular, applies when there is no way of identifying the probabilities of all future events. See Giovanni Dosi, "Sources, Procedures, and Microeconomic Effects of Innovation," *Journal of Economic Literature* 26, no. 3 (1988): 1134, and Mervyin King, *The End of Alchemy: Money, Banking, and the Future of the Global Economy* (New York: W. W. Norton, 2016), 430.

14. Itzhak Gilboa and David Schmeidler, *A Theory of Case-Based Decisions* (Cambridge: Cambridge University Press, 2001), 212.

15. Marco Martini, "Libertà Economica," in *Soggetto e libertà nella condizione postmoderna*, ed. Francesco Botturi (Milan: Vita e Pensiero, 2003), 373–92, my translation. The paper reappraises Hannah Arendt's *The Human Condition* (Chicago: University of Chicago Press, 1958).

16. These criteria are suggested as formally illustrating requirements for rationality under uncertainty and ignorance by Gilboa and Schmeidler in *A Theory*.

17. On aspirations, see Debraj Ray, "Aspirations, Poverty, and Economic Change," in *Understanding Poverty*, ed. Abhijit Vinayak Banerjee, Roland Benabou, and Dilip Mookherjee (Oxford: Oxford University Press, 2006), 409–21, and Garance Genicot and Debraj Ray, "Aspirations and Inequality," *Econometrica* 85, no. 2 (March 2017): 489–519, available at https://doi.org/10.3982/ECTA13865; on self-control, see Douglas B. Bernheim, Debraj Ray, and Şevin Yeltekin, "Poverty and Self-Control," *Econometrica* 83, no. 5 (2015): 1877–1911, available at https://doi.org/10.3982/ECTA11374; and on hope,

see Esther Duflo, "Hope as Capability," Tanner Lectures on Human Values, Harvard University, Cambridge, MA (May 3, 2012); Paul Glewwe, Phillip H. Ross, and Bruce Wydick, "Developing Hope: The Impact of International Child Sponsorship on Self-Esteem and Aspirations," *Economics* 9 (2014), available at https://repository.usfca.edu/cgi/viewcontent.cgi?article=1000& context=econ (the link where you can start download); and Travis J. Lybbert and Bruce Wydick, "Hope as Aspirations, Agency, and Pathways: Poverty Dynamics and Microfinance in Oaxaca, Mexico," in *The Economics of Poverty Traps*, ed. Christopher B. Barrett, Michael R. Carter, and Jean-Paul Chavas (Chicago: University of Chicago Press, 2019), 153–77.

18. Jonathan de Quidt and Johannes Haushofer, "Depression through the Lens of Economics: A Research Agenda," in Barrett, Carter, and Chavas, *The Economics of Poverty Traps*.

19. Karol Wojtyła, *The Acting Person*, ed. Anna-Teresa Tymieniecka, trans. Andrzej Potocki (Dordrecht and Boston: D. Reidel, 1979), vii:11.

20. Luigi Giussani explains: "Reason . . . is life, a life faced with the complexity and the multiplicity of reality, the richness of the real. Reason is agile, goes everywhere, travels many roads. . . . Reason does not have a single method; it is polyvalent, rich, agile, and mobile." See his *The Religious Sense* (McGill-Queen's University Press, 1997), 17, originally published as *Il senso religioso* (Milan: Jaca Book, 1966).

21. Angelo Scola identifies three distinct "constitutive polarities" of personal identity: corporeity/transcendence, man/woman, and individual/ community in his "Antropologia cristiana," in Pontifical Academy of Social Sciences, *Conceptualization of the Person in Social Sciences*, *Acta* 11 (Vatican City: Libreria Editrice Vaticana, 2006).

22. Donna Hicks uses the categories of ME and I as the (psychological) framework within which to bring forth self-consciousness and sort out con-flicting relations. See Donna Hicks, *Dignity: The Essential Role It Plays in Resolving Conflict* (New Haven, CT: Yale University Press, 2011).

23. Giussani, *Religious Sense*.

24. As Karol Wojtyła wrote: "The complexity of the experience of man is dominated by this intrinsic simplicity. . . . The whole experience, and con-sequently the cognition of man, is composed of both the experience that everyone has concerning himself and the experience of other men. . . . All this tends to compose a whole in cognition rather than to cause complexity." See Wojtyła, *Acting Person*, 8.

25. In the Western tradition, the expression "heart" may immediately convey emotional and romantic meanings. Here, the word is used with the profound meaning it has in the Bible, as the symbolic center of one's identity.

However, in a very mundane sense, the muscular dimension of the heart, which is the pumping force (the spark) that makes blood circulation happen, provides a powerful analogy for naming what drives human action.

26. As Pope Francis has written: "Self-improvement on the part of individuals will not by itself remedy the extremely complex situation facing our world today. . . . Social problems must be addressed by community networks and not simply by the sum of individual good deeds." See Francis, *Laudato si'*, 219.

27. For example, in the game theoretical analysis of repeated interactions, personalized relationships are often crucial for effectively pursuing and achieving one's objectives, especially when scale economies and market power are relevant, when information is asymmetrically distributed, and when agents face ignorance and "strong" uncertainty and need to learn from others for case-based decision making.

28. See Robert Sudgen, "Thinking as a Team: Towards an Explanation of Nonselfish Behavior," *Social Philosophy and Policy* 10, no. 1 (1993): 69–89; Sugden, "The Logic of Team Reasoning," *Philosophical Explorations* 6, no. 3 (2003): 165–81. See also Michael Bacharach, "Interactive Team Reasoning: A Contribution to the Theory of Co-operation," *Research in Economics* 53, no. 2 (1999): 117–47, and *Beyond Individual Choice* (Princeton, NJ: Princeton University Press, 2006).

29. Guilhem Lecouteux offers a discussion of why an approach based on collective agency rather than rational choice theory and social preferences offers a scientifically preferable theory of unselfish behaviors, in terms of both parsimony and empirical validation, in "What Does 'We' Want? Team Reasoning, Game Theory, and Unselfish Behaviours," Groupe de Recherche en Droit, Economie, Gestion (GREDEG) Working Paper 2018–17, University of Nice Sophia Antipolis, 2018.

30. This is called the Nash Equilibrium. See John Nash, "The Bargaining Problem," *Econometrica* 18 (1950): 155–62, and "Two-Person Cooperative Games," *Econometrica* 21 (1956): 128–40.

31. In Robert J. Aumann's Nobel lecture he applies a similar approach to war and peace issues. Interestingly, he concludes the lecture with a quote from Isaiah 2:2–4 pointing to the need for a common Lord who judges the parties (that is, a "government" of a kind) for swords to be beaten into ploughshares. This conclusion suggests the importance of pre-existing substantive commonality for cooperation to occur (among nations and, in general, among agents). See Aumann, "War and Peace," Nobel Prize Lecture, Royal Swedish Academy of Sciences, Stockholm, December 8, 2005.

32. In order to provide rational explanations of actual cooperation or coordination choices, different authors consider different aspects of we reasoning,

starting from the existence of focal points that facilitate convergence. See Thomas C. Schelling, *The Strategy of Conflict* (Cambridge, MA: Harvard University Press, 1960). Other rational explanations of cooperation consider payoff transformation: In this case, material payoffs of the interaction under consideration are not the ones that actually govern individual behavior. See Ken Binmore, *Playing Fair* (Cambridge, MA: MIT Press, 1994). Agency transformation occurs when the individual agent shifts from asking the question "What should I do?" to asking "What should we do?" In this case, agents view themselves as part of a group (framing). In other cases, even if the aims of the group do not coincide with individual goals, the perceived agreement of individual goals can sustain group identification (they have a common purpose), and such group framing also tends to result in cooperation. See Bacharach, *Beyond Individual Choice*, 90, and Sudgen, "Thinking as a Team."

33. Usually this literature deals with alternative forms of we-rationality decisions in one-shot (nonrepeated) interactions. See Schelling, *Strategy of Conflict*, Sugden, "Thinking as a Team," and Binmore, *Playing Fair*. We-rationality decisions are also applied to an individual's decisions over time by defining that individual as a set of time-contingent "I" spanning past and future. See Bacharach, *Beyond Individual Choice*, 89.

34. Different authors provide different interpretations for the shift from I reasoning to we reasoning—for example, mutually assured team reasoning (Sugden, "Thinking as a Team") or circumspect team reasoning (Bacharach, *Beyond Individual Choice*); still, the "I" and the "we" mindsets remain alternatives to each other. However, it may be rational to repeatedly shift from one rationality frame to the other, as in Alessandra Smerilli, "We-Thinking and Vacillation between Frames: Filling a Gap in Bacharach's Theory," *Theory and Decision* 73, no. 4 (2012): 539–60.

35. *Liberus*, Latin for "free," means "son"; that is, bonds and personal freedom are inextricably intertwined.

36. Home is what we name the place where we belong (indicating not ownership, but belonging!). Home is at once a physical, material space and a space for symbolic relations and communication.

37. "Homo sum, humani nihil a me alienum puto" (I am a human being, I consider nothing that is human alien to me). So wrote Publio Terenzio Afro in the first century AD.

38. Wojtyła, *Acting Person*, 294.

39. Paul VI, *Populorum progressio*, encyclical letter (March 26, 1967), sec. 6, as translated by Benedict XVI in *Caritas in veritate*, encyclical letter (June 29, 2009), http://w2.vatican.va/content/benedict-xvi/en/encyclicals /documents/hf_ben-xvi_enc_20090629_caritas-in-veritate.html, sec. 18.

40. Paul VI, *Populorum progressio*, 16.

41. Stephanie Nann et al., "Cambodian Patients' and Health Professionals' Views Regarding the Allocation of Antiretroviral Drugs," *Developing World Bioethics* 12 (2012): 96–103. Most patients expressed the view that the drugs should be used for the patients who are most important from a familial point of view, namely, when the family contains small children and/or is already in a precarious financial condition.

42. Arendt, *Human Condition*, 18.

43. Truth cannot, by definition, be "my" truth against "yours"; it cannot be decided by majority voting, yet it can be experienced and verified, as its most typical feature is humility (that is, it is being related to "earthly" experiences, as the Latin root *humus* indicates).

44. I would like to thank Clemens Sedmak for helping me focus on this concept and the related literature. Frankfurt's "robust concern" view is that this kind of love is neither affective nor cognitive; it is volitional. See B. Helm, "Love," in *The Stanford Encyclopedia of Philosophy*, ed. Edward N. Zalta (Fall 2013 edition), https://plato.stanford.edu/archives/fall2013/entries/love/. From the perspective of this chapter, love is all of the above, and more.

45. Charta 77 was a civic movement (informal, not meant to be an opposition party) in the Czechoslovak Socialist Republic, named after the document Charter 77 of January 1977, which called for respect of human and civil rights in Czechoslovakia and throughout the world. The reactions of the Czech government to that document were very strong; many Charta 77 signatories—including Havel—were imprisoned (in and out of prison for many years).

Charta 77 is a milestone of the nonviolent resistance movement in Communist Eastern Europe.

Havel was elected president of Czechoslovakia in 1989.

46. Václav Havel, *The Power of the Powerless: Citizens against the State in Central-Eastern Europe* (Armonk, NY: M. E. Sharpe, 1985).

47. As Pope Francis has written: "Human beings, while capable of the worst, are also capable of rising above themselves, choosing again what is good, and making a new start, despite their mental and social conditioning. We are able to take an honest look at ourselves, to acknowledge our deep dissatisfaction, and to embark on new paths to authentic freedom. No system can completely suppress our openness to what is good, true and beautiful. . . . I appeal to everyone throughout the world not to forget this dignity which is ours." See Francis, *Laudato si'*, 205.

48. We study formerly addicted people in Italian rehabilitation communities, Californian convicts attending the Guiding Rage into Power (GRIP)

programs, and vulnerable schoolchildren in periurban areas of Goma, Democratic Republic of the Congo, and Kigali, Rwanda. See Simona Beretta and Mario A. Maggioni, "Time, Relations and Behaviors: Measuring the Transformative Power of Love-Based Community Life," Working Paper No. 421, Kellogg Institute for International Studies, University of Notre Dame, May 2017.

49. See http://insight-out.org/index.php/programs/grip-program.

50. This result is robust for alternative estimation techniques and the inclusion of an endogenous behavioral measure of altruism. See Mario A. Maggioni, Domenico Rossignoli, Simona Beretta, and Sara Balestri, "Trust Behind Bars: Measuring Change in Inmates' Prosocial Preferences," *Journal of Economic Psychology* 64 (December 2017): 89–104.

51. Pope Francis, Address to the United Nations General Assembly (New York, September 25, 2015).

FOUR

Genuine Development

Reflections on Agency and Passivity

Dominic Burbidge

Shortly after Kenya's 2013 elections, I traveled to Siaya County in the western part of the country to assist with the work of an NGO providing the means for receiving a high school education to those orphaned by the AIDS epidemic. While there, I had the opportunity to visit the home of one of the campaigners for the recently elected governor of the county. Following the promulgation of the 2010 constitution, Kenya has switched to a devolved system of government that transfers key areas of public service provision to forty-seven counties spread across the country.[1] The newly created position of governor has become highly coveted, helping meet a deep, long-term desire to offset the winner-takes-all approach to central government politics. The violence that followed Kenya's disputed 2007 election was widely described as a product of a constitutional system that had made the president all-important and, therefore, had left large swathes of the country neglected.[2] In an attempt to even things out, the country supported a constitutional alternative that reduced the president's powers and decentralized fourteen important functions of government to the county level, among them the entire healthcare system.[3] In addition, the new constitution requires all levels of government to engage in public participation when making decisions in order to increase community buy-in and provide better access to community knowledge.

Despite all these positives, when sitting with one of the campaigners for the recently elected governor of Siaya County, he explained to me that many people in the county had become upset that the governor was not a good listener. Since being elected, the governor had been ignoring the advice of those closest to him and was often openly dismissive when dealing with local residents. Some blamed this on the way in which family connections had helped spread recognition of his name during the campaign and the way that his victory had in part been due to his financial advantage over other candidates. Disappointment was growing because, although the constitution had changed the legal structure of local government to make it more important and locally accountable, there was little change to be seen in elected representatives.

Is this a development failure? Certainly if one speaks to pundits of Kenya's devolution process one is often met with the phrase "The only thing we devolved is corruption." The dominant theory among the political class of Nairobi seems to be that giving local government access to core functions that were previously centralized has compromised their delivery by means of creating an unprecedented number of intermediaries who want to get their hands on state revenue. For these critics, rationalization of public services should be a process of centralization whereby the hardest decisions are made by the most competent and as many processes as possible are standardized (what we could term the Prussian model). Under this framing, one must make a choice between efficiency at the center and localized political inclusion in a zero-sum fashion, with all aware that it is the former that leads to real progress.

And this is the view one can easily fall into when visiting the staff of the newly formed county governments across the country. Meeting those involved in healthcare in Taita Taveta, a county in Kenya's southeast, I was struck by the way in which staff were made up of the young and the old, but no one in between. Working in local government was seen as something for those unable to get into central government offices in Nairobi; there were fewer chances for promotion, smaller budgets to work with, and much less job status. Indeed, Nic Cheeseman and I were so disappointed in county government personnel's sense of the value of their own work that we once wrote in the Kenyan newspaper the *Daily Nation* to complain that we need to spend more money on local government offices to make them more attractive places to work.[4] I somewhat regret that article, however, because the important point is not changing the distribution of material privileges but changing the perception among government employees of what privilege is. Being closer to the people you are helping means you can grow more in the virtue of passivity, which is perhaps the most fundamental privilege that needs to be recognized in development studies the world over.

The real complaint against the governor of Siaya County was not that constitutional change had not immediately led to material improvement for citizens. The complaint was as it was first presented: that he was not a good listener. The capacity of leaders to listen and reflect is paramount in judging their skill at leadership in many pre-colonial African traditions. Therefore, Siaya—a part of Kenya populated by those of Luo ethnicity—chimes with the broader East African history of *leading through judging*, whereby the best leader is one able to listen to both sides of a case and find a negotiated settlement that returns the parties to parity. Unilateral action by a leader is likely to sway the outcome toward one side unjustly; a good leader listens hard and then acts on behalf of the community. In the words of a Luo proverb, "Ruoth ok yiere e kom kende" (A good leader doesn't impose himself on the people).[5]

STRUCTURE AGENCY VS. AGENCY PASSIVITY

Instead of exploring what it means to listen, in development studies we have tended to listen to the voice of the underprivileged. The interest there has been on restoring a voice to the voiceless, as well as discovering stories that had previously gone undetected. A good example is Brad Weiss's *Street Dreams and Hip Hop Barbershops: Global Fantasy in Urban Tanzania*,[6] which relates the interactions and aspirations of those who run and use barbershops in Arusha, Tanzania. The book contradicts the assumed unifying process of globalization and neoliberalism by showing how local players use global trends and symbols for their own creativity, bulwarking their individual place in the world. Another interesting example is *A Man of Good Hope* by Jonny Steinberg.[7] That book recounts the migration of a Somali man from Mogadishu to Cape Town, passing through Kenya and Ethiopia. It was written after widespread concern had arisen over the xenophobic treatment of African foreigners in South Africa, and so it can be read as something of a strike against those sentiments. The account is one of persistent agency in the midst of a vortex of international upheaval, a thoroughly modern African story. The strategies and efforts employed by the protagonist are explained with the utmost accuracy, detailing the collision of structure and agency in our new world order. I once asked the author, Jonny Steinberg, how he found the subject of his book, given how unique the account was and how moving. He said he purposefully sought him out in South Africa, knowing there were Africans who had come to the country from all corners of the continent. Steinberg interviewed his protagonist many times and went back to visit all of the places the man had traveled through in his journey to Cape Town. That is an impressive labor of love and shows the fineness behind some of the literature's most cunning critiques of globalization. Another key example is *Expectations of Modernity* by James Ferguson.[8] The author explores the lifestyle responses of miners of the Zambian copper belt to the global fall in copper prices that had occurred in the 1970s, presenting the study as an "ethnography of decline." In Ferguson's account, Africans are made to adapt and shift in the face of forces beyond their control. Nevertheless, while the broad narrative is one of missed opportunities and frustrated ambitions, the creativity of people's adaptation to new circumstances provides the basis for deeper reflection on human agency on the continent.

These contributions take the developing world as a torn place of international power struggles where persons as agents do the best they can with what they have. Theirs is an agency that strikes back at the structure unraveling to undermine and punish them for being peripheral to its logic.

The framework is thoroughly Marxist in that it is principally a structural critique of society that assumes a full flourishing of agency only when such structures are broken down and replaced. Such an assessment may surprise. Do not these authors and others like them precisely demonstrate the agency that lies behind global forces, ready to pounce with cunning? Yes, they do. But that is itself to defer to structure as the dominant operating force. Under the predominant view in development studies, social structures have scientific truth, while agency is the *exception to the rule*. Development studies cries for an increase in the frequency of exceptions but fails to refute the enduringly high status given to the perceived "center." Therefore, the current dominance of the structure agency paradigm in development studies is part of the process of hegemonic subordination of the global south.

Karl Marx took a materially determining view of the person whereby the person's place in history is fully explained by the relations of the factors of production, which lie outside his or her control. Labor can be understood only in its relation to land and capital, never on its own terms.[9] While Thomas Aquinas believed that wages should be commensurate with the labor effort used in the production process, Marx argued that wages are at the mercy of the forces of supply and demand. In the Industrial Revolution, advances in capital proved the most determining factor, lowering the number of people needed to produce each item and therefore diminishing the value of labor over time. Under such analysis, it is fitting that the scattered shards of remaining human agency are to be found at the periphery of the global order. While those at the center have succumbed to the regimentation dictated by the need for ever-greater efficiency gains, those less incorporated into capitalism walk along the edge of the cliff: they are too valueless to be sucked in, yet any stumble will cause them to fall and be forgotten.

If, therefore, it looks as if the writing of agency in the developing world is a process of affirming the value of the local, think again. In fact, the structure agency distinction is one in which agency is fundamentally beholden to structure.[10] That is, agency is defined in terms of the absence of structure or the creation of new structure. Likewise, structure is the absence of agency or the creation of new agency (the conditioning of agency). As *exceptions to the rules dictated by structure*, agency in the developing world will ultimately conform to the scientific logic of materialist forces. Marx viewed social change as fully determined by its structure, such that a revolution to genuinely shift the status quo would only occur when determined by the stages of history. Whether one can help

Marxism by becoming Marxist was an idea foreign to Marx. There was no writing back to neoliberalism in him and no historiographical assault that he believed could break down neocolonialism. Insofar as one accepts these categories in the first place, one is bound by their logic of material determinacy, completely overriding philosophical depth to the human person. Understanding of agency as "class struggle" or "the human capacity for self-directed action" ultimately falters when grounded in a theory of the relations of the factors of production, which submits a teleological materialism as a cheap substitute for an exploration of human nature—its tastes, desires, wisdom, shortcomings, and choices.[11]

To replace the structure agency framework, I therefore humbly propose an agency passivity framework. *Passivity is the practice of enjoying things as they are.* It runs counter to all social science arguments of power dynamics, for it says that something is done by you through the acceptance of others' wills and others' choices. It is a defense of weakness without any promise of future strength, while Marxism is a defense of weakness with a promise of future strength. Under the agency passivity framework, agency is purposeful rather than powerful. To act is to pursue purpose; to be passive is to enjoy another's purpose.

Passivity tastes bitter to the Marxist, for it is a declaration of human compatibility with the forces that are said to undermine human welfare. In the agency passivity framework, there is no such thing as power per se, and one cannot pursue power as a thing in itself but can only do or receive *particular things.* Its critique of power mirrors the critique of money as, by definition, not something that one can pursue for its own sake. Money, as a means to other things, can be pursued only for the sake of those other things. One who pursues money for its own sake fails to understand what money is, like a man amassing ration cards without knowing the war has finished and that such cards are now defunct. Or like a man with dementia hurriedly looking for his car keys even though he no longer owns a car. The pursuit of power is like that: it detaches the means from an end and pursues the means thinking them an end. To continue the analogy with money, Marxism fails in this way to understand what money is, for by taking the factors of production rather than human intention as fully explaining the production process, the theory yields transferable equivalence between the factors, for which the measuring unit reigns supreme as the organizer and empty reason why things are done. Things are produced because that is in accordance with the process of history, not because of what they are in themselves. The goal of human flourishing remains sparsely defined, as with Hegel's account of historical change, upon which Marx's notion of the stages of history is based.

Under the agency passivity framework, goals are defined by the agent in line with the capacities of human nature. Rather than agency being parasitic on structure, it is passivity that is parasitic on agency: coming to accept, coming to cherish, finding the value in another taking direction, even sometimes for one's own affairs.

THE USEFULNESS OF PASSIVITY TO THE DEVELOPING WORLD

I therefore argue for something very strange indeed that I believe can break new ground in our understanding of human dignity and the practice of human development. It is the thesis that development is enhanced through the exercise of passivity. There are three reasons for this:

1. Passivity allows one to see different yet mutually beneficial societal goals.
2. Development is best understood as a process of identifying and respecting vocations.
3. To listen well is already to achieve something, for it changes the listener.

Let us consider these in turn. First, *passivity allows one to see different yet mutually beneficial societal goals.* The point is best explained, I believe, through the work of Amartya Sen. Sen is famous as an advocate of fair economic development for the developing world. What fewer commentators observe is that his intellectual journey started with deep criticism of homo economicus assumptions of the rational individual as one who maximizes self-interest. In the article "Rational Fools," published in 1977, Sen explains that under the prevailing approach of behavioral economics we must assume we are all aiming at the same thing, which can be computed through a single metric of welfare.[12] The reality, however, is that an individual's choice "may reflect a compromise among a variety of considerations of which personal welfare may be just one."[13] Both moral motivations and nonchoice sources of information must be treated on their own terms and fully incorporated into decision-making models. How can moral motivations be incorporated into economic theory? The point is to recognize that any rational action is pursued by means of human intention, which may well have a normative goal. Therefore, it is not possible to fully understand the reasons for economic behavior minus those moral intentions. Notwithstanding, Sen's view is that this need not be an inhibitor to economic analysis. Rather, it is the prevailing approach based on the homo economicus assumption, which is contradictory and yields limited insight because it makes impossible reductions of the human person that fail to explain reality. Purely self-interested behavior is an assumption that is internally contradictory and a model that fails tests of external validity when set against the real world.[14] If everyone were to act in their material self-interest, there would be no coordinated economic activity at all.

A key contribution Sen makes is that realizing freedom in setting personal goals as well as developmental goals is in keeping with the freedoms that undergird a successful economy.[15] Just as we value a free market for its ability to facilitate an equilibrium between supply and demand and, over time, reduce transaction costs, we should value moral freedom in debating and deciding what development is. By bringing persons' decision-making deliberation into economic analysis, we discover the true depth of possibilities for human coordination. Of course there are limits to what counts as a good exercise of freedom, as well as room for healthy criticism of what is not morally reputable, but an economy that instead reestablished every interaction as based on material self-interest would go too far in the other direction and end up reductive and limiting. For Sen, inclusion of moral discussion on the functionings of the human person and the wider purposes toward which economic activity is orientated does not discoordinate. Rather, it is the lack of such freedoms that tend to produce want and dependency in the economy, just as the simplification of identities and political positions, rather than their dialogue, threatens peace.[16] An interesting example is that of famine, for which Sen argues that food hand-outs can be damaging to the process of recovering from famine if they heavily distort market logic; it is better to employ people, as this allows them to economically flourish from within their existing social context, helping to retain the community norms and supports that do so much to mitigate the effects of disaster.[17] A community needs to retain its freedom in forming values and goals if its members are to participate fully in the development process.

Sen deploys the term "agency" generously and calls for its restoration as part of a fairer and more democratic world order. He is operating from within the existing structure agency framework of development studies. However, because of the extent to which he relies on a notion of human capability that is creative in its normativity, not just productive in its materiality, he glides away from Marxist adherence to capacity measured through the relations of factors of production. While the Marxist tradition distinguishes structure and agency in a way that renders the concept of agency parasitic on global economic structure, Sen's approach renders the concept of structure parasitic on agency. For Sen, economic goods are relevant *in the ways they are put to use*. It is as if he takes every variable in the Marxist equation and adds a coefficient of human agency. Economic progress and advantage is thus "a *relationship* between persons and goods" such that "utilities are reflections of one type of relation between persons and goods."[18] In contrast to economists' previous fixation on a money-based notion of social welfare, Sen's bigger picture involves Aristotelian appreciation of the faculties of the human person and their realization in the activities that put goods to use. Such an approach provides space for pivoting development studies's fixation on structure-agency to a new paradigm of agency-passivity. In having switched structure to become parasitic on agency, Sen breaks the contemporary mold of development studies and, in turn, creates room for possible discussion of passivity in the development process. As I have sought to explain elsewhere, Sen's approach develops "methodological openness to heterogeneity of decision procedures among actors."[19] What this means is that the hefty role played by agency—especially at the community level—requires that the development practitioner reflect on the diverse ways of thinking and ways of being of communities that, in turn, shape their societal goals. When Sen talks of the capabilities approach, we can therefore add as one human capability listening: *the identification of different but mutually beneficial societal goals*. Good listening requires passivity, making passivity one skill among others that directly aids the development process.

To whom should we be passive? The answer is our second point: *development is best understood as a process of identifying and respecting vocations.* In a UN-Habitat handbook for city leaders, I argued with colleague Nic Cheeseman that the management of municipal government is complicated by at least three roles that are often in tension.[20] The first is the government administrator, who sees reform as an internal process of better meeting goals in tax revenue, managing transfers from central government, and streamlining the work of government departments. The second is the economist, who is concerned with overall economic coordination, whether taxation is inhibiting business activities, and what items can be optimally provided as a public service versus as a product of the free market. The third is the politician, who seeks a strong state–society relationship, public support for reform processes, and manageable time frames for citizens to see benefits from the taxes that they pay. The politician can also provide moral leadership in times of crisis and social strain, an idea quite foreign to the roles played by the other two. While all three solve problems, politicians additionally redefine problems.

The particularities of these roles are only falsely described as commensurate. Often when seeking to reform government in the developing world, consultants automatically assume that a consolidation of roles will help remove corruption and enhance accountability, failing to realize that this often collapses community understandings of particular roles and responsibilities. To give an example, the attempt to make the Kenyan parliament more balanced with respect to gender led to proposals of party lists and proportional representation in place of constituency-based representatives under a first-past-the-post system (the proposed reforms of the Duale Bill). While this would have helped meet NGO concern over gender balance, it would have eliminated, overnight, the community role of MPs as leaders of local development goals. While it is true that in Kenya the office of MPs and their associated Constituency Development Fund are riddled with corruption, that is not in itself assurance that a centralization of political representation would be cleaner or fairer.

Although diverse roles in the development process can be complicated and hard for the newcomer to understand, they can complement each other and often turn out to be interdependent. We sometimes have to play a particular role when tackling a social problem, and for that we need to be okay if our assigned duty is not magnanimous. The economist is not a politician, and that is okay. A virtue of passivity allows us, over time, to distinguish between such vocations as the military and the police, the nurse and the doctor, the builder and the architect. As the philosopher Alasdair MacIntyre quotes Stuart Hampshire:

> So great has been the influence within contemporary moral philosophy of Hume, Kant, and the utilitarians that it has been possible to forget that for centuries the warrior and the priest, the landowner and the peasant, the merchant and the craftsman, the bishop and the monk, the clerk who lives by his learning and the musician or poet who lives by his performances have coexisted in society with sharply distinct dispositions and virtues.... Varied social roles and functions, each with its typical virtues and its peculiar obligations, have been the normal situation in most societies.[21]

Human flourishing is a process of actively creating diversities through deference to specializations. Rather than seeing development as a process of centralization, we should see it as a process of identifying vocations whereby the advance of an economy requires the evolution of specialties that generate distinct yet coordinating notions of role and responsibility. For this advance to occur, a key virtue is that of passivity, for it rejects the idea of development as a power conflict between structure and agency and instead provides space for the particular differences in others' community roles and how they can flourish on their own terms with their own goods in mind. A virtue of passivity says that *development is best understood as a process of identifying and respecting vocations.*

Given the soreness of the human condition in many parts of the world, a call for passivity may be resented on the grounds that it seems to amount to a policy of "do nothing." This is wrong on three counts. First, passivity is being advanced here as one virtue among many; for those who work toward development it is something that in no way inhibits the real things they do within their vocational role (the agency part) and simply helps them coordinate this role with others. Second, it is the structure agency framework that, through its assumption that the human condition is materially determined, removes reason for action. This we find in post-Marxist university cultures whereby society and the campus community are explained as sites of inevitable power struggle in the face of which humans are mere corn in the wind.[22] The resulting melancholy persists despite major economic advances in the developing world, for it is based on presumptions of human nature and the means of production, not on how things really are.

It is the structure agency framework that therefore determines that human efforts are ultimately ineffectual, not the agency passivity framework. Kelvin Knight discusses the difficulties of Marxist teleology's taking away any real notion of agency and notes that it leaves only two options remaining: "One is the way of existentialism (of Heidegger, Sartre, Foucault), according to which possibilities are unconstrained, freely constructible, and objects of choice. The other way is to understand possibilities as socially and historically constrained and to understand individual human actors as already conditioned by upbringing and situation."[23] The former redefines the realm of agency to self-defined selfhood, a tautological agency with no connection to real things or other selves. The latter lets structure carry the day, for it says that agency is *that part of the human being that gets conditioned.* Indeed, in the structure agency framework, every type of human action is imagined as wound up in constructed, conditioned, and co-opted aims; there is no pure human intention. Every attempt and ambition of the charitable sector is doubted as self-serving; every political act is reinterpreted as pursuing self-interest, not the common good. To beat this argument we must find an example of pure human intention that is unconditioned. The answer is passivity: enjoying things as they are. Passivity is the very antithesis of the structure agency presumption of ubiquitous power struggle. It is intelligent appreciation of the way things are working, without seeking to impose one's own interests on operations.

And so the third counterargument to the suggestion that passivity amounts to "doing nothing" is also the final point of this chapter's argument: *to listen well is already to achieve something, for it changes the listener.* While the dominant approach in development studies seeks to throw off the structuration that conditions the developing world, the agency passivity approach seeks to throw off the ignorance and lack of virtue that are putting painful distance between one person as helper and the other as vocation holder. Listening well to the practices and realities of those different from oneself is an encounter that threatens to change one's definitional aims. One then stands as a giant that sees past the walls that bind those who think of life as a power struggle.

Development studies has suffered from assumptions of zero-sum power relations in its attempt to examine the way structure and agency clash. The idea of the developing world is thus made to conform to a Marxist logic of center versus periphery, whereby those at the edge have no say and will have a say in years to come only if they play the same game as those at the center. From this viewpoint, the development practitioner is ultimately thwarted by the logic of the system, because any attempt to change how things are done cannot override the structure's logic. Amartya Sen breaks with this trend, however, by showing that structure is instead parasitical on agency in that genuine human freedoms in fact undergird all economic activity. Therefore, only through interactive engagement with human intentions and community norms can one grasp the true essence of development as a process of human flourishing through the exercise of multidimensional human faculties. Goods are valuable through their use, so progress comes through ending inhibitions to human capabilities, allowing for creative and meaningful use of the material.

To consolidate and expand this greater attentiveness to the role of agency in the development process, this chapter has proposed an "agency passivity" framework to replace the "structure agency" framework that pervades development studies. It has shown that there are three main values to a virtue of passivity when doing and studying development: (1) passivity allows one to see different yet mutually beneficial societal goals; (2) development is best understood as a process of identifying and respecting vocations; and (3) to listen well is already to achieve something, for it changes the listener. Those seeking to accelerate economic development across the world in a fairer manner may be surprised by this apparent advocacy of inaction. However, the call is rather to recognize the multiplicity of roles and the responsibility at the level of local community that provide the basis for any meaningful economic development. In order to respect and enhance agency in the developing world, there is a need to reorient all our understandings of the human condition. Human progress is understandable not through a utility metric but through community specializations with tailored notions of role and responsibility. The developing world is good not as an in-between stage toward progress but as good per se.

NOTES

1. Dominic Burbidge, *An Experiment in Devolution: National Unity and the Deconstruction of the Kenyan State* (Nairobi: Strathmore University Press, 2019).

2. Robin Burgess et al., "The Value of Democracy: Evidence from Road Building in Kenya," *American Economic Review* 105, no. 6 (2015): 1817–51, available at https://doi.org/10.1257/aer.20131031.

3. Joel D. Barkan and Makau Mutua, "Turning the Corner in Kenya," *Foreign Affairs*, August 10, 2010, available at https://www.foreignaffairs.com /articles/east-africa/2010-08-10/turning-corner-kenya.

4. Nic Cheeseman and Dominic Burbidge, "Are Leaders or Legislation the Silver Bullet for Counties to Succeed?," *Daily Nation*, October 1, 2016, available at http://www.nation.co.ke/oped/Opinion/are-leaders-or-legislation -silver-bullet-for-counties-to-succeed/440808-3402006-fmthhwz/.

5. Asenath Bole Odaga, *Luo Proverbs and Sayings* (Kisumu, Kenya: Lake Publishers and Enterprises, 1995), 100.

6. Brad Weiss, *Street Dreams and Hip Hop Barbershops: Global Fantasy in Urban Tanzania* (Bloomington, IN: Indiana University Press, 2009).

7. Jonny Steinberg, *A Man of Good Hope* (London: Jonathan Cape, 2015).

8. James Ferguson, *Expectations of Modernity: Myths and Meanings of Urban Life on the Zambian Copperbelt* (London: University of California Press, 1999).

9. For example, the value placed on labor by laborers themselves.

10. See, for example, the most powerful inspiration for structure-agency approaches for the study of history: E. P. Thompson, *The Making of the English Working Class* (London: Victor Gollancz, 1963). Similarly, as applied to Kenya, see Colin Leys, *Underdevelopment in Kenya: The Political Economy of Neo-Colonialism, 1964–1971* (London: Heinemann, 1975).

11. Kelvin Knight, "Agency and Ethics, Past and Present," *Historical Materialism* 19, no. 1 (2011): 145–74, 145, 159.

12. Amartya Sen, "Rational Fools: A Critique of the Behavioral Foundations of Economic Theory," *Philosophy & Public Affairs* 6, no. 4 (1977): 317–44.

13. Ibid., 324.

14. Dominic Burbidge, "The Legacy of John Nash and His Challenge to *Homo Economicus*: Why Now Is a Good Time to Study Economics," *Public Discourse*, May 27, 2015, available at http://www.thepublicdiscourse.com/2015/05/14340/.

15. Amartya Sen, *Development as Freedom* (Oxford: Oxford University Press, 1999).

16. Amartya Sen, *Identity and Violence: The Illusion of Destiny* (New York: W. W. Norton, 2006).

17. Sen, *Development as Freedom*, 177–78.

18. Amartya Sen, "Equality of What?," The Tanner Lecture on Human Values, Stanford University, Stanford, CA, May 22, 1979, 216.

19. Dominic Burbidge, "Space for Virtue in the Economics of Kenneth J. Arrow, Amartya Sen and Elinor Ostrom," *Journal of Economic Methodology* 23, no. 4 (2016): 396–412, 404.

20. Dominic Burbidge and Nic Cheeseman, "Expanding Municipal Revenues," in *Finance for City Leaders Handbook*, ed. Marco Kamiya and Le-Yin Zhang (Nairobi: UN-Habitat, 2016), 16–27.

21. Alasdair MacIntyre, *Ethics in the Conflicts of Modernity: An Essay on Desire, Practical Reasoning, and Narrative* (Cambridge: Cambridge University Press, 2016), 81–82.

22. See Nathan Heller, "Letter from Oberlin: What's Roiling the Liberal-Arts Campus?," *New Yorker*, May 30, 2016, available at https://www.newyorker.com/magazine/2016/05/30/the-new-activism-of-liberal-arts-colleges, and Dominic Burbidge, "The University of Revolution" and "The University of Subjectivism," in Burbidge, "Listening: An Antidote to the Modern University's Incoherence," *Public Discourse*, June 2, 2017, available at http://www.thepublicdiscourse.com/2017/06/19426/.

23. Knight, "Agency and Ethics," 169.

PART II

Dignity, Well-Being, and Flourishing:
Relating Objective and Subjective Dimensions

FIVE

The Lived Experience of Dignity

Matt Bloom and Deirdre Guthrie

While philosophers and theologians have been studying dignity for centuries, psychologists have largely overlooked the concept of dignity. In a search of published research over the past decade in the ten leading journals in social, cognitive, experimental, and clinical psychology we found no published articles on the topic. Even when we broadened the search to include all psychological research journals and closely related concepts such as respect, we found only 191 articles over the past ten years. But still nothing on dignity.

To address this gap in psychological research, we have launched a longitudinal study of the lived experience of dignity. One of our primary research goals is understanding the psychological dimensions of dignity. More specifically, we want to understand what people think, feel, and do when they experience themselves as having or not having dignity and also what causes people to experience that their dignity has been honored or impugned. We studied international humanitarian and global health (H/GH) professionals because people in these professions have dedicated their lives to the service of others. Dignity is essential in the work of these professionals: their mission includes an ethical commitment to accompany the victims of structural violence and help support or restore the sense of dignity of these affected persons.

In this chapter we present a preliminary conceptual model for understanding the psychological dimensions of the experience of dignity. This model emerged from a synthesis of existing research and from a grounded-theory research study with more than two hundred H/GH workers. This chapter follows our own journey through this research. We first describe the conceptual framework we developed to guide our research. This framework hypothesizes some of the core psychological dimensions of dignity. We then describe our qualitative research in which we gathered data about people's dignity-related experiences. This study enriched our conceptual framework and provided a new model of how dignity-related experiences are shaped by social interactions. Our primary goal in this chapter is to provide an initial framework to guide future research on the lived experiences of dignity.

IDENTITY AND DIGNITY

The basic elements of human psychological experience are thoughts (cognition), feelings (affect), and behaviors (conation, which also includes behavioral intentions that may not emerge in behaviors). All psychological phenomena comprise one or more of these basic elements. To develop our framework for the psychological experience of dignity, we began by drawing upon existing theories that define dignity as a person's intrinsic worth as a human being.[1] Our first hypothesis, therefore, was that, at its most basic, the psychological experience of dignity comprises the thoughts and feelings an individual has that are related to her sense of her own worthiness or adequacy as a person. Based on this initial assumption, we posited that a person's identity is the psychological "home" or core of experiences of dignity. Identity is one of the foundational concepts in psychology going back to its inception. William James, one of the founders of the field, posited that our identity includes the material self, the "me" that experiences ourselves and the world around us, and the thinking self, the "I" that can think about those experiences to understand and reflect on who we are as individual persons.[2] Although James did not directly implicate dignity, he proposed that a person's sense of self-worth is an essential part of identity and, furthermore, that self-worth is determined, at least in part, by "the good or bad positions one holds in the world."[3] Since that time researchers have continuously studied identity, and contemporary scholarship has reached consensus around several of its fundamental properties. We hypothesize that four of these properties are foundations of the lived experience of dignity.

First, researchers now define "identity" (synonyms include self-concept, self-image, and self) as the multifaceted and dynamic way a person understands or, as we describe more fully, narrates who he is, how he came to be that person, and how he fits into the world in which he lives.[4] Identity comprises the attributes, characteristics, and meanings people ascribe to themselves to answer basic existential questions such as "Who am I?" and "Why do I exist?"[5] It contains elements that may be regarded as unique to the self (i.e., the individual self) and also elements that link or embed the self with other individuals and groups (i.e., collective selves). These collective selves may include self-understandings in relation to other individuals (e.g., self as a child of particular parents or life partner to a specific individual), in relation to social roles (e.g., self as occupying a work role or that of a parent), or as members of particular social or cultural groups (e.g., self as a member of a racial or ethnic community or as an adherent to a particular religious tradition). Because identities are self-defining concepts, they form the bases for the ways people think about themselves, their relationships, and their places in the contexts in which they live. As such, a person's identity is a powerful determinant of a wide range of her thoughts, feelings, and behaviors,[6] and we argue that it is the psychological "home" of experiences of dignity.

Second, as James proposed, self-evaluation is regarded to be a fundamental feature of identity.[7] Self-evaluation is an innate and automatic process of making judgments about the worthiness and adequacy of many different kinds of constructs, including the self.[8] Self-esteem or self-worth, which reflects people's overall appraisal of whether "they are worthy or unworthy human beings," is regarded as the core self-evaluation.[9] Others include self-efficacy (a person's belief in his ability to succeed in specific situations) and self-comparison (a person's judgments of his social status), which are shaped by self-esteem. Scholars now maintain that a fundamental human need is to have a positive sense of self, that is, to have an identity that is comprised of positive self-evaluations and an overall sense that she is a person of worth and value.[10] Research on self-esteem and self-worth, for example, link them to a wide range of important outcomes that support the lived experience of dignity, including happiness or subjective well-being, resilience, adjustment to change, quality of relationships, and well-being over a lifespan.[11]

Third, a large and growing body of research indicates that a person's identity is structured both neurologically and cognitively in the form of a narrative or life story.[12] This research shows that a person's identity is an internalized, evolving story that each person creates about his or her life to integrate lived experience in ways that create purpose and meaning. Beginning in adolescence, an individual starts crafting this ongoing story about his life and experiences, and he continues authoring and reauthoring this story over the remainder of his life course.[13] This life narrative or, more properly, *narrative identity*, "reconstructs the autobiographical past and imagines the future in such a way as to provide a person's life with some degree of unity, purpose, and meaning . . . [and creates] a coherent account of [her] identity in time. Through narrative identity, people convey to themselves and to others who they are now, how they came to be, and where they think their lives may be going in the future."[14] Our identity, then, is more than a list of characteristics and other "facts" we ascribe to ourselves. Rather, it is a rich set of stories that we weave together to make sense of our lives, to give meaning to what we have done and what has happened to us, and to "reconcile who we imagine we were, are, and might be in our heads and bodies with who we were, are, and might be in the social contexts of family, community, the workplace, ethnicity, religion, gender, social class, and culture writ large."[15] Thus, in addition to being the psychological home of her experiences of dignity, a person's narrative identity also comprises the scaffolding of those salient, dignity-related experiences by which that person arrives at her self-evaluations.

Researchers have focused on the structure of narrative identities and how they are related to such important outcomes as growth, development, and well-being. Two structural features, coherence and authenticity, have emerged as especially important for understanding a wide range of outcomes. Coherence represents the extent to which a narrative identity brings disparate personal characteristics, life experiences, social interactions, role engagements, and other life elements together into an integrated and *positive* narrative identity.[16] Said differently, coherence is the extent to which a narrative identity "expresses how the individual person, who seems to encompass so many different things in a complex social world, is at the same time one (complex and even contradictory) person."[17] A central aspect of coherence is how he interprets whether his life has "added up" to something positive, to a life that he regards as worthwhile. Research indicates that people with coherent selves are much more likely to have positive self-evaluations.[18] People with less coherent identities are less capable of coping with change or with negative social encounters such as ostracism and other forms of rejection, in part because their sense of themselves has ruptured and remains fragmented.[19] The struggle to form a coherent narrative identity often coincides with a sense of ruptured dignity or self-worth. More coherent narrative identities are, we posit, consistent with experiences of having personal dignity.

The second feature of narrative identity, authenticity, refers to the extent to which, in a given social and cultural context, an individual feels that she can express her true self.[20] Social science research shows that people value their "true selves" above other constructs of the self.[21] Authentic expression—being able to express thoughts, feelings, and behaviors that we believe arise from or are consistent with our true selves—results in higher levels of subjective well-being, greater meaning in life, and greater life satisfaction.[22] Authenticity is a socially embedded experience. The extent to which a person can be authentic is determined, in significant ways, by the nature of the social interactions and cultural contexts in which that person acts. Authenticity can be thwarted, for example, when an individual feels compelled by other people, by the constraints of roles she must play, or by social conventions to act or feel or think in ways that are not consistent with her identity. Feeling that one's identity is validated by esteemed others facilitates greater authenticity. Authenticity is thus determined in part by the coherence of a person's narrative identity and also by the social contexts in which that person strives to act on and act out her life and her identity. People who experience greater authenticity deal better with adversity, persevere in the face of challenges, are more resilient, and respond better to self-esteem threats, status challenges, and other forms of mistreatment by other people.[23] We posit that being able to narrate one's true self is another aspect of experiences of one's dignity.

The final basic property of identity is that a person's sense of self is always shaped in significant ways by the people they interact with and the cultures they live in, including their access to opportunities within those contexts.[24] The desires to be loved and to belong are basic human needs.[25] To survive and thrive, people need to form and maintain at least a few stable, positive, caring interpersonal relationships and to feel they belong to the cultures they live in. People need to feel accepted and affirmed by others. Rejection is one of the most potent social experiences because it challenges a person's sense of personhood and basic human worth. Consequently, what we know and think about ourselves—that is, our identity—is shaped significantly by what other people (both individuals and groups) tell us about ourselves and what we surmise from their behavior about what they think and feel about us. While the expression of self (i.e., the specific emotions, thoughts, and behaviors that are experienced) varies across time and context, our self-concepts seem to be universally endowed with both agency and reflexivity; that is, we come to know who we are through our perceived impact on our world and through the way we mirror each other, affirming or denying possible selves. "Human beings are acutely responsive to how other people perceive, evaluate, and feel about them. . . . Positive and negative reactions from others often affect how people perceive and feel about themselves, their perceptions of other people, and the quality of their interpersonal relationships."[26] Additionally, the identity we author about ourselves is shaped in significant ways by the metastories articulated by the cultures we live in and by the norms held by those cultures about what kinds of selves, and self-stories, are acceptable, worthy, and honorable. Arthur Frank, adapting Pierre Bourdieu's concept, describes this as a *narrative habitus*, "the intuitive, usually tacit sense that some story is for us or not for us; that it expresses possibilities of which we are or can be part, or that it represents a world in which we have no stake."[27] The fundamental idea is that the relationships and cultures we are immersed in tell us what kinds of identities we *should* have, and they also tell us whether certain of our fundamental identity characteristics (e.g., our gender, race, socioeconomic status, or occupational category) are acceptable or not and, most profoundly, whether the person we are is acceptable or not.[28]

These four properties—identity is self-knowledge and self-understanding, identity comprises self-evaluations of one's status as a person, identities are structured around life narratives, and identities are socially embedded—form the basic elements of our conceptual framework of the psychological experience of dignity. We hypothesize that the process of how we come to know who we are is inseparable from our lived experience of dignity.

CONCEPTUAL INSIGHTS FROM GROUNDED-THEORY RESEARCH

For the second phase of our research we launched a qualitative study to explore how people understand and experience dignity. We conducted semistructured qualitative interviews with 207 international H/GH professionals. All participants worked for either an international humanitarian or a global health organization. International humanitarian participants were posted in Africa, Asia, the Middle East, East Asia, or South Asia; GH professionals were posted in Central America. Service tenures ranged from one year to more than thirty; 52 percent of participants were women, and 48 percent were men; 63 percent were U.S. citizens. We asked a variety of questions about their current work, including a subset designed to explore both their own experiences of dignity and how they understood the dignity-related experiences of the affected persons they worked with. Then a team of three researchers who were naïve to our conceptual framework engaged in qualitative analysis of these interviews, moving from open coding to establishing initial themes to axial coding to connect themes and then to create a final framework of conceptual insights. Four key insights emerged from this study.

First, our participants' responses to questions about dignity indicate that they think about their own and other people's dignity primarily in terms of a person's self-concept. One of the most prevalent patterns in the data emerged from responses to questions such as "What does a person experience when they feel they have dignity?" or "What is a person thinking or feeling when they have a sense of dignity?" Two consistent themes across almost all responses were (1) that dignity resides in the way a person thinks of himself and (2) that a positive sense of one's own value or worth as a human being is essential for experiences of dignity. While participants readily acknowledged that other people could shape a person's sense of dignity, the sense or experience of dignity was always described in terms of a person's self-understanding and self-evaluations. This statement by a humanitarian worker is representative of many that we heard: "It really doesn't matter if *I* think they have dignity, they have to think that about themselves, experience it in their own heart and mind. It is what *they* think about themselves that matters." Participants emphasized that, although H/GH workers were committed to acting in ways that honored the dignity of the affected persons they worked with, what mattered most was how those persons experienced the actions of H/GH workers, that is, whether the affected persons felt that their dignity was being honored. Although most participants could articulate a definition of dignity—for example, that each person has intrinsic worth as a human and that the intrinsic value of all persons is equal—they understood the experience of dignity as residing inside a person, in the way that that person thought and felt about herself. Tania Groppi's chapter in this volume provides an example of how an organization supports experiences of dignity by supporting a person's identity. At L'Arche the intrinsic dignity of all persons is a core value, but simply asserting this truth is not enough: for Jean Vanier and the L'Arche community it is essential that all persons *experience* their innate value.

Second, our participants told many stories indicating that authenticity—a person's experience that his fullest or true self is honored and feeling good about "who they really were"—is central to how they understood their own experiences of dignity and how they understood the dignity-related experience of the affected persons they work with. These stories of authenticity were, however, almost always embedded with themes related to personal agency. For example, themes related to the right and capacity to make one's own life choices or the freedom and ability to make one's own decisions about how to live one's life were often connected with experiences of authenticity. This response from one participant is illustrative of many responses: "Dignity for me means I can make the choices *I* feel are best, and those choices are not just tolerated, but they are honored and seen as good by other people in my life." Agency was particularly important in responses about the dignity of others. This response is typical of those we heard from many participants: "I think a person feels dignity when they can live the life they choose, the life they think is best for *them*, the life that fits best for who they are and what they want to be." These descriptions of agency were usually offered when participants were speaking about the dignity of marginalized persons when such marginalization arose from their gender, religious beliefs, sexual orientation, or other personal characteristics that were central to these people's identity. Participants emphasized that authenticity and agency for these persons meant being able to live in ways that were consistent with their true selves, beyond but including without fear of being ostracized or persecuted, but more fully with a sense of self-acceptance and pride in being who they are. Agency, then, was seen as more than freedom to choose and more than the capacity to make the choices one wants to make. Agency was being able to live and act in ways one felt were consistent with one's true self and to be self-confident and validated by others in that enactment. One of our global health participants provided a compelling example of authentic agency. Historically, farmers who live in poverty would wait for hours, even days, in health clinics hoping to eventually be granted admission to the clinic so they or their families could receive healthcare. The experience of accompaniment with the GH workers began to restore and strengthen the sense of authentic agency among some of these farmers. Rather than capitulating to being overlooked or ignored, they advocated for their rights to healthcare in these clinics. Advocating for themselves was a poignant enactment of authentic agency.

Third, central to H/GH workers' own experience of authenticity was the notion of enacting and embodying *virtue*, particularly the virtue of social justice, which serves as a strong motivational source for these workers. They described virtue as sustaining integrity and motivation in their lives, guiding them toward purposeful action, and thus safeguarding human dignity. Identity presumes a dynamic relationship between the "I" and one's purposeful action that is consistent. Our participants' own experience of dignity was described as manifest, in part, when their authentic selves and their belief systems were mirrored intelligibly in their experiences, actions, lifestyles, and behaviors with others. That is, our participants' narratives reflected a greater sense of meaning, purpose, and positive self-evaluations when those narratives offered coherent storylines in which their feelings, thoughts, and actions were consistent with their core life values and beliefs. However, one of the characteristics of international H/GH work is that it creates a feeling of disjointedness for many H/GH professionals overwhelmed by the burden of witnessing suffering on such a scale. The psychosocial labor that is involved in dedicating one's work life to providing service to others can involve a shrinking of oneself as a professional foregrounds their awareness of and sensitivity to the other and minimizes their own experiences. This is enacted to achieve "accompaniment" over "charity," but on a personal level it obscures agency and can create a climate in which professionals constantly question their own right to well-being. The challenge they articulated was how to honor both the dignity of others and their own. There was a strong tendency to sacrifice their own well-being in service of others.

Fourth, our participants told a variety of stories about how other people and groups impacted their experiences of dignity or the experiences of others. Many spoke in detail about how their actions and those of other H/GH workers might impact the experiences of dignity of the affected persons they work with. The responses of participants clearly conveyed that they thought of dignity as a socially embedded experience. Almost all of their stories about dignity took place in social contexts in which interactions and relationships with other people and groups were essential for experiences of dignity. We asked probing questions about how the actions of others shaped a person's experiences of dignity, especially of how actions might increase or decrease others' sense of their own dignity. Almost all of the descriptions of the social dimension of dignity linked back to the first insight—that is, that the actions of others impacted their dignity when those actions influenced the way they think about themselves. Here again, the experience of dignity was understood in terms of a person's self-evaluation. Participants described, for example, how some persons (e.g., children, women, and sick or injured persons) might be particularly vulnerable to the invidious actions of powerful others that could make vulnerable persons devalue themselves. Some participants shared examples of courageous individuals who maintained a sense of their own dignity in the face of oppression or discrimination, again situating dignity in terms of a person's self-concept.

We theorize that our participants' descriptions of how their dignity was impacted in social interactions fell along a continuum that we present in figure 5.1. Participants told many stories in which they expressed the

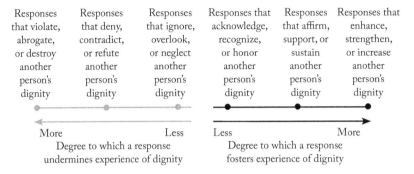

FIGURE 5.1. Responses to Dignity

idea that dignity-supportive interactions begin by acknowledging the value of others. These stories described what participants regarded as the necessary baseline for the way they interacted with others. That is, they asserted that, at a bare minimum, their interactions with others should also convey a "basic respect" for the others' dignity. These professionals sought both to understand—as best they could—the cultures of those they worked with and to act in ways that honored those cultures. For example, providing time and appropriate space for daily prayers, adjusting leaders' behaviors related to local gender norms, or removing shoes before entering a home are examples of ways H/GH professionals strove to honor local cultures. More important for our participants were responses that moved toward the positive end of the continuum. They described the need to actively affirm or support the dignity of others through responses such as including affected persons in the process of planning new H/GH initiatives, giving them autonomy over important decisions, and actively seeking to be held accountable to these persons. Almost all of our participants described their ultimate objective as acting in ways that enhance, strengthen, and increase the dignity of others. They acknowledged the ongoing challenges of achieving this highest standard for their actions, but pursuing this level of excellence was clearly at the heart of their commitments and passions for their work.

More distressing, our participants also shared stories as to how the dignity of these persons had been denied or refuted, perhaps due to unconscious bias, including the denial of equal human rights to women or members of ethnic minority groups and the exclusion of certain subgroups from access to basic life goods, such as healthcare or full participation in work. Intentionality seemed to be a crucial line of demarcation on both ends, but particularly for interpretations of negative actions. The most negative actions were those that were interpreted as intentionally or consciously annihilating or abrogating the dignity of others. Human rights abuses such as human trafficking, physical and mental violence, and torture were used to illustrate these most grievous responses against the dignity of others.

Our goal in this project was to develop an initial conceptual model that would provide a foundation for research on the lived experience of dignity. One of our core propositions is that a person's identity is the center of psychological experiences of dignity. We drew upon four fundamental features of identity, what we now restate as identity-related capacities, that are innate to all persons: our capacity for self-knowledge and self-understanding, our capacity to evaluate our status and group membership as worthy, our capacity to narrate a coherent and authentic life story, and our capacity to successfully navigate through the constraints and challenges imposed by various social contexts (public, private, and intimate). We now add a fifth capacity that emerged as especially important for H/GH professionals, a capacity that simultaneously affirms both the self and others if enacted from a place that honors the dignity of both parties. Our hope is that this framework will encourage future studies of the lived experience of dignity.

NOTES

    1. Christopher McCrudden, "In Pursuit of Human Dignity: An Introduction to Current Debates," in *Understanding Human Dignity*, ed. McCrudden (Oxford: Oxford University Press, 2014), 1–61, and Daniel P. Sulmasy, "The Varieties of Human Dignity: A Logical and Conceptual Analysis," *Medicine, Health Care, and Philosophy* 16, no. 4 (November 2013): 937–44.
    2. William James, *The Principles of Psychology*, 2 vols. (New York: Henry Holt, 1890; repr. 1918). Citations refer to the 1918 edition.
    3. Ibid., 306.
    4. Robyn Fivush, "The Development of Autobiographical Memory," *Annual Review of Psychology* 62, no. 1 (2011): 559–82, and Dan P. McAdams

and B. D. Olson, "Personality Development: Continuity and Change over the Life Course," *Annual Review of Psychology* 61, no. 1 (2010): 517–42.

5. Mark R. Leary and June Price Tangney, "The Self as an Organizing Construct in the Behavioral and Social Sciences," in *Handbook of Self and Identity*, ed. Leary and Tangney (New York: Guilford Press, 2003), 3–14, and Walter Mischel and Carolyn C. Morf, "The Self as a Psycho-Social Dynamic Processing System: A Meta-Perspective on a Century of the Self in Psychology," in Leary and Tangney, *Handbook of Self and Identity*, 14–46.

6. Fivush, "Development of Autobiographical Memory"; Leary and Tangney, "The Self as Organizing Construct"; McAdams and Olson, "Personality Development"; and Mischel and Morf, "The Self as Psycho-Social Dynamic."

7. James, *Principles of Psychology*.

8. Abraham Tesser, "Self-Evaluation," in Leary and Tangney, *Handbook of Self and Identity*, 275–90.

9. Jennifer Crocker and Laura E. Park, "Seeking Self-Esteem: Construction, Maintenance, and Protection of Self-Worth," in Leary and Tangney, *Handbook of Self and Identity*, 291.

10. Ibid., and Tesser, "Self-Evaluation."

11. Andrew J. Howell, "Self-Affirmation Theory and the Science of Well-Being," *Journal of Happiness Studies* 18, no. 1 (2016): 1–19; Dan P. McAdams, *Handbook of Identity Theory and Research* (New York: Springer, 2011); S. Katherine Nelson, Joshua A. K. Fuller, Incheol Choi, and Sonja Lyubomirsky, "Beyond Self-Protection: Self-Affirmation Benefits Hedonic and Eudaimonic Well-Being," *Personality and Social Psychology Bulletin* 40, no. 8 (2014): 998–1011; and Claude M. Steele, "The Psychology of Self-Affirmation: Sustaining the Integrity of the Self," in *Advances in Experimental Social Psychology*, ed. L. Berkowitz (New York: Academic Press, 1988), 21:261–302.

12. Jerome S. Bruner, "A Narrative Model of Self-Construction," *Annals of the New York Academy of Sciences* 818, no. 1 (1997): 145–61; Fivush, "Development of Autobiographical Memory"; McAdams and Olson, "Personality Development"; S. C. Prebble, D. R. Addis, and L. J. Tippett, "Autobiographical Memory and Sense of Self," *Psychological Bulletin* 139, no. 4 (2013): 815–40; and Jefferson A. Singer, "Narrative Identity and Meaning Making across the Adult Lifespan: An Introduction," *Journal of Personality* 72, no. 3 (2004): 437–60.

13. Tilmann Habermas and Susan Bluck, "Getting a Life: The Emergence of the Life Story in Adolescence," *Psychological Bulletin* 126, no. 5 (2000): 748–69.

14. Dan P. McAdams and Kate C. McLean, "Narrative Identity," *Current Directions in Psychological Science* 22, no. 3 (2013): 233.

15. Dan P. McAdams, "Personal Narratives and the Life Story: Theory and Research," in *Handbook of Personality: Theory and Research*, 3rd ed., ed. Oliver P. John, Richard W. Robins, and Lawrence A. Pervin (New York: Guilford Press, 2008), 242–43.

16. Jack J. Bauer, Dan P. McAdams, and Jennifer L. Pals, "Narrative Identity and Eudaimonic Well-Being," *Journal of Happiness Studies* 9, no. 1 (2006): 81–104, and Kenneth J. Gergen and Mary M. Gergen, "Narrative and the Self as Relationship," in *Advances in Experimental Social Psychology*, ed. L. Berkowitz (San Diego: Academic Press, 1988), 21:17–56; Singer, "Narrative Identity."

17. McAdams, "Personal Narratives and the Life Story," 244.

18. Dana Royce Baerger and Dan P. McAdams, "Life Story Coherence and Its Relation to Psychological Well-Being," *Narrative Inquiry* 9, no. 1 (1999): 69–96, and McAdams and Olson, "Personality Development."

19. Jennifer D. Campbell, Sunaina Assanand, and Adam Di Paula, "The Structure of the Self-Concept and Its Relation to Psychological Adjustment," *Journal of Personality* 71, no. 1 (2003): 115–40, and Jennifer L. Pals, "Narrative Identity Processing of Difficult Life Experiences: Pathways of Personality Development and Positive Self-Transformation in Adulthood," *Journal of Personality* 74, no. 4 (2006): 1079–1110.

20. William E. Davis and Joshua A. Hicks, "Maintaining Hope at the 11th Hour: Authenticity Buffers the Effect of Limited Time Perspective on Hope," *Personality and Social Psychology Bulletin* 39, no. 12 (2013): 1634–46; Susan Harter, "Authenticity," in *Handbook of Positive Psychology*, ed. C. R. Snyder and Shane J. Lopez (New York: Oxford University Press, 2002), 382–94; and Michael H. Kernis and Brian M. Goldman, "A Multicomponent Conceptualization of Authenticity: Theory and Research," *Advances in Experimental Social Psychology* 38 (2006): 283–357.

21. Rebecca J. Schlegel, K. A. Hirsch, and C. M. Smith, "The Importance of Who You Really Are: The Role of the True Self in Eudaimonia," in *The Best within Us: Positive Psychology Perspectives on Eudaimonia*, ed. A. Waterman (Washington, DC: American Psychological Association, 2015), 207–25.

22. Nelson et al., "Beyond Self-Protection"; Rebecca Schlegel, Joshua A. Hicks, Laura A. King, and Jaimie Arndt, "Feeling Like You Know Who You Are: Perceived True Self-Knowledge and Meaning in Life," *Personality and Social Psychology Bulletin* 37, no. 6 (2011): 745–56.

23. Kristine Anthis and Joseph C. LaVoie, "Readiness to Change: A Longitudinal Study of Changes in Adult Identity," *Journal of Research in Personality* 40, no. 2 (2006): 209–19; Ozlem Ayduk et al., "Regulating the Interpersonal Self: Strategic Self-Regulation for Coping with Rejection Sensitivity," *Journal*

of Personality and Social Psychology 79, no. 5 (2000), 776–92; Jeni L. Burnette et al., "Mind-Sets Matter: A Meta-Analytic Review of Implicit Theories and Self-Regulation," *Psychological Bulletin* 139, no. 3 (2013): 655–701; Claudia M. Haase, Jutta Heckhausen, and Carsten Wrosch, "Developmental Regulation across the Life Span: Toward a New Synthesis," *Developmental Psychology* 49, no. 5 (2013): 964–72; Todd B. Kashdan and Jonathan Rottenberg, "Psychological Flexibility as a Fundamental Aspect of Health," *Clinical Psychology Review* 30, no. 7 (2010): 865–78; Patrick E. McKnight and Todd B. Kashdan, "Purpose in Life as a System that Creates and Sustains Health and Well-Being: An Integrative, Testable Theory," *Review of General Psychology* 13, no. 3 (2009): 242–51, available at https://doi.org/10.1037/a0017152; Pals, "Narrative Identity Processing"; and Michelle R. vanDellen, W. Keith Campbell, Rick H. Hoyle, and Erin K. Bradfield, "Compensating, Resisting, and Breaking: A Meta-Analytic Examination of Reactions to Self-Esteem Threat," *Personality and Social Psychology Review* 15, no. 1 (2013): 51–74.

24. Susan M. Andersen and Serena Chen, "The Relational Self: An Interpersonal Social-Cognitive Theory," *Psychological Review* 109, no. 4 (2002): 619–45; Gergen and Gergen, "Narrative and the Self"; and Naomi Ellemers, Russel Spears, and Bertajn Doosje, "Self and Social Identity," *Annual Review of Psychology* 53 (2002): 161–86.

25. Roy Baumeister and Mark Leary, "The Need to Belong: Desire for Interpersonal Attachments as a Fundamental Human Motivation," *Psychological Bulletin* 117, no. 3 (1995): 497–529; and C. S. Dweck, "From Needs to Goals and Representations: Foundations for a Unified Theory of Motivation, Personality, and Development," *Psychological Review* 124, no. 6 (2017): 689–719.

26. Laura Richman and Mark Leary, "Reactions to Discrimination, Stigmatization, Ostracism, and Other Forms of Interpersonal Rejection: A Multimotive Model," *Psychological Review* 116, no. 2 (2009): 365.

27. Arthur W. Frank, *Letting Stories Breathe: A Socio-Narratology* (Chicago: University of Chicago Press, 2012), 53.

28. Bruner, "Narrative Model," and *Making Stories: Law, Literature, Life* (Cambridge, MA: Harvard University Press, 2003).

SIX

Participation, Human Dignity, and Human Development

The Challenge of Establishing a Causal Relationship

Robert A. Dowd

As other contributors to this volume suggest, there seems to be a growing consensus that human development and awareness of human dignity are inextricably linked. Yet there is much work to be done if we are to develop a better understanding of how they are linked. If human development and human dignity are related, is there a causal relationship? If one causes the other, which causes which, what exactly is the causal mechanism, and how would we know?

In this chapter I seek to disentangle these concepts, discuss how they are related in practice, and suggest how we may assess the effects of one on the other. I propose that while the two may be mutually reinforcing, human development, which I define as sustained improvements in the quality of life people enjoy as indicated by, but not limited to, advances in health, education, and financial security, typically begins with a growing awareness of human dignity, an appreciation for the inherent value of oneself and others.[1] In other words, an awakening to one's human dignity and that of others in one's community is the spark of human development. Of course, this begs the question "What 'sparks the spark,' or how are people awakened to their dignity?" As others do in this volume, I propose that relationships that are respectful and encouraging awaken people to their dignity. Assuming that dignifying ways of relating with others can be modeled and replicated in development projects through inclusive practices that allow people to share their experiences, shape their own development goals, and participate in efforts to realize these goals, the question is then "How would we ever know that such participatory practices are, in fact, dignifying?"[2]

Drawing on the experience of the University of Notre Dame's Ford Program in Human Development Studies and Solidarity in Uganda, I propose that attempts to identify and measure the effects of participatory practices that are intended to awaken people to their dignity must integrate behavioral variables (what people do) and attitudinal variables (how people account for what they do). Instead of interpreting their behaviors for them, social scientists interested in understanding what initiates changes in people's awareness of dignity must find ways to allow people to interpret their own behaviors. While it is important to be mindful of the biases that may lead people to over- or underattribute their behavior to certain factors when asked by others to explain changes in their behaviors, we are likely to get more reliable assessments of changes in awareness of dignity by incorporating explanations put forward by the very people whose behavior has changed.

The remainder of this chapter continues as follows. I begin by describing how development organizations devoted to promoting human development and human dignity may end up undermining their objectives by failing to adopt or remain faithful to participatory practices. I go on to define the terms "dignity" and "human development." After proposing how they are related and how participatory practices form the connective tissue of that relationship, I describe and discuss the Ford Program's efforts to understand whether a project devoted to increasing awareness of human dignity in rural-central Uganda through participatory and inclusive practices had its desired effect. I conclude with suggestions for future research.

THE CHALLENGE OF PROMOTING HUMAN DIGNITY AND HUMAN DEVELOPMENT

Many organizations devoted to human development claim that they are dedicated to promoting greater awareness of human dignity among the people with whom they work.[3] As Paul Perrin notes in his chapter for this volume, there are many agencies and organizations that reference dignity in their mission statements. Many are faith-based, and others are not. While it is not always clear exactly what these organizations mean by "dignity," several implicitly affirm the assertion that human development cannot be reduced to increases in material wealth.[4] Some seem to take for granted that the nonmaterial transformation that occurs *within* individual persons (e.g., growth in a sense of self-worth/self-esteem/self-confidence and capabilities or their potential to affect their own well-being and that of their communities) is important and somehow related to their material well-being and the flourishing of their communities.

However, even well-meaning organizations devoted to promoting human dignity and human development may adopt practices that undermine their objectives. One possible reason is that they wrongly conceive of the causal relationship between human dignity and human development. By this I mean that they may operate under the assumption that it is human development that leads people to grow in awareness of their dignity. This very well might be the case. Then again, it very well might not be the case. In any case, this assumption is likely to have significant consequences. If an organization assumes that human development is the spark of dignity rather than the other way around, it is likely to devote more resources toward achieving material results or outcomes than toward inclusive participatory practices. In my view, this undermines the "dignifying" potential of the development process.

A lack of patience may also undermine an organization's attempts to promote human dignity and human development. This lack of patience may be due to donors' pressure for results and outcomes, or it may have arisen because those representing development organizations have not been adequately prepared for the time and attention that truly inclusive and carefully designed participatory practices entail. An organization may discard or rush consultation and participatory practices because of pressure for material outcomes. And when an organization gets the causal relationship wrong, assuming that development outcomes and material conditions lead to dignity, people become the objects rather than the subjects of development. They become the "beneficiaries" rather than the protagonists in the development process. In my view, this renders development projects incapable of promoting awareness of dignity. In fact, projects that drift into emphasizing material outcomes or "results" and deemphasizing the processes by which they are achieved may diminish people's awareness of their dignity and even exacerbate their feelings of inadequacy and dependency.[5] How material outcomes are achieved, however positive such outcomes may be for physical/material well-being, is as important as the outcomes themselves if promoting dignity and human development, rather than mere increases in material wealth, is our objective.

Another reason that organizations may adopt practices that undermine their objectives to promote human dignity and human development concerns frustration with conceptualization and measurement. Even if changes in people's awareness of their dignity can be measured by assessing changes in their self-worth or self-esteem, it is not always obvious that such changes have taken place, why they have taken place, and/or what may be the consequences of their having taken place. If we were to approach people and ask them whether they have experienced an increase in a sense of their self-worth and capabilities due to their participation in a particular "development" program, there is a high likelihood that we would get an unreliable answer.[6] Participants may indicate that there has been such an increase because they sense that this is the answer we desire or because they think that this is the answer that will be rewarded with the continuation of a program from which they benefit.[7] They may have difficulty responding at all because they lack the vocabulary necessary to describe something so highly abstract as an increase in awareness of their dignity, even in their own language. They may also be unaccustomed to sharing deeply about their lives with anyone, particularly researchers like us who have just shown up at their doors.[8] The point here is that organizations may conclude that it is a waste of time and resources to invest in participatory practices if they think their effects cannot be measured.[9] There is a need for conceptual and analytical clarity.

THE RELATIONSHIP BETWEEN HUMAN DIGNITY AND HUMAN DEVELOPMENT

Because "dignity" has often been used in different ways, it is important to be clear about what I mean here by the word and the assumptions I make concerning its nature. Much as other contributors to this volume, I define "human dignity" as the value or worth that every human being has in equal measure by virtue of his or her existence. It cannot be earned or forfeited by the one who possesses it, nor can it be increased or decreased by the actions of others. While I believe that a Creator-God is the source of this universal human dignity, in my view one need not believe in God to believe that human beings have inherent value. It is important to be clear about three other key assumptions I make.

First, although I assume everyone has dignity to the same degree and it cannot be increased or decreased, I propose that people can be more or less aware of their human dignity and respectful of the dignity of others. Changes in awareness of human dignity are, in my view, essentially changes in a person's inner disposition or view of himself in relation to other people. A person may view himself as having more value, less value, or the same value as other people. The views of self that we have are necessarily social or relational products. In other words, how we see our "selves" is at least partly the result of how other people seem to see us or how other people have led us to believe we should see ourselves.[10] How parents, teachers, and peers treat a person during the early or most formative years of her life is likely to have a significant and lasting impact on her awareness of her own human dignity, her estimation of her own value relative to other people.

Second, I assume that the awareness of dignity that a person has or how a person sees herself in relation to others is not necessarily fixed. Certainly there are denigrating experiences that can leave, quite literally, permanent scars. People may spend a lifetime attempting to work through such experiences so as to have a healthy sense of self-worth. But of course, the opposite may be true. People may be taught from an early age to think they are inherently better than others, often because of their race, ethnicity, nationality, religion, or some other inherited, acquired, or assigned identity. They may also be led to think they have more dignity than others because of the wealth they possess or social status they have achieved.[11]

Third, while there may be limits to the extent to which aware-ness of one's dignity can be increased, particularly if one has lived long with a low level of self-worth, I assume that one's awareness of one's dignity or value may be increased through respectful encounters.[12] In many ways this echoes Martha Nussbaum's emphasis on the connec-tion between respect and dignity.[13] Here I build on Nussbaum's thought and propose how one actually encounters another respectfully. While that may seem self-evident, it is worth thoughtful elaboration. I propose that one encounters another respectfully when, among other things, one seeks to know or learn from another's experience. In this way, a respect-ful encounter requires attentiveness. However, ultimately the degree to which an encounter increases one's awareness of her dignity depends on the degree to which she perceives it as respectful. In other words, a respectful encounter must be not only the intention of the one initiating the encounter (e.g., I intend to respect you by encountering you) but also received as such by the one being encountered (e.g., you feel respected because of our encounter).[14]

"Human development," like "dignity," is a contested term. How-ever, unlike in the case of dignity, there is a widely accepted measure of human development, though not without its critics. This measure is the HDI, which implies that human development is possible only when people enjoy good health, are well educated, and have enough resources to live the kinds of lives they have reason to value.[15] These indicators of material conditions are thought to allow people to build their capabili-ties and when and where they are increasing or improving their human development. In short, it is assumed that human development is taking place if people are living the kinds of lives they have reason to value and that certain conditions—life expectancy, educational attainment, and income—are good indicators of the extent to which people are able to live the kinds of lives they have reason to value. For Sen, whose work inspired the development of the HDI, it is crucially important for people themselves to play a role in envisioning and creating these conditions.[16] The question is this: What leads people who suffer because of low levels of human development to begin envisioning themselves and their communities differently and playing a role in creating conditions they envision for themselves and their communities?

As noted above, I assume that how a person sees herself in relation to others, something we might call her "inner disposition," is the key to human development. If a person sees herself as having relatively little value, human development is impossible. This is because, unlike mere economic development, human development is a participatory process that requires a person to see herself as capable, and people who see themselves as having relatively little value are likely to see themselves as largely incapable. In my view, this does not mean that human dignity or value depends on having the capability to "do" anything.[17] Human beings are not valuable because of what they do.[18] Human dignity is about being rather than doing. "Doing" does not give people human dignity. However, people who have a low awareness of their dignity are likely to feel incapable, that they cannot "do" much. Therefore, efforts to promote awareness of dignity are likely to require practices that invite people to recognize their capabilities. Here, like Nussbaum, I define "capabilities" widely with the assumption that human beings are capable in different ways and that each and every person, regardless of age and physical or intellectual limitations, is capable in one way or another.[19] The intention of respectful encounters is not to get people to think that they are capable of anything or everything regardless of their age, education, and physical or mental state, but that they are capable of *something* valuable.

In my view, participatory practices, characterized by human encounters that respectfully invite a person to recognize her capabilities, can change a person's inner disposition and promote her awareness of her dignity, and it is this awareness that makes human development possible.[20] A great deal has been written on the merits of participatory practices.[21] Further, Amartya Sen, in *Development as Freedom*, stresses the intrinsic importance of participatory practices for human development.[22] Although he does not use the word "dignity," it appears to me that he in effect implies that the freedom to affect or influence one's own "development agenda" is what makes the development process dignifying: "Even a very rich person who is prevented from speaking freely, or from participating in public debates and decisions, is deprived of something she has reason to value. The process of development, when judged by the enhancement of human freedom, has to include removal of this person's deprivation. Even if she had no immediate interest in exercising the freedom to speak or participate, it would still be deprivation of her freedoms if she were to be left with no choice on these matters."[23]

While little empirical research has been devoted to understanding the effects of participatory practices on one's awareness of her human dignity, not to mention her awareness of the effects of human dignity on development outcomes, there is a great deal of evidence to suggest that participation in agenda-setting and decision-making processes promotes self-esteem and a sense of efficacy.[24] Therefore, there is good reason to believe that when people are invited to share their perspectives on the challenges they face, their experiences, and the kind of future they envision, they will conclude that they "count," or that, since others have assumed that they have value, they must have value. Because other people see them as worth encountering, they may begin to see themselves as worthy. Because other people assume that they have desires for their future and are capable of influencing their future, they may begin to see themselves as capable. While we cannot expect the inner dispositions of people whose experiences and desires have been dismissed for a long time by others, including so-called development experts, to change overnight, consistently applied practices of inclusion that emphasize the importance of participation and have real consequences on a community's development agenda can be encouraging and can begin to get people to see themselves differently. They can prompt people to become protagonists rather than spectators in their own development. If so, we might be able to say that the participatory practices characterized by respectful human encounters have changed people's inner dispositions and are dignifying.

There is a need for more empirical research on participative practices and their effects on development outcomes. The challenge is that such research requires time, resources, and a great deal of patience, knowing that it is extremely difficult to ever really know how participatory practices affect inner dispositions and development outcomes. We cannot directly measure awareness of dignity or changes in awareness of dignity because we cannot directly observe inner dispositions. We must infer change in awareness of dignity based on proxies or their effects.

Many social scientists assume that there are two types of proxies for inner dispositions, such as awareness of dignity. One focuses on attitudes or self-assessment, and the other focuses on behaviors or observation.[25] Self-assessment generally entails survey research and in-depth interviews. For example, interviewers may ask people questions about their sense of self-worth or self-esteem before an intervention or compare responses to such questions from people who were randomly assigned to participate in a program or intervention with responses given by those who were not. Those who focus on behavior may assess behavior before and after an intervention or compare behaviors of people who are part of a randomly assigned intervention with those who are not.

Because self-assessment is considered notoriously unreliable, many social scientists prefer behavioral over attitudinal research.[26] The operative assumption here is that actions speak louder than words, or, in other words, if we want to know what people think or how they feel, we should observe what they do rather than relying on what they say. For example, we should observe how they spend their time and/or their money. Even well-designed survey research, focused on what people say about what they think or how they feel, may suffer from social desirability effects. Respondents may over-report (or under-report) certain inner dispositions, including their sense of self-worth and self-efficacy (their sense of being able to affect their future or that of the community in which they live), if they think that such a response is likely to be rewarded (e.g., with the continuation of a program from which they have benefited).

While it may be safe to assume that actions almost always speak louder than words, it is not always obvious what actions mean or what motivates people to engage in certain behaviors rather than others. Ilaria Schnyder von Wartensee's chapter in this volume provides an example of qualitative research that seeks to understand the results of a randomized control trial (RCT). That RCT clearly showed that women entrepreneurs who had mentors had more profitable businesses than those who participated in skills training workshops, but it was unable to explain why. Behaviors always beg the question "Why?" The inner dispositions that behaviors reveal are not necessarily obvious. How do we know why a person spends an increasing amount of time on his business or on civic affairs in his community? How do we know why a person spends more money on her education or that of her children? How do we know why a person contributes more of his time volunteering in the community or more of her money to helping people she considers less fortunate than herself? In psychology, the attempt to understand the inner dispositions that behaviors reveal and the process by which people come to decide what behaviors reveal about inner dispositions is known as attribution theory.[27]

As important as observation of behavior is for estimating awareness of dignity, research on attribution theory clearly confirms that people may change their behavior not because of a change in their inner dispositions but because they desire to please, they expect to be rewarded, or they fear punishment.[28] In other words, social desirability is not just a problem for those who do survey- or interview-based research. It is also a problem for those who do behavior-focused research. In both cases, we are left with unreliable estimates of people's awareness of their dignity.

The question we are left with is "How do we know what changes in behaviors really mean, that is, what they reveal about the inner dispositions or motivations of those whose behavior has changed?" In the end, it is clear that there is no way to avoid the need to interpret behavior and behavioral change. The question is "*Who* should decide what behaviors or changes in behavior mean?" The case of the Ford Program's work in rural-central Uganda, described in the section that follows, illustrates some of the challenges described above.

THE FORD PROGRAM'S EFFORTS TO PROMOTE HUMAN DEVELOPMENT THROUGH PARTICIPATORY PRACTICES

In 2008 the Ford Program in Human Development Studies and Solidarity at the University of Notre Dame's Kellogg Institute for International Studies entered into a partnership with Uganda Martyrs University to work with people in twelve villages of central Uganda. The program's intention was to facilitate a process that would increase villagers' awareness of their dignity and their own wisdom and capabilities and also improve their standard development indicators (e.g., income and physical health). In a sense, the project was devoted to testing a hypothesis that respectful participatory practices would spark their awareness of their dignity, which, in turn, would result in improvements in their standard human development indicators. The project had a seven-year timeline, and outside financial investments ended in 2014. There are at least two important lessons we can take away from the project. First, if participatory practices are to be characterized by respectful human encounters, plenty of time and carefully trained "accompanimenteurs" are necessary. Second, if we are to measure the effects of participatory practices on awareness of dignity and, in turn, awareness of dignity on human development, we must find ways of integrating behavioral variables (what people do) and attitudinal variables (how people account for what they do).

The project began with a baseline survey intended to establish pre-existing development indicators as well as people's sense of their own capabilities and the extent to which they looked to outsiders for solutions to the challenges they faced. Responses indicated that many people did not think of themselves as capable of addressing their own development challenges, which, in this farming community, included low agricultural productivity. As one respondent told the project manager, "We cannot manage these things. For us, whatever you tell us to do, we will do. But we cannot manage to plan these things ourselves."[29] Many people assumed that, since we were academics and had financial resources, we must also have the answers to their problems. People tended to look to outsiders, particularly religious institutions and other non-governmental organizations, to solve their problems. Residents told us that many development projects had been launched in the area in past decades. However, it was clear that most of them had been "top-down" in nature. For example, according to villagers, one NGO drilled several shallow boreholes and installed pumps to provide access to water without any input from the community.[30] This seemed to be common practice. There was little consultation, so the people in the villages had largely been the objects (or recipients) rather than the subjects (protagonists) of such initiatives. Many villagers noted that they lacked much formal education and deferred to those who had more formal education. It seemed that people had come to think of themselves as "unqualified" to address their own problems and deferred to "experts" with more formal education and to outsiders with resources.

Of the 301 heads of households interviewed in the baseline survey, just over 37 percent indicated that they thought there was no way they could change their lives for the better. Many women, especially, lacked a sense of self-worth and efficacy, indicating that they did not think of themselves as particularly capable of doing much to improve their personal well-being or that of their families. In part, this was a product of their low levels of education. As one woman noted, "I have not been to school. I cannot do much. Why do you ask me questions?"[31] While it is important to recognize that the pull of tradition and custom may explain the women's behavior, what they told us suggests that they desired change that they did not see themselves as capable of effecting. More than half the female household heads interviewed said that they felt incapable of improving the lives of their households or of helping to improve their communities.[32]

With the assistance of the Uganda Martyrs University Outreach Program staff who had worked in Nnindye for several years, villagers across the twelve villages established a Parish Development Council (PDC) that was also known as the Parish Project Council (PPC). The PPC was to be a means for villagers to participate in the process of their development. The PPC membership consisted of representatives elected from each of the twelve villages as well as representatives of local government (i.e., the local village councilor and the subcountry councilor). The PPC was intended to link together the villages of the Nnindye Parish and to connect the parish to Uganda Martyrs University Outreach Program staff who were facilitating the project. Members of the PPC were expected to play a crucially important role in the project. In addition to the university personnel involved in the project, members of the PPC were expected to respectfully encounter their fellow villagers, solicit their input on their parish's development agenda, and invite them to participate in efforts to realize that agenda. It was hoped that the PPC would be an instrument of inclusive participation that would allow people to set their own development priorities. We hypothesized that, having a voice in setting their own development priorities, people would feel valued, awakened to their own dignity, and devoted to participation in efforts to realize such priorities. Among the priorities set by the PPC were (1) to increase agriculture yields and, in so doing, (2) to increase people's incomes, savings, and investment.

As the project came to an end in 2014, there had been several changes in the community. Three of the most significant changes included a dramatic increase in agricultural production, an increase in incomes derived from agricultural production, and the establishment of several small savings and lending communities. Many of the farmers who had experienced the greatest gains in production and incomes were women. Most of these women started up small savings and lending communities with the assistance of Catholic Relief Services, Uganda Martyrs University, and the Ford Program.[33] These savings and lending groups, actually called Savings and Internal Lending Communities, or SILCs, provided their members with small loans that many of the members used to improve their farms and start up small businesses.

THE CHALLENGE OF ASSESSING THE EFFECTS
OF THE FORD PROGRAM'S EFFORTS

Despite these observable positive material outcomes or changes in the villages, we wanted to know whether there was any evidence to suggest that people had grown in awareness of their own dignity, sense of self-worth, and capabilities due to their participation in the project. Did the work of the PPC realize its intended effect? With this objective in mind, we commissioned a qualitative study led by Ilaria Schnyder von Wartensee that included in-depth interviews and focus groups with people whose levels of participation in the project varied greatly.[34]

It did not take long for us to realize the great challenges we faced in determining whether the project in any way affected people's awareness of their dignity in the community.[35] Assuming that a direct question about changes in their awareness of their dignity or sense of self-worth and capabilities due to the project would not elicit a reliable answer, Schnyder von Wartensee asked people instead to describe their experiences in broad terms.[36] We were curious as to whether they would describe self-worth-enhancing experiences or an increased sense of efficacy. When asked whether and how they found the project helpful or what they found most meaningful about it, very few respondents, if any, responded in ways that could be interpreted to mean that they had grown in awareness of their own worth, efficacy, or capabilities. They instead focused on the material changes in their lives, increased incomes, savings, and investment in their small businesses.

While it is possible that most people did not describe their participation in the project in terms that would imply that it had been "dignifying" because they simply did not experience it as such,[37] we could not help but wonder whether their behaviors were speaking louder than their words. We wondered whether this might be particularly true of women. After all, they had taken the initiative to participate in the project. They had worked hard on their farms and cooperated with each other in sharing new farming techniques and in marketing their produce. They formed SILC groups largely on their own, with only minimal assistance from Catholic Relief Services, Uganda Martyrs University, and the Ford Program. It would seem hard to believe that these behaviors and outcomes were not caused by or did not cause an increase in their awareness of their worth, efficacy, or capabilities. They seemed noticeably proud of their individual and communal achievements.

Nonetheless, just as it would have been premature for us to conclude that there had been no increase in awareness of human dignity because people did not describe their experiences in this way, it would have been precipitous to conclude that the behavioral changes we witnessed across the twelve villages indicated an increase in the villagers' awareness of their dignity. After all, many respondents complained about the PPC. They described it as an elite group detached from the remainder of the community. Several respondents experienced the PPC not as serving as an instrument of respectful encounters but as a bureaucratic organization that seemed interested in imposing its will on the villages of Nnindye.[38] There is some evidence that the PPC drifted from its original purpose. It was clear that some residents of Nnindye experienced the PPC as a detached pseudogovernmental institution rather than a group of people dedicated to serving as "accompanimenteurs" who would initiate and sustain respectful encounters that invited their fellow villagers to recognize their dignity.[39] This might cause us to wonder whether anyone who would speak more positively of their experience of participation and its effects on their sense of their own value and capabilities might have been exaggerating because they did not want to offend those responsible for the project.

While recognizing the challenge that social desirability presents, there is good reason to think that only people themselves know why they behave the way they do. Therefore, our task as social scientists is to find ways of increasing the likelihood that people will provide accurate or truthful explanations of their behaviors. Besides the case of the Ford

Program's work in Uganda that I described above, let us imagine an intervention designed to promote a sense of self-worth and capabilities in low-achieving secondary school students. Imagine that some schools were randomly selected to have their students participate in what we might call the "self-worth and capabilities program," while others were not. If we find that, on average, students who participated in the program improved their academic performance much more than students who did not, would we be able to reasonably infer that the self-worth and capabilities program was effective? Without considering the sample size and other factors that might have impacted validity, it would seem premature to conclude that the program explains the improvement in students' academic performance. Even if it did, can we be sure that it triggered behaviors that improved students' academic performance because it enhanced their awareness of their human dignity, or could the change be attributed to other factors? The question remains: Did these students experience a greater sense of their self-worth and capabilities due to the program *and* did this experience lead to their improved academic performance (via more time spent on homework or studying for exams)? Can we be sure of the causal mechanisms at work just by examining the academic performance of students?

While it is easy to understand why changes in behavior or outcomes, such as the formation of SILCs or improved academic performance, are thought more reliable than survey responses, it is important to recognize that behaviors do not necessarily speak for themselves. We may interpret behaviors in different ways. There is a real danger of overestimating or underestimating the extent to which a change in students' behavior is due to a change in their awareness of their human dignity if the researcher alone is interpreting the meaning of such behavior. This danger would be particularly acute if the researcher were not familiar with the cultural context of the people whose behavior he was interpreting. However, even if the researcher is familiar with the cultural context, I propose that a study that does not allow people to explain or account for changes in their own behavior is more likely to result in error than a study that does.

While we social scientists generally recognize the importance of both behaviors and self-assessment, we too often fail to bring them together in our research and analysis. In other words, we may observe behavioral and attitudinal change and ask people generally about their situations in life, levels of self-worth, or sense of capabilities; however, we do not necessarily ask people to interpret their own behavior. Those of us who are interested in assessing whether a particular program or intervention increases people's awareness of their dignity may assume that the best we can do is to infer such increases from their effects, namely, changes in behavior, including the ways people relate to each other.[40] It is reasonable to assume that "what people do" is a more reliable indicator of their awareness of their human dignity than "what people say" or how they respond to survey questions. We would expect a person's behavior to change as her sense of self-worth and capabilities increases. For example, we may expect students to exhibit better study habits (and perhaps improve their academic performance on exams), small business owners to invest more time and energy in their businesses (and perhaps increase the income they generate from their businesses), and people with chronic illnesses to visit their local health clinics to get needed medications (and perhaps live longer and less painful lives) if there has been an increase in their awareness of their dignity. The assumption is that people who have experienced an increase in awareness of their dignity will demonstrate that awareness by taking greater initiative on behalf of their personal and communal well-being.[41]

While it is reasonable to infer increases (or decreases) in people's awareness of their dignity based on changes in their behavior, I agree with those who argue that there are significant problems with an approach to assessing people's awareness of their human dignity that is not informed by the subjective experiences of the people whose behavior has or has not changed.[42] First, there are substantive problems with such an approach. When researchers completely discount the experiences of human subjects and assume the sole authority to interpret their behaviors, they are likely to overestimate or underestimate the changes in awareness of dignity those behaviors signify. While recognizing the hazards of relying on survey research and self-assessment alone, we should also recognize the hazards of interpreting other people's behaviors for them, particularly across different cultures. Second, there are problems on grounds of principle with an approach that ignores the experience of those whose behavior (and awareness of their dignity) is in question. When we decide for others whether they have experienced a growing awareness of their own dignity, we violate their dignity.

Nonetheless, there is good reason to place behaviors at the center of attempts to assess changes in people's awareness of their dignity. This is in large part because of the social desirability bias that is likely to affect responses to survey questions and in-depth interviews about changes in people's self-worth and sense of capabilities. However, it is also because of the challenges of communication and the limitations on vocabulary, particularly across cultures. Even after conducting focus groups to develop a survey instrument or generate questions for in-depth interviews, we may struggle to know whether people are responding to a question that we intend to ask. Further, a focus on general feelings of self-worth may pick up on the extent to which people perceive themselves as fulfilling cultural expectations rather than on their awareness of their human dignity. For example, a study conducted across nineteen countries found that self-esteem among teenagers and young adults was largely based on the extent to which they saw themselves fulfilling the dominant values of their cultural environments.[43] Should we allow each culture (or, more specifically, influential leaders in each culture) to decide the bases of human dignity just as in the case of self-esteem? I think not, and the terrible and often deadly consequences of doing so are readily apparent.

While I am not suggesting that we should abandon self-assessment when studying changes in people's awareness of their human dignity, I am arguing that self-assessment should be focused on explaining behaviors rather than on general life situations and feelings of self-worth or capabilities. If a woman has joined a small savings and lending community, we need her to explain this decision, and we also need her to explain whether and how being part of such a group has affected her own sense of self-worth and capabilities. If a student's study habits have changed, we need her own explanation of why they have changed and, if there is evidence that her academic performance has improved as a result, we also need her to describe whether and how such a change in performance has affected her sense of self-worth and capabilities.

Besides studies that link particular behaviors and self-assessment of such behaviors, longitudinal studies are crucial to the future of research focused on assessing the causes and effects of someone's awareness of her human dignity. Even if a study were to consider a person's behaviors together with her own assessment or explanation of those behaviors in order to assess a project's impact, the analysis would be inadequate without a good measure of that person's behaviors before the project. This is what the Ford Program's central Ugandan study lacked, and it is a central reason that we cannot be certain whether the project promoted, or failed to promote, a greater awareness of dignity among the people who participated.

In this chapter I have proposed that participatory practices, which are characterized by respectful human encounters, make the development process "dignifying." I have pointed to previous scholarship to support the plausibility of this proposition.[44] There is a great deal of evidence to suggest that participation in agenda-setting and decision-making processes promotes self-esteem and a sense of efficacy, a sense that one counts and is capable of doing something positive.[45]

Nonetheless, based on the Ford Program's experience in Uganda, I have pointed to the difficulty of remaining faithful to participatory practices. There is evidence that the PPC, intended to be an instrument of respectful encounters that invite people to recognize their own dignity, did not fulfill its objective. There is also evidence that project staff experienced a lack of clarity about the importance of human encounters. They felt inadequately prepared to foster such encounters while also experiencing pressure to produce material results. After all, transferring skills and generating concrete results were the focal points of their previous training. Assuming that inadequate budgets or donors' pressure for results may often be responsible for the jettisoning of participatory practices, characterized by respectful encounters, it seems that there is a need to educate donors about the importance and potential benefits of remaining faithful to such practices and the patience required to do so. Further, if respectful encounters are what make participatory practices "dignifying," there need to be sufficient personnel and appropriate training so as to make such encounters a reality. The interpersonal skills of project staff are just as important as their technical skills.

Yet even if we remain true to participatory practices and invest the time, personnel, and training necessary for their faithful implementation, measuring the effects of such practices remains the great challenge. There can be no doubt that more research is necessary and that we must continue to develop rigorous methods to test our hypotheses about the effects of participatory practices on people's awareness of their human dignity and human development. In this chapter I have proposed that the research frontier includes finding ways to mitigate the social desirability bias when seeking explanations for behavior changes offered by the very people whose behavior has changed. In my view, conducting this type of research calls for partnerships between research institutions, funding agencies and foundations, and organizations responsible for implementing development projects in various parts of the world. Such partnerships have the potential to help us achieve a better understanding and, more importantly, become increasingly effective in promoting awareness of human dignity and creating the conditions that allow for truly human development.

NOTES

1. For analytical clarity, I define "human development" in terms of the widely accepted Human Development Index (HDI), which focuses on life expectancy at birth, literacy, and income.

2. By "dignifying," I do not mean that dignity is created or bestowed but that people grow in awareness of the dignity they already possess by virtue of their existence.

3. In its mission statement, Catholic Relief Services states, "We are motivated by the Gospel of Jesus Christ to cherish, preserve, and uphold the sacredness and dignity of all human life." See http://www.crs.org/about/mission -statement. Jacqueline Novogratz, founder and CEO of Acumen, writes of the work of the organization she founded, "I believe we have the chance to build a world where all individuals have the chance to live with dignity." See "Jacqueline Novogratz: For Changing the Way the World Tackles Poverty," *Asia Game Changers Awards*, Asia Society, 2019, https://asiasociety.org/asia -game-changers/jacqueline-novogratz. Other organizations include the International Federation of the Red Cross, the International Rescue Commission, Oxfam International, and UNICEF.

4. It is important to note that some organizations imply that dignity is something they can give people or that advances in material wealth, health, and education are dignifying.

5. This may be attributed to donors' pressure to achieve material "results" or other factors.

6. Derek L. Philips and Kevin J. Clancy, "Some Effects of Social Desirability in Survey Studies," *American Journal of Sociology* 77, no. 5 (1972): 921–44.

7. Ivar Krumpal, "Detriments of Social Desirability Bias in Sensitive Surveys: A Literature Review," *Quality and Quantity* 47, no. 4 (2013): 2025–47.

8. This is a challenge that Ford Program researchers faced when we attempted to assess changes in awareness of dignity in central Uganda. In the local language, Luganda, there is no word that translates as "dignity" and no proximate word that people in the villages would be accustomed to using for such an abstract concept.

9. In his chapter in this volume, Paul Perrin notes that this challenge has led many scholars to reject the use of the term "dignity" since measurement of change in something so underspecified and abstract is assumed impossible.

10. Clemens Sedmak, "Human Dignity, Interiority, and Poverty," in *Understanding Human Dignity*, ed. Christopher McCrudden (Oxford: Oxford University Press, 2013).

11. One may argue that such people actually have a poor sense of their own dignity as illustrated by their need to "prove" their superior dignity.

12. It is important to recognize that there may be medical or psychological conditions that constrain one's awareness of dignity. Clinical depression, for example, certainly affects the awareness of one's dignity. In this chapter, I assume mental health in the normal range.

13. Martha Nussbaum, "Human Dignity and Political Entitlements," in *Human Dignity and Bioethics: Essays Commissioned by the President's Council on Bioethics*, ed. Adam Schulman (Washington, DC: President's Council on Bioethics, 2008), 351–80.

14. Here it is worth noting the importance of cultural awareness and cultural sensitivity when designing development projects, especially practices intended to promote awareness of dignity.

15. For a description of the HDI, see United Nations Development Programme, *Human Development Report 2016: Human Development for Everyone*, http://hdr.undp.org/sites/default/files/2016_human_development_report.pdf.

16. Amartya Sen, *Development as Freedom* (New York: Anchor Books, 1999).

17. This line of argumentation is different from that of Nussbaum's "Human Dignity," in which she suggests that capabilities are necessary for dignity. Of course she defines "capabilities" widely and argues for the importance of recognizing different types of capabilities. In other words, Nussbaum

believes that every living being is capable in some way and, therefore, deserving of respect.

18. This runs against much of what is called "Western Culture," which implies that a person's value depends on what he or she can do or potentially do (e.g., the reason an infant or child may be seen as valuable). Thus people who are able to "do" less, particularly the disabled or elderly, come to feel less valuable. In this sense, I would argue, their dignity is disrespected and violated.

19. Nussbaum, "Human Dignity," 351–80.

20. While I propose that human dignity does not require capabilities (for people have human dignity in equal measure regardless of what they are capable of doing), I propose that human development requires "a sense of capability." This is because I assume that human development is something that people do for themselves (but not by themselves). If human development is taking place, people are envisioning their future and participating in efforts to realize the future they are envisioning. While advances in human development may in turn increase awareness of dignity, creating a virtuous cycle, I propose that it all begins with the spark of dignity. Human development begins with human encounters that are deeply encouraging and, in essence, dignifying.

21. Anirudh Krishna, Norman Uphoff, and Milton Esman, *Reasons for Success: Learning from Instructive Experiences in Rural Development* (West Hartford, CT: Kumarian, 1998); Solava Ibrahim and Sabina Alkire, "Agency and Empowerment: A Proposal for Internationally Comparable Indicators," *Oxford Development Studies* 35, no. 4 (2007): 379–403; Irene Guijt and Robert Chambers, "PRA Five Years Later," in *The Participation Reader*, ed. Andrea Cornwall (London: Zed Books, 2011); and Linje Manyozo, "The Pedagogy of Listening," *Development in Practice* 26, no. 7 (2016): 954–59.

22. Sen, "Development as Freedom," 36–37.

23. Ibid., 36–37.

24. Henry E. Brady, Kay L. Schlozman, and Sidney Verba, *Voice and Equality: Civic Volunteerism in American Politics* (Cambridge, MA: Harvard University Press, 1995), 320–54, and Anirudh Krishna, "Introduction: Poor People and Democracy," in *Participation and Democracy*, ed. Anirudh Krishna (Cambridge: Cambridge University Press, 2008), 324.

25. Ulrich Ortho and Richard W. Robins, "The Development of Self-Esteem," in *Current Directions in Psychological Science* 23, no. 5 (2014): 381–87; Todd F. Heatherton and Carrie L. Wyland, "Assessing Self-Esteem," in *Positive Psychological Assessment: A Handbook of Models and Measures*, ed. S. J. Lopez and C. R. Snyder (Washington, DC: American Psychological Association, 2003), 219–33.

26. Abihijit V. Banerjee and Esther Duflo, *Poor Economics: A Radical Rethinking of the Way to Fight Global Poverty* (New York: PublicAffairs, 2011), and Dean S. Karlan and Jacob Appel, *More Than Good Intentions: Improving the Ways the World's Poor Borrow, Save, Farm, Learn, and Stay Healthy* (New York: Plume, 2011).

27. Fritz Heider, *The Psychology of Interpersonal Relations* (Hillsdale, NJ: Lawrence Erlbaum and Associates, 1958).

28. Kelly Schaver, *An Introduction to Attribution Processes* (New York: Routledge, 1983).

29. Quote from an interview conducted by the project manager with a resident in November 2008.

30. When the Ford Program and Uganda Martyrs University began working in the villages, they found eleven of twelve boreholes unused because, according to villagers, the pumps had been broken for several months.

31. Quote from an interview conducted by the project manager with a resident in November 2008.

32. Ibid.

33. These small savings and lending communities followed Catholic Relief Services' Savings and Internal Lending Community (SILC) model. Between 2012 and 2014, 29 SILC groups in the area had been formed with assets totaling over $22,000 and almost $16,000 in outstanding loans.

34. Ilaria Schnyder von Wartensee, "At the Root of Participatory Approaches: Uncovering the Role of Accompaniment," *Development in Practice* 28, no. 5 (2018): 636–46.

35. Our first and perhaps biggest challenge was the fact that the baseline was conducted in such a way that we could not recontact baseline respondents so as to assess the change in individuals' responses to the same questions before and after the project.

36. Schnyder von Wartensee, "At the Root," 11–13.

37. Ibid.

38. Ibid.

39. Ibid.

40. This has become increasingly true in economics and political science.

41. See the chapter in this book by Wydick, Dowd, and Lybbert, "Hope and Human Dignity."

42. Gabriella Berloffa, Giuseppe Folloni, and Ilaria Schnyder von Wartensee, *At The Root of Development: the Importance of the Human Factor* (Milan: Fondazione per la sussidiarietà, 2012), and Paolo G. Carozza, "Human Rights, Human Dignity, and Human Experience" in *Understanding Human Dignity*, ed. Christopher McCrudden (Oxford: Oxford University Press, 2013).

43. Maja Becker, Vivian L. Vignoles, and E. Owe, "Cultural Bases of Self-Esteem: Seeing Oneself Positively in Different Cultural Contexts," *Personality and Social Psychology Bulletin* 40, no. 5 (2014): 657–75.

44. Krishna, Uphoff, and Esman, "Reasons for Success," 379–403; Guijt and Chambers, "PRA Five Years"; and Manyozo, "Pedagogy of Listening," 954–59.

45. Brady, Schlozman, and Verba, *Voice and Equality*, 320–54.

SEVEN

Hope and Human Dignity

Exploring Religious Belief, Hope, and Transition
Out of Poverty in Oaxaca, Mexico

Bruce Wydick, Robert A. Dowd,
and Travis J. Lybbert

Hope has a fundamental and integral relationship with human dignity. Simply put, people who are aware of their own human dignity are hopeful because they believe they are capable of shaping their future for the good by doing good. Its opposite, hopelessness, is incompatible with human flourishing, not only because hopelessness is in itself an undesirable state but also because hopelessness discourages progress toward a better state though its power to quash aspirations and demotivate positive human action. Individuals may live in material poverty, but poverty is both magnified and perpetuated when accompanied by hopelessness. Hope, in contrast, gives birth to aspiration, and aspiration to a sense of purposefulness that can enable human flourishing.

In this chapter we address this relationship between hope and human dignity. Specifically, how are a person's capacity to aspire and her sense of agency related to human dignity and human flourishing? Moreover, how does the nature of spiritual and religious belief influence hopefulness? We address these questions by exploring and unpacking the basic components of hope: the capacity to aspire, the conceptualization of personal agency and responsibility, and the ability to conceptualize pathways to a better state. Using the framework of the economic model developed in Lybbert and Wydick (2018), we then apply this conceptualization of hope to a field experiment we carried out among 601 women who were part of a faith-based microfinance lending program in Oaxaca, Mexico.[1] We argue that hope is fundamental to human flourishing and dignity and that a better understanding of hope as a motivational and inspirational force of the soul can inform both our understanding of poverty and the design of effective programs to alleviate poverty.

In his classic work on the psychology of hope, Rick Snyder decomposes hope into *goals, agency,* and *pathways.*[2] His characterization of hope gives us a framework for thinking about the relationship between hope and human dignity and, in turn, how spiritual belief may influence both of these. While Snyder's work is of a secular nature, it is possible to find evidence of a relationship between human flourishing and Snyder's components of hope in the earliest biblical writings of the Hebrew scriptures and the New Testament. Different Christian traditions, however, have emphasized different facets of scripture and offered diverse interpretations of scriptural references to hope. As a result, Christian understandings of the nature of hope, its manifestation in religious practice, and its influence on individual behavior vary widely within and across Christian denominations and faith communities.

In this chapter we compare and contrast the theological roots of hope within the context of Snyder's hope framework.[3] We also share results from a field experiment built on Snyder's framework, which interface strongly with themes of religious belief and human dignity. We designed and implemented this experiment with a microfinance lender in order to test whether a spiritually based intervention designed to elevate levels of hope is able to (1) increase hopefulness as measured by psychological indicators and (2) generate significant effects on key economic variables such as microenterprise expansion and business income. In this study of indigenous women in Oaxaca, which we describe in detail later, we have found that baseline values of hope, optimism, and agency display strong religious correlations. However, our results also demonstrate that it is possible to bridge these differences through a hope intervention. We use these results to explore the relationship between religious belief, hope, and human flourishing and dignity. We find that if a spiritually based intervention nurtures greater hope and hope is integral to human flourishing and human dignity, then we may be able through such an intervention to conceptualize a relationship between human dignity and spiritual beliefs as mediated by hope.

HOPE, AGENCY, AND HUMAN DIGNITY

We define hope along the lines of Jürgen Moltmann and Jon Sobrino, as the belief that the future may be different from the present in desirable ways.[4] Hope can be passive, as when people wait for an external force to produce a desirable state for them, or it can be active, as when people take it upon themselves to do what is necessary to realize a desirable state. In this section we explore the theme of hope in Judeo-Christian theology, but we begin with the understanding of hope by the ancient Greeks. This progression from the Greek to the Judeo-Christian conceptualization of hope is particularly noteworthy because of the stark contrast between the two. Indeed, in the vast span of human history, our collective understanding of hope as part of the human experience has never been so radically altered as it was in the transition from Greek mythology and philosophy to Judeo-Christian theology and practice.

Greek mythology largely framed human existence as driven inexorably by fate. The Greek understanding of hope is expressed in the story of Pandora's box. In this story, which provides an explanation for the presence of evil and trial in the world, Zeus seeks to torment mankind by giving Pandora, the first human on earth, a box filled with all the evils of this world. Although he forbids her from opening the box, he knows that curiosity will ultimately prompt her to open the box. When she does, all of the evils in the box escape and begin tormenting the world— all the evils, that is, except hope, which remains trapped inside. To the modern reader, the logical interpretation of this final outcome is that hope remains to help mankind confront and conquer evil and trial. Yet this interpretation imposes too much of our contemporary worldview on the ancient myth. The only interpretation consistent with the Greek philosophy is that if fate controls our destiny, hope is worse than foolish; it is the ultimate and most enduring evil because any sense of human agency is fundamentally illusory.[5] Thus, in the juxtaposition of hope and fate, hope was seen as a human weakness, even a vice. Indeed, it would be inconceivable in ancient Greece to view hope as many view it today, as fundamentally good, even virtuous.

This radical shift in our view of hope in the Western world traces back to the emergence and growth of Judeo-Christianity, which articulates a worldview in which human agency plays a central role in tandem with the guidance, will, and grace of God. Nonetheless, this shift toward understanding hope as inherently good left considerable space for differences in emphasis and application. Thus, not everyone influenced by a Judeo-Christian worldview applies hope in the same manner. Some Christians apply hope by emphasizing the importance of waiting: waiting for God to do something or waiting for a miracle or some direct divine intervention in their lives to deliver them from an undesirable state. Some have associated this "passive hope" with some Christian denominations and communities, where hope can lie in manifestations of the supernatural in the form of a patient faith that perseveres in praying and waiting for deliverance or healing. Other Christians may apply hope in ways that require their personal action in cooperation with the divine as a means of deliverance from some undesirable state. We refer to this as "active hope." Active hope can be manifest in variants of Pentecostalism in the form of the "prosperity gospel,"[6] but it is also embedded in the liberation theology of developing-world Catholicism.[7] People who exude this kind of hope envision their personal lives or their communities to be more fulfilling, secure, just, and peaceful in the future and devote themselves to cooperating with God and others in order to realize this vision. In this worldview, hope quickly becomes a source of inspiration, motivation, and even salvation. Moreover, manifestations of active hope may move beyond a self-absorption with personal gain to a more general sense of both personal and communal health and well-being. A positive conceptualization of hope and related future-oriented traits is apparent throughout the Hebrew scriptures. This strand of the Judeo-Christian tradition sees goals, aspirations, and planning as virtues that can enable human flourishing, though human plans should be inspired and influenced by the will of God (see, e.g., Proverbs 16:3 and 16:9). Both the Old and New Testaments speak directly of the importance of hope. The book of Proverbs, for example, admonishes us that "Where there is no vision, the people perish."[8] Proverbs contains other counsel, regarding the importance of planning and purposefulness,[9] which is balanced with the value of submitting individual plans to the greater will of God and to wise human counsel.

Other strands of scripture relate the importance of hope. Psalm 9:18 states, "For the needy shall not always be forgotten, and the hope of the poor shall not perish forever." Jeremiah 29:11 reads, "For I know the plans I have for you, declares the Lord, plans for welfare and not for evil, to give you a future and a hope." In Luke 1:37, Jesus tells his disciples, "For nothing will be impossible with God." And in 1 Corinthians 13:13, the Apostle Paul lists hope among the paragon of virtues with faith and love.

In sharp contrast to the Greek vision, this particular Judeo-Christian worldview conceptualizes human agency as fundamental to this set of virtues, which is central to human flourishing and dignity. Early in Genesis, God speaks to humankind, saying: "Be fruitful, and multiply, and replenish the earth, and subdue it: and have dominion over the fish of the sea, and over the fowl of the air, and over every living thing that moveth upon the earth."[10] Such declarations of human agency run freely through both the Hebrew and Christian scriptures, often paired with accountability for the natural consequences of choices within this agency. In other instances, human agency is seen as subject to divine accountability.[11]

The ability to think outside of historical patterns, to question established norms, and to conceptualize different paths to achieve an objective is arguably less overt in the Judeo-Christian scriptures and tradition, but it is implicit in many of the admonitions of scripture, in which creativity, skill, and individual giftedness are consistently praised.[12] One of many examples in the Hebrew scriptures is seen in Nehemiah's organization of the Jewish people during the rebuilding of the wall after the return of the Jews from the Babylonian exile, particularly in Nehemiah's ingenuity in overcoming obstacles and opposition.[13] There is also a sense in the New Testament, in particular, that one component of human and even spiritual flourishing involves the choice of creative, even divinely inspired, pathways in the context of human agency. The Apostle Paul emphasizes in Ephesians, "We are his workmanship, created in Christ Jesus for good works"[14] and tells us to "Work out your salvation with fear and trembling."[15] We also see examples of creativity and innovation in Jesus's own admonition against putting new wine into old wineskins[16]— which reflects his support for the free, creative, and productive use of resources[17]—and in the creative pathways forged by Paul in bringing the Christian gospel to the Roman world as led by the Holy Spirit.[18]

In the faith of biblical Christianity, hope originates from multiple sources, including hope for an eternal heaven, described as "hope of eternal life, which God . . . promised before the ages began,"[19] and hope for God living within the believer: "Hope does not put us to shame, because God's love has been poured out into our hearts through the Holy Spirit, who has been given to us."[20] To the extent that the latter forms a vital component of hope for the believer, human agency is not a contradiction of the sovereign will of God, but rather the will of God is summoned to act within human beings in the context of their human agency. As such it breeds a capacity to aspire, a belief and even acceptance of one's "locus of control" as divinely appointed.[21] In the context of human agency, the divine will allows for creativity, thinking "outside the box," new pathways around obstacles, and inspiration and direction from the Spirit when we are making choices and taking action. The submission, then, of individual aspirations, agency, and pathways to divine wisdom, guidance, and influence, indeed the submission of one's own recognized agency to *divine* agency, is a vital component of a biblical view of human flourishing. The recognition of all human beings and their human agency—their capacity for moral choices and creativity, their capacity to be smaller imitators of the divine, and their capacity for the indwelling of his Spirit—is an affirmation of human dignity.

AGENCY AND HOPE IN PROTESTANT AND CATHOLIC CHRISTIANITY

The best-known (and more recent) elucidation of Christian perspectives on human agency is Max Weber's *The Protestant Ethic and the Spirit of*

Capitalism, which argues that the personal conservatism, thrift, and work ethic characteristic of Calvinist northern Europe fostered the emergence of modern capitalism and the region's relative economic prosperity.[22] Implicit in Weber's work is the observation that a sense of human agency, at least at a crucial point in the history of the European Industrial Revolution, was generally greater among Protestants than among Catholics, whom he viewed as distinctly proactive and passive, respectively, in their relationship to divine will. The Protestant ethic viewed human choices as principal sources of human flourishing based on scriptural evidence: "Diligent hands will rule, but laziness ends in slave labor."[23] "Whoever watches the wind will not plant—whoever looks at the clouds will not reap."[24] "For the Spirit God gave us does not make us timid, but gives us power, love and self-discipline."[25] "I can do all things through him who gives me strength."[26] A more submissive posture toward the divine can also be supported with scripture, but the dominant Protestant interpretation of the scriptural canon as a whole has tended to emphasize the centrality of human agency.[27] This emphasis on agency comes with an equal emphasis on the principles of love of God and neighbor and on submission to the divine will.

It is important to recognize that Weber's explanation for the rise of modern capitalism and the contrast he draws between the attitudes and behaviors encouraged by Protestantism versus those encouraged by Catholicism are not without their critics. Some have argued that the roots of modern capitalism pre-date the Reformation by pointing to an emphasis on agency in northern Italian city-states during the fifteenth century.[28] The emphasis on agency in these heavily Catholic settings occurred either despite Catholicism or, to some extent, because of the way Catholicism was applied at the time. Our point here is simply to recognize that both Protestantism and Catholicism may be applied in ways that encourage or discourage "active hope" and the human agency that flows from such hope.

As we have noted, the Christian scriptures include many passages that may be used to encourage human initiative and hope for a better life in this world (and not just in the next). However, there are also passages that seem to discourage human initiative and encourage people to focus exclusively on a better life in "the world to come" (i.e., heaven). In this sense, Christianity is multivocal, and Christian leaders, as well as members of the churches they lead, have a choice as to which of these voices in their scriptures and traditions they choose to emphasize.[29] They may choose to give greater weight to those voices in scripture and tradition, encouraging attitudes and behaviors that call upon human agency to improve the well-being of their families and communities, or they may emphasize those voices that encourage more passive approaches, which deemphasize human agency and more strongly emphasize the sovereignty of God over human events.

Although there are many exceptions, there is evidence to suggest that, at various points in time and in many parts of the world, Protestant leaders and members of their communities have given greater weight than Catholic leaders and members of their communities to those voices in Christian scripture and tradition that emphasize human choice and initiative. Indeed, since Weber wrote *The Protestant Ethic*, other studies have found Protestant Christianity in many contexts to place greater emphasis on human choices and agency than does Catholic Christianity.[30] Protestantism has been thought to place more emphasis on human freedom within the religious hierarchy, privileging the unmediated authority of scripture over the authority of church leaders. The structure of Protestant churches is more conducive to human agency, as church organization tends to be more horizontally than vertically organized. Because Protestant churches are typically less hierarchical than the Catholic Church, they provide more leadership opportunities for their ordinary members, including women.[31] Along with an emphasis on the importance of individual choices, the leadership opportunities that many Protestant churches afford their members may give Protestants the chance to build the self-confidence and social skills that serve them well in economic activities and civic affairs outside of church.[32] Yet, without dismissing the basic theological and organizational differences between Catholicism and Protestantism and the findings of previous studies, it is important to recognize the diversity within Protestantism and Catholicism, particularly at the local level, and to refrain from making overly sweeping generalizations about the effects of Protestantism and Catholicism on human agency.

The relationship between religious faith and human agency is complex. We certainly recognize that Catholicism does not always and everywhere discourage human agency and Protestantism does not always and everywhere encourage such agency. The relative passivity of evangelicals in Latin American revolutionary movements in the face of Catholics who were motivated to action by different strains of liberation theology provides merely one counterexample. Indeed, there is evidence of variation across time and place in how Catholicism as well as Protestantism may be applied to social, economic, and political life.[33] Since there is evidence of variation across time and place in how both Catholicism and Protestantism are applied to social, economic, and political life, there is reason to think that there is something about time and place that explains why Protestantism or Catholicism is lived out in ways that are more or less encouraging of human agency.

In liberation theology, hope is manifest in the mediation of human beings to usher in the reign of God on earth.[34] In this view of hope, human agency is critical to fulfilling the will of God for the poor. As Gustavo Gutierrez (1993) expresses,

> We may say that there is an *act of hope* and an *act of hoping* and that both must be made concrete in the act of service to the poor in order to provide access to an understanding of the Reign [of Christ]. The object of hope is the object of the hope of the poor in this world—an end to their misfortunes, an opportunity for life, a just configuration of this world that oppresses them. The signs that the poor hope for are those that already offer them a little life and enable them to hope that life is possible. . . . Hope always has the structure of victorious action against what opposes it.[35]

Thus, in liberation theology we see a strain of thought that runs counter to strains of Catholicism that are more accepting of status-quo political structures; and, while possessing implications for collective action that contradict the political views held by most mainstream Protestants, this strain contains a similar emphasis on human agency.

HOPE AND POVERTY IN ECONOMIC LIFE

For the vast majority of people throughout human history, poverty— often crushing, desperate poverty by modern Western standards—has defined daily life. Given the trivial rates of improvement in material conditions that prevailed until the past few centuries,[36] this was as true for the average citizen of the city-states of ancient Greece as it was for the disciples of Jesus or commoners of the Middle Ages. In the sweeping history of the mythology and theology of hope we provided above, the reality of grinding poverty amidst concentrations of relative wealth and power among the elite must have fundamentally shaped conceptualizations of hope and human dignity. In this section we briefly explore modern perspectives on hope and poverty through a World Bank project that sought to understand poverty through the eyes of the poor.

In the 1990s, inspired by the work of Amartya Sen, the World Bank undertook an ambitious project to document how the poor themselves view poverty. This Voices of the Poor project provides a nuanced and qualitative complement to the standard objective and quantitative measures and definitions of poverty that development economists typically use. This research effort mined all of the dictated text collected in this project for references to the word "hope" and its derivatives. By analyzing all of the terms the poor used in conjunction with these references to hope, it is possible to gain some insight into how the poor today think about and experience hope and its counterweight, hopelessness.

Figure 7.1 depicts the content of hopeful statements made by the poor as a word cloud in which the size of the word is proportional to the number of references to hope linked to it. While there are several patterns that could be plumbed in these statements, there is one dominant pattern we wish to highlight: the common targets or sources of hopefulness of these desperately poor individuals from around the world are remarkably similar to the targets and sources of those who are comfortable or even wealthy. Moreover, this cloud makes clear how multidimensional the experience of hope is for the poor. When viewed from a position of relative material comfort, it is easy to let the material plight of the poor blind us to the social, spiritual, and emotional dimensions of life and the relationships that bring meaning and purpose—not only to the poor, but also to the rest of us. This seems to be corroborated by a recent survey of World Bank researchers that concluded that "development professionals assume that poor individuals are less autonomous, less responsible, less hopeful, and less knowledgeable than they in fact are."[37] When we focus our attention on the material needs of the

FIGURE 7.1. Words Invoked in Hopeful Statements from Participants in the World Bank's Voice of the Poor Project

poor, we can ignore the deeper dimensions that provide them meaning and purpose—and hope.

Evidence from the Voices of the Poor project also helps to underscore important differences in the specific manifestations of hope, and especially hopelessness, among the poor. Powerlessness is often cited by the poor as a primary source of hopelessness. This is particularly true among those who are or have been victimized. Many poor describe living only for today due to a perceived lack of anticipated opportunities tomorrow or even a lack of imagination about the future generally. The observation that the poor derive hope from similar sources as the rich but suffer many different forms of hopelessness suggests a version of hope akin to Tolstoy's famous opening line in *Anna Karenina*, which refers to happiness: *Hopeful* families are all alike; every *hopeless* family is *hopeless* in its own way.[38]

THE OAXACA HOPE PROJECT: UNDERSTANDING DIFFERENTIAL IMPACTS BETWEEN CATHOLIC AND PROTESTANT MICROFINANCE BORROWERS

In this section we describe a randomized controlled trial that sought to leverage hope among indigenous women in Oaxaca, Mexico. In our intervention we hoped to tap into the deeply meaningful and yet, in many ways, less tangible forms of hope in order to encourage entrepreneurship among these women as they managed various microenterprises. We found significant differences in our baseline measures of hope between Catholic and Protestant women, but the intervention was, at least in the short term, able to narrow these differences.

A Description of the Project

In May 2015 we launched a randomized controlled trial among 601 indigenous women who procured microfinance loans with Fuentes Libres, a Protestant evangelical faith-based microfinance institution based in Oaxaca, Mexico. Oaxaca is one of the poorest states in Mexico, and, while known for a rich culture of art, cuisine, and architecture, it is also beset by numerous social and political problems. Fuentes Libres carries out microlending among its borrowers through a network of more than fifty community banks. The women we worked with both saved and borrowed at the banks, and there was joint liability for loans at the community bank level: if a woman failed to repay a loan, other members of the bank were liable for the loan via their deposits with the community bank. Loans from Fuentes Libres are typically in the range of US$200 to US$1,000, and the loans are used to augment investment in microenterprises. The kinds of enterprises women operate with the banks' help vary, but common activities include selling food on the streets or in small eateries, producing or retailing children's and women's clothing, and operating small convenience stores. Fuentes engages in other interventions as well, working with abused women and providing other kinds of spiritual formation and counseling; it uses a holistic approach to economic development that is oriented around the idea of human dignity and human flourishing.

Our randomization was carried out in the two main centers of Fuentes's program activity, Oaxaca City and Salina Cruz.[39] Fifty-two community banks were included in the study, and the banks were put into matched pairs based on the size of the group, the age of the group, the ages of the women in the group, the group's business activities, and the women's having a common loan officer. Each bank in a matched pair was then assigned to the letter A or B, and a coin was flipped to determine which twenty-six banks, the As or the Bs, would be selected into the treatment or the control group, where the coin flip determined that the B banks' customers were selected for treatment. The A banks' customers would receive this treatment for twelve months after the beginning of the intervention.

The intervention consisted of a "hope treatment" based on Snyder's three components of hope: goals, agency, and pathways.[40] First, a film crew from California State University at Sacramento produced a documentary featuring four of the most successful women in the Fuentes microlending program. In the thirty-five-minute film women told their stories of being lifted out of poverty, in part through the help of the community bank loans. Women using the community banks who were selected for the treatment group viewed the documentary at the time of the baseline survey and found the film to be inspirational and uplifting.

After the film, each woman was given a three-by-eight-inch refrigerator magnet showing the three components of hope (*aspiraciones, abilidades, y avenidas*) along with three corresponding Bible verses related to aspirations, agency, and pathways.[41] Below these verses were spaces for the women to write their goals for community bank saving and sales for their enterprises as well as a long-term goal such as a major business expansion or sending a child to high school or a university.

During the five weeks after the screening of the documentary and the completion of the baseline survey, the women in the treatment group were engaged with a Bible-based curriculum centered around the three components of hope: in the first week, the importance of having goals and aspirations; in the second, the recognition of their gifts and abilities (agency); and in the third, training in conceptualizing new avenues for their businesses, or thinking "outside of the box." The fourth week involved performed case-study exercises, and a preliminary one-month follow-up survey was taken in the fifth week after the baseline survey and documentary screening. Taken as a whole, the intervention was designed to provide a biblical basis for fostering aspirations, agency, and the ability to conceptualize pathways out of poverty and to appeal to both Catholic and evangelical women in the community banks.

We expected that the Catholic and evangelical women might respond in subtly different ways to the treatment. Historically, Oaxaca is predominantly Catholic, but over the centuries the Catholicism of the area has blended with traditional indigenous beliefs; however, the area's evangelical Protestant churches are newer and tend to manifest a more vibrant and modern manifestation of the Christian faith. Because the intervention was carried out by a nonprofit organization rooted more strongly in the Protestant evangelical tradition, we thought it likely that the Bible-based curriculum might appear to be more novel to the Catholic women than to the evangelical Protestant women.

Results

In a work we published in 2019, we present results from the five-week follow-up survey that show the impact of the hope intervention.[42] We estimate its impacts using an ANCOVA (analysis of covariance) estimator that controls for the baseline values of the impact variable as well as other characteristics of the women in the study. We have two major sets of results, one on psychological impacts related to the components of hope and the second on microenterprise variables that include reported savings as well as sales and profits of the women's enterprises.

As we reported in the 2019 study, we find that the intervention increased aspirations by 24.4 percent among women in the treatment group based on an index of questions created to capture differences in the capacity of women to aspire.[43] Point estimates also increased in happiness, optimism, agency, pathways, and future orientation, although, unlike the increase found in aspirations, these estimations were not significant at the 95 percent level of confidence. We created indexes of seven measures of hope, including all of the above and of the basic three components of hope, and they all increased significantly at the 90 percent and 95 percent levels, but this was largely driven by the substantial increase in aspirations.

The impact of the hope intervention on business performance shows some interesting effects. While we found no impact on employees at five weeks, plans for new employees, or hours spent in the enterprise, we did find that sales increased by 17.7 percent in the treatment group, and profits increased by 19.1 percent; however, both of these point estimates had confidence intervals that contained zero at the 90 percent level. A business performance index shows point estimates of a positive effect of about 0.1 standard deviations, but this is statistically insignificant.

What is perhaps most interesting about our results, however, was the difference in baseline levels of our psychological variables between Catholic (74 percent) and Protestant evangelical (26 percent) women in the sample and the impact of the intervention on these differences. Protestant evangelical women at baseline showed levels of optimism that were 0.29 standard deviations higher than those of the Catholic women ($p < 0.01$). Their levels of aspiration were far higher than those of the Catholic women, a difference of 0.21 standard deviations ($p < 0.05$). The evangelical women were also reported to be happier (based on a happiness index) by 0.16 standard deviations ($p < 0.10$) and had a greater sense of agency by 0.14 standard deviations (though this was not statistically significant). A three-variable hope index shows a baseline difference in favor of the Protestant evangelical women of about 0.15 standard deviations, and our seven-variable hope index shows a difference of about 0.17 standard deviations. In other respects, the two groups of women were similar in risk aversion, future orientation, and business variables.

The most stunning result of our experiment, nevertheless, was that the impact of the intervention was exceptionally strong for the Catholic women and had essentially zero impact on the Protestant evangelical women. The differences in impact on psychological variables can be seen in figure 7.2. Note that point estimates for the impact of the hope intervention on Protestant evangelical women are very close to zero, and confidence intervals at every level contain zero. However, the impact estimates for Catholic women are far more positive: impacts of about 0.30 standard deviations in the area of aspirations, 0.12 standard deviations in agency, 0.23 standard deviations in future orientation, 0.17 standard deviations in optimism, 0.21 standard deviations on our Hope3 index, and 0.27 standard deviations on our Hope8 index.

Figure 7.3 shows that our hope intervention had virtually zero impact on business variables among the Protestant evangelical women; a business performance index was even slightly negative. In contrast, the figure shows a 0.28 percent increase in sales and a 0.26 percent increase in profits for Catholic women. On other variables such as savings and employees (but not hours devoted to business) the effects were positive but insignificant.

The increasingly influential field of behavioral economics—a blend of economics and psychology—will shape policies and programs aimed

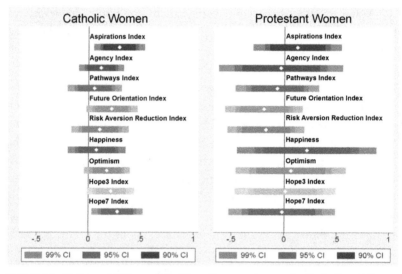

FIGURE 7.2. Estimated Effects of the Hope Intervention on the Catholic and Protestant Women in Our Study in Terms of Psychological Measures after One Month in the Microfinance Groups

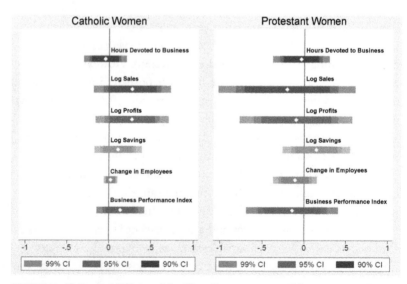

FIGURE 7.3. Estimated Effects of the Hope Intervention on Microenterprise Performance Measures after One Month for Catholic and Protestant Women in the Microfinance Groups

at alleviating poverty in both developed and developing countries for decades to come. This field has begun to generate insights into how people form aspirations and how these aspirations affect their livelihoods and well-being. Building on "hope theory" in psychology, we took the triad of aspirations, pathways, and agency as the conceptual basis of hope and explored the relationships among religious belief, hope, and poverty. We found that baseline differences between Catholic and Protestant indigenous women in Oaxaca largely reflect differences in hope and agency that are consistent with the patterns described by Weber and others. We also found that a Bible-based curriculum structured around developing aspirations, agency, and pathways out of poverty significantly reduced these differences.

Our study raised important questions about the nature of spiritual beliefs, how these beliefs affect one's conceptualization of hope, and how this conceptualization of hope influences human flourishing and human dignity. At first glance, the lower levels of aspirational hope found among Catholic women relative to Protestant women at our study's baseline would seem to indicate that Catholicism causes lower levels of hope than does evangelical Protestantism. But, this may be a misleading interpretation. Can we be sure that the Protestant women did not choose to become Protestants because they were more hopeful or wanted to exhibit greater agency in the first place? In other words, there may be a self-selection phenomenon at work that prevents us from concluding that Protestantism is more hope-inducing than Catholicism.

While further study is necessary, the findings we present in this chapter also suggest that hopefulness and human agency can be induced through the use of religious messages, especially among people for whom such messages are new. The religious messages we designed to induce hope were likely familiar to many Protestant women but less so to the Catholic women in the study. This novelty of the hope intervention may partly explain the relatively large impact such messages had on hopefulness among these women. Although meant to appeal to both Catholic and Protestant women, the intervention was viewed by many as "Protestant" in nature and was implemented by Protestant evangelicals working for evangelical faith-based organizations. Thus, what we appear to see, at least in the very short term, is a group of Catholic women who were strongly impacted by a Protestant-leaning intervention that emphasized human agency.

Christian orthodoxy teaches the virtue of an aspirational hope that encourages human agency with a fidelity to the principles of love for God and neighbor, as well as the virtue of a wishful hope that places faith in the beneficent agency of God. While different traditions have emphasized the former or the latter to varying degrees, particularly in different contexts, nearly all denominational leaders are likely to advocate for some degree of balance between the two. A better understanding of this balance will be of benefit to faith-based development practitioners who favor a holistic approach to poverty intervention that emphasizes not only the release of material constraints but the addressing of internal and spiritual concerns both as ends unto themselves and as means to poverty reduction.

Scripture states that "where there is no vision, the people perish."[44] The capacity to aspire, the ability to conceptualize pathways to a better state, a healthy conception of human agency, and the navigation of these pathways are fundamentally related to human flourishing and human dignity. The lesson from our research is that developing hope and its components represents a fundamental process in the cultivation of human dignity and human flourishing and that this is possible through spiritually based interventions that can accompany other kinds of "tangible" interventions, such as those related to women's empowerment and microfinance. Future research and practice can more deeply explore this relationship in a wide array of poverty interventions.

NOTES

1. Travis J. Lybbert and Bruce Wydick, "Poverty, Aspirations, and the Economics of Hope," *Economic Development and Cultural Change* 66, no. 4 (2018): 709–53.

2. Rick C. Snyder, *The Psychology of Hope: You Can Get There from Here* (Simon and Schuster, 1994).

3. Ibid.

4. Jürgen Moltmann, *Theology of Hope: On the Ground and Implications of a Christian Eschatology* (Minneapolis: Fortress Press, 1964; rpt. 1993), and Jon Sobrino, *Where Is God? Earthquake, Terrorism, Barbarity, and Hope* (Maryknoll, NY: Orbis Books, 2004).

5. Jürgen Moltmann, "Hoping and Planning: Future Anticipated through Hope and Planned Future," *Cross Currents* (1968): 307–18. For other important interdisciplinary work on hope, see J. R. Averill, G. Catlin, and K. K. Chon, *Rules of Hope* (New York: Springer, 1990); Ernst Bloch, "The Principle of Hope," *Studies in Contemporary German Social Thought* 1 (Cambridge: MIT Press, 1986), 1320; L. A. Curry et al., "Role of Hope in Academic and Sport Achievement," *Journal of Personality and Social Psychology* 73, no. 6 (1997): 1257; Jaklin Elliot, "What Have We Done with Hope? A Brief History," in *Interdisciplinary Perspectives on Hope*, ed. J. Elliot (Hauppauge, NY: Nove Science Publishers, 2005), 3–45; Maria Miceli and Cristiano Castelfranchi, "Hope: The Power of Wish and Possibility," *Theory and Possibility* (2010): 251–76; A. D. Ong, L. M. Edwards, and C. S. Bergeman, "Hope as a Source of Resilience in Later Adulthood," *Personality and Individual Differences* 41, no. 7 (2006): 1263–73; C. R. Snyder, "Hope Theory: Rainbows in the Mind," *Psychological Inquiry* 13, no. 4 (2002): 249–75; C. R. Snyder, *The Psychology of Hope: You Can Get There from Here* (New York: Simon and Schuster, 1994); and C. R. Snyder et al., "The Will and the Ways: Development and Validation of an Individual-Differences Measure of Hope," *Journal of Personality and Social Psychology* 60, no. 4. (1991): 570.

6. Katherine Attanasi and Amos Yong, *Pentecostalism and Prosperity* (New York: Palgrave Macmillan, 2012).

7. Sobrino, *Where Is God?*

8. Prov. 29:18 (Authorized King James Version, the only translation of the Bible used in this work).

9. Prov. 15:22 and 16:23.

10. Gen. 1:28.

11. For example, Gen. 3:17–19; 1 Sam. 15:11; Matt. 12:36–37; and Rom. 14:12.

12. E.g., Exod. 35:35; Col. 3:23; and Rom. 12:6.

13. Neh. 6:1–7:3.

14. Eph. 2:10.

15. Phil. 2:12.

16. Matt. 9:17.

17. Matt. 25:14–30.

18. Acts 20–28.

19. Titus 1:2.

20. Rom. 5:5.

21. Arthur Bandura, *Social Learning Theory* (Englewood Cliffs, NJ: Prentice Hall, 1977).

22. Max Weber, *The Protestant Ethic and the Spirit of Capitalism* (New York: Scribner, 1904).

23. Prov. 12:24.

24. Eccles. 11:4.

25. 1 Tim. 1:7.

26. Phil. 4:13.

27. The distinction in human agency in Spanish is sometimes described as the difference between "Si Dios quiere" (If God wills it) versus "Sí, Dios quiere" (Yes, God wills it). Where the former implies a submission to and acceptance of the (unknown) will of God (who is perceived to control all events), the latter implies human agency in carrying out what is perceived to be the will of God.

28. Hartmuth Lehmann and Guenther Roth, *Weber's Protestant Ethic* (Cambridge: Cambridge University Press, 1993), and Gordon Marshall, *In Search of the Spirit of Capitalism* (New York: Columbia University Press, 1982).

29. Alfred Stepan, "Religion, Democracy, and the Twin Tolerations," *Journal of Democracy* 11 (2000): 37–57.

30. Robert Woodberry, "The Missionary Roots of Liberal Democracy," *American Political Science Review* 106 (2012): 244–74; Jorg Spekunch, "Religion and Work: Micro-Evidence from Germany," *SOEP Paper Series* (Berlin: 2010); and Robert Woodberry, "Pentecostalism and Economic Development," in *Markets, Morals, and Religion*, ed. J. B. Imber (New Brunswick, NJ: Transaction, 2008).

31. Robert Putnam, *Bowling Alone: The Collapse and Revival of American Community* (New York: Touchstone, 2000).

32. Sidney Verba, Kay Lehman Scholzman, and Henry Brady, *Voice and Equality: Civic Volunteerism in American Politics* (Cambridge, MA: Harvard University Press, 1995).

33. Monica Toft, Daniel Philpott, and Timothy Shah, *God's Century: Resurgent Religion in World Politics* (New York: W. W. Norton and Company, 2011); Robert Dowd, *Christianity, Islam, and Liberal Democracy: Lessons from Sub-Saharan Africa* (New York: Oxford University Press, 2015); and Robert Dowd and Ani Sarkissian, "The Roman Catholic Charismatic Renewal and Civic Engagement in Sub-Saharan Africa," *Journal for the Scientific Study of Religion* (online first, March 24, 2018).

34. See Ignacio Ellacuría and Jon Sobrino, *Mysterium Liberationis: Fundamental Concepts of Liberation Theology* (Maryknoll, NY: Orbis Books, 1993).

35. Gustavo Gutierrez, "Option for the Poor," in Ellacuría and Sobrino, *Mysterium Liberationis*.

36. Angus Madison, *The World Economy: A Millennial Perspective* (Paris: Development Centre of the Organisation for Economic Cooperation and Development, 2001).

37. World Bank, *World Development Report 2015: Mind, Society, and Behavior* (Washington DC: International Bank for Reconstruction and Development/World Bank, 2015), 188.

38. The English translation of what Tolstoy wrote is this: "Happy families are all alike; every unhappy family is unhappy in its own way." See Leo Tolstoy and David Magarshack, *Anna Karenina* (New York: New American Library, 1961).

39. For an expanded description of the research design, see Travis J. Lybbert and Bruce Wydick, "Hope as Aspirations, Agency and Pathways: Poverty Dynamics and Microfinance in Oaxaca, Mexico," in *The Economics of Poverty Traps*, ed. Christopher B. Barrett, Michael Carter, and Jean-Paul Chavas (Chicago: University of Chicago Press, 2019) and *NBER Working Paper W22661* (2016).

40. Snyder, *The Psychology of Hope.*

41. Ps. 37:4; Phil. 4:13; and Prov. 3:6.

42. Lybbert and Wydick, "Hope as Aspirations."

43. Ibid.

44. Prov. 29:18.

PART III

Dignity and Institutionalized Practices

EIGHT

Contextualized Participatory Monitoring and Evaluation

Paul Perrin

The international Humanitarian Charter—as expressed in 2004 by what is arguably the most widely known and respected effort to promote quality of humanitarian efforts, the Sphere project—is based on two core beliefs: "First, that all possible steps should be taken to alleviate human suffering arising out of calamity and conflict," and second, that "those affected by disaster have a right to life with dignity."[1] The first belief is intuitive and would seem to comprise the very concept of humanitarian relief; why, then, is there a need for the second core belief—that of the notion of dignity? The Sphere standards go on to say that "dignity entails more than physical well-being; it demands respect for the whole person, including the values and beliefs of individuals and affected communities, and respect for their human rights, including liberty, freedom of conscience and religious observance."[2] Notably, in the 2011 update of the Sphere Handbook, the prominence of the notion of dignity increased from previous versions: the order of the two core beliefs as referenced above was reversed, placing the core belief of the "right to life with dignity" first, while the frequency of use of the word dignity increased from 14.7 per 100 pages in the 2004 version to 18.8 per 100 pages in the 2011 edition.

DIGNITY IN THE PRACTICE OF INTERNATIONAL DEVELOPMENT: BUZZWORD OR MEANINGFUL DRIVER?

The notion of dignity is also at the core of the Universal Declaration of Human Rights, predicated as it is upon a "recognition of the inherent dignity . . . of the human family."[3] This bold declaration has echoed in many proclamations of international humanitarian relief and development entities. Indeed, when U.S. president Barack Obama laid out his vision of the U.S. Agency for International Development in terms of dignity, he stated that "our U.S. Global Development Policy—the first of its kind by an American administration—is rooted in America's enduring commitment to the dignity and potential of every human being."[4] The importance of the concept of dignity in international development and humanitarian work is further underscored by the peppering of the term in statements of the missions and values of many key international nongovernmental organizations (see examples in table 8.1), not to mention the myriad nonprofits that include the term in their very names.[5]

The term "dignity" is virtually omnipresent in international development and humanitarian settings; yet dignity as a measurable construct is strikingly absent given its seeming thematic centrality to the disciplines. It is apparent from the activities of many humanitarian organizations that dignity has been relegated to a nebulous, purposefully underdefined word and that few—if any—service-providing organizations have attempted to operationalize a definition of dignity, let alone doing so in ways that are concretely measurable. One organization has even taken to providing "dignity kits"—their preferred moniker for hygiene kits—in humanitarian settings[6] and, in so doing, confidently asserting that dignity can be distributed to the suffering masses in the form of humanitarian goods. Michael Marmot sums up the quandary nicely, stating: "If we cannot define dignity precisely, we will have trouble measuring it. If we cannot measure it, how will we know if we are achieving it?"[7]

TABLE 8.1. Dignity in the Humanitarian Consciousness

Organization	Dignity Quote[1]	Context of Quote
ActionAid	"Our programs focus on advancing women's rights, the right to education, the right to food, the right to security during conflict and emergencies, the right to life with **dignity** in the face of HIV/AIDS, and the right to just and democratic governance."	Mission Statement[2]
Action Contre la Faim	"Committed to principled humanitarian action, ACF restores **dignity**, self-sufficiency, and independence to vulnerable populations around the world."	"About Us" Statement[3]
American Jewish Joint Distribution Committee	"The American Jewish Joint Distribution Committee (JDC) is the world's leading Jewish humanitarian organization, committed to ensuring that every Jew is able to live in a safe and secure environment with a sense of **dignity**."	"Our Commitment" Statement[4]
American Refugee Committee	"We help people survive conflict and crisis and rebuild lives of **dignity**, health, security and self-sufficiency."	Mission Statement[5]
CAFOD	"We believe that everyone in the world has the right to live their lives with **dignity**."	"Who We Are" Statement[6]
CARE	"We seek a world of hope, tolerance and social justice, where poverty has been overcome and all people live with **dignity** and security."	Vision Statement[7]
Catholic Relief Services	"We are motivated by the Gospel of Jesus Christ to cherish, preserve and uphold the sacredness and **dignity** of all human life."	Mission Statement[8]
Concern Worldwide	"We envision a world . . . in which everyone is treated with **dignity** and respect."	"Who We Are" Statement[9]

(continued)

TABLE 8.1. (*Continued*)

Organization	Dignity Quote[1]	Context of Quote
Danish Refugee Council	"People's right to a life with **dignity** takes precedence over politics and principles.... We insist on the right of the individual to use his or her own abilities to shape his or her own life with **dignity**, in interaction with others."	"Vision and Values" Statement[10]
Episcopal Relief & Development	"Hearing God's call to seek and serve Christ in all persons and to respect the **dignity** of every human being, Episcopal Relief & Development serves to bring together the generosity of Episcopalians and others with the needs of the world."	Mission Statement[11]
Freedom from Hunger	"Freedom from Hunger brings innovative and sustainable self-help solutions to the fight against chronic hunger and poverty. Together with local partners, we equip families with resources they need to build futures of health, hope and **dignity**."	Mission Statement[12]
Global Communities	"We envision a world where everyone has the freedom, means and ability to live and prosper with **dignity**."	Vision Statement[13]
Habitat for Humanity	"We believe that no one lives in **dignity** until everyone can live in **dignity**."	Mission Principles[14]
Handicap International	"We work alongside people with disabilities and vulnerable populations, taking action and bearing witness in order to respond to their essential needs, improve their living conditions and promote respect for their **dignity** and fundamental rights."	"About Us" Statement[15]
Helen Keller International (HKI)	"HKI believes that ... everyone—from the people we serve to our partners and staff—deserves to have a voice and to be treated with respect and **dignity**."	"Our Values" Statement[16]

TABLE 8.1. (*Continued*)

Organization	Dignity Quote[1]	Context of Quote
HelpAge International	"Our vision is of a world in which all older people can lead **dignified**, active, healthy and secure lives."	Vision Statement[17]
InterAction	"Our mission is to ... ensure human **dignity** for poor and vulnerable populations worldwide."	Mission Statement[18]
International Federation of the Red Cross and Red Crescent Societies (IFRC)	"Contributing to the maintenance and promotion of human **dignity** and peace in the world."	Vision Statement[19]
International Organization for Migration (IOM)	"IOM acts with its partners in the international community to ... uphold the human **dignity** and well-being of migrants."	Mission Statement[20]
International Orthodox Christian Charities	"We envision that, by God's grace, IOCC will respond, without discrimination, to those who are suffering and in need, to enable them to continue to improve their own lives and communities and to have means to live with **dignity**, respect and hope."	Vision Statement[21]
International Rescue Committee (IRC)	"The IRC is committed to freedom, human **dignity**, and self-reliance."	Mission Statement[22]
Islamic Relief	"Islamic Relief endeavours to protect life and **dignity**."	"Our Work" Statement[23]
Lutheran World Relief	"Empowered by God's unconditional love in Jesus Christ, we envision a world in which each person, every community and all generations live in justice, **dignity** and peace."	Vision Statement[24]

(*continued*)

TABLE 8.1. (*Continued*)

Organization	Dignity Quote[1]	Context of Quote
Médecins Sans Frontières	"We respect patients' autonomy, patient confidentiality and their right to informed consent. We treat our patients with **dignity**, and with respect for their cultural and religious beliefs."	Core Principles Statement[25]
Mercy Corps	"We believe in the intrinsic value and **dignity** of human life."	Core Values Statement[26]
Norwegian Refugee Council	"Preserving **dignity**: The displaced people we work with are strong, **dignified** and resourceful. Most are able and willing to fend for themselves. But sometimes, when a person has lost everything, it can be hard to retain a sense of **dignity** and confidence. We work with them to make sure that the support they and their families receive is adjusted to their particular needs."	"Who We Are" Statement[27]
Oxfam International	"We work with people living in poverty striving to exercise their human rights, assert their **dignity** as full citizens and take control of their lives."	"What We Do" Statement[28]
Relief International	"Our mission is simple: We partner with some of the world's most vulnerable communities to relieve poverty, ensure well-being and advance **dignity**."	Mission Statement[29]
Trócaire	Trócaire envisages a just and peaceful world where people's **dignity** is ensured and rights are respected."	Vision Statement[30]
United Methodist Committee on Relief	"We believe all people have God-given worth and **dignity**."	"About Us" Statement[31]

TABLE 8.1. (*Continued*)

Organization	Dignity Quote[1]	Context of Quote
UNICEF	"We help children . . . to live their lives with **dignity**."	"Who We Are" Statement[32]

1. These statements were current as of September 2016 but may evolve over time. Boldface added by editors.
2. https://www.interaction.org/member/actionaid-international-usa.
3. http://www.actionagainsthunger.org/about/acf-international.
4. http://www.jdc.org/about-jdc/our-commitment.html.
5. http://arcrelief.org/about/.
6. http://cafod.org.uk/About-us/What-we-do.
7. http://www.care.org/about/mission-vision.
8. http://www.crs.org/about/mission-statement.
9. http://www.concernusa.org/about/who-we-are/.
10. https://drc.ngo/about-drc/vision-and-values.
11. http://www.episcopalrelief.org/who-we-are/mission-and-mandate.
12. https://www.freedomfromhunger.org/about-us.
13. http://www.globalcommunities.org/aboutus.
14. http://www.habitat.org/how/mission_statement.aspx.
15. http://www.handicap-international.us/about.
16. http://www.hki.org/our-impact/about-us/mission-and-goals.
17. http://www.helpage.org/who-we-are/our-values-and-ambitions/.
18. https://www.interaction.org/2012-annual-report-who-we-are.
19. http://www.ifrc.org/en/who-we-are/vision-and-mission/.
20. https://www.iom.int/mission.
21. https://www.iocc.org/about/our-mission.
22. https://www.interaction.org/member/international-rescue-committee.
23. http://www.islamic-relief.org/about-us/.
24. http://lwr.org/mission-vision-and-values.
25. http://www.msf.org/en/msf-charter-and-principles.
26. https://www.mercycorps.org/about-us/our-mission.
27. https://www.nrc.no/who-we-are/our-impact/.
28. This has since been updated. https://orgsync.com/21673/custom_pages/2546.
29. http://www.ri.org/our-mission.
30. https://www.trocaire.org/about/how-we-work.
31. http://www.umcor.org/UMCOR/About-Us.
32. http://www.unicef.org/about/who/index_introduction.html.

While the term enjoys lofty status in the lexicon of international development, human rights, and humanitarianism, as Carozza and Sedmak highlighted in the present volume's introduction, it is by no means without its detractors. The arguments contesting the concept of dignity are particularly salient in the conversation of monitoring and evaluation, for, in the minds of many scholars, dignity is a concept that is nothing more than "feel-good philosophical window-dressing," "a substitute for hard thinking," or "incurably theological."[8] Noted bioethicist Ruth Macklin threw down the gauntlet when she declared dignity "a useless concept"— one that could be substituted for more meaningful concepts—in a *BMJ* editorial that continues to be a point of debate.[9] Building on Macklin's arguments, Steven Pinker laid out three additional fundamental objections to the term "dignity," claiming that it is relative, fungible, and often harmful, pithily calling dignity "the sizzle, not the steak."[10] Moreover, Pinker argues that undignified behavior and other external projections of dignity to an outside world (such as clothing), what Pinker calls "the signs of dignity," can lead to "dignity illusions" in the observer.[11] One author, commenting on the use of the term in development discourse, exclaimed that "it is the height of arrogance to think dignity [of poor and suffering people] needs our protection."[12] Ultimately, the term seems to be the subject of lively debates whenever it is raised in scholarly settings.[13] All of these objections have validity and must not be simply brushed aside when discussing the utility of the concept for monitoring and evaluation (M&E) purposes.

The arguments against the concept of operationalizing human dignity in development practice may be fair but not necessarily fatal. On the flip side of the debate, one of the key arguments in favor of an actual, meaningful concept of dignity is that we respond to it in contexts and ways that other concepts cannot fully encompass.[14] Indeed, much research in a variety of disciplines has been undertaken to provide meaningful definitions of dignity in an attempt to delineate its fuzzy edges. An in-depth review of the literature surrounding dignity broadly categorized the conceptual definitions into two main forms: human dignity, with which all persons are endowed simply by virtue of being sentient human beings or (in religious terms) by virtue of their relationship to a creator-god, and social dignity, which can be maintained or threatened through social interaction.[15] Jonathan Mann adds another consideration to the equation by identifying the two components of a person's dignity as the internal ("how I see myself") and the external ("how others see me").[16] Mann further states that "violations of dignity are pervasive events with potentially devastating negative effects on physical, mental and social well-being."[17]

Further solidifying its endurance in the development and humanitarian consciousness, a recent World Humanitarian Summit dedicated one of its five themes to dignity, which it described as "empower[ing] people to cope and recover with dignity through humanitarian action that puts people at its heart, delivers equally for women and girls, reaches everyone, invests in youth and children, and protects and enables people as the primary agents of their own response."[18] In this paradigm, dignity is inseparably linked with participation. One of the ways in which communities often participate in development work—although it should never be mistaken for the end-all and be-all of participation—is through M&E efforts.

The arguments laid out in this chapter, as well as other chapters in this volume, are based on the notion that, indeed, dignity gains meaning only through the respect accorded to it (through what Carozza and Sedmak refer to as "dignity-enacting practices" in the introduction to the present volume). Building on this notion, the interaction with human dignity can and should be explicitly taken into account in assessing the success of international development practice, if indeed this concept is so central to the core of the missions of so many organizations occupying this space. The remainder of this discussion will focus on the importance of linking M&E and the recognition of dignity, presenting a few examples of how this has taken place in international development practice and proposing a high-level path forward in taking steps toward more meaningfully integrating this concept in M&E in development.

THE ROLE OF MONITORING AND EVALUATION IN THE DIGNITY CONVERSATION

The credibility of international humanitarian and development action is often threatened by perceptions of lack of impact, poor coordination, waste and inefficiency, corruption and fraud, political motivation for assistance, and a lack of professionalism.[19] As a result of these realities, the international aid system is particularly vulnerable to the risks of moral hazard, perverse incentive (i.e., relief agencies' perpetuating adverse conditions to ensure continued "business"), and inappropriate choice (i.e., agencies' taking on jobs for which they are not qualified).

Agencies that are working with vulnerable populations have a duty to use money as effectively as possible. Because development and humanitarian needs are so great, for decades it was often taken for granted that virtually any action taken to address human suffering would have a positive effect, whether large or small. This presumption began to be more systematically challenged in the aftermath of the previous decade's global recession and shifting geopolitical power loci. There were strong indications that international development and humanitarian budgets could not be sustained in the face of growing public skepticism unless implementers could demonstrate that aid was making a real difference, causing a likely permanent shift in the international relief and development environment. Well-publicized stories of ineffective aid threatened to undermine legitimate life-saving and dignity-affirming efforts that are often less visibly documented.[20] One of the characteristics of this emergent environment was an increased pressure to demonstrate results, including the impact, of humanitarian and development programming. It is believed that a greater focus on results ensures that we are generating the best value from our programmatic investments and thereby strengthening agency competitiveness. Without continually assessing the impact of programming, humanitarian and development agencies, whether newly created or seasoned, constantly run the risk of making mistakes, being misguided, or sometimes even deliberately abusing the trust that is placed in them. In spite of all of the challenges and realities noted above, the majority of donors to international nongovernmental organizations (INGOs) are working to be disciplined in their approach and are serious about their commitment to achieving results in the lives of the people they serve by promoting a culture of rigorous M&E to better understand the impact of humanitarian programming.

Assessing the quality of international development and humanitarian work is a concept that is at its most meaningful when applied to the lives of individual participants or communities.[21] Nora Jacobson's review of dignity and health concludes with the plea that although much work has been done to better understand the concept of dignity, work on dignity "should now strive for greater explanatory power" to understand perceptions, causal relationships, and mechanisms related to dignity and health.[22] Given the past and the evolving new realities, this is an ideal time for promoting measurements around the recognition of dignity in international development and humanitarian settings as a way of maintaining the focus of measuring the effects of such programming on the experience of vulnerable populations. Finding better ways to understand and assess the effects of international development programming on perceptions of human dignity and subjecting the measurement to rigorous statistical analysis may be a viable surrogate outcome and impact indicator, which could provide insight into where additional investments might be warranted and what types of programming or conditions are correlated with an increased sense of dignity. Moreover, depending on how it is defined and operationalized, it may be more sensitive to change in the shorter term than other valid impact measurements.

PRACTICAL EXAMPLES OF DIGNITY IN MONITORING AND EVALUATION

While recognition of dignity can easily be conceptually associated with international development outcomes,[23] research actually demonstrating such a link is more difficult to come by. Perceptions of dignity have been better researched in clinical settings, particularly among adult populations that are terminally ill, disabled, and older.[24] The following case studies are early examples of how the dignity dialogue intersects with M&E in the practice of international development and, ultimately, how dignity-oriented M&E can influence the structure of development and humanitarian activities themselves. Each case study discussed below adopted a different approach to examining the recognition of dignity in these contexts.

UNDERSTANDING DIGNITY THROUGH SELF-REPORTED MIXED-METHODS APPROACHES

A recent examination of NGO efforts through focus groups among conflict-affected recipients of aid across the Middle East revealed a pervasive sense that, whilst vast initiatives were under way and NGOs were actively providing assistance, recipients did not feel that these efforts were made in a way that respected their dignity. Tellingly, respondents gave an average ranking of 3.5 out of 10 when asked to what extent they were treated with respect and dignity by NGOs.[25] Based on these and other findings, the report concluded that "humanitarian NGOs ... sometimes fail to match their actions to their words, ... [and] true accountability is ... perhaps the greatest challenge for NGOs, as well as for governments and the UN."[26]

Conflict-affected Afghanistan in the first decade of the twenty-first century provides a textbook example of the pitfalls associated with a lack of perceived accountability among the affected population in a humanitarian effort—positive M&E reports notwithstanding. One study identified a significant disconnect between how local communities perceived humanitarian activities and the views of the humanitarian and larger aid communities, resulting in general frustration with and widespread criticism of aid agencies.[27] While the Afghans surveyed noted the numerous interventions being perpetrated upon them—which ostensibly were devised to benefit the people—the study authors concluded that "the fact that NGOs, as a category of civil society, have fallen from the role of heroes to that of villains in the space of a few years is an indication that something is amiss with the category as a whole either in what it provides (which may no longer correspond to popular expectations) or in how it provides it."[28] Perceptions of poor quality of aid response in Afghanistan have been confirmed in subsequent studies.[29] Confidence in international NGOs among the populace of Afghanistan has been steadily dropping over time, with only 44 percent of the Afghan public reporting confidence in 2015 as compared to 64 percent and 56 percent in 2007 and 2011, respectively.[30] While there is no research that directly links perceived poor quality of response with security incidents, these perceptions certainly cannot ameliorate the fact that Afghanistan has become the single most dangerous country in the world for aid workers, with 1,084 aid workers victimized between 1997 and September 2016[31] and the vast majority of incidents occurring since the Donini report was released in 2006.[32]

When examining these and other realities in the NGO world, the most recent World Humanitarian Summit concluded that "there was a recognition that the continued provision of relief alone is not feasible and there is consensus on the need to find innovative ways of more sustainably meeting people's needs with dignity ... and more needs to be done to improve results in practice."[33]

Another relatively recent example of how a dignity lens helped change the perception of M&E involved a 2011 study among older adult internally displaced persons (IDPs) in the Republic of Georgia, where conflict in both the early 1990s and again in 2008 left sizeable populations of both "protracted" and shorter-term IDPs living in both urban and nonurban environments.[34] With regard to the situation in Georgia, the United Nations Security Council stressed "the urgent need to alleviate the plight of refugees and internally displaced persons and the need for a perspective of life in security and dignity in particular for a new generation growing up outside Abkhazia, Georgia."[35] This yearning for a greater respect for dignity was borne out by the findings of the qualitative portion of the study, in which older IDPs noted that they were "drowning in nihilism," deeply depressed, or even wished for death due to the lack of respect for them and their lack of control of their situations. Noting the emergence of this theme of dignity in the qualitative portion, the study team incorporated a scale developed and validated to assess respect for dignity among displaced populations in the West Bank, Gaza, and the Caucasus region.[36] The tool comprises the domains of *autonomy* (i.e., a sense of independence and control; the ability to make one's own decisions; functional capacity), *worthiness* (i.e., feeling important and valuable in relation to others; being treated as such by others), *self-respect* (i.e., respect both for oneself and others; being responsible and reliable), and *self-esteem* (i.e., continuity of self, role and legacy preservation, maintenance of pride and a sense hopefulness and a "fighting spirit"). The survey using this tool, which involved 900 older IDPs in the regions of Samegrelo, Shida Kartli, Mtskheta-Mtianeti, and Tbilisi, found that the strongest predictor of elevated dignity recognition scores was lower depressive symptom scores, followed by higher levels of function, lower anxiety scores, better health status, and higher cognitive ability.[37] Surprisingly, what might be considered more traditional humanitarian indicators, such as accommodation type, current socioeconomic status, access to water and sanitation, and access to household items, were weaker predictors after being controlled for the other predictors in the model.

These data suggested that when attempting to use recognition of dignity as an outcome measure, our understanding of what constitutes a necessary response might become more nuanced than a model based on Maslow's hierarchy of needs that seems to implicitly drive much humanitarian and development work today.

UNDERSTANDING DIGNITY THROUGH NARRATIVE APPROACHES

Development organizations are under increasing pressure to better understand the experiences of project participants as a means for improving project outcomes and ensuring increased accountability to communities.[38] Quantitative data collection methods, such as the ubiquitous survey, provide easily comprehensible and synthesizable information but, in the way they are administered, are now often considered "extractive data gathering processes," which can inhibit engaging in the "dynamic process of listening and responding to beneficiaries."[39] This is because they are highly predetermined, often by parties external to the community in question, and the information shared by the survey participants is foisted upon them by the structure of the survey itself. Therefore, and although such data collection activities are meant to serve vulnerable populations, these activities rob local populations of their voice and the opportunity to share their experiences in their own ways. Although not intended as such, survey participants often perceive NGOs as not actually interested in their lives and as caring about their experiences only insofar as they can be categorized, aggregated, and depersonalized. In my experience as a researcher and evaluator frequently interacting with respondents, some even see this process as dehumanizing and disrespecting their human dignity. Acknowledging this, many key players in providing international aid strongly advocate for more participatory processes for M&E. The World Bank, for instance, has stated that "participation adds value— the more participatory the process, the more value can potentially be added to the program . . . as participation in evaluation facilitates consensus-building and ownership of evaluation findings, conclusions, and recommendations."[40]

Likewise, development evaluation experts are beginning to embrace the notion of complexity—the idea that change processes are often nonlinear or unpredictable a priori, notwithstanding the fact that traditional M&E approaches often assume otherwise. To date, however, there has been little agreement on what types of tools can provide this information in a way that complements the existing M&E systems that are required by donor agencies. Traditional methods cannot hope to fully address the critical challenges of complexity while maintaining rigor and fostering dignity through participation in M&E.[41] Fortunately, there are cracks of light that hint at "creative and sometimes unorthodox approaches [that] will be required to measure project achievements in complex and/ or insecure environments."[42] Catholic Relief Services (CRS) has piloted one promising new methodology—SenseMaker (SM)—which is a methodology and software suite that helps analyze short narratives and self-signified data and is based on the premise that "one can monitor through data, but also through dialogue."[43]

Traditional storytelling methods, such as telling "success stories," are appealing to development agencies due to their human touch and their more grounded approach to discussing impacts. Indeed, a body of researchers feel that narrative methods such as storytelling offer a "powerful mode of human expression" that "accommodates diverse voices and perspectives"; contrasted with traditional evaluation approaches that are "imposed from outside, the storytelling approach emerges organically from within [one's] organization, projects and participants."[44] Narrative methods are emerging as a "powerful way to exchange and consolidate knowledge" because research suggests that this approach "builds trust, cultivates norms, transfers tacit knowledge, facilitates unlearning, and generates emotional connections."[45] These advantages are not lost on many evaluators, who have begun to incorporate narratives into the process of evaluating public services and international development work.[46] However, these approaches are not without challenges in that they often suffer from a lack of scalability, pose a strong challenge for aggregation,[47] and are subject to bias and lack of credibility if not systematically and deliberately collected following scientific principles;[48] to wit, some of the larger NGOs may implement six or seven projects in more than a hundred countries annually, and a repository of narratives of even a fraction of such scale and breadth quickly becomes unwieldy and difficult to analyze.

Seeking to harness the power of the narrative while also looking toward scale and aggregated analysis, CRS implemented a multicountry pilot of the SM tool and approach for capturing and analyzing narratives. CRS sought to test the approach because SM seemed to combine the advantage of self-signified stories with the value of doing large-scale statistical analysis that allows the exploration of patterns and metrics using the codes, along with a qualitative database of stories. Indeed, the stated applications of the SM approach have been "organizational aggregation from diversity, rolling baselines, cross-organizational comparisons, and understanding the unanticipated."[49] In short, SM generates detailed, "disintermediated" stories that can be aggregated to provide insight on the development impact of CRS programming that will be of use to staff working at different levels across the agency.

Like traditional qualitative research methods, the SM approach uses an open-ended question prompting beneficiaries to describe their experiences with a development project in a way that people naturally narrate their experiences. Unlike traditional methods, however, these stories, or "micronarratives," are gathered in large volumes in a rigorous way to correct for bias, and beneficiaries themselves then assign meaning to (or "signify") their own stories using a set of pre-defined "signifiers," or codes, rather than having an external "intermediary" assigning meaning to their stories, as is the case in conventional qualitative analysis. This mass capture of fragmented material that is self-signified at the point of origin provides quantitative data in addition to the qualitative story.

This approach has been pioneered in the development sector by Cognitive Edge (which developed the SM software package for analyzing and visualizing stories) and Irene Guijt,[50] and it has been piloted by GlobalGiving, IRC, the United Nations Development Programme (UNDP), Girl Effect, and Vredeseilanden/VECO. Using this approach, GlobalGiving has created a central database of 57,000 beneficiary stories that they claim are easier to manage than standard quantitative indicators because they are easily aggregated at the agency level, analyzable using both qualitative and quantitative methods, and agnostic to program area (thus allowing for easier cross-sector comparisons).[51] Moreover, because SM enables those on the receiving end of CRS interventions to conceptualize and speak about those interventions' impact for themselves rather than through a pre-determined framework of metrics, it greatly advances the opportunity for beneficiary accountability in a way not possible with other approaches. Indeed, GirlHub reported that one beneficiary who participated in an SM exercise explained that the approach better respected the dignity of beneficiaries because it differed from traditional methods in which "people come and they do a survey, but they're asking questions that are important to them, not what is important to us."[52] SM analysis of stories has demonstrated that what the community identifies as important elements of impact is often different from what the experts and program implementers have identified.[53] UNDP's experience at the program level has demonstrated that this approach can be more responsive than surveys to shifting attitudes, subtle behavior changes, or hardening of beliefs. Moreover, UNDP has demonstrated cost savings over more expensive impact evaluations while also allowing them to move "beyond how many people we've reached or how many 'likes' we had to what is the extent of perception changes we're seeing as a result of various campaigns."[54]

CRS worked to build on the experience and work of others in SM who have built their approaches on established scientific theories. In 2015 CRS launched the three-country, one-year SM pilot, which was implemented in five phases: (1) preparation, (2) training, (3) micronarrative gathering, (4) sensemaking, and (5) dissemination and pilot reflection. The goal of the pilot project was to assess the utility of adding the SM methodology to the agency's well-developed internal systems for M&E as a way of fostering participation and better addressing complexity. The pilot focused on examining the implementation of partner relationships and experiences in India, understanding the relative experiences with various value-chain approaches among coffee farmers in Colombia, and probing the pathway to prosperity amongst rural populations in Nicaragua.[55]

In all three initial pilot cases, some surprising findings emerged that challenged initial project assumptions and required staff to understand differently how change occurs and what matters for people. In Colombia, for example, project staff had initially assumed that the "massive specialized" markets would not be valued by farmers. However, the data showed that the stories from the subset of farmers who were exposed to such markets were largely positive. This has prompted staff to explore further what this value chain offers farmers and to translate those insights into other value-chain relationships. In Nicaragua, CRS staff were interested in the emergence of six distinct pathways to and from prosperity from farmers' stories. Climate change and microfinance were themes strongly linked to negative stories related to prosperity pathways.

The staff in Nicaragua were also surprised by the large number of stories that indicated the continued desirability of an agriculture-based livelihood, as project staff had expected more of the participants to favor nonagricultural futures. In India an important emerging finding was the level of importance respondents attached to social connections, relationships, and community engagement. This result has triggered discussions on how such a finding should inform the next phase of the project. In all three cases traditional M&E approaches had also been implemented that had failed to reveal these findings, which were observed only through the voice and experiences of the populations in question. In some cases, SM also contributed to confirming existing strategies or assumptions.

CRS has found thus far that using SM is not without its challenges. For one, analysis of the data requires a paradigmatic shift for professionals, even (or perhaps especially) those who are experts in quantitative or qualitative methods. CRS staff with advanced statistical and ethnographic training at times struggled with the design and analysis aspects of SM, which are less scientific and more artistic. Using SM in a more open-minded setting versus one dominated by linear thinking will require a different kind of process, a different manner of stakeholder engagement for analysis and interpretation, and reflection on the competencies required going forward. Likewise, considerable up-front investments of time and capacity building are necessary when compared with more traditional approaches to M&E. This means that, at present, SM could not be easily employed for rapid studies in new contexts. Because of these challenges, CRS is currently using SM to complement the routine, more traditional performance M&E systems rather than to replace them.

In light of the above, a critical examination of the pilot and reflection on it revealed that under certain conditions and project time frames, the SM methodology can be a useful tool that can complement the conventional M&E systems of a development agency. Based on this analysis, CRS, its partners, and communities concluded that the SM pilot: (1) gave a greater voice to project participants; (2) provided useful insights into why change is or is not occurring—insights that are beyond the reach of traditional M&E approaches; and (3) helped planners to better understand some of the factors that are affecting their activities in complex, unpredictable environments.[56] CRS has expanded the use and understanding of the SM methodology through a second round of pilots, which have resulted in expansion of the methodology to eight additional countries and to new topical areas.[57]

Building on these experiences with the methodology, one promising avenue to explore is to use SM not just as a means for fostering perceptions of dignity in M&E by encouraging participation but also as a means to assess the recognition of human dignity itself. This will allow the benefits of a structured framework for dignity without overly constraining people's experience in sharing their experiences of living the concept of dignity. In so doing, we can bring to pass a paradigm that challenges "the dominance of quantitative statistical information as the sole, authoritative source of knowledge . . . so that we embrace much richer ways of thinking about development and of assessing the realities of what is happening closer to the ground."[58]

A WAY FORWARD: SEEKING TO BETTER UNDERSTAND RECOGNITION OF DIGNITY

Interesting and compelling as these case studies are, a few scattered examples of seeking to measure and operationalize recognition of dignity do not a body of knowledge make. There remains a collective need to better define, assess, and improve recognition of dignity in all humanitarian settings. The temptation in environments where basic needs are met is to claim "mission accomplished." There remains the question of how the equation might change if recognition of dignity were the primary outcome of interest for humanitarian interventions and if the quality of development and humanitarian efforts were partially examined through the lens of dignity experiences.

As it stands in the fields of international development and humanitarian assistance, dignity is simultaneously a supremely powerful notion and a remarkably weak buzzword. On the one side, the term is at the forefront of how many major international entities working in the field articulate their purpose, given the recognition that the term encapsulates the essence of what their work seeks to accomplish, beyond simply keeping people alive. On the flipside, "dignity" as a term is a poster child of what Cornwall has coined "development's buzzwords," about which the author eloquently wrote:

Development's buzzwords gain their purchase and power through their vague and euphemistic qualities, their capacity to embrace a multitude of possible meanings, and their normative resonance. The work that these words do for development is to place the sanctity of its goals beyond reproach. . . . Buzzwords aid this process, by providing concepts that can float free of concrete referents, to be filled with meaning by their users. In the struggles for interpretive power that characterise the negotiation of the language of policy, buzzwords shelter multiple agendas, providing room for manoeuvre and space for contestation.[59]

Humans are complex creatures, and therefore dignity is a complex construct. For that reason, one of the questions of prime importance to tackle first from a standpoint of international development practice is whether there is a universal objective construct of dignity that has cross-cultural and cross-individual significance. It is highly likely that certain elements of the dignity construct will vary in quality and in importance from culture to culture, but research should seek to determine both which elements of dignity are highly context-specific and whether there are elements of the experience of dignity that resonate across the globe in most, if not all, contexts. This is a tall order for any construct, but if—as the mission statements, guiding principles, and visions of so many humanitarian entities attest—we are truly serious about dignity, it is time to work toward assuring recognition of dignity in our work by restoring the notion from buzzword to a meaningful impetus for humanitarian and development work. The quality assurance triangle comprises the three points of defining quality, measuring quality, and improving quality.[60] Similarly, a "dignity assurance" triangle can be adopted that describes the processes of clearly defining recognition of dignity, systematically and properly assessing recognition of dignity based on that definition, and using the measurement to continually improve the respect for dignity in international development practice; this approach could be adopted within organizations, within countries, and at the global level to bring meaning to the concept of dignity in development programming.

The few attempts to develop such measures represent important steps forward in defining and measuring recognition of dignity on a global scale. However, if a universal definition and measurement of recognition of dignity is revised or devised, such a measurement would also need to be rigorously validated cross-culturally while also allowing for the addition of cultural variations in perceived dignity through rigorous mixed-methods research.[61] Alternatively, if such a measure is not forthcoming, adopting narrative approaches such as SM—which allow our understanding of dignity to be driven by individual lived experience with the construct rather than a universal metric—would be feasible and would constitute a worthy line of exploration.

While not necessarily probable, it is possible that perceiving international development and humanitarian assistance through a "dignity assurance" lens could fundamentally change the way we approach providing such assistance. Alternatively, it could confirm that what we have been doing all along is indeed fostering recognition of dignity in the most optimal way.

Until such processes are in place and until recognition of dignity gains real operational meaning so as to direct the flow of resources, the NGO community cannot credibly advocate for the dignity of the people they serve among donors and host governments. Furthermore, NGOs cannot hope to fully understand the impact they are or are not having on those they are meant to serve. Ultimately, the term must emerge from its political and theological uses[62] if it is ever to enjoy meaningful and broad operationalization in development and humanitarian settings. Conceptualizations of dignity may also need to focus less on the external material manifestations and behaviors and more on the internal experience of dignity and assaults thereupon.

NOTES

1. The Sphere Project, *Humanitarian Charter and Minimum Standards in Disaster Response* (Geneva: Oxfam Publishing, 2004), available at http://www .sphereproject.org/content/view/27/84.

2. Ibid.

3. United Nations General Assembly, *Universal Declaration of Human Rights* (New York: United Nations, 1948).

4. White House Office of the Press Secretary, *Fact Sheet: The President's Global Development Council* (Washington, DC: White House, 2012), available

at http://www.whitehouse.gov/the-press-office/2012/02/09/fact-sheet
-president-s-global-development-council.

5. Such as Dignity Danish Institute against Torture, Dignity Founda-
tion, Embrace Dignity, Dignity for Children Foundation; Human Dignity
Foundation; Dignity International; Life with Dignity, Human Dignity Trust,
Building Dignity, and so on.

6. Libby Abbott et al., *Evaluation of UNFPA's Provision of Dignity Kits
in Humanitarian and Post-Crisis Settings* (New York: United Nations Population Fund, 2011).

7. Michael Marmot, "Dignity and Inequality," *Lancet* 364 (2004): 1019–
22, available at http://www.lancet.com/journals/lancet/article/PIIS0140-6736
(04)17075-X.

8. Charles Foster, "Putting Dignity to Work," *Lancet* 379, no. 9831 (2012):
2044–45, available at https://doi.org/10.1016/S0140-6736(12)60885-X.

9. Ruth Macklin, "Dignity Is a Useless Concept," *BMJ* 327, no. 7429
(2003): 1419–20, available at https://doi.org/10.1136/bmj.327.7429.1419.

10. Steven Pinker, "The Stupidity of Dignity," *New Republic*, May 2008,
available at http://www.newrepublic.com/article/the-stupidity-dignity.

11. Ibid.

12. J. Brooks, "Dignity vs. Humanity," in *FundRaising Success* (2008).

13. See, for instance, the online comments in response to Macklin's piece.

14. Foster, "Putting Dignity to Work."

15. Nora Jacobson, "Dignity and Health: A Review," *Social Science and
Medicine* 64, no. 2 (2007): 292–302, available at https://doi.org/10.1016/j
.socscimed.2006.08.039.

16. Jonathan Mann, "Dignity and Health: The UDHR's Revolutionary
First Article," *Health and Human Rights* 3, no. 2 (1998): 30–38.

17. Ibid., 35.

18. World Humanitarian Summit, *Restoring Humanity: Global Voices
Calling for Action*, 2016, available at https://consultations.worldhumanitarian
summit.org/bitcache/e29bc4269edb7eaeceb5169a8f41275327a701c8?vid=
555558&disposition=inline&op=view.

19. Humanitarian Accountability Partnership International, *HAP 2007
Standard in Humanitarian Accountability and Quality Management* (Geneva:
HAP, 2007), available at http://www.hapinternational.org/pool/files/hap
-2007-standard(1).pdf.

20. William R. Easterly, *The White Man's Burden: Why the West's Efforts
to Aid the Rest Have Done So Much Ill and So Little Good* (New York: Penguin
Press, 2006); Michael Maren, *The Road to Hell: The Ravaging Effects of Foreign*

Aid and International Charity (New York: Free Press, 1997); David Rieff, *A Bed for the Night: Humanitarianism in Crisis* (New York: Simon and Schuster, 2002); and Fiona Terry, *Condemned to Repeat? The Paradox of Humanitarian Action* (Ithaca, NY, and London: Cornell University Press, 2002).

21. S. Campbell, M. Roland, and S. A. Buetow, "Defining Quality of Care," *Social Science and Medicine* 51 (2000): 1611–25, available at http://www.sciencedirect.com/science/article/pii/s0277953600000575, and Emergency Capacity Building Project, *Impact Measurement and Accountability in Emergencies: The Good Enough Guide* (Oxford: Oxfam, 2007).

22. Jacobson, "Dignity and Health."

23. H. K. Armenian, *In War and Peace: Health with Dignity* (Beirut: American University of Beirut, 2005).

24. H. M. Chochinov et al., "Dignity in the Terminally Ill: A Cross-Sectional, Cohort Study," *Lancet* 360, no. 9350 (2002): 2026–30, available at https://doi.org/10.1016/S0140-6736(02)12022-8.

25. Edmund Cairns and Naomi Meneghini-Relf, *For Human Dignity: The World Humanitarian Summit and the Challenge to Deliver* (Oxford: Oxfam International, 2015), available at https://policy-practice.oxfamamerica.org/static/media/files/bp205-for-human-dignity-world-humanitarian-summit-080715-en.pdf.

26. Ibid., 24.

27. Antonio Donini, *Humanitarian Agenda 2015: Afghanistan Country Study* (Medford, MA: Feinstein International Center, 2006), available at http://fic.tufts.edu/publication-item/humanitarian-agenda-2015-principles-power-and-perceptions/.

28. Ibid., 11.

29. P. Benelli, A. Donini, and N. Niland, *Afghanistan: Humanitarianism in Uncertain Times* (Boston, MA: Feinstein International Center, 2012), available at http://fic.tufts.edu/assets/Afghan-uncertain-times.pdf; A. M. Rivas, *Health and Education in Afghanistan: 10 Years After—Quantity Not Quality* (Kabul: ACBAR Policy Series, 2011), available at http://reliefweb.int/sites/reliefweb.int/files/resources/10010547981111.pdf; and World Humanitarian Summit, *Restoring Humanity*.

30. Sayed Masood Sadat et al., *A Survey of the Afghan People* (Washington, DC: Asia Foundation, 2015), available at https://asiafoundation.org/resources/pdfs/Afghanistanin2015.pdf.

31. Humanitarian Outcomes, The Aid Worker Security Database, 2016, available at https://aidworkersecurity.org/.

32. Donini, *Humanitarian Agenda 2015*.

33. World Humanitarian Summit, *Restoring Humanity*.

34. C. Robinson el al., *Aging in Displacement: Assessing Health Status of Displaced Older Adults in the Republic of Georgia* (Baltimore: Johns Hopkins School of Public Health, 2012), available at http://chca.org.ge/_FILES/2017/10/25/278182c5f42fe435ef3d89633402ddcae81901214a82c44eca546d92e9a5d537.pdf.

35. W. Kalin, "Legal Aspects of Return of Internally Displaced Persons and Refugees to Abkhazia, Georgia" (Washington DC: Brookings Institution, 2007), available at http://www.brookings.edu/speeches/2007/1129_georgia_kalin.aspx.

36. R. Khatib and H. Armenian, "Developing an Instrument for Measuring Human Dignity and Its Relationship to Health in Palestinian Refugees," *World Medical and Health Policy* 2, no. 2 (2010): 35–49; Maya Simonyan, "Dignity and Health-Related Quality of Life of Adult Residents of Yerevan," (master's thesis, American University of Armenia, Yerevan, 2007).

37. Paul Perrin, "'Drowned in Nihilism': Dignity and Health among Older Adults Displaced by Conflict in the Republic of Georgia" (PhD diss., Johns Hopkins Bloomberg School of Public Health, 2013).

38. O. Barder, "Evidence and Scale," notes for remarks to the CIFF Board, London, May 16, 2014; A. Blum, "The Peace Bridge to Nowhere," *Foreign Policy* (2014), available at http://www.foreignpolicy.com/articles/2014/09/22/peace_bridge_to_nowhere_aid_accountability_conflict_disaster; World Bank, "Learning and Results in World Bank Operations: How the Bank Learns" (Washington DC: IEG World Bank Group, 2014); and J. Watts et al., "Institutional Learning and Change: An Introduction," *ISNAR Discussion Paper* 3-10 (The Hague: International Service for National Agricultural Research, 2003).

39. Lachlan Groves, *Beneficiary Feedback in Evaluation* (London: U.K. Department for International Development, 2015), available at http://betterevaluation.org/sites/default/files/Beneficiary-Feedback-Feb15a.pdf.

40. C. Gerrard, D. Hill, L. Kelly, and E. Wee-Ling Ooi, *Sourcebook for Evaluating Global and Regional Partnership Programs: Indicative Principles and Standards* (Washington, DC: World Bank, 2007), available at http://siteresources.worldbank.org/EXTGLOREGPARPROG/Resources/sourcebook.pdf, 21.

41. Clodagh Miskelly, Annie Hoban, and Robin Vincent, *How Can Complexity Theory Contribute to More Effective Development and Aid Evaluation?* (London: Panos London, 2009).

42. U.S. Agency for International Development, *USAID Evaluation Policy* (Washington DC: USAID, 2011), available at https://www.usaid.gov/sites/default/files/documents/1868/USAIDEvaluationPolicy.pdf, 8.

43. Jennifer Lentfer, "Imposing Risk-Averse Behaviour?," *Broker* (2012).

44. Sylvia Sukop, Joseph Tobin, and Gustavo E. Fischman, *Storytelling Approaches to Program Evaluation* (Los Angeles: California Endowment, 2007), 2.

45. Deborah Sole and Daniel G. Wilson, "Storytelling in Organizations: The Power and Traps of Using Stories to Share Knowledge in Organizations," *Training and Development* 53 (1999): 1–12.

46. K. Pottie et al., "Narrative Reports to Monitor and Evaluate the Integration of Pharmacists into Family Practice Settings," *Annals of Family Medicine* 6, no. 2 (2008): 161–65, available at https://doi.org/10.1370/afm.815.

47. Mudie Salm, "Stories," *Better Evaluation*, accessed January 2, 2018, http://www.betterevaluation.org/en/evaluation-options/stories.

48. Richard A. Krueger, "An Introduction to Using Stories in Research," University of Minnesota, Minneapolis, accessed January 2, 2018, https://richardmaryanne.files.wordpress.com/2015/07/an-introduction-to-story telling-in-research.doc.

49. I. Guijt and J. Hecklinger, "Making Sense of Sensemaker: Evaluating Development Initiatives through Micro-Narrative Capture and Self-Tagging in Kenya," PowerPoint presentation, American Evaluation Association, 2010, available at https://www.globalgiving.org/jcr-content/gg/landing-pages/story-tools/files/microsoft-powerpoint---makingsenseofsensemaker.pdf.

50. D. Casella et al., "The Triple-S Project SenseMaker Experience: A Method Tested and Rejected," Triple-S Working Paper 9 (2014); I. Guijt et al., "Evaluation Revisited: Improving the Quality of Evaluative Practice by Embracing Complexity" (Wageningen, Netherlands: Wageningen UR Centre for Development Innovation, 2010); and I. Guijt and T. Wind, "Evaluating Communicating for Influence: Guidance Notes for IDRC Grantees on Using Sense-Maker® to Evaluate Research Communications and Uptake" (IDRC, 2013).

51. Maxson, "*Real Book.*"

52. Girl Effect, "Unearthing the Wisdom."

53. Guijt and Hecklinger, "Making Sense of Sensemaker."

54. UNDP Regional Center for Europe and CIS, *Stories for Development.*

55. Catholic Relief Services, "Findings of the CRS SenseMaker Learning Pilot—Colombia" (Baltimore: CRS, 2015a); Catholic Relief Services, "Findings of the CRS SenseMaker Learning Pilot—India" (Baltimore: CRS, 2015b); and M. V. Gottret et al., "Findings of the CRS SenseMaker Learning Pilot—Nicaragua" (Baltimore: CRS, 2015).

56. Ibid.

57. M. V. Gottret, "Understanding and Assessing Resilience: A Sensemaker-Based Methodology" (Baltimore: CRS, 2017), available at https://

www.crs.org/sites/default/files/tools-research/learning-brief-sensemaker
_resilience-tool.pdf.

58. Lentfer, "Imposing Risk-Averse Behaviour?"

59. Andrea Cornwall, "Buzzwords and Fuzzwords: Deconstructing Development Discourse," *Development in Practice* 17, nos. 4–5 (2007): 471–84, available at https://doi.org/10.1080/09614520701469302.

60. L. M. Franco et al., "Sustaining Quality of Healthcare: Institutionalization of Quality Assurance," QA Monograph Series 2, no. 1, Bethesda, MD, 2002. Published for the U.S. Agency for International Development by the Quality Assurance Project.

61. For instance, the approaches described by J. K. Bass, P. A. Bolton, and L. K. Murray in "Do Not Forget Culture When Studying Mental Health," *Lancet* 370, no. 9591 (2007): 918–19, available at https://doi.org/S0140-6736(07)61426-3, and by P. A. Bolton et al. in "Interventions for Depression Symptoms among Adolescent Survivors of War and Displacement in Northern Uganda," *JAMA* 298, no. 5 (2007): 519–27.

62. See, for example, the debates raging over the term in end-of-life debates.

NINE

The Role of Human Dignity
in Integral Human Development

Martin Schlag

Development is more than economic growth. In this chapter I will argue that human development requires religion and religious freedom in order to be truly integral. Where there is religious freedom there is more space for human dignity. Obviously I am not saying that someone who is not religious cannot respect human dignity; furthermore, not being religious is precisely an attitude also protected by religious liberty.

In modern democracies, religion can be freely exercised as long as it is not incompatible with human dignity. We believe in religion "within the boundary of human dignity," to slightly modify Kant's expression.[1] Human dignity has been, in theory and in practice, a decisive motor of economic, social, and political development. It articulates itself institutionally and structurally by directing all socially relevant human activity toward the common good, especially politics and business. Concern for the poor and underprivileged leads us to include the marginalized in the production, distribution, and consumption of wealth. This implicit option for the poor was the historical starting point for the creation of the Christian concept of human dignity in the early Church, as I will show at the end of this chapter.

Thus religion can add and has added something very important to the understanding of human dignity. Human dignity plays an essential role both in opening up space for religion in modern liberal democracy and in promoting political and economic development. This role is expressed differently in the U.S.–American and in the European traditions. I will try to explain this difference. Throughout, my chapter is focused on Catholic social thought, and I will therefore try to find ways in which the originally Christian concept of human dignity can be made fruitful for civil law and for business even though the Church has renounced direct or indirect political power.

INTEGRAL HUMAN DEVELOPMENT AND RELIGIOUS FREEDOM

The Concept of Integral Human Development

First I turn to the concept of development that goes beyond mere economic growth. Amartya Sen, for instance, defines his capability approach to development as a focus "on human life, and not just on some detached objects of convenience, such as incomes or commodities that a person may possess, which are often taken, especially in economic analysis, to be the main criteria of human success." He seriously departs "from concentrating on the *means* of living to the *actual opportunities* of living."[2] On a somewhat different but substantially similar line, Angus Deaton concentrates on "well-being" that comprises "all things that are good for a person, that make for a good life."[3] This includes income and wealth, health and happiness, education, democratic participation, and the rule of law. The list Deaton presents is quite long compared to the triad the UN Human Development Index requires for human development: long and healthy life, knowledge, and a decent standard of living.[4] The definition by the UN is like a secular blueprint of the one given by Pope Benedict XVI in his encyclical *Caritas in veritate* on integral development. According to Catholic social thought, economic growth, in order to be fully human development, needs faith and positive affirmation of human life in families that are open to children.[5] Quoting three documents published by Pope Paul VI, Benedict XVI merges their three messages into the overall aim of integral human development: the well-known (and much-criticized) encyclical on the regulation of birth, *Humanae Vitae*, defends the openness of married couples to life; the well-known (and much-praised) encyclical on the development of peoples, *Populorum Progressio*, calls on Christians to contribute to international development; and, finally, the apostolic exhortation on the proclamation of the gospel, *Evangelii Nuntiandi*, propounds the beauty of announcing the good news and penetrating deeper into its contents.[6] All three together—life, economic growth, and faith—form the Catholic concept of integral human development. Furthermore, in *Caritas in veritate* Benedict XVI underscores the message that faith presupposes a radical openness to truth. Truth alone can set us free. He further points to the ethical dimension of development without which technology quickly becomes soulless and progress degenerates into dangerous manipulation.

The Role of Faith and Religious Liberty in Human Development

As I stated at the beginning of this chapter, in my reflections I would like to use the concept of integral human development as propounded by Catholic social thought.[7] Specifically I would like to concentrate on the role of the Christian faith, religious freedom, and human dignity in development. Faith is an important dimension of human life, be it in the positive sense of professing a creed or in the negative sense of not being forced into any religious establishment. Most if not all people would agree that living in accordance with one's conscience and free from impositions is a very important—perhaps even the most important—dimension of a fulfilled human life. Even if the struggle for mere survival is existentially pressing and inescapable on the level of basic animal needs, human life is guided by individual insight and free choice, that is, by reason and will. For the vast majority of people on this earth, this intellectual and spiritual dimension of human life includes a horizon of beliefs and transcendent values that we call religion. Religion is handed down to us through traditions; their contents, however, are individually appropriated and made one's own through inner consent. This is certainly true for the Christian tradition during the first centuries up to the emperor Constantine: the early Church Fathers underscored the impossibility of coercion in religious matters because religious violence produces only simulation and is unworthy of God. The inner act of trust in God's word and his revelation ("act of faith") can only be free. This insight, together with the axiom of human dignity, led the Catholic Church at the Second Vatican Council to declare religious freedom as a civil right.[8] Government should neither impose nor impede individual and collective manifestations and practices of religion. This harmonious and cooperative separation of state and religion is based on the Catholic conviction that both church and civic government derive their authority from God and have different competences: the church in spiritual affairs, the government in secular or civic ones. In practice, this distinction is not always easy to make; however, the principle is clear and is founded on Christ's command to give to Caesar what belongs to Caesar and to God what belongs to God.[9] Catholic social thought further teaches the moral ascendancy of the Christian faith over merely secular reason and also teaches that the authority of the Church judges all political actions by strictly moral (not political) standards insofar as the salvation of souls and the defense of human rights require. This competence refers to the infraction of moral absolutes that forbid the violation of a person's dignity, especially his right to life, freedom, and property and the basic tenets of the confession of Christ and life in Christ. Christianity, like other post-axial religions,[10] may even require that we renounce immanent goods we cherish for our material, social, and personal well-being in order to conserve the transcendent meaning of our lives, thus giving greater importance to spiritual aims than to material goods. Nevertheless, apart from these extreme moments of martyrdom, the Christian faith greatly contributes to human flourishing and to happiness on earth, and thus to development, by fostering the virtues and because of the unity of nature and grace. Human nature is directed toward its supernatural fulfillment. Even though human life is possible without grace, grace infuses supernatural charity and thereby leads virtuous human life to its perfection. Grace heals and elevates cultured human life to fulfillment.

Also, from a secular point of view, faith and spirituality are important for human development. Development is a shared public-private effort resulting both from long-term government intervention and from farsighted private initiative. For this one needs good governance.

Governance both in polities and in businesses is applied ethics. Governance requires strategy, and that, as a long-term horizon of an organization, is an inevitably ethical affair: it requires aims and goals that have the quality of ends. Ends of actions are open to ethical evaluation because they are not merely technical means (logic of utility) but also constitute the raison d'être of an entity (value logic). A mission statement is thus an ethical program. Besides, business strategy requires an ongoing balance between conservation and innovation. There are rules for this, but rules do not admit an infinite regress: there is no infinite chain of rules on the application of rules. It is impossible to govern organizations strategically only by rules. One needs the right values and all the virtues, particularly the virtue of practical wisdom.

Values without spiritual foundations, however, wither away like cut flowers in a vase. The Enlightenment was an attempt to maintain Christian values without Christ. As Alasdair MacIntyre has shown in theory—and as the course of Western history has in practice—that is not possible, at least not in the long run.

In this sense, religious moral messages are cultural factors worth taking into account both in politics and in business, also by mere standards of well-understood self-interest: after the collapse of the great ideologies, the only remaining creators of culture are the big world religions. Businesses that neglect religion completely might be making a strategic error.

Transformative Accommodation of Religion in Secular Society

The massive immigration of Muslims to Europe and elsewhere has precipitated reflections on the way religion should express itself in the Western public and, in consequence, has led our society to reflect on its own secularity. An example of such a reflection is the proposal by former archbishop of Canterbury professor Rowan Williams to use the concept of human dignity for a "transformative accommodation" of Sharia law in the English legal system.[11] Williams was aiming to defend the rights of religious groups and of religion as such in the public sphere of secular society.[12] He was thinking of a coalition of religions under the leadership of Christianity to achieve exemptions from civil law for reasons of conscientious objection. Without using the Catholic expression "natural law," the idea of a set of binding moral norms before and above positive law is apparent in his words. They are inspired by the conviction that our identity in society is not exhaustively defined by only one form of belonging. There are at least two ways in which we belong to a society: one is through citizenship in a civil legal order; the other—for believers—stems from a "non-negotiable level of reality" that is defined by a covenant between God and creation.[13] Nonbelievers may have other forms of belonging that shape their identity. These two forms of belonging (citizenship and religious belief) do not exclude but rather complement and condition each other. The harmony between the two orders is endangered by religious fanaticism and extremism (which negates independent civil citizenship) on the one hand and, on the other hand, by the attempt of secular states to create an exclusive monopoly on defining public identity by purely secular standards. Contrary to this secular monopoly, modern civic governments should realize that it is religious and other forms of social diversity that allow identity to take shape. We define our identity not only by referring to bigger entities like nations but also by feeling at home in communities, for instance, in religions. Smaller entities that create identity need not apply to governments for permission to come into being but have an original right to exist. Therefore, belonging to one of these groups should not diminish or curtail our civic rights and duties in an overarching legally constituted society. Williams redefines the function of the rule of law in the secular state, and it is in this context that he uses the concept of human dignity:

> The rule of law is thus not the enshrining of priority for the universal/abstract dimension of social existence but the establishing of a space accessible to everyone in which it is possible to affirm and defend a commitment to human dignity *as such*, independent of membership in any specific human community or tradition, so that, when specific communities or traditions are in danger of claiming finality for their own boundaries of practice and understanding, they are reminded that they have to come to terms with the actuality of human diversity—and that the only way of doing this is to acknowledge the category of "human dignity as such," a nonnegotiable assumption that each agent (with his or her historical and social affiliations) could be expected to have a voice in the

shaping of some common project for the well-being and order of a human group.[14]

Williams envisages competing legal systems in one and the same society that vie with each other for their citizens'/members' loyalty.[15] However, each of these systems must comply with the requirements of human dignity, for example, the individual rights of women must not be curtailed or violated. In practice, we could imagine a system like that in some American states, in which the canonical marriage of Catholics is recognized as legally valid by the state legislature. Extending this to Sharia law should be possible as long as human dignity and individual freedom are respected, says Williams. In a facultative and alternative way, those norms of Sharia law that concur with the values of human dignity and freedom could be applied to Muslims by English courts and administration. Some Muslim women have severely criticized Williams's proposal as dangerously naïve and utterly irresponsible. In practice, it would abandon female members of Muslim minority groups to a legal order that systematically and on principle treats women as inferior beings.[16] Here I am not advocating for the implementation of Williams's proposal but underscoring the importance human dignity plays in the European discourse on religious rights.

Williams's criteria for inclusion are in coherence with the jurisdiction of the European Court of Human Rights, according to which religious practices must "be worthy of respect in a democratic society and ... not incompatible with human dignity."[17] This formula serves as a kind of threshold test for the applicability of Article 9 of the European Convention of Human Rights, which protects religious freedom. In Europe, human dignity functions legally as a kind of metaprinciple for all human rights contained in the European Convention of Human Rights. Human dignity plays a central normative role as a legal concept in the European juridical tradition, albeit in different degrees according to the national system involved. Its clearest formulation is to be found in the German Basic Law in which human dignity is enshrined as the highest constitutional norm.

In contrast, the U.S. Supreme Court, in its detailed jurisdiction on religious freedom, has not returned to the *topos* of human dignity.[18] This is no coincidence. The U.S. Constitution does not contain human dignity as a formal legal concept, nor has the Supreme Court developed a human right to dignity, as it has done rights to privacy, freedom, due procedure, equality, and so on. Human dignity in the United States is thus a "legal alien" and in no way the highest constitutional norm. Leon R. Kass has explained the situation: "In contrast to continental Europe and even Canada, human dignity has not been a powerful idea in American public discourse, devoted as we are instead to the language of rights and the pursuit of equality. Among us, the very idea of 'dignity' smacks too much of aristocracy for egalitarians and too much of religion for secularists and libertarians. Moreover, it seems to be too private and vague a matter to be the basis for legislation or public policy."[19]

Nevertheless, the notion of human dignity has also been pivotal in American public discourse and in the development of U.S. law. I refer to the *word* "dignity" *and* the underlying *concept* of respect for the individual human person, as well as the moral prohibition against instrumentalizing anyone, treating him or her as a mere means. The appreciation for individual human dignity in the United States has led to institutional and structural consequences in laws, politics, and also business. Suffice it to mention the civil rights movement and the ensuing laws against slavery, racism, and segregation; against experiments on nonconsenting patients; against the exploitation of workers; and against drugs, prostitution, and self-mutilation. They are all expressions of respect for human dignity even though they are clad in the language of individual rights or the protection of society. Human dignity serves as a secondary juridical argument in legislation, administration, and jurisdiction that adds clout to the primary normative arguments based on the rights of the U.S. legal tradition. Human dignity thus exercises an indirect normative influence primarily in new fields such as bioethics and bio law.[20]

THE INSTITUTIONAL ARTICULATION OF HUMAN DIGNITY

Human Dignity in Business and Economy

Human dignity has also played an important role in business ethics in the United States, perhaps because it is a relatively new field of applied ethics and less attached to the U.S. legal tradition than strictly juridical questions. Business ethics thus tends to be a field that is wide open to international discourse.

Starting with a seminal article written by Robert W. Johnson in 1949, human dignity has played a decisive role in rethinking the relationship between owners, management, and employees.²¹ Johnson referred to an essentially Christian notion of human dignity seen as intrinsically shaped by the relational character of the human being. His insights, however, were mainly ignored and gave way to a more technical and skill-oriented approach in business management education. It was only and especially after the financial crisis in 2007 that the intellectual movement really began to place the human person at the center of all social and economic dealings. This conviction has found expression in calls to rethink the way business works. Human dignity and the common good have been invoked as guidelines. In this context we must mention, among others, Domènec Melé, Michael Naughton, Alejo José G. Sison, and Joan Fontrodona, who have promoted both personalism (human dignity) and the common good as pillars of business and organizations.²²

All of these authors are influenced by Catholic social thought and frequently refer to it. In the literature we find a shared conviction that the principles of human dignity and the common good express two sides of the same coin: the personalist principle refers to the individual dimension, the common good principle to the relational dimension of the human person. As individuals we are born with inalienable rights that are not granted to us by society or political authority but are recognized and protected and, therefore, cannot be revoked by those who hold power. Human dignity, to the contrary, means that we possess and exercise our individual rights on our own authority as human beings. In the German constitutional tradition, human dignity has therefore been called the "right to rights."²³ On the other hand, from the very moment of our conception we are inserted and born into relationships. As persons our lives are not fully human, we cannot develop as humans or flourish culturally, without interaction with our fellow human persons. We depend on others who, in their turn, depend on us; we are intertwined, and this mesh of lives and this communality of dependencies is the common good. The common good is the *bonum communionis*, the good of sharing and living together. People who in no way interact with each other do not together form a common good.

The Common Good and Integral Human Development

The common good is more than the sum of individual goods. It is a good of its own kind, which we could call the "good of communality" or the good of being together. The common good exists only as a shared experience of life. Thus, contrary to individual goods, it grows through consumption. An example might make the idea clearer: the food we eat diminishes the more people partake of it, and each morsel of food that an individual eats is exclusively his. However, the more people eat together in friendship, the greater the experience of sharing a common meal becomes. This act of sharing and eating together is the common good of the meal. The food is a divisible good that must be attributed to individuals in order to be of effect and diminishes through consumption. The common good of the meal is not the food but the fact of eating together. The common good grows through consumption, just as muscles expand when they are exercised. I once heard a Chinese comparison between heaven and hell that expresses the idea of the common good: hell is a room with a big table full of bowls of delicious steaming rice. People sit around the table, and each has chopsticks in his or her hands to eat the rice. However, the chopsticks are so long that nobody is able to eat; instead, each pokes the others in the eyes each time they attempt to feed themselves with the chopsticks. There ensues a constant and bitter fight, and consequently people starve in front of the bowls of food. Heaven is quite different: the room is the same, the table with the rice bowls is the same, even the chopsticks are just as long and cumbersome. However, instead of fighting, the diners feed each other in sublime harmony. They have a real common good. The common good is not the sum of individual goods but a product of multiplication. In a sum, if one of the numbers in the series is zero, the sum remains the same; the zero does not take away from the sum of the others. In multiplication, if one of the factors is zero, the result is always zero even if the other factors are enormous. In an analogous way, if the dignity of a human person is downtrodden in any form of community of persons—a business firm, a married couple, or a group of friends, for example—the common good is destroyed.[24] It is easy to see how important these ideas are for the notion of integral human development. Without a clear orientation toward the common good, there is no development. What does this specifically mean? Are there concrete applications of this for the markets and for businesses?

Applications of the Common Good Principle in Business

Businesses, when they are ethically conducted, in and of themselves contribute to the common good without any additional extrinsic orientation toward it. However, being ethical is never an easy affair, and it certainly does not come automatically. It is a cultural and anthropological achievement. Being ethical requires a firm orientation toward the common good, which is the aim of all social ethics, business ethics, and law. So we seem to end up in a tautology: being ethical requires the common good, and the common good requires ethical behavior. However, no tautology comes to bear in this case because the common good logically comes first. With this I mean to say that private rights to property, to free commerce, and to other moral principles and social institutions are justified by their efficiency and contribution to a peaceful common life. Friendship among humans comes first, as Thomas Aquinas has beautifully expressed it, in an unknowing inversion of Thomas Hobbes *ante litteram*: "*Homo naturaliter est omni homini amicus*" (Every man is naturally friendly toward all other men).[25] Certainly, in our modern and largely anonymous world, this friendship might not be felt immediately, but its aggregate effects are nevertheless tangible. Extreme individualism that excludes consideration for others and isolates people from one another is incompatible with business as a moral calling.

Directing business toward the common good means, among other consequences, that profit maximization cannot be the only aim of businesses; they bear a social and ecological responsibility. Needless to say, profit is an irrefutable goal of any business, but a business's aim is also to create an atmosphere of intense and decent work that goes beyond profit and makes as many people as possible share in the value during the process of production and not only afterward through redistribution. The common good implies respecting the workers' rights as they have developed over the past century. Additionally, in the era of globalization there is a growing awareness of the need to include the poor in the production, distribution, and consumption of wealth.[26]

This program of inclusion resonates strongly with the social teaching of Pope Francis. The pontiff from Argentina defines "poverty" as exclusion from an important aspect of dignity: "There is no worse material poverty, I am keen to stress, than the poverty which prevents people from earning their bread and deprives them of the dignity of work."[27] His calls to "resolve the structural causes of poverty" are constant: "Welfare projects, which meet certain urgent needs, should be considered merely temporary responses. As long as the problems of the poor are not radically resolved by rejecting the absolute autonomy of markets and financial speculation and by attacking the structural causes of inequity, no solution will be found for the world's problems or, for that matter, to any problems. Inequity is the root of social ills."[28]

These words link human dignity with agency and work: earning one's bread through work increases one's self-esteem and respect in society. Certainly, esteem (be it self-esteem or that granted by others) and respect are not the same as dignity. Esteem and respect have to do with (self-)recognition, whereas dignity is something that can be neither granted nor taken away, prevailing even in the face of public scorn and shame. Nevertheless, dignity has to do with integral human flourishing and fulfillment, an important part of which normally is constituted by good and honorable relationships in society. Therefore, it is not surprising that business plays an important role in this vision of the pope: "Business is a noble vocation, directed to producing wealth and improving our world. It can be a fruitful source of prosperity for the areas in which it operates, especially if it sees the creation of jobs as an essential part of its service to the common good."[29]

In these words we discover an immediate connection with the common good. Pope Francis actually redefines the notion of the common good from the perspective of the preferential option for the poor:

In the present condition of global society, where injustices abound and growing numbers of people are deprived of basic human rights and considered expendable, the principle of the common good immediately becomes, logically and inevitably, a summons to solidarity and a preferential option for the poorest of our brothers and sisters. This option entails recognizing the implications of the universal destination of the world's goods, but, as I mentioned in the

Apostolic Exhortation *Evangelii Gaudium*, it demands before all else an appreciation of the immense dignity of the poor in the light of our deepest convictions as believers. We need only look around us to see that, today, this option is in fact an ethical imperative essential for effectively attaining the common good.[30]

Clearly, there are limits to the common good rhetoric. When politicians speak a lot about the common good, they probably wish to raise taxes, which, as we know, does not always stimulate growth or contribute to social justice. More often than not, it serves to finance an overgrown bureaucracy, to maintain a class of rentiers who live off the interests of public debt, or is wasted in inefficient public expenditure. However, the Pope's words should stimulate an examination of conscience, because specifically Christian culture begins with love for the poor.[31] Any pagan can love the rich, but Christ explicitly exhorts his followers to invite to our gatherings those who cannot reciprocate. This radical inversion of the antique social pyramid was fundamental for the development of the concept of human dignity in the Western world in the early Christian era. Human dignity is an authentically Christian concept that was formed through a combination of the Roman legal and social concept of *dignitas* and the biblical notion of *imago Dei*. Its revolutionary potential was primed by the notion of the gratuity of grace and equality in Christ. The early Fathers of the Church created this explosive charge and made it the foundation of antique society: it blew up the Roman social pyramid of honor. In the pagan world dignity was earned through prowess in battle. First a Roman man had to prove his virtue, he acquired merit, and then he was granted dignity.[32] In the Christian view, God gives dignity freely. As his adopted children in Christ, we need not earn it, but once we have received this dignity of divine filiation we are called to a moral life of virtue through which we merit the eternal reward.[33] Human dignity in the Christian sense thus possesses a minimum (ontological) expression that cannot be lost: every human being, by the mere fact of existing, possesses it. There is, however, also a maximum (moral) expression of dignity, to which we are called and which we cannot attain without God's grace and the gifts of the Holy Spirit: holiness, a virtuous and saintly life, independent of whether we are "free or slave, Greek or Jew, man or woman."[34]

Historically speaking, the first Christians came mainly from the lower levels of ancient society. This message was especially attractive to them. With Michael Rosen we can consider Christianity as a propulsive force in the "expanding circle narrative" regarding the idea of human dignity: formerly a quality confined to social elites, it expanded out and down until it referred to all humans.[35] And thus the circle of religious freedom, human dignity, and integral development closes conceptually but remains an open challenge for our actions.

NOTES

1. Immanuel Kant, *Religion within the Boundary of Pure Reason*, first published in German in 1793 under the title *Die Religion innerhalb der Grenzen der bloßen Vernunft*.

2. Amartya Sen, *The Idea of Justice* (London: Penguin Books, 2010), 233.

3. Angus Deaton, *The Great Escape: Health, Wealth, and the Origins of Inequality* (Princeton, NJ: Princeton University Press, 2013), 24.

4. See United Nations Development Programme, "Human Development Index (HDI)," http://hdr.undp.org/en/content/human-development-index-hdi.

5. See Benedict XVI, encyclical letter *Caritas in veritate*, June 29, 2009 (Vatican City: Libreria Editrice Vaticana, 2009).

6. See Benedict XVI, *Caritas in veritate*, 15, and Paul VI, encyclical letter *Humanae Vitae*, July 25, 1968; encyclical letter *Populorum Progressio*, March 26, 1967; and apostolic exhortation *Evangelii Nuntiandi*, December 8, 1975.

7. For a study on development and human dignity according to Catholic social thought, see also Charles M. A. Clark, "From *The Wealth of Nations* to *Populorum Progressio* (On the Development of Peoples): Wealth and Development from the Perspective of the Catholic Social Thought Tradition," *American Journal of Economics and Sociology* 71, no. 4 (2012): 1047–72. For more general notions on the creation of wealth and Catholic social thought, see Helen Alford, Charles M. A. Clark, S. A. Cortright, and Michael J. Naughton, eds., *Rediscovering Abundance: Interdisciplinary Essays on Wealth, Income, and Their Distribution in the Catholic Social Tradition* (Notre Dame, IN: University of Notre Dame Press, 2006).

8. The process that led up to the Second Vatican Council's declaration on religious freedom, *Dignitatis Humanae*, was long and complex and is not the subject of this chapter. For a short introduction, see Kenneth D. Whitehead,

Affirming Religious Freedom: How Vatican Council II Developed the Church's Teaching to Meet Today's Needs (New York: St. Pauls, 2010); a detailed account is given by Joseph Lecler in *Toleration and the Reformation*, 2 vols. (London: Longmans, 1960).

9. See Matt. 22:21, Mark 12:17, and Luke 20:25.

10. The expression "post-axial" was introduced by Karl Jaspers in his book *Vom Ursprung und Ziel der Geschichte* (Munich: Piper, 1949). Since then it has become a standard notion in the sociology of religion. For further reading, see Robert N. Bellah and Hans Joas, eds., *The Axial Age and Its Consequences* (Cambridge, MA, and London: Belknap Press of Harvard University Press, 2012). An axial religion is characterized by the discovery of the preeminence of divine transcendent values over immanent human ones.

11. Rowan Williams, "Civil and Religious Law in England: A Religious Perspective," in *Islam and English Law: Rights, Responsibilities and the Place of Shari'a*, ed. Robin Griffith-Jones (Cambridge: Cambridge University Press, 2013), 20–33.

12. Williams might be slightly too accommodating regarding the Sharia, especially in the European context. The European Court of Human Rights (ECHR) has declared Sharia incompatible with the European Convention on Human Rights. See the sentence of the ECHR, handed down on February 13, 2003, in the Refah case: http://www.google.de/url?url=http://hudoc.echr.coe.int/app/conversion/pdf/%3Flibrary%3DECHR%26id%3D003-698131-706228%26filename%3D003-698131-706228.pdf&rct=j&frm=1&q=&esrc=s&sa=U&ved=0ahUKEwjB0sa6gc7RAhXDuBoKHYsgDoAQFggUMAA&usg=AFQjCNENIF434ODND4xg_jJCPs4QVoF-jw.

13. Williams, "Civil and Religious Law in England," 23.

14. Ibid., 30.

15. Ibid., 32.

16. See Elham Manea, *Women and Shari'a Law* (London and New York: I. B.Tauris, 2016), 91–95.

17. See Christopher McCrudden, "Dignity and Religion," in *Islam and English Law: Rights, Responsibilities and the Place of Shari'a*, ed. Robin Griffith-Jones (Cambridge: Cambridge University Press, 2013), 94–106. Here McCrudden quotes the sentence of the ECHR in *Campbell and Cosans v. United Kingdom* (1982), 4 EHRR 293, para. 36.

18. For a general overview, see Richard J. Regan, *The American Constitution and Religion* (Washington, DC: Catholic University of America Press, 2013), 25–41. In this chapter I do not intend to make an elaborate comparison or distinction between the United States and Europe but rather to hint at the differences in an illustrative manner.

204 THE PRACTICE OF HUMAN DEVELOPMENT AND DIGNITY

19. Leon R. Kass, "Defending Human Dignity," in *Human Dignity and Bioethics: Essays Commissioned by the President's Council on Bioethics*, ed. President's Council on Bioethics (Washington, DC, 2008), 297–331.

20. See Carter Snead, "Human Dignity in US Law," in *The Cambridge Handbook of Human Dignity: Interdisciplinary Perspectives*, ed. Marcus Düwell, Jens Braarvig, Roger Brownsword, and Dietmar Mieth (Cambridge: Cambridge University Press, 2014), 386–93.

21. Robert W. Johnson, "Human Relations in Modern Business," *Harvard Business Review* 27 (1949): 521–41.

22. Domènec Melé, "Integrating Personalism into Virtue-Based Business Ethics: The Personalist and the Common Good Principles," *Journal of Business Ethics* 88 (2009): 227–44. Melé gives an overview of the *status quaestionis* of business ethics, proposing an integration of personalism into virtue ethics through the dual principles of the dignity of the human person and the common good; for an overview of theories on the organization of businesses, see Domènec Melé, "The Firm as a 'Community of Persons': A Pillar of Humanistic Business *Ethos*," *Journal of Business Ethics* 106 (2012): 89–101. In the light of virtue ethics and Catholic social tradition, Melé proposes community as the correct notion for the building of relationships in firms. Everything in the firm is directed toward the common good. See also Alejo José G. Sison and Joan Fontrodona, "The Common Good of Business: Addressing a Challenge Posed by *Caritas in veritate*," *Journal of Business Ethics* 100 (2011): 99–107. The authors take up the challenge posed by Pope Benedict XVI to rethink business. They propose the common good as the framework for this change. The same authors expand on these notions in Alejo José G. Sison and Joan Fontrodona, "The Common Good of the Firm in the Aristotelian-Thomistic Tradition," *Business Ethics Quarterly* 22, no. 2 (2012): 211–46. The authors continue their reflections by applying the notion of the common good of the firm to the different players and roles in the firm; see Alejo José G. Sison and Joan Fontrodona, "Participating in the Common Good of the Firm," *Journal of Business Ethics* 113 (2013): 611–25, and Alford et al., *Rediscovering Abundance*, which contains useful reflections on Catholic social thought in the American cultural context.

23. See Christoph Enders, *Die Menschenwürde in der Verfassungsordnung* (Tübingen: Mohr Siebeck, 1997), 501.

24. See Alberto Lo Presti, "Bene comune," in *Dizionario di Economia Civile*, ed. Luigino Bruni and Stefano Zamagni (Rome: Città Nuova, 2009), 80–89.

25. Thomas Aquinas, *Summa Theologiae*, II-II, q. 157, a. 3, ad 3. Centuries later, Thomas Hobbes would write: "*Homo homini lupus*" (Every man is a wolf

for all other men) in *On the Citizen*, ed. Richard Tuck and Michael Silver-thorne (Cambridge: Cambridge University Press, 1998), 3.

26. See, for instance, Rüdiger Hahn, "Inclusive Business, Human Rights and the Dignity of the Poor: A Glance Beyond Economic Impacts of Adapted Business Models," *Business Ethics: A European Review* 21, no. 1 (2012): 47–63.

27. Francis, "Address to the Centesimus Annus Pro Pontifice Foundation," May 25, 2013, http://w2.vatican.va/content/francesco/en/speeches /2013/may/documents/papa-francesco_20130525_centesimus-annus-pro -pontifice.html.

28. Francis, apostolic exhortation *Evangelii Gaudium* (Vatican City: Libreria Editrice Vaticana, November 24, 2013), 202. In a footnote the pope adds: "This implies a commitment to 'eliminate the structural causes of global economic dysfunction,'" citing Benedict XVI, "Address to the Diplomatic Corps," January 8, 2007, http://w2.vatican.va/content/benedict -xvi/en/speeches/2007/january/documents/hf_ben-xvi_spe_20070108 _diplomatic-corps.html, 73. It is noted that I have changed the quotation from the official English translation at the Vatican website: I have translated the first word of the final sentence of the quotation as "inequity," because the official translation says "inequality," which is incorrect. The Spanish original speaks of *inequidad*, meaning inequity or unjust inequality, not *desigualdad*, meaning inequality.

29. Francis, encyclical letter *Laudato Si'*, May 24, 2015, 129.

30. Ibid., 158, quoting Francis, *Evangelii Gaudium*, 186–201.

31. See Francis, "Address to Participants in the Ecclesial Convention of the Diocese of Rome," June 17, 2013, http://w2.vatican.va/content/francesco /en/speeches/2013/june/documents/papa-francesco_20130617_convegno -diocesano-roma.html.

32. See Josiah Ober, "Meritocratic and Civic Dignity in Greco-Roman Antiquity," in *The Cambridge Handbook of Human Dignity: Interdisciplinary Perspectives*, ed. Marcus Düwell, Jens Braarvig, Roger Brownsword, and Dietmar Mieth (Cambridge: Cambridge University Press, 2014), 53–63.

33. St. Paul develops a Christological anthropology with the aim of universalizing salvation beyond the limits of the Jewish race (Rom. 3:21–31). Not the human person, but Christ, is the true image of God, the firstborn of creation (Col. 1:15–20). We are images of Christ, God's image, through our incorporation into Christ through baptism (Rom. 8:18–30 and 1 Cor. 12:12–13). All people can belong to Christ, even those who do not belong to the Jewish race: this is Paul's message, not a reduction of the dignity of

Christians alone. Reading this into Paul would be an anachronistic projection of modern problems into the scriptures. It would be *eisegesis* and not *exegesis*.

34. Gal. 3:28.

35. See Michael Rosen, *Dignity: Its History and Meaning* (Cambridge, MA: Harvard University Press, 2012), 8.

TEN

Reciprocity and Trust as the Telos of the Market

The Civil Economy Perspective

Luigino Bruni

It is true that certain living creatures, as bees and ants, live sociably one with another . . . and therefore some man may perhaps desire to know why mankind cannot do the same.

—Thomas Hobbes, *Leviathan*

Homo homini natura amicus (Man is by nature friend to man).
—Antonio Genovesi, *De iure et officiis*

If we seek the original meaning of the Latin word *dignitas*, dignity, we find that "dign" and "dignus" meant "merit." From merit comes "deserving," and also "decent" and "decor." So dignity requires merit, and esteem, for the person with dignity. Not all forms of cooperation respect the dignity of all partners involved. The invention of the market economy has been mainly the introduction of a new form of cooperation among equals, which represents a true human innovation if measured in terms of dignity. Reciprocity is the telos (true nature) of the market, at least in that philosophy of market and civil society known as the civil economy.

In this chapter I will present and discuss the civil economy idea of cooperation and trust and then conclude with a discussion of the market seen as cooperation among equals with dignity.

THE CIVIL ECONOMY TRADITION

In the eighteenth century, the goal of the Neapolitan school of civil economy was mainly (though not exclusively)[1] the development of a civil and Franciscan humanistic ethics built around the concept of *philia* (civil friendship) but also influenced to some extent by Christian *agape* (love).[2] We can also think of the Neapolitan tradition as a development of the same cultural humanism that began with Aristotle and was then taken further with the Roman republican thought of Cicero, Sallust, and Seneca. The same project was later picked up and "Christianized" by Aquinas and by the Franciscan school until the synthesis of civil humanism in the fifteenth century. After the Renaissance and into modernity, we observe the first real break in this tradition, which we have termed "classic," when, in the passage from Martin Luther to Thomas Hobbes, life in common was reformed on new anthropological grounds. We have already mentioned how *philia* would then evolve (or regress) into market exchange.

The Neapolitan school of civil economy, thanks to the critical role of mediation played by Giambattista Vico (who transformed this tradition from classic into modern, yet without subscribing to Hobbes's anthropological arguments), made the last significant attempt to graft the classic tradition into modernity by offering a view of the market as reciprocity, *fides* (faith), and *philia*. This tradition never became prevalent in the modern social sciences. Nonetheless, it remains alive today, and it has continued to flow "underground" through this important stretch of time.

In this chapter I consider the possibility of conceiving of the market as a civil fraternity. I have championed this theoretical claim for about a decade now, together with the economist and philosopher Robert Sugden, who, while also drawing from David Hume, Adam Smith, Friedrich Hayek, and James Buchanan, found in Antonio Genovesi as well as in the civil economy an important source of inspiration for a different ethos of the market.[3]

At the center of Genovesi's thought and the tradition of the civil economy is the notion of "mutual assistance," a qualified form of reciprocity that was considered to be the telos of the market. The idea of the market as mutual assistance makes the working of the market somewhat less mysterious than does the Smithian metaphor of the invisible hand. Anyone who has had the experience of teaching economic theory knows with what surprise students typically react when they find themselves confronted, pretty immediately, with the logic of market exchange. In people's minds a sort of mercantile fallacy seems to exist that is more pervasive than ordinarily thought (or at least more so than we economists ordinarily think). This fallacy has various manifestations that lie in the background of common sense in the understanding of economic matters. A first and deeply rooted fallacy consists in conceiving political economy as a sort of household management: it consists in picturing the economy of a large collectivity (state, city, etc.) as more or less like the economy of a family (the Greeks' *oikos-nomos*). If a family undergoes a moment of crisis, parents have to solve the crisis (by working more, saving, redistributing wealth and resources within the family, etc.); similarly, one could think, if a state undergoes an economic crisis, politics can and must solve the problems and can, for instance, find a solution to world poverty simply by redistributing wealth from the more affluent to the poor. Reasoning in these terms, one falls into this mercantile fallacy by carrying out the same reasoning as those seventeenth-century economists who understood national economy as like domestic economy and ascribed the most critical role to politics and to the king.[4]

A second "fallacy" is more directly related to the nature of the market. This consists in thinking of the market as a "zero-sum game" (an exchange in which there is a given cake, and the various slices are ascribed through negotiation to the participants in the game). This was also originally a mercantile idea according to which commerce (international commerce in particular) was thought of as enriching one part (those importing gold and silver) and impoverishing another (which, in the exchange, lost gold or silver). This second fallacy is what leads those who have little understanding of economic theory to deny the idea that when the market exists and functions properly all those involved in the exchange may have the chance of improving their initial position (although not all in the same way, as asymmetries may exist). As a matter of fact, if one thinks of the market as based on individual interests, what comes to mind are cases in which a subject benefits in an opportunistic way to the detriment of another.

By focusing on mutual assistance and collective advantage, as we have seen, Genovesi directed his students to look at the market (and, in general, at civil society) as a large space in which there are opportunities to trade that lead to mutual advantages (the most important of which consists in creating markets capable of replacing feudal society).[5] This view of the market makes it harder to understand the linkage between mutual interest and the common good because the actor's intention in this case is also oriented to the advantage of those with whom he or she interacts on the market. In mutual assistance—unlike in Smith's theory of the invisible hand—a direct connection arises between the agents' intentions and the effects of their actions. The possibility of friendship, or *civil fraternity*, as a market paradigm also derives from this approach: the market has a certain moral content (and morality directly refers to intentions), and well-functioning societies require that this moral sense be fostered and made explicit.

In the civil economy, a market that shows a moral and fraternal attitude does not necessarily imply (nor does it exclude) the renunciation of one's own material gain to the benefit of one's partner in the exchange. Genovesi explains that it is possible to maintain a fraternal attitude toward those taking part in a market exchange, without necessarily having to embrace altruism.

For this reason, the civil economy is different from today's prevailing understanding of market relations. Two aspects mark this distinction and indicate its significance. The first aspect, clearly visible in Smith's theory of the "butcher, the baker, and the brewer," is the idea that partners in a market exchange are mutually indifferent and that the market, when competitive, in the words of philosopher David Gauthier, is a "morally free zone"—that is, a zone in which there are no moral constraints.[6] In such an approach, which we have referred to as Smithian, the beneficial consequences of the markets in terms of development and wealth are nonintentional. In this sense, market relations are not substantially *social*.

We must observe that if there is a sphere of genuinely social human relations, it exists outside the market and is characterized by relational forms that cannot be found within market interaction. In fact, economists, yesterday as today—even those who are more tightly inscribed within the official tradition of economics—typically believe that this sphere of "genuine" social relations may exist only in family life, in friendship, and in various forms of civil commitment; however, ordinarily, these spheres have been thought of as having nothing, or too little, to do with the economic sphere. This is a point on which the tradition of the civil economy differs from the Anglo-American tradition, which has become mainstream.

HOW TO ANALYZE SOCIALITY IN ECONOMICS

Aside from "mutual indifference," or social neutrality, there is a second dimension that characterizes the conventional notion of the market and is significant for the sake of our discussion about the ethos of the market. This second dimension is not so much the product of Smith's own thought but rather of the post-Smithian developments in economic science in recent decades. I am referring to the idea that the concern, or the unconcern, of an individual for another is a matter of *individual preferences*. To say that a certain person A has a concern for another person B basically means that, according to A's preferences, B will attain a higher level of consumption or income and that, as a consequence of these preferences, A is willing to *sacrifice* part of his or her own consumption (or income) in order to improve B's situation.[7]

According to this perspective—which is still present today in the strands of economics that deal with behaviors that are not self-interested—being genuinely social means having "other-regarding" preferences, that is, being willing to sacrifice part of one's own advantages for the benefit of others. In contemporary economic theory, social (or other-regarding) preferences are normally translated by assuming a certain degree of altruism, that is, a person's positive concern for the consumption or well-being of another.

Recently, more specific models have been developed, often based on experimental lab evidence. For instance, Gary Bolton and Axel Ockenfels have found that people (some people, at least) have preferences that are sensitive to differences between their own income and the income of others; they have found, in other words, that people are "inequality averse."[8] In "Incorporating Fairness," Matthew Rabin has suggested, instead, that preferences are informed by "reciprocity," leading people to reward those who behaved "kindly" to them in the former round of an interaction (assuming a sequential game) and to punish those who didn't.

What these theories have in common is that the element that determines whether preferences are "social" is typically revealed by one's willingness to sacrifice one's own interest in order to reward or punish others; also, it should be noted, such models represent an important innovation in economic theory, and they must be met with satisfaction by those wishing to enrich the anthropological basis of economic and social science. The basic game in these models (which are for the most part experimental or theoretical) is the so-called Trust Game.[9] If we reduced the game to its most basic structure, it could be illustrated as follows in figure 10.1.

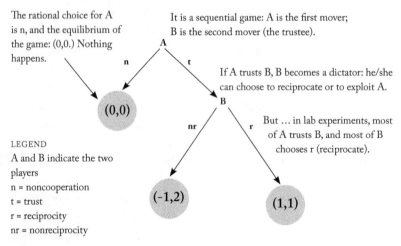

The rational choice for A is n, and the equilibrium of the game: (0,0.) Nothing happens.

It is a sequential game: A is the first mover; B is the second mover (the trustee).

If A trusts B, B becomes a dictator: he/she can choose to reciprocate or to exploit A.

But ... in lab experiments, most of A trusts B, and most of B chooses r (reciprocate).

A

n   t

(0,0)

B

nr   r

LEGEND
A and B indicate the two players
n = noncooperation
t = trust
r = reciprocity
nr = nonreciprocity

(-1,2)   (1,1)

FIGURE 10.1. The Trust Game

Standard theory (rational choice theory) excludes the possibility that A may rationally trust B since it assumes that if A chooses to trust B (*t*), A knows that B will then compare 2 with 1 and eventually decide not to reciprocate A's trust, thus resulting in A's receiving −1 (below 0, which represents the status quo).[10] Therefore, the only equilibrium of the game, in a nonrepeated framework, is (0,0): A ends the game after the first move (*n*).

The theory of social preferences, in turn, envisions the possibility that A may rationally trust B based on the assumption that if A believes B to have social preferences (and believes, therefore, that B might reciprocate A's initial kindness at his own expense in the second round), A may play "*t*" in the expectation that B, in view of his social preferences, may play "*r*," thus reaching the equilibrium (1,1), *where both agents are better off compared to the status quo* (0,0).

This theory certainly seems in line with Genovesi's understanding of the economy, but with an important difference. Rabin's theory (and in general most of the theories of reciprocity based on social preferences)[11] allows one to reach the cooperative outcome in a trust game[12] because the theory (and, hence, also the game's payoffs)[13] includes this kind of social preference, which reflects a sort of mutual sacrifice. Here the status quo is (−1,2) and both agents renounce something in order to reward a "social" behavior of the other player (see figure 10.2).

What difference is there compared to the civil economy perspective? Considering the theory of *social preferences* we will see that *in fact* the

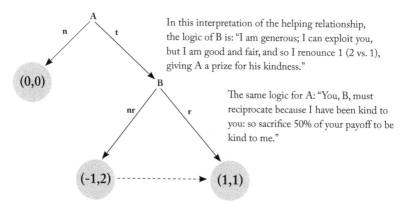

In this interpretation of the helping relationship, the logic of B is: "I am generous; I can exploit you, but I am good and fair, and so I renounce 1 (2 vs. 1), giving A a prize for his kindness."

The same logic for A: "You, B, must reciprocate because I have been kind to you: so sacrifice 50% of your payoff to be kind to me."

FIGURE 10.2. The Trust Game: The "Sacrifice" Frame

relation between the agents does produce a mutual benefit. But—and this is the point—the intentional content of the relation is not mutual advantage, but rather the punishment or reward of one player according to the other's preferences. In these models and games there is no notion of a "joint action" or of "mutual advantage"; the players remain separate and independent individuals.

On the other hand, taking inspiration from the civil economy tradition, we may describe the Trust Game (and trust phenomena in general) in a different way. Let us go back to the representation of the Trust Game: in this picture, figure 10.3, I have again highlighted two outcomes: (0,0) and (1,1). A "Genovesian" view of the civil economy suggests that the players, in order to regard the game in a correct and civilly fruitful way (dotted arrow), ought to compare (0,0) and (1,1). It is as though the agents had to maximize a sort of "social utility function," as if they formed a single agent, who, confronted with the choice between (0,0), (–1,2), and (1,1), would definitely choose (1,1), because it yields a higher sum result (2 > 1). Society can function only when it regards the civil game (including the market) as a passage between a certain uncooperative status quo (0,0) and one that entails a mutual advantage (1,1) without lingering in opportunistic dynamics during the second phase of the game.

Here there is no sacrifice but rather a renunciation of opportunism based on the common awareness that opportunism would leave both

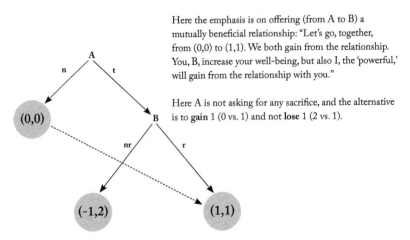

Here the emphasis is on offering (from A to B) a mutually beneficial relationship: "Let's go, together, from (0,0) to (1,1). We both gain from the relationship. You, B, increase your well-being, but also I, the 'powerful,' will gain from the relationship with you."

Here A is not asking for any sacrifice, and the alternative is to **gain** 1 (0 vs. 1) and not **lose** 1 (2 vs. 1).

FIGURE 10.3. The Trust Game: The "Mutual Benefit" Frame

players stuck in the status quo. B is not rewarding A for his kindness (by choosing to reciprocate); B is reciprocating only A's intention to carry out together an operation that is mutually advantageous. Indeed, it is important that each agent have good reasons to believe the other is not an opportunistic player, not a "cheeky" one (a "birbo" in the Italian word of Genovesi), because when this happens the entire construction of the civil economy falls apart, together with civil and economic development—as history often has shown and still shows, unfortunately, even in the land of Genovesi.

The difference between a theory à la Genovesi and the theory of social preferences might appear of little importance; in fact, it becomes very important as soon as we try to analyze even the most ordinary relational dynamics as they occur in the market. In these cases, each agent "objectively" benefits from taking part in the market (here the "invisible hand" works properly). But according to the notion of morality and sociality entailed in Rabin's theory and in the theory of "strong reciprocity," for instance, the baker is not "social," or even moral, for the fact of choosing simply to sell bread to anyone who wishes to buy bread (as opposed to not selling it), because he makes no "sacrifice" in making this choice. In the same way, a customer is not "moral" when he buys bread. In the theory of social preferences, which today is gaining increasing popularity among theories trying to inject economics with a moral content, there is no place for genuine and moral reciprocity within "normal" market transactions unless someone makes sacrifices: "civil" bakers are not enough; bakers must also reward and punish their customers at their own expense. In this sense, we are left with market theory as a morally neutral zone where we cannot ordinarily experience genuinely social relations. The civil economy, as we have seen, has maintained a different vocation and considered, even considers, the economy as intrinsically civil because the meeting of persons to trade with a friendly and non-opportunistic attitude is already a moral pursuit.[14]

The distinction between a Genovesian approach to market sociality and the theory of social preferences is important for the analysis of those cases in which the market's ability to function depends on trust. Let us consider a context in which contracts are not "enforceable," that is, where there are no institutions (or no reputational effect) guaranteeing that the other will do her part even when there is an incentive to behave in an opportunistic manner. We may think of all those sequential games (even nonrepeated) in which one player must act before the other; imagine a situation in which goods must be delivered before they are paid for. How can we explain the frequency of these types of transactions (in spite of what the standard theory would predict)? The theory of social preferences would explain this by requiring, as in a sort of trust tame, that B reward the kindness shown by A in the first round by renouncing part of her own gain, to the benefit of A.

Even though in this case the relation is mutually advantageous (the exchange does take place), B is asked to sacrifice part of her gains for A (provided that B has a high enough degree of inequality aversion, or that B is sufficiently sensitive to A's motivations, or both).[15] This theory entails a radical distinction between economic exchanges that take place through "enforceable" contracts and exchanges in which such contracts cannot be implemented: mere self-interest operates in the first, altruism and sacrifice in the latter. To me, this seems to be an overly demanding requirement and, above all, one that confines the market's "morality" to exceedingly narrow domains, like a "fill-in" in a normality that remains substantially immoral.

Let's recap. The conventional way of conceiving market relations today is characterized within economic (and social) theory by two great contrapositions: the market versus the social and self-interest versus altruism.[16] The conceptual framework of modern and contemporary economic theory doesn't offer a way of conceiving a relationship between individuals *simultaneously* as a mutually advantageous exchange in which neither party wishes to act altruistically or to renounce a slice of economic benefit *and* as a genuinely social interaction whose moral value is determined by its social content. I strongly believe that the absence of such a possibility has the effect of limiting our understanding *both* of the market *and* of human relations in general.

In fact, if we remain in contemporary economic theory, on the one hand we cannot describe market relations as a genuine form of reciprocity given the fact that they are aimed at mutual advantage—consider how many pages have been written by philosophers and economists to defend the claim that "true sociality" begins where pure market relations end, thus making the market and the world increasingly less humane. On the other hand, as a different face of the same coin (theory), economic theory (and even social theory) is unable to represent nonmarket relations as mutually advantageous, like those shared by friends or family members; this is to say that if an exchange yields mutual advantages, it is immediately transformed into something that is essentially less noble: the relationship turns into a mere contract, a relationship with a "mercenary" quality.[17]

This chapter is an attempt to move past this dualistic vision, which so far has benefited neither the market (which, so frequently depicted as immoral, is increasingly reflecting its portrayal) nor the nonmarket (where the habit of associating family and friendship with pure gratuitousness often masks relations dominated by power as well as pathologies of all kinds: gender issues within traditional communities are a good example of this danger).

MUTUAL ASSISTANCE VERSUS MUTUAL ADVANTAGE

In order to continue developing our discussion on the civil economy as a possible market paradigm for today, we must still come to terms with an objection that, if not properly addressed, may end up being fatal. We have argued that the basic idea of Genovesi's message to his interlocutors, yesterday as today, has been that when agents operate in the market they must be motivated by the intention of "being helpful to each other." Within the market economy, however, individuals always tend to act in such a way as to be helpful to one another; otherwise their exchange would not take place. What, then, is the great difference and novelty of Genovesi's approach? Is it ultimately a mere difference of language? Smith was certainly well aware that the market can function and expand because people pursue ways of being useful to each other and the market relies on this mutual utility rather than on the "benevolence" of fellow citizens.

The mechanism that allows coordination of the actions of the various agents in the market, who try to be useful to one another, is the *price system*: from this mechanism and from the signals that prices incorporate, each agent is induced to be useful to others. Such "utility" is measured by the willingness to pay for the goods and services on offer. This is an essential feature of the market system, as argued by the liberal tradition. This feature allows the development of the "knowledge division," which is no less important or essential in the market economy than is Smith's "division of labour": in large-scale economies it is impossible for each citizen to gather all the information that the price of a good "incorporates" and hence to figure out the value of one's own activities. Such information may be transferred only through the price system (in a well-functioning market). In the market economy, due to this informational problem, the only way to be truly helpful to others—as Hayek, along with all those who embrace contemporary economic theory, would argue—is to elaborate price signals efficiently and to act in a way as to optimize one's resources. If this is the case, what does it mean to act, as Genovesi says, with the intention of being helpful to each other?

For Smith, in order to be consistent with the proper functioning of a free society and with the market economy, any moral or social discussion concerning the market must be consistent with the idea that individuals choose their own economic activities in response to price signals.[18] The question thus becomes "How can we reconcile the idea of the market as mutual assistance with this basic principle of the market economy?" Not answering this question would amount to saying that Genovesi's civil economy is possible only in small pre-modern communities or within some marginal parts of the market economy—a message we cannot subscribe to.

My suggestion (in agreement with Sugden), which emerges from our discussion so far, is that market interaction (we could say "contracts") can be understood and represented as that which makes the parties into a collective agent with reference to the particular joint action that is the object of the contract. From this perspective, which is a legitimate translation of the view of the market held by the civil economy, the contract binds each party in the contract to do his or her part in order to achieve their common objective. This objective is the joint benefit that derives from the contract, indeed within the specific limits defined by the transaction. In doing his or her part, each agent is moved by the intention to take part in a combination of actions directed to the benefit of the entire "team." Hence, when a potential customer turns to the baker, the content of his intention may be expressed and deconstructed as a proposal of this kind: "I offer you to undertake a joint action that will benefit both of us: you help me to satisfy my need for bread, and I help you to satisfy your need for money. Together we perform this joint action, we form this (temporary) team."

If the two reach an agreement, the customer will intentionally wish that the baker also benefit from the exchange, and vice versa.[19] Therefore, each has the conscious intention to be "helpful to the other." *The mutual advantage lies inside the transaction*, whose content is thus not limited to the pre-condition of the commercial agreement.

This is one way of making Genovesi's notion of mutual assistance compatible with the market economy. However, it should be noted that from this perspective, collective action (or mutual assistance) comes into existence *during* the execution of the contract; it is not offered beforehand as motivation *for* the contract. In choosing which contract to subscribe to in order to satisfy one's needs, each individual is free to choose a partner based on his or her own preferences and on price signals. For instance, the implication that a customer might choose a certain baker for the purpose of helping him (for example, because the baker is going through a moment of economic crisis) finds no place in the logic I have outlined so far.

Only when the contract is sealed does the customer's commitment to the common aim actually begin. So, for example, Genovesi (and I, too) would not advise an entrepreneur this way: "Choose provider A because he's going through rough times even though his prices are higher than B's." The entrepreneur's choice can (and must, in a way) follow price signals (in a well-functioning market), and only once he has chosen his providers freely can he behave as someone who belongs to the same team. Therefore, the analysis of exchange as mutual assistance is compatible with the acknowledgment of the role of signals in the market.[20]

What differences, then, are implied by this view of the market? What added value does it carry, compared to the standard or Smithian view? First of all we ask how the subjects involved *perceive* the relation and the overall human experience of market transactions. Reading the contract as a collective action (and not just as mutual indifference) changes the "affective tone" of the relation. Even if market relations are associated with feelings of friendship and benevolence, it is possible that Smith's *correspondence of sentiments* might arise—which is, according to Smith, one of the greatest sources of well-being.[21] On the other hand, reading and living the market as mutual indifference—or, worse, as opportunism—is something that in the long run makes economic life sad and scarcely habitable.

But someone might object, wondering whether it is possible that market relations can be fraternal when the parties involved stand on a plane of objective economic inequality (in terms of income, contractual power, etc.). To answer, we look back at Smith's example of the customer and the baker. Could their relationship be described as "fraternal" if, for instance, the baker were to have a small bakery in the suburbs and the customer were a rich city banker? Or, conversely, if the baker worked for a large, profitable chain of bakeries and the customer were a poor student?[22] The first answer is also a question in itself: *Why shouldn't it be possible?* There is no doubt that, on the one hand, fraternity and friendship are more easily established among equals (in economic and social terms, and even in terms of age), but, on the other hand, it seems equally true that if civil society wished to develop sentiments of friendship and mutual assistance, it would also need to favor and to allow its members to develop a friendly disposition toward those who differ from them in various respects, including economic profiles. No one can prevent a person from living out a concrete economic encounter (between equal or unequal parties), here and now, as a fraternal one even if his general judgment on a certain firm and economic system may be very critical.

Can we work to build a more fraternal, global economy while *simultaneously* living out fraternal economic relations here and now? Is it possible, for instance, to work in fair trade and at the same time to have a positive relation with the airline flying us to Brazil (better yet if with low-pollution emissions)?

We could pose a different but related question: How far does the commitment to act fraternally toward the other party in the contract *extend*, especially in those (frequent) cases of incomplete contracts, *unenforceable* or *one-shot* (in which there is no reputational effect in play)? The answer depends on how we conceive of mutual assistance and common intention. We move between two extremes. The more frugal of the two would lead us to consider that collective intention consists of reaching a mutual benefit *given the preferences, the information, and the beliefs of each agent at the time of the contract.* Such a restrictive interpretation of reciprocal assistance, under closer examination, does not bring us much further than the antiquated mercantile ethics of *caveat emptor* (buyer beware). Given the opposite extreme, however, one might argue that the two parties must define the common benefit in terms of a common notion of well-being. For instance, a barman might have doubts as to whether he should offer the tenth shot of grappa to a customer who is already intoxicated or to the youngster who is about to drive home after a night at a club. If, in fact, market relations are intended as mutual assistance, the parties may incur moral responsibilities toward each other, responsibilities that extend beyond what a contract would prescribe. A similar point, yet even more strict, may be raised with regard to economic relations that take place *over time*.

RECIPROCITY AND MUTUAL DIGNITY AS THE TELOS OF THE (CIVIL) MARKET: SMITH AND GENOVESI RECONCILED

There are, however, points of contact between Smith's political economy and Genovesi's civil economy. Let us return to the considerations of the baker. Smith's main message, embodied in the parable of the benevolence of the butcher, is very different from those of mainstream economics, including Amartya Sen's interpretation.[23] In the logic of Smith's vision of the market, the primary motivation for action *is* self-love, even though *in fact* everyone's self-interested actions combine to create mutual benefit.[24] The idea that economic agents should understand their interactions as mutual assistance is characteristic of an older tradition of natural-law philosophy, from which mainstream economic thought turned away in the later eighteenth century. Nevertheless, there is a sense in which this idea is implicit in some of Smith's writings and in the writings of many other major economists from the eighteenth century to the present day. In this context, Smith's most famous passage on the butcher should be interpreted, taking seriously the final sentence of the passage: "Nobody but a beggar chuses [*sic*] to depend chiefly upon the benevolence of his fellow-citizens."[25]

This sentence gives sense to the entire passage. Smith is telling us that the market allows us to satisfy our economic needs without dependency, with *dignity and self-respect*. The market gives each of us the freedom to act on our own interests, subject to the constraints imposed on us by other people's acting on theirs. Market relations are free horizontal relations

between equals: the tradesman and his customer are symmetrically posi-
tioned with respect to a mutually beneficial transaction, in contrast to the
asymmetric relationship of inferior and superior between the beggar and
the person from whom he begs. By virtue of this property, the market supports the virtues of independence and moral equality. That market relations
are characterized by impersonality and mutual unconcern is not a matter
for regret: it is intrinsic to their role in promoting independence. In a pre-
commercial society, Smith argues, a wealthy man has little choice but to
spend most of his income on servants, each of whom is at his personal command. In a commercial society, in contrast, the equivalent income will be
spent on an array of luxury goods produced by the combined work of many
different tradesmen. In this way, the rich man contributes to the maintenance of a large number of people, none of whom is dependent on him.

The meaning and crucial role of Smith's invisible hand can be properly understood within the general framework of the entirety of his
work.[26] The latter part of this famous statement on the invisible hand—"I
have never known much good done by those who affected to trade for
the public good"[27]—is everything but ironic. It instead reveals clearly
the relation between private and common goods, individual virtue (prudence) and public happiness. It is not, of course, the *only* mechanism of
creation of the public welfare; it is just the *main* one.

The previous sentence on the invisible hand has to be read together
with the following:

> A revolution of the greatest importance to the public happiness was
> in this manner brought about by two different orders of people who
> had not the *least intention* to serve the public. To gratify the most
> childish vanity was the sole motive of the great proprietors. The
> merchants and artificers, much less ridiculous, acted merely from a
> view to their own interest, and in pursuit of their own pedlar prin-
> ciple of turning a penny wherever a penny was to be got. Neither of
> them had either knowledge or foresight of that great revolution
> which the folly of the one, and the industry of the other, was gradu-
> ally bringing about.[28]

To Smith, whose writing here is similar to that of Genovesi regarding
his civil economy, the *first and foremost capability* of a commercial society

is to create the conditions that allow poor people to quit the condition of beggars and enter into market relationships of equality in dignity. It is the market that is the main instrument of empowerment for deprived persons. So *self-help through the market* is for Smith an essential market virtue, probably the most important, but it does not seem to be a Senian virtue of the market. As discussed in particular in a 2013 article of Bruni and Sugden, within the *practice* of a market that is structured by mutual benefit, each individual's wants and aspirations are relevant to others only insofar as they can be satisfied in mutually beneficial transactions.[29] A person who expects his trading partners to account further for his interests is restricting his own and other people's opportunities for mutually beneficial transactions. Hence, it is a Smithian "market virtue" to accept without complaint that others will be motivated to satisfy your wants, or to provide you with opportunities for self-realization, only if you offer something that they are willing to accept in return. Reciprocity among people with equal dignity is the telos of the market. Smith's denigration of the person who chooses to depend on other people's benevolence upholds this virtue.[30] A person who acts on the basis of this virtue will not only avoid appealing to other people's benevolence; she will also avoid asking others to reward her for producing goods that those others do not value.

Therefore, in this context, not only is Smith's idea of the market different from Sen's, but also are their theories of poverty and deprivation—the foundation of Sen's capabilities theory—different. Sen's global representation of both Smith's *Wealth of Nations* and *Theory of Moral Sentiments* is to call for more motivations (other than self-interest) operating in society, and so softens the principal role of self-interest in the subjective conditions of being rescued from poverty. The whole of Smith's discourse on poverty and deprivation cannot be understood without considering this *virtuous* role of the market in liberating people from poverty traps. Without taking seriously this *basic capability of the market*, as Sen does, we cannot fully grasp Smith's economic and social philosophy. Freeing poor people from the benevolence of landlords, using their self-love instead of benevolence, is the main contribution of the market to a more civilized society.

I have claimed that it is possible to look at the market as a domain of interactions—that is, those comprising the civil economy—which considers economic interactions to be at once moral and mutually advantageous and where sociality and morality do not deal with a particular kind of motivation but with joint intentions and actions. And finally, I have argued (without demonstrating it here) that in considering the market as relationships among people with equal dignity, Smith and Genovesi are very similar.

What this approach calls for is a mature way of thinking about markets. Normal economic dealings require not greed, competition, or self-interest but mutual advantage and civil fraternity. Fraternity is, in fact, the *forgotten principle* of modernity. When the founders of modernity announced the new principles of the new world—*liberté, egalité, fraternité*—they pronounced something crucial: individual freedom and social equality are not enough to build the new post–ancien régime society because neither liberty nor equality produce a "bond," or relationships *among* persons. Market society has endeavored to invent a new bond of society, but the paradoxes of happiness on the one hand and inequality on the other reveal that the nexus is too frayed and must be reinforced by a new form of civil fraternity. It is not a fraternity of shared familial bloodlines and clan ties or a fraternity of closed and discriminating communities. Rather, it is civil fraternity *together* with freedom and equality. This fraternity, or civil friendship, on the part of the members of a community implies participation in a common destiny, being united by a link less exclusive and elective than intimate friendship but capable of generating feelings of reciprocal sympathy, which can and even should be expressed in ordinary market transactions. A vision of the market that penetrates all civil domains and is based on reciprocity fosters more dignity and respect in the society as a whole.

NOTES

1. This tradition had several modern sources, such as Isaac Newton, John Locke, and Giambattista Vico.

2. Luigino Bruni, *The Genesis and Ethos of the Market* (London: Palgrave, 2012); Bruni, "On the Concept of Economia Civile and Felicitas Publica: A Comment on Federico D'Onofrio," *Journal of the History of Economic Thought* 39, no. 2 (2017): 273–79; Bruni and Stefano Zamagni, *The Civil Economy* (London: AgendaPub, 2016).

3. This chapter shares many arguments with Luigino Bruni and Robert Sugden, "Fraternity: Why the Market Need Not Be a Morally Free Zone," *Economics and Philosophy* 24, no. 1 (2008): 35–64; and Bruni, *Genesis and Ethos*.

4. Today, on the contrary, we know—thanks in particular to Friedrich Hayek—that the government plays only a small part in the relaunching of the economy and in its orientation since the largest role is played by millions of separate subjects who possess only fragmentary information (as demonstrated especially by Hayek in the twentieth century).

5. Genovesi's critique of offering mere assistance to the poor is well known, and we find it also in the *Lezioni*: his politics involved creating opportunities so that the poor could work, hence overcoming the feudal logic of benefactors and beneficiaries.

6. David Gauthier, *Morals by Agreement* (Oxford: Clarendon Press, 1986), 84.

7. Mutual indifference (in the Smithian or Rawlsian sense) is represented in this game by the absence of "pro-social" or "other-regarding" preferences.

8. Gary Bolton and Axel Ockenfels, "ERC: A Theory of Equity, Reciprocity, and Competition," *American Economic Review* 90 (2000): 66–93.

9. In the version of the game that is commonly employed in lab experiments analyzing reciprocity and fairness, there are normally two players, A and B, who are asked to interact within a sequential game. A has two options available: to trust B or to not trust B, in which case the game ends straightaway (in this case, for example, the initial endowment may be divided between the two, e.g. 10 euros, 5 euros each). If A decides to trust B, they then move on to the second phase of the game, where B has full control: the money sum is multiplied (e.g., by 3, giving 30), and B can decide whether to keep the money entirely (thus not reciprocating the trust previously received from A) or to give something back to A. Incidentally, we should note that lab evidence basically contradicts what standard economic theory would predict. Similar games or variations of the Trust Game include the so-called Investment Game (A receives 10 euros and, if he or she does not trust B, B gets nothing and A keeps all) and the Gift-Exchange Game (where A and B receive the same sum, and they simultaneously have to decide whether or not they trust each other).

10. It must be noticed that in this representation, the payoffs (0,1 through 1,2) are expressed in terms of monetary (or material) rewards, not in terms of utility or preference satisfaction—an assumption that is also required by the other games we have previously introduced.

11. E. Fehr and S. Gachter, "Fairness and Retaliation: The Economics of Reciprocity," *Journal of Economic Perspectives* 14, no. 3 (2000): 159–81.

12. In fact, this kind of literature employs games, like the Trust Game or the Ultimatum Game, which are different from the Prisoner's Dilemma partly because they are sequential (and nonsimultaneous). However, the relational logic of interaction remains essentially the same.

13. The game is illustrated by assuming that the objective (or utility) functions of the agents and, hence, their preferences (the utility function represents the preferences of the players) are more complex than those employed by the standard theory. For example, according to standard neoclassic theory, the utility function of A is equal to $U_a = f(I)$, where I is the income or material payoff in the game, which is the *only* variable in the agent's function: there is no motivation other than I (or consumption or, in general, material rewards). On the basis of this function and of the standard assumption of nonsatiation (more is better than less), the game equilibrium (0,0) is eventually achieved. If, instead, we assume, along with Rabin and other social preferences authors, that agents are also concerned about inequality in income distribution (inequality aversion) and/or about the motivations of their partners in the game (kindness), we will adopt a more complex utility function to calculate the game's payoffs (payoffs are simply a representation of the agents' objective function, which reflects their preferences). In addition to $U_a = f(I)$, such function will also contain other variables (thus allowing one to embed these other dimensions in the agents' preferences). For instance, in its very basic form, a function that embodies psychological elements can be indicated as $U_a = f(I + a)$, where a represents these other components of the agent's preferences, that is, the nonmaterial aspects that nonetheless motivate the agent and affect utility (in fact in the models a represents several different parameters covering the various aspects of each single theory: inequality aversion, reciprocity, etc.). See Matthew Rabin, "Incorporating Fairness into Game Theory and Economics," *American Economic Review* 83 (1993): 1281–1302.

14. Dragonetti's ethics of virtue, for instance, despite having been developed outside the logic of "collective rationality" and despite centering on the individual person, still is an expression of concern for the *common good* and of a view of society whose components are bound to each other.

15. B's ability to reciprocate might depend on his or her degree of inequality aversion, which, in this case, would operate independently of A's motivations (this line of thought derives from Fehr and Gachter, "Fairness and Retaliation"), as well as from the desire to "reward" the motivations that led A to take a risk by trusting B. (This line of thought originates in Rabin, "Incorporating Fairness.") Recent models combine both explanations. For a survey of the different explanations, refer to Luca Stanca, Luigino Bruni, and Luca Corazzini, who outline the results of an experiment trying to further

investigate the relation between B's behavior and A's motivations in "Testing Theories of Reciprocity: Do Motivations Matter?," *Journal of Economic Behavior and Organization* 71, no. 2 (2009): 233–45.

16. Such contrapositions are not perfectly overlapping. For instance, there are some market analyses where the agents seem to act on the basis of social preferences, but at the same time there are some reductionist theories that explain even the most intimate relations in terms of maximization of self-interest.

17. Giacinto Dragonetti, *A Treatise on Virtues and Rewards* (London: Johnson and Payne, 1969), Italian first edition, *Delle virtù e de' Premi* (Naples: Beccaria, Cesare, 1768).

18. See, for instance, Adam Smith's argument about the salaries of mine workers in *An Inquiry into the Nature and Causes of the Wealth of Nations*, ed. R. H. Campbell, A. S. Skinner and W. B. Todd (Oxford: Oxford University Press, 1976/1776).

19. This approach to the market works well when looking at long-term economic interactions (consider, for instance, the contracts in a firm).

20. A view like Genovesi's does not lead to the creation of informal economies between "friends," wherein commercial partners are chosen for reasons of "friendship"; in time such operations can often lead to a lack of economic sustainability. I believe that the challenge posed by experiences of the social economy, like fair trade or ethical finance, is to combine price signals with an authentic spirit of fraternity. If, on the contrary, these two levels are mixed (and one chooses a provider because he is a "friend" or because it is "part of the project"), this may be a dangerous path to choose. While this choice is not necessary to make the market a civil realm, we should recognize that a certain willingness to do something more might be warranted in order to fix distortions and make the market even more civil.

21. Adam Smith, *The Theory of Moral Sentiments*, ed. A. L. Macfie and D. D. Raphael (Oxford: Oxford University Press, 1759).

22. This point opens up an interesting discussion about the logic of altruistic punishment, which is present in the theories that make use of social preferences, such as "strong reciprocity": in these models and experiments the subjects reject offers they consider unfair (in an ultimatum game, for instance) at their own expense. For example, if A offers B to share 8—2 out of 10—B will often refuse in order to punish A (when, if B refuses, they both gain zero). My own approach would be to discourage such refusals, because this aversion to inequality, which we all have, should not be encouraged because it leads persons to miss out on mutually advantageous exchange opportunities.

23. Amartya Sen, *Development as Freedom* (New York: Knopf, 2000).

24. Sympathy and benevolence are central to Smith's *Theory of Moral Sentiments* but play only minor roles in his economic analysis.

25. Smith, *Wealth of Nations*, I.2.2.

26. Luigino Bruni and Robert Sugden, "Fraternity: Why the Market Need Not to Be a Morally Free Zone," *Economics and Philosophy* 24 (2008): 35–64.

27. Smith, *Wealth of Nations*, IV.2.9.

28. Ibid., III.4.17, italics added.

29. Luigino Bruni and Robert Sugden, "Reclaiming Virtue Ethics for Economics," *Journal of Economic Perspectives* 27 (2013): 141–64.

30. "Chuses to" is important here. Smith is not denigrating dependence on others when people have no other means of subsistence. Benevolence is one of the central virtues of Smith's theory of moral sentiments, but it is not a *market* virtue in our sense.

ELEVEN

Human Dignity, Development Policies, and the EU's Human Rights Conditionality

Lorenza Violini and Giada Ragone

In this chapter we aim to answer the following questions: Is human dignity a fundamental value that can influence policy makers when dealing with problems related to development? If yes, is it necessary to institutionalize and define this value (and the principles subtended), or, vice versa, can its influence simply be detected when analyzing the practices of national and international institutions in the field of development?

Such questions arise because of the difficulties that scholars encounter when trying to identify the specific content of the principle of human dignity, especially when the legal discourse on human dignity is grounded in its role in the judicial adjudication of case law. In this context, indeed, some legal scholars tend to underestimate the role played by the principle itself. In fact, facing the different—and sometimes even contradictory—positions judges take when interpreting human dignity, they are led to the conclusion that it is an inconsistent concept. This is undisputed: there might be, of course, in the broad area of litigation, some inconsistencies or misinterpretations of the principle. But can we assume that judges are the ultimate evaluators of the viability of a value as important as human dignity? Is there another point of view from which to investigate the merit of the principle and its link to human development and rights promotion?

Such an alternative was envisaged by Jeremy Waldron. In his attempt to connect human dignity—understood as a comprehensive, foundational aspect of all rights—with humanity, Waldron says that the answer to the question of the nature of human dignity cannot be explored solely by looking at the lists of rights and principles present in international and national instruments as interpreted by the judiciary. On the contrary, he says, "There may be other ways in which dignity will turn out to be important in our understanding of human rights"[1] and—one might add—of human development.

If one takes seriously the hypothesis that there are other ways to approach the multifaceted question of the nature of human dignity and its relation to human rights (and human development), one can look to the field of human rights (or political) conditionality, applied at the European level, as an excellent case study. More specifically, in this chapter we will try to show that the protection of human dignity has been a basic goal orienting the policy of the European Union, consisting in the swapping of economic and diplomatic advantages to third countries for respect of human rights. This was clear, in particular, when the policy originated, when it did not have a specific legal basis, thus giving evidence of the foundational nature of dignity.

We will start our analysis by examining the essence of human dignity as a basis for the protection of fundamental human rights; we then explore the links between dignity, humanity, and development, both in general and with a specific focus on the political conditionality of the EU in its relations with third countries.[2] In this chapter we conclude that, as the history of conditionality in Europe shows, development policies should have a solid basis in a sound understanding of human dignity; human dignity, in turn, cannot be limited to statutory writings and judicial interpretation. It must be translated into coherent political action that must derive from a very practical, concrete, contextual, and prudential practice.

DIGNITY AND RIGHTS: A *PRACTICAL* MATTER

Human dignity is a central principle in modern Western legal systems at all levels of government. With profound roots in theology, philosophy, and anthropology, it was first positively declared at the international level in the Universal Declaration of Human Rights of 1948. After that decisive step was taken, dignity found fertile ground in Europe to grow as a *foundational* principle of democratic constitutions, based on human rights. Against this common historical background, and lumped together with the desire to avoid mistakes of the past, European countries built in their constitutions a "common constitutional tradition" that included dignity among its basic values, as evidenced in the Lisbon Treaty and the Charter of Fundamental Rights.

Foundational as it may be, the definition of "human dignity" remains a hot topic among philosophers and legal scholars. Arthur Schopenhauer[3] tagged the Kantian definition of dignity contentless because he thought that it lacks a real ethical basis. Later on, Steven Pinker, in opposition to the 2008 Report on Human Dignity issued by the President's Council on Bioethics, did not hesitate to write an article titled "The Stupidity of Human Dignity."[4] Moreover, it is not only the content of dignity that is perceived as problematic; even the method of identifying this content is still under debate. Scholars, looking for a specific and univocal definition of dignity, may in fact follow a philosophical or logical path, interpret the different norms of positive law, or go chasing case law, trying to identify a common thread that connects and gives unity to the countless decisions of the courts at a global level. From the historical point of view, the very path legal scholarship has undertaken to cross this forest shows different starting points: some scholars, such as Jeremy Waldron, chose to start from Roman law,[5] or even from the Bible and from Jewish tradition, as David Kretzmer did;[6] others stressed the importance of Christian philosophy and took as a milestone the well-known definition of *persona* and its dignity framed by Boethius ("*Rationalis naturae individua substantia*");[7] and others, in turn, undertook the hard task of reconstructing the meaning of dignity starting from the post–World War II era and the Universal Declaration of 1948, already cited.

Following this last stream of thinkers, one cannot avoid citing Jacques Maritain. According to the French natural law philosopher, an agreement was reached in the United Nations Assembly as to a list of rights simply because "no one asked why." Of course, Maritain took this *why* very seriously, as the cornerstone of his reasoning, and reached the conclusion that the agreement was a *practical* and not a theoretical one. Today, almost seventy years after that discussion, one may still agree with Maritain's vision. Jurists have a practical attitude toward rights, and, as to our topic, dignity shares the same destiny as all human rights, the destiny of having a specific practical function: to continue to inspire the human attempt to make human life flourish, a goal never fully achieved.

This is the reason why human dignity is strongly connected to policy. Policy makers have to accomplish their tasks pursuing the ultimate goal of helping people and societies to achieve a reasonable level of development in order to benefit humanity. But, since the concept is so highly contested, what does it mean to pursue the protection of human dignity in different social and economic contexts?

Another philosophical position may identify a reasonable answer to such a multifaceted question, following a suggestion offered by Maritain. In "The Concept of Law," H.L.A. Hart wrote: "The continued reassertion of some form of natural law doctrine is due in part to the fact that its appeal is independent of both divine and human authority, and to the fact that despite a terminology with much metaphysics, which few could now accept, it contains certain elementary terms important for the understanding of both morality and law."[8] Hart's statement inevitably includes human dignity among these "elementary terms" that need to be restated. Both Maritain and Hart moved toward a similar *practical—as opposed to metaphysical*—attitude toward the basic principles of law. As a consequence, human dignity can be understood as an undeniable element of any legal system. This fact—one is tempted to say—provides a useful tool for elaborating solutions.

Aiming to restate human dignity "in simpler terms" so that it may be useful to the development of persons and societies, we can proceed in our reasoning by wondering: In which sense can we today approach the *complex* issue of the protection of human dignity *in simpler terms?* Can complexity and simplicity be reconciled? Taking on this challenge, we would suggest the following reflections, based, first of all, on a very simple term: humanity.

HUMANITY AS THE ULTIMATE CORE OF
THE PROTECTION OF HUMAN DIGNITY

Taking for granted that "simple," in philosophical and legal discourse, cannot be understood as either *easy* or *trivial*, let us first adopt a "simple," intuitive anthropological vision of human dignity that focuses on *humanity*. On this basis, dignity can be understood as pertinent not only in the material (biological) aspect of life but also in its diachronic one, that is, the time span from birth to death. In the following paragraphs, we will speak of dignity in simpler—and practical—terms within a fundamental rights charter and development policies. However, it is undeniable that it is mainly in the case law of courts that we find the recognition of human dignity before birth and after death. A well-known example of the state's duty to protect human dignity after death is seen in the *Mephisto* case, in which the German Constitutional Court gave a negative answer to the question of whether freedom of art would justify a violation of the protected human dignity of a deceased actor. At the end of its opinion, the Court reasons, "The duty imposed on all state authority by Article 1 of the Basic Law to protect the individual from attacks on his dignity does not end with death."[9] Legally speaking, here we face a comprehensive vision of human dignity that encompasses a strong duty of protection by state authorities.

Entering now into the "internal" boundaries of life, it is worth noting that dignity ought to be respected in all personal decisions. Dying with dignity is often requested by advocates of euthanasia as an expression of the desire, the very human aspiration, not to be conditioned in one's own behavior by any reason imposed by others. And of course, not only the end of life is affected by this desire. In *Casey v. Planned Parenthood*, the U.S. Supreme Court held: "Our law affords constitutional protection to personal decisions relating to marriage, procreation, contraception, family relationships, childrearing and education. These matters, involving the most intimate and personal choices a person may make in a lifetime, choices central to personal dignity and autonomy, are central to the liberty protected by the XIV Amendment."[10]

What is interesting for our purposes is that the court immediately afterward says: "At the heart of liberty is the right to define *one's own concept* of existence, of meaning, of universe and of the mystery of human life." This latter quotation may suggest that dignity, in its tight connection with liberty, involves a whole set of issues related to human life and to "the pursuit of happiness" typical of every human being. The right to freely dig deep into reality, philosophy, and religion is embedded in one's own personal dignity; dignity, in turn, implies the right to search everywhere for some sparks that can shed light on the mystery of life. In this sense, one can say that human rights as a whole are instrumental to such a search. When they are respected, the human person is free to flourish and to pursue the full development of his humanity, according to his human experience.[11]

HUMANITY AS THE ULTIMATE CORE OF THE UNDERSTANDING
OF DEVELOPMENT AND THE FRAMING OF DEVELOPMENT POLICIES

The attempt to connect human dignity, understood as a comprehensive, foundational aspect of all rights, to humanity (human life, from birth to death) raises the question of development. The link between dignity, human rights, and development can be best traced when analyzing the European Charter of Fundamental Rights. This paramount document is absolutely relevant to our argument for two reasons. First, in its pages dignity plays a central role as the basis of the most important rights identified by Western constitutionalism. Indeed, the charter identifies dignity as the first and foremost principle under which are included and encompassed the right to life, the right to the physical and mental integrity of the person (encompassing the free and informed consent of the person; the prohibition of eugenic practices, in particular those aiming at the selection of persons; the prohibition on making the human body and its parts a source of financial gain; and the prohibition of the reproductive cloning of human beings), and also the prohibition of slavery, forced labor, torture, and inhumane or degrading treatment or punishment. Secondly, the charter recognizes that the full flourishing of human beings is not only a matter of single rights but also deals with the provision of development policies and goals. Indeed, in Article 37 the document makes explicit references to principles of sustainable development. This link between dignity, rights, and development—stated in the relatively recent charter—has very interesting roots in European history and practice, as it is visible in foreign policies under the name of "political conditionality."

THE ORIGIN AND DEVELOPMENT OF THE EU'S
HUMAN RIGHTS CONDITIONALITY POLICY

The EU's human rights or political conditionality[12] offers an interesting benchmark of the concrete application of the principle of human dignity "in simpler—and practical—terms." As mentioned above,[13] "conditionality" refers to European trade and cooperation in development policies characterized by the swapping of economic and diplomatic advantages with third countries in return for respect of fundamental freedoms, democratic reforms, and improvements in human rights performance.[14]

The first step toward this kind of policy dates to 1977,[15] when the European Community revoked promised payments of development aid from the government of Uganda after the dictator Idi Amin Dada committed a cruel massacre of civilians.[16] At that time, EC relations with Uganda were governed by the Lomé I Convention, a treaty signed in 1975 by the European Community with forty-six African, Caribbean, and Pacific (ACP) developing countries. According to the convention, ACP states had preferential access to the Common Market and received financial aid from the European Development Fund. The treaty concerned economic issues and did not establish human rights standards as conditions for access to its advantages, nor did it provide any sanctions in case of human rights violations carried out after the convention took force. Due to this legal framework, the community's decision to reverse Uganda's privileges was not without legal difficulties. It was far from clear that the community could suspend already promised development aid on the basis of the violations of human dignity, human rights, and democracy, all principles absent from its primary and secondary law. Nonetheless, the EC Council stated that development aid to Uganda would not reinforce or prolong the deprivation of fundamental rights and therefore withdrew it.[17]

This case is absolutely relevant to our discourse. Here European policy makers, in the absence of a formal legal basis or binding duty, felt the need to adopt measures capable of sanctioning the commission of severe human rights violations. We cannot avoid asking the reason for this behavior. It can be said that the European Community withdrew its economic aid because it did not want to be considered an accomplice to crimes carried out by Uganda's government. However, this can be only a part of the story. It is also important to note that the European reaction can be considered a sign of the very nature of human dignity. The withdrawal came as a consequence of the perceived inconsistency and injustice of granting financial aid and/or benefits to a dictatorship that was denying respect, dignity, and other rights to human beings, thus thwarting the very purpose of development policies and aid: to help governments and persons "develop" their lives to the full extent of human flourishing. Returning to the conclusion of the present case, it is clear that the EC's courageous choices were the "starting point for the discussion on integrating human rights clauses into EU external policy."[18]

In the years that followed, the community sought to establish a formal legal basis for its human rights conditionality policies in the Lomé Convention. The first attempt, Lomé II in 1980, failed, but the Lomé III Convention of 1985 stated that measures should be taken in case of systematic violations of fundamental human rights by a party. Five years later, the community included the first operative human rights clause in a cooperation agreement: the European Economic Community (EEC)–Argentina agreement of 1990.[19] Since then, human rights (HR) clauses have become standard in agreements with third countries. One of the most important and innovative developments in these clauses was made in the agreement between the EEC and the Republic of Albania in 1992. On this occasion, the EC and Albania designated respect for human rights as an essential element of the treaty.[20] By so doing, the EC created "a strong legal basis for reaction to Human Rights violations."[21] Indeed, Article 60 of the Vienna Convention on the Law of Treaties established that the violation of a provision essential to the accomplishment of the object or purpose of the treaty would enable the parties to terminate the treaty itself or suspend its operation in whole or in part, without any further explanation in the agreement. "As this provision was also used in agreements with the Baltic States, it came to be known as the 'Baltic clause.'"[22] This clause evolved into the "Bulgarian clause"[23] and was integrated into many other agreements.[24] It took nearly twenty years after the Uganda case, "but the EC did arrive at a firm clause enabling reactions."[25]

Through its case-by-case approach, the EU has developed, and currently has available, a range of HR conditionality clauses, some permitting the withdrawal of privileges in the event that the beneficiary country violates human rights and democratic principles (negative conditionality clauses), others in the area of trade preferences, providing positive incentives to countries that comply with HR (and other) norms (positive conditionality clauses). HR conditionality evolved from a simple tool to suspend treaty relations with third states violating human rights, a sort of contract termination clause, to an autonomous instrument of foreign policy and cooperation with development, consisting of the practice of using human rights as a factor in the allocation of aid budgets, usually as a part of "political" or "good governance" conditions. According to Grainne de Burca and Paul Craig, HR conditionality can nowadays be considered "one of the key legal instruments deployed by the EU in pursuit of human rights goals."[26] Many criticisms have been raised against this EU policy concerning the effectiveness of conditionality,[27] the difficulty of agreeing on the concrete content of the human rights protected by clauses, and, above all, the lack of EU legitimacy in introducing human rights clauses within trade or commercial agreements.[28] In some cases, the clauses are used as autonomous instruments of foreign policy, and their presence in trade agreements is seen as inappropriate as they go beyond the scope of trade affairs.

Nonetheless, it must be said that the EU is virtually unique in its policy of including human rights conditionality clauses in its international agreements. Some of the free trade agreements of the European Free Trade Area (EFTA) have copied the EU model with conditionality clauses, including nonexecution clauses and dispute settlement clauses. But there are no other direct analogies to the EU's conditionality policy. And "the idea of tying trade policy benefits to the compliance with HR clauses may make trade agreements more effective to achieve HR objectives than general HR treaties that do not include any sanctions in cases of noncompliance. [At least] trade agreements may be a very good choice as an incentive for compliance with human rights principles."[29]

At the beginning of this chapter we asked whether human dignity can be considered a principle capable of influencing policy makers when dealing with problems related to development. As the above analysis suggests, there must be a positive answer to this question. Indeed, at least in the Western world, human dignity has to do with the deep character and nature of legal systems and their roots. It might not be possible to define, once for all, the content of human dignity or to institutionalize it into regular policies. Nonetheless, what human dignity requires is "detectable" by reflecting on practice. In particular, within the broad landscape of development policies, it can be identified using the same method scientists use to identify dark matter, that is, a sophisticated form of indirect detection. Its existence and relevance to the legal system emerge each time a new unresolved problem arises.

This is exactly what can be deduced from the Uganda case. On that occasion, even in the absence of a legal basis for intervention, it became instinctive for the European Community to acknowledge and to appeal to a metaphysical or metalegal principle that incorporates the aspirations of justice present in human hearts and in society. This event gave evidence of a very simple idea: it was not acceptable to keep giving financial support to a political system that did not share the community's basic respect for human rights and for justice. As a consequence, one can perceive that cooperation and development policies are not only a matter of material economic aid but must also be functional toward the enhancement of a whole series of values. Among them, the flourishing of human dignity is paramount, even when not explicitly cited. The decision to suspend aid to Uganda was a form of intervention that derived from the tendency to preserve justice without legal intervention, but law cannot exist without humans' tendency toward justice. The translation in the legal terms of the so-called conditionality clauses was, in essence, only a second step, the first being the tension of all human beings—among them political decision makers—to act in compliance with that "complex of needs and evidences that are at the basis of any human person."[30] In other words, the subsequent codification resulted in a sort of transformation of a principle of natural law into a positive prescription. We could call this case "the case against positivism" and, at the same time, the case "against treating human dignity as an abstraction."[31]

When international agreements subscribed by the EU have clauses that explicitly protect human rights and democracy and give economic benefits to third countries that respect such values, considering the origins of these courageous legal choices, one cannot avoid going back to the *dark matter* that made itself apparent in the Uganda case.

NOTES

1. J. Waldron, "Is Dignity the Foundation of Human Rights?," in *Philosophical Foundations of Human Rights*, ed. R. Cruft, S. M. Liao, and M. Renzo (Oxford: Oxford University Press, 2015), 117.

2. We use "third countries" to refer to states that are not members of the European Union.

3. A. Schopenhauer, *On The Basis of Morality* (Indianapolis, IN: Hackett, 1995).

4. S. Pinker, "The Stupidity of Dignity," *New Republic*, May 28, 2008.

5. J. Waldron, "Is Dignity the Foundation of Human Rights?," New York University Public Law and Legal Theory, Working Paper No. 374, January 2013, 25.

6. D. Kretzmer, "The Religious and Philosophical Background of Human Dignity and Its Place in Modern Constitutions," in *The Concept of Human Dignity in Human Rights Discourse*, ed. D. Kretzmer and E. Klein (The Hague: Kluwer Law International, 2002).

7. Boethius, "De duabus naturis" 3, Patrol. Lat. LXIV 1345.

8. H.L.A. Hart, *The Concept of Law* (Oxford: Oxford University Press, 2012), 188.

9. Bundesverfassungsgerichtsentscheidung (BVerfGE) 30, 173 (1971), Article 5.3, first sentence.

10. *Casey v. Planned Parenthood*, 112 S. Ct. 2791 (1992).

11. Paolo G. Carozza, "Human Rights, Human Dignity and Human Experience," in *Understanding Human Dignity*, ed. Christopher McCrudden (Oxford: Oxford University Press, 2013), 615–29.

12. In this chapter we do not refer to the so-called pre-accession conditionality, which is also considered a kind of political conditionality that is the requirement of meeting certain conditions (among others, democracy and the rule of law) by candidate member states in order to enter the European Union.

13. Refer to the introduction to this chapter.

14. See, among the others, T. Dolle, "Human Rights Clauses in EU Trade Agreements: The New European Strategy in Free Trade Agreement Negotiations Focuses on Human Rights—Advantages and Disadvantages," in *The Influence of Human Rights on International Law*, ed. N. Weiss and J. M.

Thouvenin (Berlin: Springer, 2015); L. Bartels, *The Application of Human Rights Conditionality in the EU's Bilateral Trade Agreements and Other Trade Arrangements with Third Countries*, a study requested by the European Parliament, Directorate General External Policies of the European Union (Brussels, 2008); L. Bartels, *Human Rights Conditionality in the EU's International Agreements* (Oxford: Oxford University Press, 2005); T. A. Borzel and T. Risse, "One Size Fits All! EU Policies for the Promotion of Human Rights, Democracy and the Rule of Law," paper prepared for the Workshop on Democracy Promotion; K. E. Smith, "The Use of Political Conditionality in the EU's Relations with Third Countries: How Effective?," *European Foreign Affairs Review* 3 (1998): 253; J. Harrison and A. Goller, "Trade and Human Rights: What Does 'Impact Assessment' Have to Offer?," *Human Rights Law Review* 8 (2008): 587; and F. Schimmelfenning, S. Engert, and H. Knobel, "Costs, Commitment and Compliance: The Impact of EU Democratic Conditionality on Latvia, Slovakia and Turkey," *JCMS* 41, no. 3 (2003): 495. See also S. Angioi, "Genesi ed evoluzione del 'principio di condizionalità' nella politica commerciale e nella politica di cooperazione allo sviluppo della comunità europea," *Rivista internazionale dei diritti dell'uomo* 2 (1999): 458; A. Di Marco, "Le clausole di condizionalità politica alla luce degli accordi di associazione: Il recente caso siriano," *I quaderni europei*, online working paper (2011), 31, available at www.cde.unict.it/sites/default/files/31_2011.pdf.

15. See Dolle, "Human Rights Clauses," 213.

16. See Smith, "Use of Political Conditionality," 259, and E. Fierro, *European Union's Approach to Human Rights Conditionality in Practice* (The Hague, 2003), 43.

17. See the statement of the council: Bull. EC of 21.06.1977.

18. Ibid.

19. See Framework Agreement for Trade and Economic Cooperation between the European Economic Community and the Argentine Republic, OJ L 295, 26.10 (1990), 67–73. Article 1 (*Democratic Basis for Cooperation*) reads: "Cooperation ties between the Community and Argentina and this Agreement in its entirety are based on respect for the democratic principles and human rights which inspire the domestic and external policies of the Community and Argentina. The strengthening of democracy and regional integration are the basic principles of this Agreement and are a concern shared by both Parties. Implementation of this Agreement shall be ensured by encouraging economic and social development by means of trade, economic, agricultural, industrial and technological cooperation."

20. Agreement between the European Economic Community and the Republic of Albania, OJ L 343, 25.11 (1992), 2–9. Article 1 affirms: "Respect

for the democratic principles and human rights established by the Helsinki Financial Act and Charter of Paris for a new Europe inspires the domestic and external policies of the Community and Albania and constitutes an essential element of the present agreement."

21. See Dolle, "Human Rights Clauses," 217.

22. Ibid.

23. The Bulgarian clause (1993) states as follows: "(1) The Parties shall take any general or specific measures required to fulfill their obligations under the Agreement. They shall see to it that the objectives set out in the Agreement are attained. (2) If either Party considers that the other Party has failed to fulfill an obligation under the Agreement, it may take appropriate measures. Before so doing, except in cases of special urgency, it shall supply the [Council] with all relevant information required for a thorough examination of the situation with a view to seeking a solution acceptable to the Parties."

24. Other important steps in the evolution of HR clauses are described in Bartels, *Human Rights Conditionality*, 23.

25. See Dolle, "Human Rights Clauses," 217.

26. Grainne de Burca and Paul Craig, preface, in Bartels, *Human Rights Conditionality*, III.

27. See Smith, "Use of Political Conditionality," 253.

28. See Bartels, *Human Rights Conditionality*, 238, and Bartels, *Application of Human Rights Conditionality*, 18.

29. Dolle, "Human Rights Clauses," 223.

30. See Carozza, "Human Rights, Human Dignity and Human Experience," 625.

31. Ibid., 615.

PART IV

Case Studies of Dignity in Practice

TWELVE

Dignity in Accompaniment

Integrated Healthcare in the Sierra Madres

Steve Reifenberg and Elizabeth Hlabse

A dirt road winds through the Sierra Madre Mountains in southern Chiapas, en route to the rural village of Salvador Urbina. Traversing a lush, humid, tropical landscape punctuated by coffee plantations and forests of tall broadleaf evergreens, the road at times parallels a winding river. There are lovely vistas, with waterfalls framed by hanging vines and orchids.

On the border with Guatemala, Chiapas is Mexico's poorest state. Over 75 percent of its population lives in poverty, with more than 30 percent living in conditions of extreme poverty.[1] Coffee production is the major industry in the southern part of Chiapas, and much of the rural population relies on coffee for work. In recent years a yellow-orange fungus, coffee leaf rust, has decimated coffee bushes, damaging much of the coffee production and worsening economic hardship. Not surprisingly, healthcare in the isolated rural villages of Chiapas has been among the worst in Mexico. However, an innovative model of healthcare delivery and community engagement is helping transform this scenario.

Gladys, a community health worker, makes her rounds, going from home to home in Salvador Urbina, her community of about 1,500 people tucked away in the mountains, literally at the end of the road. It's 8:15 in the morning, and Gladys arrives at the home of a patient, a woman in her 50s diagnosed with tuberculosis. The woman's youngest son opens the door, excited to see Gladys. His mother waits in bed, with not yet enough strength to walk to the door, left alone to tend to daily chores. Laundry hangs from the ceiling, and it's clear that the child has been busy at work, making the morning tortillas and keeping up with the household work while his mother recuperates. A kettle whistles. The boy offers Gladys coffee and a tortilla, ushering her to sit beside his mother, who smiles, encouraged by Gladys' presence. Gladys asks about her week: whether there have been any changes in her symptoms and whether the woman has taken her medicine. The boy pipes up, noting a day when his mother had forgotten a dose. Yet Gladys is quick to console her, reminding her patient that before long she will feel well again and be able to resume her daily routine. Refilling the pillbox, Gladys promises to return the next week. This is the first of six visits Gladys will make in Salvador Urbina that day.

In daily practice, Gladys is part health worker, part social worker, part community builder, all the while a mother to four and a *mama de casa*, a homemaker. One day a week, Gladys makes her rounds as a community health worker. She visits patients with chronic diseases such as hypertension, diabetes, epilepsy, and tuberculosis (TB), ensuring that they take their medication (which for patients with TB is typically an eight-month regimen). To numerous patients and families, Gladys brings hope. She breaks through the isolation that characterizes illness for many in this rural town. She connects them with healthcare, ensuring that they get the necessary routine check-ins and helping those with more serious conditions to access appropriate treatment. Though an educator, teaching her patients about their health, nutrition, and behavioral modifications, Gladys spends much of her visits listening to her patients talk about their needs, concerns, daily troubles, and joys.

Gladys is one of many community health workers, or *acompañantes*, in Chiapas. Her work is possible through *Compañeros en Salud* (CES), a Mexican-based nongovernmental organization (NGO), founded in 2011 that aims to build a model of excellence for rural primary care in partnership with the Ministry of Health (MOH). *Acompañantes* like Gladys collaborate closely with young doctors, called *pasantes*, working in local clinics. In the Sierra Madre Mountains of Chiapas, CES has worked to place motivated *pasantes* in ten local MOH clinics that formerly were abandoned.

CES envisions its model as one of accompaniment, which animates the organization and guides the work of both the doctors and the community health workers. There is simultaneously a top-down and a bottom-up process in play. CES identifies talented professionals completing medical school and motivates them to move to rural areas where there have long been few doctors, ensuring that the *pasantes* have the material support and mentorship that is likely to make them more successful in their new roles. At the same time, CES trains local community members, building a critical mass of ten or so *acompañantes* in each community. Key to CES's work is connecting the efforts of the *pasantes* and the *acompañantes* in ways that are mutually reinforcing.

Accompaniment, for CES, is about human relationship—connections between *acompañantes* and patients and between doctors and patients, as well as relationships across local communities and regional and national systems of care. Accompaniment is a model not only of integrated healthcare but, more broadly, of human development. Taking into account the person and the context in which the person lives, accompaniment affirms the dignity of patients and healthcare providers alike. Through an approach of empathy and deep listening—of walking with patients from their initial diagnoses through their plans of treatment—accompaniment empowers patients to become agents in promoting their own health. Through the example of CES, we find that dignity in accompaniment is experienced in the centrality of relationships and in integrated models of care that take into account patients' social, emotional, and spiritual needs in the context of local cultures, values, and ways of life. Hence, accompaniment is not just about effective medical care but about understanding the complex interrelationships that influence health and treatment and that can bring about systemic transformation. Beginning with patient experience, accompaniment generates insight for systems change, informing necessary improvements for policy and healthcare systems so that personalized quality healthcare might be realized for even the most marginalized populations.

PUTTING ACCOMPANIMENT IN CONTEXT

Accompaniment informs and is informed by the community health worker (CHW) model, an approach being implemented by health organizations across the globe that prioritizes local patient care with policy implications. Increasingly, evidence points to the model's effectiveness in realizing positive health outcomes. CHWs serve as access points to preventative, diagnostic, and medical treatment services, especially for isolated and underserved areas. Their long-term impact is reflected in individuals' and communities' improved health and nutrition-related behaviors,[2] which is helping to curb and prevent certain diseases like diabetes and to improve treatment adherence for those with diseases like HIV and multidrug-resistant TB.[3]

The CHW model facilitates more integrated care, as reflected in improvements in patients' psychosocial outcomes, their experience of hope, and their ability to resume existing social roles.[4] Qualitative studies show that the emotional support and direct assistance of CHWs, including for nonmedical needs (for instance, advising patients on insurance and financial support), positively impact patients' well-being.[5]

Through preventative care, CHWs have brought about sustainable economic benefits. In contrast to caregivers in a hospital setting, CHWs provide care at lower costs in patients' homes and community clinics. Their localized care contributes to "building and strengthening the communities in which they operate" while they also act as advocates to regional and national governments and related authorities on behalf of communities' needs for medical infrastructure and services.[6] CHWs have helped realize positive economic returns, in some cases as much as a tenfold return on investments, given the increased productivity and employment of a healthier population and diminished reliance on emergency services.[7]

Accompaniment, while similar to the CHW model, focuses more specifically on concepts of human dignity. Interestingly, well before it became part of the global health discourse, the conceptualization of accompaniment emerged from theology and philosophy. Fr. Gustavo Gutierrez, a Catholic priest and theologian from Peru who is generally considered the father of liberation theology, described accompaniment as a pathway for realizing the preferential option for the poor. More recently, theologians have described a theology or spirituality of accompaniment. Roberto Goizueta, James Bretzke, S.J., and Kim Lamberty write about accompaniment from within the context of Latino communities, the slums of Seoul, Korea, and in Haiti, respectively.[8] More recently, social scientists have been taking an interest in this trend.[9]

As a model for global health and human development, accompaniment is still in its nascent stage. CES is supported in realizing an accompaniment approach by its partner organization, PIH, a global health organization dedicated to partnering with local communities, national governments, and international actors to build capacity and strengthen health systems across resource-poor settings.[10] Several other organizations, primarily faith-based ones, identify accompaniment as a key principle in their work, among them Lutheran World Relief, the Mennonite Christian Peacemaker Teams, International Peace Brigades, and Catholic Relief Services and its sister organizations in Caritas International. An accompaniment approach is also present organically among a number of smaller grassroots organizations. And a small, but growing, body of literature explores the theory behind accompaniment in international organizational practice.[11] The defining characteristics of accompaniment become clear in examining the CES approach.

CES IN CHIAPAS: COMBINING A BOTTOM-UP AND TOP-DOWN APPROACH TO CAPACITY BUILDING

Some significant challenges exist in the Mexican public health system, especially in relationship to the provision of rural health. Considered by the World Bank as an upper-middle-income country, Mexico produces a large number of doctors each year and is noted among developing countries for its more developed health infrastructure, including the universal right to healthcare.[12] In 2001, Mexico launched the People's Insurance (*Seguro Popular*, or SP) to improve low-income families' access to health services, including emergency care and high-cost interventions.[13] By

2012, more than 50 million individuals had been incorporated. Despite the increasing number of doctors and nurses, specialized care is centralized in larger cities, and there is limited access to care in rural and geographically isolated areas.[14] For reasons of financial and personnel resources and the dynamics of poverty, tremendous gaps exist between the rights guaranteed by law and their realization. Despite Mexico's precedent of the universal right to healthcare, countless resource-poor communities face a lack of access to quality care and treatment.

To address the challenge of staffing rural clinics, the Ministry of Health (MOH) has for more than eighty years operated the *pasantía* program, which requires graduating medical students to complete a mandatory year of service giving primary care prior to receiving their medical licenses.[15] Nearly one-third of public primary care clinics are staffed by *pasantes*, and as many as three-quarters of *pasantes* are assigned to rural health centers.[16] Nonetheless, these young doctors typically receive little to no training specific to their field placements and little continuing medical education or support once they are in the field. *Pasantes* are often isolated and faced with running remote, insufficiently stocked clinics with patients suffering from major illnesses. Because *pasantes* are given preferences as to their service sites based on their academic performance in medical school, very often the poorest and most remote clinics receive those *pasantes* with the lowest grades, or in many cases do not receive anyone at all.

In this context, CES innovated the accompaniment model. Recognizing that universal access to healthcare depends on the equitable distribution of well-trained and -supported healthcare providers, CES worked with the MOH to identify communities in the Sierra Madre region that had public clinics but lacked full-time physicians.[17] The organization recruited graduates from Mexico's best medical schools to spend their service year in clinics in remote rural areas and, in so doing, shifted the paradigm: it assigned to these clinics top-performing medical graduates and equipped them with the necessary resources, so now the rural sites are no longer perceived as punishment for poor student performance.

Currently CES operates through ten rural public clinics in the Sierra Madres. Staffing and supplying clinics beyond the standard issue, CES ensures that clinics have in stock over a hundred medications in order to treat the majority of diseases, which can then be managed at the community level. The model of effective coverage treats patients with debilitating diseases, ranging from epilepsy to schizophrenia, TB to rheumatologic diseases. These treatments are available in communities for the first time, at no cost to patients. CES helps doctors and clinics to offer more specialized care, providing clinicians with necessary supplies, supplementary medicines, and diagnostic equipment, and forecasting needs to avoid times when these are out of stock.

ACCOMPANIMENT AS A PATHWAY FOR DIGNIFIED HEALTHCARE

Through extended relationships of care between *acompañantes*, *pasantes*, and patients, accompaniment gives centrality to the person. Beginning with the experience of the patient, accompaniment acts across several levels to protect and advance dignity in practice. First, it gives priority to equity and to delivering healthcare to the poorest and most marginalized patients. Second, accompaniment engages in processes of deep listening, empathy, and mutuality. This gives way to an integrated model of care involving patients, healthcare practitioners, and communities that generates insight for systemic change, informing policy and practice.

The deep listening, empathy, and mutuality required of accompaniment become possible through the training and support offered to *pasantes*. These young doctors are introduced to the field by former *pasantes* who stay with them during their first two weeks, and new *pasantes* receive ongoing clinical support and medical education throughout their service year. They are trained to learn from their patients how to understand health and healing as well as to adapt their language to the patients' level of understanding.[18]

The director of CES, Dr. Hugo Flores, describes the organization's approach to training doctors and *acompañantes* in empathy:

> We teach doctors to consider themselves in the situation of the patient, and help them to realize that blaming a patient for his or her lack of understanding is not an option. We teach our doctors that there are different ways people make sense of our world, our bodies, and the processes of disease, as well as the concept of healing. . . .

We teach our doctors that in the Sierra we are the outsiders, and need to learn the language of our patients.[19]

Pasantes learn to hold their expertise gently, bringing forth the resources of medicine and their professional practice in a way that is responsive to the needs and values of their patients.[20] They visit patients in their homes and check in if a patient misses a follow-up appointment. Working closely with the *acompañantes*, who are all members of the local community, *pasantes* learn where and how their patients live. They come to know their patients' families and share in their stories. Together, *acompañantes* and *pasantes* enter a process of mutual learning and teaching that sustains their work. Gladys, the *acompañante* in Salvador Urbina described earlier, reflects on how each day she tries to put herself in her "patients' shoes." She strives for empathy, to enter into the feeling of the other.[21] For *acompañantes* and *pasantes*, this empathy goes hand in hand with mutuality. Hence, when challenges come into play, the *pasantes* are less likely to think they have all the solutions; instead, they work with the patients to understand possible solutions and appropriate plans of treatment.

While the empathetic listening and mutuality involved in accompaniment reflect the qualities of mentorship, which are described in Ilaria Schnyder von Wartensee's chapter in this volume, accompaniment differs from mentorship in that it moves beyond the caretaker and patient relationship to generate insights for organizational behavior as well as more systemic change involving the broader community.

Deep listening allows for the possibility of integrated care by considering the multiple interrelated needs of the person, involving the surrounding community, and empowering the patient to act on behalf of her health and well-being. Through empathy and mutuality, *acompañantes* and *pasantes* work to create relationships of trust in which patients feel safe and able to share their concerns and needs about their health as they understand it. One *acompañante* described how working with a community member's struggles with depression helped the *acompañante* understand and address her own battles with depression. Together, they began to chart a path of working toward the patient's mental and physical health and well-being that provided great benefit to the *acompañante* as well. Recognizing the broader need for mental healthcare, in January 2016 CES launched a training program for *acompañantes* in psychosocial and cognitive therapy strategies. This integrated approach helps patients to grow in understanding of their health and to incorporate their values and practices in the treatment and healing processes. In this way, accompaniment empowers patients to become agents working for their health and well-being. Physician writer Atul Gawande captures the CES approach to accompaniment in healthcare when he cautions against an overreliance on technical answers: "We've been wrong about what our job is in medicine. We think our job is to ensure health and survival. But really it is larger than that. It is to enable well-being. And well-being is about the reasons one wishes to be alive . . . . The vital questions are the same: What is your understanding of the situation and its potential outcomes? What are your fears and what are your hopes?"[22]

For CES, the primacy of the person informs an approach to healthcare that reflects the integrated needs, values, and aspirations of the patient. By asking the "vital questions" and listening deeply to patients' responses, *acompañantes* and *pasantes* learn with their patients how to work toward the patients' health and well-being. Direct patient care translates to organizational learning. Community health workers and *pasantes* integrate lessons learned from shortcomings in patients' access to care in order to improve access—as is seen, for example, in CES's efforts to accompany patients to overcome obstacles faced in receiving referral care at local hospitals—into a conscious effort to bring operations to scale and to build effective systems. The experience of CES highlights how the organization, by accompanying patients, comes to understand broader systemic needs and begins to advocate for policy changes so as to better realize integrated, patient-centered care.

COMMUNITIES OF ACCOMPANIMENT
AND REALIZING ONE'S RIGHTS

In the accompaniment model, the realization of one's rights, including the universal right to healthcare, begins in relationships of mutual learning and education among doctors, *acompañantes*, and patients. Through a continual process of learning and gaining insight, they come not only to understand the right to healthcare, its meaning and implications, but also to perceive more clearly the dignity of the human person that underlies and animates this right. Accompaniment has resulted in transformative change across communities in the Sierra Madre of Chiapas. Patients are not only coming to better understand their health and wellbeing, but they also are coming to a fuller recognition of the contributions they as individuals can make to their communities. In Salvador Urbina, a rural township located about seventy miles from the CES central office in Jaltenango, the CES team recently celebrated the graduation of eleven new *acompañantes*. On a basketball field in the town's central plaza, a small concrete riser served as the stage for each newly trained *acompañante*—ten women and one man—to receive a diploma. Upon receiving his or her diploma, each *acompañante* explained what this training experience had meant. Their message was consistent: they had developed a commitment to be good *acompañantes*, the desire to keep learning, and an enormous appreciation for being given the opportunity to be of service to their community. As one graduate stated, "It is a great blessing to have a mission to serve and to give hope to others."

Although community health workers typically might be envisioned in their roles with respect to their patients, the graduation ceremony made clear that *acompañantes* are expanding their conception of how they contribute to their communities. Their remarks were public commitments—before the wider community of Salvador Urbina—to be of service to others, especially to those most in need. Through their work, the *acompañantes* administer critical care, reducing the threat of serious illness and preventing the high costs of late treatment. They fill a serious gap in health coverage, helping deliver healthcare to the most marginalized populations, meanwhile personalizing the care. Many of the *acompañantes*, who seemed so comfortable sharing their reflections on stage in Salvador Urbina, had never spoken in public before. They later said it had been an anxiety-producing situation, yet they were proud that they had been able to publicly share their contributions and commitment. Their reflections bring to light the mutually transformative impact of accompaniment in practice.

These *acompañante* graduates shared that there are few places where ordinary members of the community find encouragement and a space to speak about their dedication and service, as well as their aspirations for the community. Moreover, in the Sierra, women have few job opportunities outside their households. Work as an *acompañante* is part-time employment, with modest compensation in the form of a basket of food each month. Yet by caring for others in a more deliberate and public way, the *acompañantes* have come to recognize that their contributions matter; they learn to take care of patients and apply this skill set to care for their families, their communities, and themselves; and some described how they have begun to share with their spouses the responsibility of maintaining their households.

Accompaniment, nevertheless, also brings tension, as the efforts of *acompañantes* are embedded in broader structural issues, existing inequalities, and power dynamics. Inevitably, problems arise when *acompañantes* enter their new roles. Their newfound recognition can result in discontent among other community members and sometimes new power dynamics. As many of the *acompañantes* are women, problems can also arise within households as the women, traditionally homemakers, take on new roles. Accompaniment doesn't resolve these issues. Like any pathway for human development, it is necessarily embedded in existing socioeconomic structures while also risking the rupture of certain traditional ways of life, social norms, and cultural practices.

TRANSLATING ACCOMPANIMENT: BRINGING A PATIENT-CENTERED APPROACH TO SCALE

In beginning with individual patients and caring for them throughout the process from diagnosis to treatment, *acompañantes* and *pasantes* gain a distinctive set of insights about the broader systemic requirements necessary for patient-centered healthcare. Accompaniment thus necessarily leads to organizational and policy insights regarding how to care for the integrated needs of patients at scale, and, as such, it highlights the path for integrated systemic change. CES advocates for policy change by not merely pointing at the deficiencies but by focusing on specific, discernable areas of improvement and working in partnership with government to create pathways for improvement.

In Chiapas, for example, despite the improvements in patient care in communities where CES operates, the patients with more serious illnesses who require referral to specialists are often encumbered by the shortcomings of the broader healthcare context and the dynamics of rural poverty. Patients referred for surgery often face various stumbling blocks from complex documentation to delays in the timing of their first appointments. A patient might travel for hours, spending her monthly wage on transportation and missing days of work, to arrive at the surgical hospital and discover that the doctor is absent or unavailable. Patients sometimes must wait so long for surgery that their lab results or pre-surgical evaluations become out of date, requiring that they start the entire process yet again. Differing hospital procedures make the situation yet more confusing for patients and for those doctors—in many cases *pasantes*—referring them for care.

In an effort to improve patients' access to more specialized care, CES looked at PIH's pioneering efforts in Haiti, where the local PIH organization, *Zamni Lasante*, had built a Right to Health Care Program (RHC) to accompany patients from rural areas through the process of receiving specialized medical care. The RHC program manages logistics for the patients, coordinating their transportation from rural areas to more urban health facilities, helping them find lodging near the hospitals, and offering comprehensive personal assistance to patients as they navigate the broader healthcare system. In order to develop the RHC Program, CES had to navigate that system and to build a program of comprehensive assistance: it learned the hospital referral process; developed relationships with important stakeholders including surgeons, social workers, and schedulers; and identified where and how it could most effectively use its resources and contacts to ensure patients' care, even tracking down those patients who had been lost to follow-up.

To facilitate the RHC, CES identified where patients might most easily have lab work completed, which hospitals had availability, and how best to overcome obstacles. The program began with a dedicated physician, logistics coordinator, and driver. As the program has evolved through an increasingly extensive network of personal relations and sophisticated understanding of barriers, the RHC has more effectively navigated obstacles to patient care, working case by case and learning from each patient's needs.[23] As of June 2016, the program employed five team members working with more than six hospitals, including the two hospitals in Chiapas that provide tertiary care. The program teaches *pasantes* how to navigate patient referrals and anticipate obstacles in the system. The increasing availability of communications, particularly through instant messaging with WhatsApp, has made it easier to communicate with multiple sites, inquiring as to where care is readily available and helping hospitals to prepare for a patient's care before he or she arrives at the hospital.

The RHC is a model of translating patients' experience to inform systemic change. By walking with patients from diagnosis to treatment and follow-up, CES *pasantes* and *acompañantes* gain a systems perspective. They perceive supply-side constraints in terms of hospital and medical provisions and demand-side constraints in terms of patients' abilities to request and receive care. They begin to identify where bottlenecks are limiting patients' care and where there are shortcomings in communication or inefficiencies between medical practitioners.

Focusing on specific realizable areas for improvement—whether in the RHC model or the *pasante* program—CES invests in creating new pathways for care and access to care. Taking these insights, CES enters into dialogue with local government officials, highlighting examples of how those insights could be replicated and realized at scale so as to make specialized medical care more accessible to patients. In its commitment to partner with government, CES inevitably enters into challenging environments in which it can be criticized for legitimizing certain insufficiencies and problems of the state and its healthcare system. Nonetheless, CES takes on these engagements willingly, recognizing that the sustainability and scalability of integrated healthcare depends on partnership.

Accompaniment charts the path for more integrated healthcare, taking into account the whole person and the whole context of the person, including systemic, social, and structural factors, with the potential for insights for organizations, policy makers, and practitioners. It is in the daily accompaniment work of *acompañantes*, social workers, nurses, doctors, and others that dignity emerges. Through empathetic listening and mutuality, accompaniment empowers patients to act on behalf of their health and well-being and that of family and community members— transforming the understanding of what it is to participate in development. At its core, accompaniment affirms the worth of the person, demonstrating how insights generated from walking alongside patients translates into possibilities of broader systemic change.

NOTES

1. Consejo Nacional de Evaluación de la Política de Desarrollo Social (CONEVAL), "Pobreza 2014, Chiapas," 2014, available at http://www.coneval .org.mx/coordinacion/entidades/Chiapas/Paginas/pobreza-2014.aspx.

2. Henry Perry and Rose Zulliger, "How Effective Are Community Health Workers?," Johns Hopkins Bloomberg School of Public Health, Baltimore, 2012, https://www.chwcentral.org/sites/default/files/How%20effective%20are %20community%20health%20workers%20%20-%20Johns%20Hopkins %20University_0.pdf. The effectiveness of CHWs for improving primary care in low-income settings is highlighted by Prabhjot Singh and Jeffrey Sachs in "1 Million Community Health Workers in Sub-Saharan Africa by 2015," *Lancet* 382, no. 9889 (2013): 363–65, available at http://www.thelancet.com /journals/lancet/article/PIIS0140-6736(12)62002-9/fulltext?_eventId=login; see also U. Lehmann and D. Sanders, *Community Health Workers: What Do We Know about Them? The State of the Evidence on Programmes, Activities, Costs and Impact on Health Outcomes of Using Community Health Workers* (Geneva: World Health Organization, January 2007), available at https://www.chwcentral.org /community-health-workers-what-do-we-know-about-them-state-evidence -programmes-activities-costs-and.

3. Adrienne LaFrance, "The Danger of Ignoring Tuberculosis," *Atlantic Monthly*, August 3, 2016, available at http://www.theatlantic.com/health /archive/2016/08/tuberculosis-doomsday-scenario/494108/.

4. Heidi Behforouz, Paul Farmer, and Joia Mukherjee, "From Directly Observed Therapy to Accompagnateurs: Enhancing AIDS Treatment Outcomes in Haiti and in Boston," *Clinical Infectious Disease* 38 (2004): S429–36; S. Shin et al., "How Does Directly Observed Therapy Work? The Mechanisms and Impact of a Comprehensive Directly Observed Therapy Intervention of Highly Active Antiretroviral Therapy in Peru," *Health and Social Care in the Community* 19, no. 3 (2011): 261–71; and M. Muñoz et al., "Community-Based DOT-HAART Accompaniment in an Urban Resource-Poor Setting," *AIDS and Behavior* 14, no. 3 (2010): 721–30.

5. D. Thomson et al., "Community-Based Accompaniment and Psychosocial Health Outcomes in HIV-Infected Adults in Rwanda: A Prospective Study," *AIDS and Behavior* 18, no. 2 (2014): 368–80; H. L. Behforouz et al., "Directly Observed Therapy for HIV Antiretroviral Therapy in an Urban US

Setting," *Journal of Acquired Immune Deficiency Syndromes* 36, no. 1 (2004): 642–45; and S. Shin et al., "How Does Directly Observed Therapy Work? The Mechanisms and Impact of a Comprehensive Directly Observed Therapy Intervention of Highly Active Antiretroviral Therapy in Peru," in *Health and Social Care in the Community* 19, no. 3 (2011): 261–71.

6. B. Dahn et al., "Strengthening Primary Health Care through Community Health Workers: Investment Case and Financing Recommendations," *World Health Organization Reports* (2015), https://www.who.int/hrh/news /2015/chw_financing/en/.

7. Direct data on the cost-effectiveness of CHWs is limited but beginning to emerge. Ideally, such data would allow for the comparison of costs and effectiveness across different levels of care in order to assess where care is best provided. Initial studies suggest that for some interventions the cost of care can be reduced significantly if managed at the community level (for instance, a study in Pakistan on the treatment of severe pneumonia by Save the Children). An August 2015 bulletin of WHO reports on the cost-effectiveness of community-based health programs: Dahn et al., "Strengthening Primary Health Care," 8.

8. Roberto Goizueta, *Caminemos con Jesús: Toward a Hispanic Latino Theology of Accompaniment* (Maryknoll, NY: Orbis, 1995); James T. Bretzke, "Faith Seeking Transformation: Theology of Accompaniment in Post-Minjung Korea," presentation at the Korean Religions Group of the American Academy of Religion Annual Convention, Atlanta, November 22–25, 2003; and Kim Lamberty, "Toward a Spirituality of Accompaniment in Solidarity Partnerships," *Missiology, An International Review* XL, no. 2 (2012): 181–93.

9. Social scientist Patrick Coy has pursued ethnographic research on several organizations' practices of "protective accompaniment" in conflict zones.

10. "Our Vision," Partners In Health, http://www.pih.org/pages/our -vision.

11. Certain convergences (and differences) have been identified between strategies of faith-based and secular global health efforts that emphasize accompaniment. See George Kane, "Breaking Bread Together: The Convergent Development of Accompaniment in Secular and Catholic Global Health Efforts," *Journal of Global Health Perspectives*, 2012.

12. In 1983 the state of Mexico amended its constitution to include the right to health protection for all people. See Felicia Marie Knaul et al., "The Quest for Universal Health Coverage: Achieving Social Protection for All in Mexico," *Lancet* 380, no. 9849 (2012): 1259–79.

13. Felicia Marie Knaul et al., "Quest for Universal Health Coverage," Comisióón Nacional de Protección Social en Salud/Seguro Popular, Catálogo

Universal de Servicios de Salud (CAUSES), 2012, http://seguropopular
.tamaulipas.gob.mx/wp-content/uploads/2013/06/CAUSES.pdf, and N. C.
Gutiérrez, "Mexico: Availability and Cost of Health Care—Legal Aspects,"
Report for the U.S. Department of Justice, LL File No. 2014-010632, July 2014.

14. Findings suggest that the impact of SP varies based on an individual's
access to healthcare facilities. For individuals in remote rural areas or near facilities with limited staffing, SP does not reduce catastrophic out-of-pocket
expenditures. Patient usage of health facilities "decreases exponentially with distance from the patient." See Jíeffrey Grogger, Tamara Arnold, Ana Sofía León,
and Alejandro Ome, "Heterogeneity in the Effect of Public Health Insurance on
Catastrophic Out-of-Pocket Health Expenditures: The Case of Mexico," *Health
Policy and Planning* 30, no. 5 (2015): 593–99, 597; see also Dahn et al., "Strengthening Primary Health," and Gutiérrez, "Mexico: Availability and Cost."

15. Andrew Van Wieren et al., "Service, Training, Mentorship: First
Report of an Innovative Education-Support Program to Revitalize Primary
Care Social Service in Chiapas, Mexico," *Global Health Action* 7, no. 1 (2014).

16. G. Nigenda, "Social Service in Medicine in Mexico: An Urgent and
Possible Reform," *Salud Publica Mex* 55 (2013): 519–27.

17. Van Wieren, "Service, Training, Mentorship," 1.

18. *Pasantes* learn via a global health training program supported by
Brigham and Women's Hospital in Boston, Harvard Medical School, and
Tecnológico de Monterrey.

19. Hugo Flores, "Catastrophic Expenditures: What It Means to Be
Poor and Sick—and the Need for Policy Accompaniment," in "From Aid to
Accompaniment," ed. P. Farmer, *PublicAffairs*, forthcoming.

20. The transformative education reflects the charge of the Lancet Commission for Health Professions Education, which suggests that medical education reform be informed by two principles: "transformative (rather than only
informative or formative) learning, and interdependent and interdisciplinary
education." See Van Wieren, "Service, Training, Mentorship," 7; J. Frenk et al.,
"Health Professional for a New Century: Transforming Education to Strengthen
Health Systems in an Interdependent World," *Lancet* 376 (2010): 1923–58.

21. Jodi Halpern, *From Detached Concern to Empathy: Humanizing
Medical Practice* (Oxford: Oxford University Press, 2001).

22. Atul Gawande, *Being Mortal: Medicine and What Matters in the End*
(New York: Henry Holt and Company, 2017), 259.

23. In 2015, according to CES data, 391 patients in CES clinics were
"accompanied" and successfully received specialized medical care at a secondary or tertiary hospital.

THIRTEEN

Being "For Others"

Human Rights, Personhood, and Dignity in Sierra Leone

Catherine E. Bolten

Can the institution of human rights legislation actually damage human dignity rather than supporting it? In this chapter I address the possibility that human rights may be a limited good in that the deployment of universal laws in particular contexts does not result in the universal protection of human dignity. I analyze two vignettes that explore the shifting ground on which people understand dignity in the small West African country of Sierra Leone and the role that human rights legislation has played in revealing and feeding frictions in the social world. In Sierra Leone, a good life is articulated as "being for others," that is, a person understands his or her worth in their nurturing linkages with other people and not as an autonomous, entitled individual. The focus on autonomy in universalist human rights doctrine threatens the basis of Sierra Leonean understandings of personhood, as being "for others" is replaced with being "for myself." A person who focuses on his or herself is deemed badly socialized and may threaten the dignity of others. The experiences of Sierra Leoneans reveal that we cannot assume that human rights and dignity are coterminous or mutually beneficial.

As an anthropologist, I examine philosophical ideas as they become manifest in daily life. Sierra Leoneans do not speak of "dignity" per se; it was never articulated in the decade (2003–12) that I conducted research in urban northern Sierra Leone, even as I was analyzing the country's transition to peace after twelve years of civil war. Rather, implicit articulations of dignity emerged when the government enacted human rights legislation, and people began speaking and acting based on their understanding of what constituted rights. Friction emerged between adults and between parents and children over whether "rights" were undermining the basis of what it meant to be "Sierra Leonean"—and thus what it meant to be human—or whether they were addressing and correcting past social abuses, namely, the elite capture of resources and power that nurtured a decade-long civil war. At issue was the possible transformation of people's understanding of their humanity from a social world that emphasized hierarchy, authority, and community to one of supposed equality and individuality. Sierra Leonean conceptions of self and community have come into contact with a universal doctrine claiming to safeguard and recognize essential humanity, unearthing and challenging previously latent understandings of what it means to be a good person living a good life. Both of the events I describe occurred in 2012, five years after human rights and child rights were officially adopted as law. In both cases, the enactment of rights conflicted with the extant social emphasis on obligations and understandings that people are human not because of the inherent qualities imbued in them but because of what they can and will do for others.

THE EMERGENCE OF "RIGHTS" IN DAILY LIFE

It was a warm September day in Makeni, the capital of the northern province of Sierra Leone, when I sat down for a conversation with my friend Abu. He was late arriving at our meeting because he had had a confrontation with his children that evolved into an argument with his wife. Abu's wife had risen early to make breakfast for the family and sent him into the neighborhood to call in the children to eat before they went to school. He was already in a foul mood when he went out to find the two boys, as they had failed to go to the neighborhood tap with their buckets to collect water for the family, their first responsibility upon awaking. It had thus been left to his wife to do it. His mood had worsened by the time he found the children and hustled them inside. The two boys refused to come home initially, though they were already running late for school, because they did not want to abandon a soccer game that had broken out on their street. They had argued with their father that one more goal would settle the contest, and then they would return. The boys took their time returning and set to gobbling down their food without acknowledging their parents. Abu was incensed, asking them, "Are you so high and mighty that you cannot greet your father before you eat in the morning? I will withhold your food this evening if you repeat this behavior!" Apparently, one boy looked at him and said, "Breakfast is our right. Dinner is our right. You cannot withhold them." They grabbed their school bags and left without another word.

After the children departed, Abu's wife confronted him. She had drawn the water and cooked; why did he have more of a right to be greeted than she did? The boys were meant to perform their simple household tasks as a form of respect for her. She was furious that Abu had used the food she had made to demand respect from the children, when she, who had cooked it, did not receive it. Abu explained that his wife's argument had more to do with her anguish that the children appeared to have lost their will to be Sierra Leonean than with anything else. The empty buckets, the lack of a morning greeting, the casual lateness, and the fact that the boys did not appreciate their food all signified that child rights laws had replaced familial solidarity and adult authority with individual autonomy and age-independent equality, which threatened the foundations of social personhood.

In essence, to be Sierra Leonean is to do things for others, to think of others first, and to be connected rather than autonomous. Sierra Leonean children are meant to be humble and helpful and to learn that being human requires learning to do things for others—and to accept sanctioning from adults if they fail. As far as Abu and his wife were concerned, rather than emphasizing an individual's inherent dignity, rights undermined it, as dignity, like personhood, is acquired rather than inherent. "They are only hurting themselves," Abu lamented. "If they refuse to be for others, they become like animals." To be for others is to understand one's life as a web one weaves with others, in mutual need and nurturing, and recognizing that one earns the ability to climb the social ladder. It is learning to be for others that makes one human. However, all adults recognize that this is difficult, and often unpleasant, as this learning involves sacrificing one's immediate desires, and often one's short-term goals, for others. Rights are attractive because they offer instant gratification. Abu's children had received pamphlets and education on their rights at school from representatives of an international rights organization, and they also gave materials to their parents about parental obligations and legal consequences for contravention. Abu's children embraced their new social positions wholeheartedly, and Abu's experience was not singular.

The second vignette occurred a few weeks later, while I was walking in Makeni with two friends, Saidu and Mohamed. A drenching rainstorm had left massive puddles and muddy roads, but the narrow sidewalks had drained and were dry. We walked single-file on the raised sidewalk, where our path was soon blocked by freshly washed clothing, which a woman had lain carefully across the surface to dry in the sun. To step off the sidewalk at that point would have meant wading through the mud. Saidu called out, "Whose washing is this? It is blocking our way!" A woman shouted from her house, "Those are my clothes. Don't touch them!" Saidu was taken aback and picked up a skirt, waving it over a puddle and asking, "Does this have more right to the sidewalk than I do?" She retorted, "You are disturbing my human rights if you get my clothes dirty!" Perturbed, he picked up the clothes and dropped them in a heap on a table next to the sidewalk. The woman launched into a tirade about how he lacked respect for her and that he was violating her human rights, and we walked off quickly. Saidu muttered about how rights had "spoiled" people for good behavior. He explained, "Before these rights, no one would disregard others facially [in such a public way]." To use a public right-of-way for personal gain was one thing—Mohamed laughed off the incident as "one woman pushing her advantage just a little"—but to claim that one had a right to do so, thus emphasizing a legal imperative to do as she wished over and above the needs of others, was another matter entirely.

What can we make of these episodes? On the surface, they are clear-cut cases of the misinterpretation of child rights and human rights, with individuals manipulating doctrines meant to protect basic human dignity in the service of winning petty quarrels with their fellows. However, these were common occurrences and highlighted what many Sierra Leoneans considered troubling trends in behavior whereby individuals persistently used the language of rights to foreground their own desires compared to those of others. Many articulated the idea that rights were damaging sociality and that children especially were not "growing up well" because rights had "spoiled them" for proper personhood. The struggle over human rights emergent in these episodes is not part of a universal movement to engage governments in recognizing the inherent qualities of personhood,[1] nor is it a matter of people's making political claims for changes in laws that will both define and respect those inherent qualities,[2] which are two arguments put forth in anthropology as to what human rights "are" and "do." These examples illustrate rights as a challenge to responsibility, harmony, obligation, and care that potentially broadens the scope of abuses that had characterized a corrupt patrimony and nurtured a decade-long civil war, rather than eliminating it.[3] By allowing individuals to act contrary to good social relations, human rights discourse and practices have the prospect of damaging individuals' potential to lead a good life, which by definition must include other people's well-being as a primary consideration. People who live without nurturing their connections to others through acts of material exchange and work become isolated from their social networks, and the fragmentation of these networks, and thus the fragmentation of care, damages everyone.

BEING "FOR OTHERS": CARE, HARMONY, AND SIERRA LEONEAN PERSONHOOD

I begin this section with child rights, as the work of learning to be for others starts in childhood. The case of Abu and his children highlights multiple frictions that emerged from the 2007 enactment of the Child Rights Act (CRA). Adults argued that the state was inserting itself between children and their parents, disrupting the proper training and

enculturation of children and thus threatening successful social repro-
duction. The wording of the CRA follows that of the UN Convention on the Rights of the Child (CRC) closely and defines children as
autonomous agents entitled to protections and guarantees beyond those
granted adults, a situation of "neontocracy," or "the rule of the child."[4]
This stands in direct contravention to Sierra Leonean gerontocracy, the
rule of the old, and disturbs the local emphasis on social connection and
obligations existing within a community,[5] in essence the obligation of
Abu's boys to contribute to their household by drawing water. Sierra
Leoneans emphasize that children are unfinished beings,[6] socially insignificant and spiritually dangerous,[7] who mature through "good training" involving laboring for the household, submitting to adult authority,
and accepting sanctioning when they are *fityay*, or acting impudently.
Adults consider these obligations essential to children's moral and social
development, without which they are not fully human. The CRA specifically banned corporal punishment, circumscribed child labor, and
gave children the right to participate in decisions affecting their welfare,
making it clear that adults could no longer engage in the "good training"
of their children.

The implementation of the CRA was swift. Abu's children brought
home pamphlets from school titled "This Is Our Law!" with smiling
children on the cover. They articulated the rights of children—rights
to an education, food, leisure, and legal representation, among others—
in simple language and stated that adults are responsible for providing
all of these things. The pamphlet also made it clear that adults had no
right to "force" children to do anything, whether simple household tasks
or taking education seriously, and that children were legally entitled to
report any adult in violation of the CRA to the Family Support Unit at
the police station. Michael Wessells and colleagues have reported many
cases in which children have done just that, resulting in fines on and
public reprimands of poor, overworked adults. They reported parents
withdrawing care from "unruly" children, as their "bad" and "wicked"
children were bankrupting them.[8]

Instead of children being products of "good training," they are now
relieved of the responsibility to work and to care for others, the quintessential qualities of "bad training." Parents are clear that it was always
historically their own responsibility to fix "bad" children, and they often

quoted the saying *"Bad bush no de fo trowe bad pikin,"* in essence, There is no bad jungle in which to throw away bad children. However, children now have legal protection for disobedience, and the law states that the only recourse parents and teachers have to this is to "keep children busy at school."[9] Teachers argue that they cannot compel unwilling children to learn, creating a vicious cycle of unformed, "bad," and "wild" children who now embody tumultuous intergenerational social relations. The social consequences are profound, as adults who no longer have the authority to train, socialize, and sanction the community's children believe they also bear no responsibility for feeding, supervising, or caring for other children. Abu's challenge to his children that he would withhold their dinner is an example of parents' resisting this behavior; however, his children could legally report him to the police for denying them adequate nutrition.

What no child could ever report, however, was whether they were no longer receiving food from their neighbors. This had been a common practice prior to the CRA, when children were not considered autonomous, fully formed humans. A teacher in his sixties called Abdul highlighted this: "When I was growing up, I was public property. Anybody in the community can correct me or punish me if I am doing something wrong, and this way I learned that even if I was not with my mother, that did not mean that she was not watching me. And those people would feed me as well, so I was like everyone's child, and so was every other child in the village." If a child's mother could not provide food, they could usually find nourishment at other homes, especially from those women who took an interest in their "good training." For many parents, the loss of community supervisory capacity and children's responsibilities was part and parcel of their children's *fityay* and of their own inability to ensure that their households maintained the necessary labor inputs. The children suffered physically due to the new law: not only were household resources lost but also the social linkage between molding and feeding was broken. Stripped of the power to sanction other people's children, people's once-common offerings of food, water, and care to their community's children are waning, highlighting an integral relationship between power and obligation that characterizes Sierra Leonean personhood. This inversion of historical childrearing practices is now alienating children from vast social networks that had fed, supervised, and trained them as an investment in the future. By rendering children autonomous, the law is effectively atomizing them and rendering them vulnerable.

The state itself has no institutions or resources for child protection; therefore, it cannot step in as a substitute support network for children who are now suffering in ways rights organizations might find inexplicable. The adoption of child rights occurred without lawmakers' knowledge of the extant framework of relationships, in which the social contract is paramount. When an adult feeds a child, a relationship of debt and obligation is created between them. The child recognizes that the adult is investing in him and that the adult will have the right in the future to call on the child for material or social support. In being for others, the emphasis is placed on putting oneself at the service of others, knowing that in time these debts will be repaid. It creates a social safety net that extends much further into the future than the simple feeding of a hungry child. However, the time frame of delayed gratification inherent in the social contract is voided by rights that emphasize the immediacy of relationships. It is imperative that a rights framework respect the dignity inherent in cultural modes of childrearing, including the realization that the right to sanction is embedded in the responsibility to feed and that these are not simple tit-for-tat actions, but actions with long-term consequences for the social contract.

The case of the woman laying her washing out on a public sidewalk and openly arguing with Saidu illuminates how the local adoption of the International Covenant on Civil and Political Rights (ICCPR) has undermined the emphasis on maintaining public harmony and unity, quintessential elements of Sierra Leonean sociality. I want to provide an immediate caution that harmony as an ideology can hide a multitude of evils if people are actively discouraged from articulating suffering, violence, or abuse in the service of those who control their social worlds.[10] However, an ideology of maintaining good public relations and a sense of unity requires a way of articulating and addressing conflict formally. "Hanging heads"—the practice of community leaders meeting to transform conflict of any sort into some kind of public consensus—once provided the primary route for ensuring grievances or conflicts, whether concealed or public, were addressed.[11] Because this process forced people to accept resolutions of their conflicts that might not be in their favor, individuals habitually acted with consideration for others lest a litany of past public sins be used against them in private negotiations.

Now that individuals have the legal "right" to consider only their own needs, even with respect to ostensibly public goods, the power of harmony to encourage people to consider others has been attenuated, and people nurture anger instead of relationships. Saidu and the lady drying her wash never resolved their argument; rather, he walked away as she shouted, both considering that they were in the right. Both of them had *wam at*, "warm hearts," meaning that they carried their anger with them, with no possibility of facing their differences and "cooling" their hearts. To carry a warm heart means that the person is acting "for" him- or herself—one's anger is one's own—and is potentially dangerous, as it opens an individual up to future conflict and "invites" that conflict to return.[12] If the people in conflict were both thinking of their obligations toward each other and of the benefits of cultivating good relationships, the conflict would never have occurred; in our case, the lady would have moved her washing or found somewhere else to put it to begin with.

Harmony was also once maintained through the process of reparations, which became particularly salient in the immediate aftermath of the civil war. The *fambul tok* (family conversation) is an old custom of gathering around the village bonfire, during which people aired any wrongs done to them and perpetrators asked for forgiveness through offers of reparations.[13] Those reparations usually involved righting the wrong that had been done, for example, a man's offering a lifetime of manual assistance to the person he had physically disabled through a vicious beating. Before these reconciliations became common due to the efforts of a Sierra Leonean lawyer, these individuals would silently avoid each other, creating agonizing silences in once lively villages and stopping both peace and reconstruction in their tracks. Before rights were established, the woman with the washing would have automatically made the small calculation that forcing others to wade through the mud would produce social consequences and that it was her responsibility not to do so. With rights enacted, that responsibility and any attendant consequences were both nullified. Public goods have become open to private abuse, and individuals, rather than considering each other as a matter of course, think primarily of themselves.

The emergence of friction, and potentially the atomization of people, is part of a larger trend within human rights in discourse and practice in Africa. Human rights legislation was not enacted through social and political trends aiming to enhance human dignity; rather, they initially emerged as political cries for help in the 1980s and early 1990s in a country crippled by debt and structural adjustment. Joseph Momoh, who was president from 1986 to 1992, ratified every UN convention that crossed his desk. He was signaling to bilateral donors that Sierra Leone was a modern country worthy of their aid and investment. Though the conventions were not adopted under his presidency, they became salient with the establishment of the Truth and Reconciliation Commission (TRC) at the end of the civil war in 2002. The TRC reached an agreement with then-president Tejan Kabbah that the commission's recommendations would be legally binding resolutions to the social and political problems that had nurtured the war.

It was at the war's end that international organizations began serious humanitarian engagements with Sierra Leone, and much of this work involved the explicit deployment of human and child rights frameworks. Through the programming of organizations dedicated to the rehabilitation of child and youth combatants in particular, discourses about the relationship between age and personal responsibility, for example, first became pronounced and salient in the social world. This began with the Lomé Peace Accords in 1999, which marked the first time that child soldiers were explicitly mentioned in a peace agreement.[14] Various UN organizations were brought in to assist the government with programming that would explicitly address the needs of demobilized child soldiers, and the resulting programming relied on "the discourse of abdicated responsibility," whereby children were legally and socially absolved of the crimes they committed during the war because they were under the age of eighteen at the time. Programming was developed through "lessons learned" from other conflicts in Africa and Latin America, rendering the implementation of and education around rights the result of multiple levels of abstractions and assumptions about the universal nature of childhood.[15] As demobilized children re-engaged with civilian communities, the universalist doctrine came into contact with local notions of childhood, reworking and remaking both children and the doctrine itself.[16] As the war receded into the distance, the more international doctrines were tempered by the realities of everyday interaction between children and adults, with children working and submitting to the authority of adults. Old hierarchies began to reassert themselves, if only because living with others was so much easier for children than the alternative, and this required being "for others."

The country also initially faced difficulties with grasping the identities of and finding futures for hundreds of thousands of "war-affected youth": young people for whom the decade of war had been their primary formative experience, even as, by definition, they took no active role in the fighting. This is where the initial implementation of rights-based frameworks for action became subject to explicit conversations at the local level. Steven Archibald and Paul Richards argue that war-affected youth took the lead in local-level "social renewal" in the rural areas and were often joined by their mothers and sisters, using a rights-based framework in conversations aimed to "reconfigure the social" with respect to their relationships with their male elders.[17] Before the war, the traditional value of being for others had been systematically abused by elders, who received the majority of tribute, loyalty, and work, and redistributed little to those in need, especially youth, whom they argued could "stand on their own feet."[18] Women and youth, who had gained confidence in their abilities after surviving the war, began speaking out in meetings, arguing for justice and fairness in moments when they previously would have been silent. Though Archibald and Richards couched these discussions in the terms of human rights, the arguments made by vulnerable groups speak more to a fundamental conception of dignity in which there is no discrepancy between being for others and being treated fairly, honestly, and with respect by community leaders.

The dignity framing was not, however, successful in transforming local contexts to a fulsome embrace of former combatants. The majority of former combatants and displaced war-affected youth who returned to their communities or attempted to integrate into new ones had to temper their quests to be treated with dignity to the immediate need to find social acceptance, which required an elaborate performance of being for others. Many former combatants were successful in reintegrating into communities if they argued that they never acted "for themselves" in the war; rather, that their agency had been subsumed to their commanders. Adopting the personas of humble strangers in a new village, many were accepted if they strove to work for the benefit of the community and paid a small token monthly to the chief—re-establishing the prewar patrimonial order rather than pushing an altered framework that was welcoming to conceptions of rights.[19] The war and its aftermath opened the possibility of thinking in terms of rights, justice, and dignity, but the extant frameworks of patrimony and gerontocracy were not easily altered, even as these frameworks enabled injustices that contributed greatly to the war.

The TRC had as a primary task addressing these abuses, and existing rights doctrines provided easy and internationally identifiable ways of moving forward. The full adoption of ratified UN treaties was a primary tenet of the TRC's final report in 2003, with a strict timeline for implementation. Four years later, the ICCPR and the Convention on the Rights of the Child became law in Sierra Leone.[20] People that I spoke to from 2010 to 2016 agreed that prewar social politics, characterized by a gerontocracy under which young people and the poor existed in relative indentured servitude, was corrupt and abusive. However, they also agreed almost unanimously that the implementation of rights in Sierra Leone did not correct these abuses; instead it shifted the framework under which individuals could disrespect or damage each other. This is not a problem of rights as an abstract philosophical concept designed to embrace and celebrate human dignity but a problem of what happens when a doctrine is enacted within contexts in which local precedents for good behavior and well-being already exist, even if they had been tarnished through abuse.

HUMAN RIGHTS AND SOCIAL PERSONHOOD IN AFRICA AND SIERRA LEONE

What is the relationship between human rights and dignity, and how can a cross-cultural examination of human rights assist in the quest to understand human dignity? The literature on human and child rights illuminates that contestations are commonplace when ostensibly universal doctrines are incorporated into diverse local social contexts. Scholars write of people in various cultural milieu seeing human rights as an "imported" discourse arriving with foreign interests, be they colonial or humanitarian.[21] In addition, the individualist assumptions of rights doctrines do not resonate in places where people are not conceived of primarily as individuals, for example, among the Swazi of southern Africa. Ethical practice in Swaziland is predicated on people's being "Swazi" first and individuals only secondarily, and ethical practice emerged from this sense of community.[22] In the case of the Dinka Agaar of South Sudan, people's individuality is subsumed to their clan membership, rendering one life essentially interchangeable for another.[23] Scholar Jeffrey Deal struggled to maintain his conception of individual lives' having unique worth when working with the Dinka, for whom any young man's life can be taken in revenge for a clan member's wrongdoing. These examples illustrate starkly what is at issue when context is ignored in favor of universal claims about how people understand their own dignity.

The primacy of the community is similar in Sierra Leone, with the attendant consequences for notions of individuality. If individuals can enact productive relationships only through their membership in communities, rather than as autonomous beings, rights may undo the capacity of those communities to, for example, produce large rice harvests or collectively look after their children.[24] The UN may have articulated individuality as a universal quality of persons, but this vision comes into conflict with social worlds where individuals draw their dignity from being part of a whole greater than themselves. Some scholars have emphasized that people often conceive of "rights" as possessing salience within *unequal*, rather than egalitarian, social relations. Harri Englund argues that the poor in Malawi made claims not as autonomous agents but by placing themselves under the authority of legitimate leaders. Dependency is the basis for specific moral and material accomplishments, making relationships themselves the basis for claiming rights.[25] James Ferguson highlights this point in what he calls "declarations of dependence," whereby in southern Africa personal autonomy is equated with atomization and isolation.[26] Only by pursuing relationships with powerful people can poor, unconnected individuals gain incorporation and membership in a social world.[27] Through these relationships of responsibility and obligation, individuals achieve their full potential as human beings.

This argument occurs in other guises, particularly as "wealth in people'" which describes the political, social, and economic measure of individuals in their relationships with others, specifically clientelism and patronage, which are salient in Sierra Leone.[28] This is where the idea of "atomization" as the outcome of rights is a possibility. The youth who argued for the need for justice in their own communities were highlighting that adults were abusing their power to sanction them and failing in their responsibility to provide, agonizing over failures of their work-based system rather than arguing for a new system based on universal morals.[29] The way people understand their personhood, and thus their conceptions of dignity, becomes clear through these analyses. The "practice" of human dignity is emphasized rather than inherent qualities so that we can understand rights, and thus dignity, within the everyday activities that people undertake within their social worlds. As new discourses change the way people think about their everyday comportment, a conversation with a friend or a walk down a street can illuminate the otherwise invisible battles taking place over what it means to be human. Though Ferguson and others talk about "unequal relationships" as a basis for rights, in Sierra Leone this is conceived as "being for others."

The converse of the generous outward thinking of being for others, "being for myself," seems unproblematic in social worlds where autonomy and individuality are assumed human qualities and comprise fundamental aspects of dignity. However, in Sierra Leone, with a long history of slavery, drought, internal warfare, and a concomitant culture of mitigating risk through investing in people, being for oneself is dangerous for more reasons than just causing petty quarrels to emerge on street corners or, in the case of children, refusing to do their chores or greet their parents. It signals not just a movement away from a framework of generosity and sanctioning that make positive social life possible but also the inversion of that framework. As Abu explained regarding his children, they become "like animals." If people possess the "right" to think of themselves first (and potentially think only of themselves) and it becomes illegal to sanction others for bad behavior—be they children who refuse to do chores or adults who casually and openly use a public good for private gain—there is no way, as many people have argued, to "see" them as humans. Humans are connected, caring, and considerate; disconnected beings are animals.

Giorgio Agamben used the example of a bandit as an individual whose existence was stripped of its political salience, leaving only his "bare life" as his being. He writes: "to 'ban' someone is to say that anyone may harm him, or [he] was even considered to be already dead."[30] This person is stripped of his political personhood and loses all the rights and consequences attending that status. Agamben's bandit appears at first to contradict the struggle over rights in Sierra Leone, as rights doctrines were intended to furnish citizens with robust political personhood and legal protections. And yet Agamben's rumination illuminates a fundamental point concerning how people recognize their personhood equally as socially and politically salient. For a banned person to be truly "dead," all individuals who have encountered that person have had to deny their personhood. And yet a person can still be denied personhood without a legal brand, such as being sent out of the spaces of human habitation. If they find others and live with them in the woods, for example, they regain some humanity through this recognition. In an example given by Archibald and Richards, elders who were alarmed when youth withdrew from the village and set up a bush camp when their grievances were not heard stated that they were potentially responsible for turning their youth into rebels through their pursuit of unjust aid redistribution policies.[31] For all the youth to retreat together signaled a demand for their individual and collective personhood, and dignity, to be recognized.

The construction of people as "animals" in Sierra Leone was first apparent to me when many former combatants described the lowest points in their lives. For many, being rebels—even if they were kidnapped and forced to kill their family members—was emotionally damaging, but not nearly as much as the further separation from those bonds, often through the deaths of their battle comrades. One former combatant was in tears while describing a time after a skirmish destroyed his unit, when he lived alone in the bush and emerged only to beg for food from villagers.[32] He was reduced to being less than human—a soul without dignity—as no one cared for him and he cared for no one, and thus his basic personhood was negated. We can think about the introduction of "rights" in Sierra Leone in a similar key, if not a similar register. In deploying rights to affirm their salience in the world, many Sierra Leoneans have experienced the clash of rights with extant understandings of personhood whereby they respond to individuals asserting their autonomy with declarations of separation from them. Abu still agreed to care for his children and feed them, even as he perceived them as demanding, ungrateful, and "like animals."

Other researchers have described different outcomes, especially between parents and children, in which parents "give up" on children who have defied them too often in asserting their own personhood. In withdrawing resources and care from their *fityay* offspring, they have atomized their children and significantly damaged their life chances.[33] Though rights in the abstract have the potential to enhance people's life chances by affirming their dignity as autonomous, unique beings, the experience of rights in Sierra Leone has diverged from this expectation. The early focus on the dignity of survivors after the war, in which communities began to form their own conceptions of a more just world in which elders owed women, youth, and children a fair and honest share of the world's productivity, was overcome by a top-down legislation of what "rights" looked like. In asserting autonomy over connectedness and what one is owed rather than what one owes others, individuals see attaining rights as a process of people's shedding the hard work of well-being and personhood through being "for others" and accepting instead a diminished life on one's own. For dignity to be truly apparent in Sierra Leone, the laws must consider how a life well lived is imagined and be willing to attend to those contours.

NOTES

1. Mark Goodale, "Human Rights after the Post–Cold War," in *Human Rights at the Crossroads*, ed. Mark Goodale (Oxford: Oxford University Press, 2013), 1–28.

2. Michael Goodhart, "Human Rights and the Politics of Contestation," in Goodale, *Human Rights*, 31–44.

3. Joseph Hanlon, "Is the International Community Helping Recreate the Preconditions for War in Sierra Leone?," *Round Table* 94, no. 381 (2005): 459–72; William Reno, *Corruption and State Politics in Sierra Leone* (Cambridge: Cambridge University Press, 2008); and Paul Richards, *Fighting for the Rainforest: War, Youth, and Resources in Sierra Leone* (New York: Heinemann, 1996).

4. David Lancy, *The Anthropology of Childhood: Cherubs, Chattel, Changelings* (Cambridge: Cambridge University Press, 2008).

5. Melissa Leach, *Rainforest Relations: Gender and Resource Use among the Mende of Gola, Sierra Leone* (Washington, DC: Smithsonian Press, 1994).

6. Susan Shepler, *Childhood Deployed: Remaking Child Soldiers in Sierra Leone* (New York: New York University Press, 2014).

7. Mariane Fermé, *The Underneath of Things: Violence, History, and the Everyday Sierra Leone* (Berkeley: University of California Press, 2001), 198.

8. Michael G. Wessells et al., "The Disconnect between Community-Based Child Protection Mechanisms and the Formal Child Protection System in Rural Sierra Leone: Challenges to Building an Effective National Protection System," *Vulnerable Child and Youth Studies* 7, no. 3 (2012): 211–27, and Michael G. Wessells et al., "The Limits of Top-Down Approaches to Managing Diversity: Lessons from the Case of Child Protection and Child Rights in Sierra Leone," *Peace and Conflict: Journal of Peace Psychology* 21, no. 4 (2015): 574–88.

9. Government of Sierra Leone (GOSL), *Compendium of the Gender Laws in Sierra Leone* (Freetown: Ministry of Social Welfare, 2007).

10. Laura Nader, *Harmony Ideology: Justice and Control in a Zapotec Mountain Village* (Stanford, CA: Stanford University Press, 1990).

11. Mariane Fermé, "Staging *Politisi*: The Dialogics of Publicity and Secrecy in Sierra Leone," in *Civil Society and the Political Imagination in Africa*, ed. John L. Comaroff and Jean Comaroff (Chicago: University of Chicago Press, 1999), 160–90.

12. Rosalind Shaw, "Linking Justice with Reintegration? Ex-combatants and the Sierra Leone Experiment," in *Localizing Transitional Justice: Interventions and Priorities after Mass Violence*, ed. R. Shaw and L. Waldorf (Stanford, CA: Stanford University Press, 2010), 111–34.

13. Lyn S. Graybill, "Traditional Practices and Reconciliation in Sierra Leone: The Effectiveness of *Fambul Tok*," *Conflict Trends* 3 (2010): 41–47.

14. Shepler, *Childhood Deployed*, 61.

15. Ibid., 63.

16. Ibid., 83.

17. Steven Archibald and Paul Richards, "Converts to Human Rights? Popular Debate about War and Justice in Rural Central Sierra Leone," *Africa: Journal of the International Africa Institute* 72, no. 3 (2002): 339–67.

18. Ibid., 345.

19. Shaw, "Linking Justice with Reintegration?," 125.

20. Catherine Bolten, "Productive Work and Subjected Labor: Children's Pursuits and Child Rights in Northern Sierra Leone," *Journal of Human Rights* 17, no. 1 (2017): 199–214, http://dx.doi.org/10.1080/14754835.2017.1315296.

21. Daniel Goldstein, "Whose Vernacular? Translating Human Rights in Local Contexts," in Goodale, *Human Rights*, 111–21; John Rusk, "Africa Rights Monitor: Structures of Neo-Colonialism: The African Context of

Human Rights," *Africa Today* 33, no. 4 (1986): 71–76; and Shepler, *Childhood Deployed*, 4.

22. Sari Wastell, "Being Swazi, Being Human: Custom, Constitutionalism, and Human Rights in an African Polity," in *The Practice of Human Rights*, ed. M. Goodale and S. E. Merry (Cambridge: Cambridge University Press, 2007), 320–41.

23. Jeffrey Deal, "Torture by Cieng: Ethical Theory Meets Social Practice Among the Dinka Agaar of South Sudan," *American Anthropologist* 112 (2010): 563.

24. A. A. An Na'im, "The Legal Protection of Human Rights in Africa: How to Do More with Less," in *Human Rights: Concepts, Contests, Contingencies*, ed. A. Sarat and T. R. Kearns (Ann Arbor: University of Michigan, 2001), 89–116; Harri Englund, "Cutting Human Rights Down to Size," in Goodale, *Human Rights*, 201; James Ferguson, "Declarations of Dependence: Labour, Personhood, and Welfare in Southern Africa," *Journal of the Royal Anthropological Institute (N.S.)* 19 (2013): 223; and Rusk, "Structures of Neo-Colonialism," 72.

25. Englund, "Cutting Down to Size," 204.

26. Ferguson, "Declarations of Dependence," 224.

27. Ibid., 225.

28. A. E. Nyerges, "The Ecology of Wealth-in-People: Agriculture, Settlement, and Society on the Perpetual Frontier," *American Anthropologist* 94 (1992): 860.

29. Archibald and Richards, "Converts to Human Rights?"

30. Giorgio Agamben, *Homo Sacer: Sovereign Power and Bare Life*, trans. Daniel Heller-Roazen (Stanford, CA: Stanford University Press, 1998), 104–5.

31. Archibald and Richards, "Converts to Human Rights?," 347.

32. Catherine Bolten, *I Did It to Save My Life: Love and Survival in Sierra Leone* (Berkeley: University of California Press, 2012), 95.

33. Wessells et al., "The Disconnect," and Wessells et al., "The Limits of Top-Down Approaches."

FOURTEEN

"The Heart to Continue"

A Case Study on Mentorship in Periurban Kenya

Ilaria Schnyder von Wartensee

I arrived in Dandora, Kenya, at the end of May after an exhausting two-day trip from South Bend, Indiana, to Amsterdam and finally to Nairobi. During the layover in Amsterdam, instead of waiting at the airport, I decided to visit the Van Gogh Museum downtown. The painting *The Potato Eaters* captured my attention.[1] The painting depicts a poor rural family struggling for daily subsistence, sharing a meager meal. In conveying their quotidian communal life, the work communicates dignity. A woman, presumably the mother, pours a beverage into each cup. Some faces seem to be expressing a desire for more; other faces are hopeful.

Vincent described the painting to his brother Theo thus:

> You see, I really have wanted to make it so that people get the idea that these folk, who are eating their potatoes by the light of their

little lamp, have tilled the earth themselves with these hands they are putting in the dish, and so it speaks of manual labor and—that they have thus honestly earned their food. I wanted it to give the idea of a wholly different way of life from ours—civilized people. So I certainly don't want everyone just to admire it or approve of it without knowing why.[2]

In Dandora a few days later, my gaze was caught by a little boy reading a piece of a journal recovered from one of the nearby piles of garbage. Surrounding him were many other children and women trying to sell their vegetables or secondhand clothes to make ends meet. The dust, the smell, and the misery of Dandora deeply hurt me. More than one hundred years since Vincent wrote to his brother, in a poor urban area of this world, I listened to the stories of women who earn their food honestly through manual labor and struggle to live with dignity. How is it possible? How do they have *the heart* to continue? I have come to find that a mutual experience of care and friendship enables these women to endure. At the core of this relationship, respect for one another's human dignity engenders a new way of living within—though not dependent on—one's situation of poverty.

Dandora is a periurban area located northeast of Nairobi, Kenya. Its four square kilometers are home to about 151,046 residents (according to the 2009 census). Dandora is well known for its immense dump, the municipal waste dump site, the primary location for the disposal of solid waste for all of Nairobi, where an estimated two thousand tons of unsorted waste is deposited daily. The dump is the origin of adverse health effects for the local population and livestock, resulting from metal contamination.[3] The burning of waste and methane fires impact the air quality, creating a toxic environment for residents. Pollution has been found in the vegetables sold in several Nairobi markets, including those in Dandora.[4] The area near Dandora is considered one of the world's most polluted places and lacks basic infrastructure and services, including adequate access to water, sanitation, roads and footpaths, electricity, and public lighting.[5] About 50 percent of children living near the area suffer from respiratory ailments, and blood lead levels exceed internationally accepted levels.[6] In addition to the unhealthy conditions and environmental degradation, the area also has elevated levels of violence, a high unemployment rate, food insecurity, uncertainty of property rights, and lack of education and healthcare facilities.

In 2011, the University of Notre Dame's Ford Family Program in Human Development Studies and Solidarity established the Dandora Human Development Program in partnership with the local Holy Cross Parish to assess the development needs and resources of Dandora's residents. Through a community engagement strategy, residents prioritized the need to learn business practices.[7] The literature shows that empowering the business capacity of young female entrepreneurs in developing countries should be a priority in socioeconomic development, since women tend to invest their business profits in their families and children (i.e., housing, health, and education).[8] In 2014 and 2015, Wyatt Brooks, Kevin Donovan, and Terence Johnson of the University of Notre Dame conducted a randomized controlled trial in Dandora to investigate whether mentoring a group of young female entrepreneurs in their business activities yielded positive effects. Their research showed that young female entrepreneurs who were mentored benefited more in the year following the conclusion of the experiment than both young female entrepreneurs who received standard business training and their counterparts in a control group—largely because nearly half of the mentees and mentors were still meeting twelve months after the mentorship program officially ended. The study does not, however, clarify why so many mentors and mentees continued to meet or whether nonbusiness factors influenced the likelihood of the sustained partnership. In this chapter I consider how the women's flourishing in the context of mentoring relationship gives us insight into how the recognition of dignity can contribute to human development.

Through narratives and qualitative data collection, the present study aims to explore the reasons that mentors and mentees continued to meet and invest in their relationship beyond the initial financial motivation. Considering the potential of mentorship, the study has found that *encouragement* and *mutual care* are key dimensions in sustained mentoring relationships. Moreover, the concepts of encouragement and mutual care convey how dignity is experienced despite undignified conditions of poverty and environmental degradation. The findings relate to the chapter in this volume of Reifenberg and Hlabse, who consider how dignity is a key feature of the accompaniment model of *Compañeros en Salud* (CES).[9] As in mentorship, quality relationships between *acompañantes* (community health workers), *pasantes* (young doctors), and patients were essential to people becoming protagonists in their own development and flourishing. The present study considers qualitatively the experience of human dignity in mentoring relationships while also identifying the unique role of female entrepreneurs in East Africa.

THE MENTORSHIP EXPERIMENT

In their experiment, Brooks and colleagues randomly assigned 372 young businesswomen to three groups: one group received a standard-ized in-class business training program, the second was assigned to meet individually with a successful local business mentor, and the third constituted a control group.[10] Random matching between mentors and mentees was conditioned on the mentor and mentee's being engaged in similar business sectors; however, it was not always possible to fulfill this condition.

Mentees were asked to meet with their mentors at the locations of the mentors' businesses on a weekly basis over the course of a month (the same length of time as the in-class program). Researchers did not provide elaborate directions but rather supplied short scripts of questions for the mentors to facilitate discussion. With respect to the in-class program, four two-hour business classes were facilitated by faculty of Strathmore University, covering conventional topics such as market-ing, accounting, cost structure, inventory management, and the creation and development of business plans. The participants in all three groups received 48 USD to participate. Mentors were selected among Dandora business owners who were over 35 years old and had been operating the same businesses for at least five years. The mentors also received a bonus of 48 USD for participating.

The study found that mentorship was effective in improving busi-ness outcomes among microenterprises. At the official conclusion of the program (after one month), 85 percent of mentees were continuing to meet with their mentors, and over the course of the following year the weekly profits of the mentees were on average 20 percent higher than those of the in-class and control groups. As the mentor-mentee relationships concluded, the positive effects of mentorship on profitability compared to the other groups began to diminish, but it is important to note that, although the experiment did not provide huge incentives to enhance mentors' motivation, 45 percent of the mentor-mentee pairs continued to meet one year after the one month specified by the study. With regard to the in-class business training, the study seems to confirm, despite the training's popularity, its modest impact on profits and sales.[11]

As to the reasons for the increase in profits among mentees, Brooks and colleagues identified switching to new, less expensive suppliers, more effective bargaining for better prices in the marketplace, and improved management of inventory, particularly during difficult periods. In some cases, mentors acted as guarantors for mentees so that they could obtain credit from suppliers or lent them money to expand their businesses.[12]

What engendered such support from the mentors? What motivated the mentors to invest time and resources in mentees without apparently receiving anything back? What did the mentors and mentees respectively gain from their relationships? What were their reasons for maintaining these relationships beyond the conclusion of the study?

THE METHODOLOGY OF THE PRESENT STUDY

The database for the experiment included a list of 198 mentees and mentors.[13] For the purposes of the qualitative study, thirty-one participants were randomly selected from this list: ten continuing mentees, nine continuing mentors, eight former mentees, and four former mentors. The participants chosen were contacted by phone. Interviews were conducted in May and June 2016 by the principal investigator and two research assistants. The interview questions were in English, and the interviewees responded in English and Kiswahili. Lasting between thirty minutes and one hour, the interviews were recorded, transcribed verbatim, and, when necessary, translated into English by the research assistants. In order to understand the local context, the principal investigator visited mentors and mentees at their workplaces. Transcripts from the interviews were coded and analyzed using a thematic analysis approach.

BACKGROUNDS

The group of female business owners (both mentors and mentees) inter-viewed participated in a range of business areas, including perishable food, clothing, tailoring, and small pharmacy management. The majority decided to enter business out of a desire for autonomy (self-employment), flexibility, and personal accomplishment. Through their respective enter-prises, the women have more money with which to support their fami-lies, particularly through paying for rent and their children's education.

Which area of business each woman pursued depended on her par-ticular talents, interests, and hobbies. Women frequently decided to start a given enterprise because relatives previously had owned businesses of the same kind and could provide support or because they observed the examples of other women already succeeding in similar ventures. The ini-tial capital required was generally low (about 1,000 Kenyan shillings/10 USD), and with their savings the women were generally able to buy stock (such as vegetables or secondhand clothes) and begin selling. The Nairobi City Council requires business owners to obtain business per-mits for small fees. Both obtaining and maintaining the license—with the requisite fees—is a stressful step for many young businesswomen.

The majority of the mentees interviewed initiated their businesses between 2009 and 2013, while the mentors had begun between 1992 and 2008. At the beginning of the experiment, the mentors and mentees did not know each other. Findings show that the mentorship relation-ships worked better when the products or services provided by the busi-nesses of mentors and mentees were similar.

THE POTENTIAL OF THE MENTORING PROCESS

In Homer's epic poem *The Odyssey*, when Odysseus left for the Trojan War, he appointed his friend Mentor to direct, wisely guide, and inspire his son, Telemachus. In contemporary parlance, a mentor is someone with the qualities of wisdom, honesty, and generosity, someone who accom-panies, guides, and supports a less-experienced and generally younger individual in her personal and professional growth. M. Polanyi classified the type of knowledge gained through mentorship as "tacit knowledge."[14]

Whereas "explicit knowledge" refers to more objective and structured knowledge (for example, of the types of skills acquired in formal business classes), tacit knowledge suggests a more informal, experiential form of skills acquisition that allows for "a fluid mix of framed experience, values, contextual information and expert insight."[15] Standard business training tends to be less efficacious because, being "standardized," it omits the context, aspirations, and needs of specific entrepreneurs.[16] Mentorship, in contrast, is practical and context-specific, giving mentees the opportunity to learn important insights about the local environment.

Tacit knowledge is closely related to the process of "learning by doing" and is transmitted through a process of socialization and internalization.[17] Walter Swap and colleagues argue that the mechanisms of mentoring and storytelling promote the transfer of tacit dimensions of knowledge.[18] Mentors educate their mentees by sharing their experiences, offering constructive feedback, serving as models, and recalling stories and challenges they encountered in the past. By doing so they "disclose important pieces of their own histories, such as critical turning points in their development."[19] As in the accompaniment process, tacit knowledge is disclosed through relationships grounded in empathy.[20] An empathetic relationship allows for the "vital questions" of a person's unmet needs to be voiced, answered, and explored together in a context of trust and deep listening. Mentorship, like accompaniment, relies on trust to foster a deeper awareness of one's needs and challenges through constructive dialogue. However, the mentoring relationship diverges from accompaniment when mentors share their own relatable stories of fear and development, which invites mentees to see themselves as agents capable of embracing their present challenges with optimism.

FINDINGS

The findings show that mentorship led to fruitful relationships for all those interviewed, including former mentors and mentees. The reasons for this relate both to the improvements in mentees' businesses and to the human enrichment of both parties, engendered in relationship.

The present study confirms the findings of Brooks and colleagues—that mentors provided key advising to mentees regarding effective ways to cut costs, helping mentees identify where to buy inventory at lower prices and how to stock supplies in larger quantities to save money. Mentors also advised mentees about methods of accounting, optimal business hours, customer relations, and product variation in order to improve business outcomes and diversify revenue sources. As one mentor pointed out: "[M]y mentee had not fully grasped the business environment, [and] it was important for me to steer her in the right direction. . . . I advised her to sell groundnuts during the cold seasons just as an added commodity to uplift her business."

Despite the overall positive outcomes, the mentoring relationship did not work for some. Confirming the findings of Brooks and colleagues, the most common explanation given by former mentors and mentees of why their relationships ended were problems in communication, coordination, and commitment (e.g., the mentors and mentees never met, or the meetings were rare; phone numbers that were lost or changed; lack of commitment or willingness to learn); or lack of mentor availability (and the consequent difficulties of developing a bond; as one mentee expressed, "We have not known each other long enough"). Interestingly, many former mentors and mentees expressed the desire to be reconnected with their former counterpart.

It could be argued that the positive responses to the interview questions were the result of participants' expectations that they would receive additional compensation. It is fairly remarkable, however, that no participant explicitly complained when compensation ended, nor did anyone express a desire to receive more money. Similarly, none of the respondents, including the former mentors and mentees, exhibited dissatisfaction or levied criticisms against the mentoring relationship. On the contrary, this study suggests that the relationships were genuinely positive for both those who continued meeting and those who had stopped meeting.

KEY ELEMENTS OF SUCCESS: ENCOURAGEMENT AND MUTUAL CARE

Encouragement: Providing the Heart to Continue

In entrepreneurial enterprises, mentoring implies a relationship between an experienced entrepreneur (the mentor) and a novice entrepreneur (the mentee), with the goal of promoting the latter's personal and professional development. According to Etienne St-Jean and J. N. Audet, mentoring relationships convey both cognitive learning (such as management and organizational skills, as well as business vision) and affective learning (including impacts on the outcomes of attitude, motivation, self-confidence, and values).[21] Those mentors who continued to meet with mentees over the course of a year offered specific technical and professional skills grounded in the local context while also involving the mentees in their networks, opening doors that the mentees would not be able to open themselves.

In their contribution to this volume, Wydick, Dowd, and Lybbert stress the crucial role of hope in stimulating the growth of female entrepreneurs.[22] Hope is fostered through the encouragement and support (affective learning) that mentors offer to their protégés during difficult times. One mentee recognized the uniqueness of the relationship by using two different metaphors—a bridge and a midwife, saying: "[The mentor] gave me strength and that morale and motivation. . . . She was a bridge to me to get to the other side. . . . She helped me to keep hope, not to give up. She encouraged my spirit . . . to go on working. . . . She is like a midwife who always helps a mother to deliver."[23]

The word "encouragement" comes from the French *coeur*, or heart. As Beretta affirms in her chapter in this volume, heart is "the spark for human action."[24] The word "heart" was in fact used by some respondents to describe the encouragement they received from their mentors to continue and to have hope: "She [the mentor] encouraged me, gave me heart to continue my business"; "[the mentor] encouraged me not to have a faint heart but to be working as there are days when the business would be low"; "[the mentee] has given me the heart to work."

By actively and receptively listening, mentors reassured mentees and strengthened their confidence, helping them to reduce their anxieties, facilitate problem-solving, and inspire perseverance and resilience. As Peter F. Wilson and Brad Johnson describe, "The mentor's courage allows the protégé to face adversity ultimately boosting self-confidence and solidifying a new identity."[25]

By being affirmed and accepted, mentees become better able to believe in themselves and to take new risks. In fact, people thrive in safe, friendly, and supportive environments; they flourish with warmth and acceptance: "When a mentor is friendly, open, approachable, and consistently encouraging, protégés are more at ease with risk-taking, more assured they can succeed, and more comfortable asking for advice and assistance."[26] This type of support is generative: "Mentoring is . . . a process of bringing into existence and passing on a professional legacy. Mentors communicate to their mentees excellence and provide a strong sense of inspirational motivation."[27] The mentoring relationship also involves the growth of certain virtues, including patience and the capacity to accept and overcome problems, especially in youth who tend to be more emotionally reactive. As one mentor explains, "I teach her [the mentee] how to be patient. . . . There was a time her business was on the low and she decided to close for two months, I called her and told her to go back to work, be patient and begin making customers . . . regardless the difficulties in order to be successful . . . These young people are never patient."

One mentee acknowledged that she enjoys the relationship with her mentor because she understands her struggles, having undergone the same experiences: "When you sit with a person who has gone through what you have gone through you feel happy because you can understand each other. . . . It is easy to sit with her because she is not opposite from you." Mentees spoke of their mentors' capacity to provide them with optimism and positivity, helping them to view their own potentialities and resources with confidence. Mentees recounted having learned that hopefulness could supplant the frustration and negativity that the unpredictability of business can generate.

An aspect of the mentors' encouragement includes how they convey determination and a work ethic to mentees through their own examples in daily work. Two mentees affirmed: "I saw it's like she is a hard working woman because as much as there is competition she is determined; the most important thing I learnt from her is that determination"; "she [the mentor] wants me to be up like her, not to sleep even one day." Mentors also reflected determination by reassuring their mentees that challenges are part of the journey and that there are better ways to face them than by stopping prematurely. Life in Dandora is difficult because of insecurity and urban violence (many interviewees recounted robberies that had occurred in the area). A young woman starting a small business from scratch must deal with additional challenges; for instance, there is the need to obtain a business permit from the Nairobi City Council. Other challenges include the fluctuation of prices, the lack of money or stock during certain periods, the need for loans and the repayment of debts, and the uncertainty generated when customers buy on credit. Many young mentees admit that it is easy to lose hope, confidence, and optimism given the uncertainty of the environment. One said: "Before the work was down, and I nearly lost hope in business," and "I used to despair when I do not make sales, but now I know that tomorrow will be a better day." One mentee expressed her anxiety over her safety: "I used to tell her that I was afraid of working here due to the robbery incidences." Through their encouragement, mentors help mentees to recognize their value and dignity: "You have to accept yourself and not lose hope. . . . If you have decided you want to venture into a business you should continue with it. This is because there are those who tend to lose hope when the business goes down. My mentor told me there will be days when it will be hot and there will be no food to sell, but one has to look for ways to run their business, accepting oneself and moving forward." As Johnson and Ridley affirm, "The most important type of affirmation . . . is an acknowledgement of a person's inherent worth."[28] Many mentees identified that the mentor took on the role of a mother or sister who helped them to feel at peace: "She is as my mother. She knows me very well; even when I am disturbed she will know. . . . At the end of the day I feel relaxed."

Encouragement is not a one-time event; rather, mentees highlight the importance of sustained relationships in which their mentors become points of reference who tirelessly reassure them. The mentors were physically present, giving their time and visiting the mentees at their businesses. As one mentee testified: "She did not abandon me at any particular point. As busy as she was when I used to visit her at a salon, she would always attend to me."

Mutual Care

Another aspect of the mentoring dynamic is the importance of mutual support between the mentor and the mentee: "Mutuality is the shared respect, trust, and affection that evolve in a reciprocally beneficial mentoring relationship."[29] An understanding of the mentorship relationship would be incomplete without recognizing how the mentor herself undergoes a process of transformation and development. Quarles van Ufford and Giri describe this dynamic: "Development is not only meant for the other, it is also meant for the self . . . both the development of the other and development of self should go hand in hand."[30] Mentors achieve personal satisfaction from imparting skills and knowledge and from receiving fresh energy, loyalty, and support from their mentees.[31] Fletcher and Ragins examine how mutual learning contributes to the development of a high-quality mentoring relationship,[32] for instance, by creating a "power with" relationship[33] instead of a "power over" dynamic characterized by more hierarchical relationships. Hence, trust becomes a central feature in reciprocal business relationships, particularly in mentorship relationships.[34] This type of caring relationship is rare, as it requires a high level of confidence from both sides to overcome the competition and envy that can manifest in the business environment and in human relationships generally. As one mentor highlights, "It is not an easily accepted [cultural practice]. This is because people view it as competition, thus assisting one to achieve a certain business goal is out of the question."

This closeness is expressed by mutual assistance in which both the mentor and the mentee benefit: "Once we started this relationship, each of us became a beneficiary." They meet, discuss, share, and develop new ideas together: "We met and discussed about business and advised each other so much. And we even decided to add cosmetics to get more profit." Both parties in the relationship bring skills that can help the other. As one mentee states: "We have assisted each other and been able to remove each other from our low points." Mentees also advise mentors on improving their business activities: One mentee said: "I have taught [the mentor] how to arrange her shelves in a certain way because she used to mix up the drugs." Mentors often offer financial help to their mentees by providing credit or by starting a joint microfinance group: "I enjoyed this program because it united us together so we talked and came up with a *sacco* [cooperative] . . . like 100 shillings . . . after two weeks we got drugs so that we don't have loopholes [gaps] in our stock."

Many mentors and mentees develop relationships that go beyond giving business advice and transform into genuine closeness: "[The mentor] does not only want to know how I am doing in business . . . but what is going on with my family, and she gives me the most appropriate advice on what is going on in my life." For the mentors, what began as narrowly conceived transfers of expertise and knowledge expanded into an investment of self through one's time and energy. They became passionately and emotionally involved. In this case, the relationship extends beyond business and enters a more personal sphere of people's lives. As one mentee described it: "It is unique. This is because some time back we had no one to ask us about the experiences in our personal life and help you by just allowing you to reveal yourselves to them. Also sometime last year we were given money which is something very rare." Likewise, another former mentee affirmed: "We used to mingle talk about family matters; sometimes she gives me fish to take to my children." In many cases, the mentee was younger and found in the mentor someone with more experience and wisdom: "As a single parent we tend to go through many challenges . . . she has children. . . . She is able to tell me whether I am moving in the right direction or a wrong one. I have gained a lot from her; she is an old lady . . . she advises me . . . she is experienced in life despite the differences in our experiences."

The story of Jenny [mentor] and Eleanor [mentee][35] is an astonishing example of a mentoring relationship that developed into a friendship. When Eleanor contracted an illness and needed to be hospitalized for six months, Jenny employed another person to run the business for Eleanor. Jenny recalls the story: "There was a time she went down. When I went there we talked and talked, and she told me she was sick and she has to be admitted [to the hospital], so I told her I will employ a girl who would be selling for her, and I will be collecting the money in the evening . . . and when she came out of the hospital, her business was doing good. That was for six months." A similar experience is remembered by Eleanor: "When I was very sick . . . I was admitted to hospital and she run my business on my behalf until I came out of hospital" [breaks down crying]. When Jenny was asked the reason for her actions, she replied, "You know, where I came from, I starved a lot and I don't want to see anyone else starve like I did. Even now in my house I have two boys I adopted. I don't even know their parents." Eleanor expressed deep gratitude: "She took me from far . . . I think I would have been very down . . . I would always start a business and it would fail. . . . I am so grateful with her."

Beginning with the findings of Brooks and colleagues' 2016 randomized control trial on the impact of mentorship among female entrepreneurs in Dandora, Kenya, this study focuses on the reasons for which some mentors and mentees continued to meet and invest in their relationships beyond the experiment's timeline. It examines the outcomes of these relationships in both economic and human terms.

The mentorship dynamic is not perfect; even though the majority of the mentor-mentee pairs reported that they had enjoyed the experience, many mentees and mentors stopped meeting a few months after the experiment officially ended, frequently because of difficulties with communication and coordination but also because of a lack of commitment. This resulted in reduced profits and, from a personal and human point of view, reduced the empowerment of the mentee.

The interviews with both former and continuing mentors and mentees revealed that encouragement and mutual care are the crucial characteristics of mentoring relationships. Several mentees spoke of encouragement using the word "heart" (for instance, "[She] gave me the heart") to describe how the relationships with their mentors changed their attitudes toward work and made their commitments stronger. This conveys the potential for a caring and affective relationship to provide a "safe haven" in which a person can truly be herself. Authentic self-expression reflects the person's dignity, her unique "way of perceiving the world," which informs a "way of living" in accord with her full potential, as explained by Bieri.[36]

The majority of mentees stated that their mentors motivated them to pursue their commitment to business despite their fears of failure and contextual difficulties, such as market unpredictability, the insecurity of the area, and the lack of initial capital. This study conveys how "whole-hearted" mentoring relationships recognize the other's dignity and the intrinsic worth of every human being. When mentees experience being recognized by their mentors for their intrinsic value, they find the strength and motivation to keep striving and to face the inevitable sacrifices, costs, and momentary despair that their entrepreneurial endeavors entail. It is interesting that at least two mentors continued helping their protégés because of a desire to raise them to the same level of success that they themselves had attained—a desire that can generate lasting change.

Moreover, many mentors and mentees continued to meet not only because the mentors gained esteem and respect from teaching younger women about their experience, but also because both parties mutually benefited from the relationship; in many cases, the bond became a genuine, close friendship. In this sense, the mentorship process fostered the unique abilities and talents of each mentee, displayed mutual beneficence, and promoted an example of equality that was seen by the entire community. This demonstrates a second reason for sustainable results: the desire to continue working together for friendship and mutual learning.[37]

In other words, the study reveals that mentoring relationships have the potential to generate experiences of human and economic empowerment. The positive effects of these experiences would be reinforced by physical places and supportive environments in which mentors and mentees could discuss their experiences. In the painting *The Potato Eaters*, the family served as a nourishing and generative haven, and Holy Cross Parish in Dandora likewise has the potential to be a fertile and dynamic ground wherein new relationships can develop and flourish, acting as a bridge and point of reference for a durable mentorship program.

Overall, the findings of this study have implications for understanding how development practice should be grounded in an approach that takes into consideration the dignity of each person involved. Relationships embedded in encouragement and mutual care are the "legs" enabling a person to "walk [on] the rough ground" of impoverished conditions.[38] Mentorship intensifies mentees' sense of dignity by reinforcing their present capabilities and strengthening their hope in the future, for both themselves and their communities. The shared trust of mentorship allows mentors and mentees to move beyond business partnerships to empathetic relationships sustaining "hearts" in the journey of development.

NOTES

The author gratefully acknowledges the support of the Kellogg Institute for International Studies, Paolo Carozza, Steve Reifenberg, Elizabeth Hlabse, Taylor Still, Wyatt Brooks, Kevin Donovan, and Terry Johnson for critical commentary, support, and encouragement. Special thanks to Kathy and Doug Ford, Robert Dowd, and in particular Jackie Oluoch Aridi, Christine Achieng, Brian Ambutsi, Brian Mukhaya, and the Dandora community for permitting me to conduct this study.

1. Vincent van Gogh, *The Potato Eaters*, 1885, oil on canvas, 82 × 114 cm, Van Gogh Museum, Amsterdam, https://www.vangoghmuseum.nl/en/collection/s0005V1962.

2. Vincent van Gogh, *The Letters* (Amsterdam: Van Gogh Museum, 1885).

3. H. Nakata et al., "Metal Extent in Blood of Livestock from Dandora Dumping Site, Kenya: Source Identification of Pb Exposure by Stable Isotope Analysis," *Environmental Pollution* 205 (2015): 8–15.

4. A. N. Mutune, M. A. Makobe, and M.O.O. Abukutsa-Onyango, "Heavy Metal Content of Selected African Leafy Vegetables Planted in Urban and Peri-urban Nairobi, Kenya," *African Journal of Environmental Science Technology* 8, no. 1 (2014): 66–74.

5. Blacksmith Institute, "The World's Worst Polluted Places: The Top Ten of the Dirty Thirty," New York, September 2007.

6. United Nations Environment Programme (UNEP). "Environmental Pollution and Impacts on Public Health: Implications of the Dandora Municipal Dumping Site in Nairobi, Kenya," UNEP, 2007.

7. Ford Family Annual Report (2013), internal document, unpublished.

8. Rachel Lock and Helen Lawton-Smith, "The Impact of Female Entrepreneurship on Economic Growth in Kenya," *International Journal of Gender and Entrepreneurship* 8, no. 1 (2016): 90–96; D. Kelley, C. Brush, P. Greene, and Y. Litovsky, *Global Entrepreneurship Monitor 2010 Women's Report* (Wellesley, MA: Babson College, The Global Entrepreneurship Research Association, 2011), available at http://ibqp.org.br/wp-content/uploads/2016/09/GEM-2010-Women-Report.pdf.

9. See the chapter by Steve Reifenberg and Elizabeth Hlabse in this volume.

10. Wyatt Brooks, Kevin Donovan, and Terence Johnston, "Local Knowledge and Managerial Ability in Kenyan Microenterprises," working paper, Ford Family Program in Human Development Studies and Solidarity, University of Notre Dame, Notre Dame, IN, 2016.

11. D. McKenzie and C. Woodruff, "What Are We Learning from Business Training and Entrepreneurship Evaluations around the Developing World?," *World Bank Research Observer* 29 (2013): 48–82.

12. Brooks et al., "Local Knowledge and Managerial Ability."

13. Ibid.

14. M. Polanyi, *The Tacit Dimension* (New York, NY: Doubleday, 1996).

15. T. H. Davenport and L. Prusak, *Working Knowledge: How Organizations Manage What They Know* (Boston, MA: Harvard Business School Press, 1998).

16. J. Hessels, M. Van Gelderen, and R. Thurik, "Entrepreneurial Aspirations, Motivations, and Their Drivers," *Small Business Economics* 31, no. 3 (2008): 323–39.

17. I. Nonaka, H. Takeuchi, and K. Umemoto, "A Theory of Organizational Knowledge Creation," *International Journal of Technology Management* 11, no. 7 (1996): 833–45.

18. Walter Swap, Dorothy Leonard, Mimi Shields, and Lisa Abrams, "Using Mentoring and Storytelling to Transfer Knowledge in the Workplace," *Journal of Management Information Systems* 18, no. 1 (2001): 95–114.

19. W. Brad Johnson and Charles R. Ridley, *The Elements of Mentoring* (New York: Palgrave Macmillan, 2004).

20. See the chapter by Reifenberg and Hlabse in this volume.

21. Etienne St-Jean and J. N. Audet, "The Role of Mentoring in the Learning Development of the Novice Entrepreneur," *International Entrepreneurship and Management* 8, no. 1 (2012): 119–40.

22. See the chapter by Bruce Wydick, Robert Dowd, and Travis Lybbert in this volume.

23. To protect the confidentiality of mentors and mentees, none of their names are given in the text or the notes.

24. See the chapter by Simona Beretta in this volume.

25. Peter F. Wilson and W. Brad Johnson, "Core Virtues for the Practice of Mentoring," *Journal of Psychology and Theology* 29, no. 2 (2001): 127.

26. Johnson and Ridley, *Elements of Mentoring*, 16.

27. Ibid., xv.

28. Ibid., 10.

29. Ibid., 34.

30. Philip Quarles van Ufford and Ananta Kumar Giri, "Reconstituting Development as a Shared Responsibility," in *A Moral Critique of Development: In Search of Global Responsibilities*, ed. Philip Quarles van Ufford and Ananta Kumar Giri (London: Routledge, 2003), 253–78.

31. T. D. Allen, "Mentoring Relationships from the Perspective of the Mentor," in Belle Rose Ragins and Kathy E. Kram, eds., *The Handbook of Mentoring at Work: Theory, Research, and Practice* (Los Angeles, CA: Sage Publications, 2007); Kathy E. Kram, *Mentoring at Work: Developmental Relationships in Organizational Life* (Glenview, IL: Scott Foresman, 1985).

32. Joyce K. Fletcher and Belle Rose Ragins, "Stone Center Relational Cultural Theory: A Window on Relational Mentoring," in *The Handbook of Mentoring at Work*, ed. Ragins and Kram.

33. Mary Parker Follett, *Creative Experience* (New York: Peter Smith, 1924).

34. Peter F. Wilson and W. Brad Johnson, "Core Virtues for the Practice of Mentoring," *Journal of Psychology & Theology* 29 (2001): 121–30; Stephen Covey, *Principle Centered Leadership* (New York: Simon and Schuster, 1992); and Chip R. Bell, *Managers as Mentors* (San Francisco: Berrett-Koehler, 1998).

35. Names here have been changed to maintain confidentiality.

36. Peter Bieri, *Human Dignity: A Way of Living* (Cambridge: Polity Press, 2016).

37. Limited to the experience of mentors and mentees in the context of Dandora, this study partially lacks generalizability of its results. More research is required to determine the efficacy of mentorship and mutual assistance in contexts where the characteristics and conditions of the actors involved may differ.

38. Ludwig Wittgenstein, *Philosophical Investigations* (Oxford: Blackwell, 1967).

FIFTEEN

L'Arche as an Experience of Encounter

Tania Groppi

On May 18, 2015, upon receiving the prestigious Templeton Prize at St. Martin-in-the-Fields, London, Jean Vanier, a man of 87 years old who was simply dressed in a navy jacket, expressed his thanks for the "magnificent award" given him "in recognition of the beauty and the value of people with intellectual disabilities. This beauty has been revealed as *we have lived together in L'Arche*," said Vanier. He continued:

> People with intellectual disabilities are the ones who are the heart of our communities; they are the ones who have revealed to so many

---

Editors' note: This chapter was prepared and accepted for publication prior to the public revelation of Jean Vanier's abusive relationships with a number of women during his lifetime. Because the focus of this chapter is fundamentally not about Vanier himself but rather about the experience of L'Arche as a movement that places the recognition of human dignity at the core of its mission and practice, we, in consultation with the author, believe that it remains a valuable contribution to the larger themes and questions explored in this book, notwithstanding the references to the life and work of Jean Vanier.

people—families, assistants and friends—their human and spiritual gifts. It is to them this prize will be given, so that many more people with intellectual disabilities throughout the world may grow in greater inner freedom, *discover their fundamental value as human beings and children of God.* They in turn will be able to help many so-called 'normal' people, imprisoned by our cultures orientated towards power, winning, and individual success, *to discover what it means to be human.*[1]

Jean Vanier is the founder of L'Arche (the Ark), an international movement of residential communities, which celebrated its fiftieth anniversary in 2014 and now numbers 149 communities in 37 countries on all five continents, including five thousand members with disabilities.[2] Each community is born out of the desire to create a place where people can feel at home—not an institution, but a *foyer*, according to the French translation—in which people with intellectual disabilities ("core people" or "core members") and caregivers ("assistants") live together, experiencing a community life inspired by the Beatitudes.[3]

L'Arche realizes a distinct vision of human development by conveying how life in common with people with disabilities involves mutual growth in and through relationship. Community is a place wherein each person can grow to become more fully him- or herself, where each member can develop his or her unique gifts; it is a place of belonging in which each person may be transformed and find human fulfillment.

As a lawyer, I sought first to illustrate L'Arche and its contribution to the enactment of human dignity and human development by focusing on its fundamental elements and core values, as identified in several "normative" documents.[4] However, I quickly discovered the deficiencies of this approach and that we must instead turn to the concrete, lived, and incarnated experience.

FUNDAMENTAL ELEMENTS AND CORE VALUES OF L'ARCHE

The "Identity and Mission Statement" provides a self-definition of L'Arche: "We are people with and without intellectual disabilities, sharing life in communities belonging to an International Federation.

Mutual relationships and trust in God are at the heart of our journey together. We celebrate the unique value of every person and recognize our need of one another."[5]

The core values are detailed by the "Charter of the Communities of L'Arche" (approved in 1993),[6] which remains in force notwithstanding certain changes in the vision reflected in more recent documents.[7] These core values are deeply rooted in the vision of a common humanity and human dignity.

Common Humanity

The first fundamental principle of the charter can be considered as the foundation of L'Arche, from which all the other principles flow: "Whatever their gifts or their limitations, people are all bound together in a common humanity. *Everyone is of unique and sacred value*, and everyone has the *same dignity* and the *same rights*. The fundamental rights of each person include the right to life, care, home, education and work. *Also, since the deepest need of a human being is to love and to be loved, each person has a right to friendship, to communion and to a spiritual life.*"[8]

Relationship and Community

From this vision of the human person, some consequences arise: "If human beings are to develop their abilities and talents to the full, realizing all their potential as individuals, they need an environment that fosters personal growth. *They need to form relationships with others within families and communities.* They need to live in an atmosphere of trust, security and mutual affection. They need to be valued, accepted and supported in real and warm relationships."[9] This fundamental principle is developed in the paragraphs on personal growth: "L'Arche communities are places of hope. *Each person, according to his or her own vocation, is encouraged to grow in love, self-giving and wholeness,* as well as in independence, competence and the ability to make choices. *The communities wish to secure for their members education, work and therapeutic activities which will be a source of dignity, growth and fulfillment for them.*"[10]

In addition, it continues: "All community members are invited to participate, as far as possible, in decisions concerning them."[11] Other aspects are included in the principles on community life: "Home life is at the heart of a L'Arche community. The different members of a community are called to be one body. They live, work, pray and celebrate together, sharing their joys and their suffering and forgiving each other, as in a family. They have a simple life-style which gives priority to relationships."[12]

Spiritual Life

Among the fundamental principles of L'Arch we find this statement: "In order to develop the inner freedom to which all people are called, and to grow in union with God, each person *needs to have the opportunity of being rooted and nourished in a religious tradition*."[13]

This principle is also developed by the paragraphs on personal growth: "*The communities wish to provide their members with the means to develop their spiritual life and to deepen their union with and love of God and other people,*" as well as in the paragraphs on the communities, according to which "L'Arche communities are *communities of faith*, rooted in prayer and trust in God. *They seek to be guided by God and by their weakest members, through whom God's presence is revealed.* Each community member is encouraged to discover and deepen his or her spiritual life and live it according to his or her particular faith and tradition. Those who have no religious affiliation are also welcomed and respected in their freedom of conscience."[14]

All those principles and values are translated into concrete practices in the everyday life of each L'Arche *foyer*, informing the organization of the times of activities, as well as working programs, routines, activities, physical care, meals, holidays, celebrations, and, more generally, the behaviors of all members. Several documents of national and regional communities of L'Arche set forth the practices to be followed in order to fulfill the organization's mission. They are especially addressed to the coordinators or to the boards, as they may be used to evaluate a community's growth and needs and to set priorities for the future. They also inform the formation of community members as coordinators and assistants.[15]

During my first visit to Trosly in February 2011, I began to recognize that L'Arche cannot be described—even less understood—as an institution, or as a federation of institutions. L'Arche cannot be described at all. It has to be lived, for L'Arche is a way of life. This is not only my personal feeling. In fact, many people spoke of the "mystery of L'Arche." A former assistant remarked that one has to be something of a poet to really understand the meaning of L'Arche: beneath the surface of the daily routines in the homes of L'Arche, there is an "obscure dimension" of life lived together with persons with learning disabilities that is difficult, if not impossible, to put into language.[16]

L'Arche is a place in which meetings between persons take place in an elemental way, as much through a look, a gesture, or a touch as through words. L'Arche is also lived on a level that is very tangible and physical. There are chores to be done and residents' baths, meals, and appointments to look after. These two levels are intimately linked. The tenderness of a glance of recognition over the dinner table between an assistant and a core member with an intellectual disability cannot be separated from the sheer physicality of washing dishes or cleaning floors together. The mystery of L'Arche lies in the relationship between those two levels, and it cannot be captured in words.[17]

Nevertheless, I will try to describe as much of this mystery as possible by relying on the direct testimonies of Jean Vanier and the assistants[18] and—as far as possible—of the persons with intellectual disabilities. The "silence" of the core members (whose testimonies are not as numerous) has to be pointed out: as many of them tend to communicate more through bodily gestures and behaviors than through verbal language, the only possibility for listening to them is to create a space in which they may be heard. As a scholar with a disability said during a workshop in Trosly, "Not only our lives and bodies, but also even a lack of voice and communication capacity, may speak so loudly."[19]

With this awareness in mind, we may now return to the foundation of L'Arche.

L'ARCHE AS A WAY OF LIFE

On August 4, 1964, Jean Vanier, a Canadian man in his midthirties, began a life of community with Raphaël Simi and Philippe Seux. Both Raphaël and Philippe were affected by intellectual disabilities, and with Jean they shared a small house in a village at the edge of the Compiegne forest in the French region of Picardie.[20] "It went very quickly. It was unexpected!" Jean Vanier remembered on the occasion of the fiftieth anniversary of the foundation:

> When I started, I cannot say that I thought it was going to grow. I had been shocked by the way in which people with disabilities were treated. They were the humiliated, the lowest, the worthless.... I met my first two companions in an institution near Meaux. They lived in horrible conditions. We started with a small very dilapidated house but we were happy. This was liberation for them, and for me too.[21]

They settled in a small stone house, decrepit and modest. They called it "L'Arche."

The idea of living together was there from day one, the idea of living happily together, of celebrating and laughing a lot, came very quickly and spontaneously. *When the idea of the poor educating us came, I don't know exactly.* The words of St. Vincent de Paul, "The poor are our masters" were always there, but when they became a reality is uncertain.[22]

Vanier reflects:

> Living with these two men with intellectual disabilities *has transformed my life.* Before I met them, my life had been governed chiefly by my head and by a sense of duty, I had created inner barriers to protect myself from my fears and vulnerability. In L'Arche, I began to learn to live from the heart. Despite some difficult moments, these forty-seven years have brought me great joy. My heart has been opened and my understanding has grown. I had learnt a great deal about the human heart and its need for, but also its fear for, relationships of love and communion with others. I have learnt much about the gospel, and about the life and person of Jesus. *L'Arche has been for me a school of love.*[23]

The fact that "L'Arche is first and foremost an experience" emerges in a very clear way from the testimonies of the assistants and is highlighted through a study conducted in 2007 at the request of L'Arche by external scholar Christian Salenson, whose research involved interviews and meetings with the members of L'Arche and questionnaires given to the members.[24]

How might we understand the experience of L'Arche? It is an experience of encounter: its members describe *L'Arche as a place where one encounters the other*, not merely as a place that cares for people. In the case of L'Arche communities, this is not necessarily obvious, as an encounter implies parity between two parties, and this cannot be found at L'Arche because there is asymmetry between assistants and people with disabilities.

The formal recognition that people are "gifts of God" and full members of the community does not provide for a satisfactory explanation. Notwithstanding this recognition, the imbalance remains evident as far as intellectual capacities, and often physical ability, are concerned. But parity may be found in places other than those usually recognized. "It is not enough simply to say that we are all human," says Salenson. "That is obviously so. But when there is such a marked imbalance, what is to be done? How is it possible for there to be a true encounter?"[25]

L'ARCHE AS AN EXPERIENCE OF TRANSFORMATION

The accounts of L'Arche assistants convey that, on the one hand, "core members" are transformed through being treated with care and love, being considered as fully human. Their anxieties and anguishes are relieved, and most of the core members finally find peace and experience a certain level of joy and happiness. For the assistants—as for Jean Vanier at the beginning of his shared life with Raphaël and Philippe—community life with the core members unveils their own weaknesses. Encountering the vulnerability of suffering, broken, and rejected people reveals the assistants' own vulnerabilities, very often hidden beneath an appearance of strength and self-confidence.[26] Though weakness could have prevented the encounter, on the contrary, it allows for a singular encounter, a constant renewal of the original experience of the first *foyer*.

At L'Arche, each person, with or without disabilities, joins the community with all of his or her experiences of both life and faith and with all of their wounds. Mutual vulnerability makes for trust—and therefore true encounters—between assistants and core members, which would otherwise be unimaginable.[27]

In community life, each person has to face his wounds. Every wound tells a story: the person that has been hurt speaks "about what it is to be human because he is someone who has, to a greater or lesser degree and not without suffering, come to an acceptance of his limits."[28]

All members of L'Arche are changed by these encounters in several ways.[29] By saying that an experience of encounter has changed them, the members of L'Arche attribute to this encounter a dynamism that comes from the other and over which they have no control: it can be considered a grace-based moment. They welcome an irruption into their lives that has the potential to change them, which is gifted by another, including the person living with a disability—an interruption that is out of their control. Then *"L'Arche is first and foremost an experience, an experience of encounter between people, some of whom are living with a disability, and this encounter is life changing for both parties."*[30] As Salenson has written:

> *At heart the founding experience of L'Arche is that weakness is a source of life.* And that instead of merely being a theory, it is a lived reality! The person with a disability is then at the centre of this reality—as an unequivocal sign and means of the experience—confronting everyone with the truth of its own history.... *The experience of personal fragility as a source of life, which in itself is an individual experience, is institutionalized in L'Arche.* The institution itself is built and never ceases to be built around that notion.[31]

The experience emerging from the narrative of the long-term assistants is that of a progressive, threefold awakening.[32] The first is the awakening of the capacity for tenderness and love. The power of the encounter with the weak reveals that human personhood is not rooted in the ability to think, understand, judge, or act. One's deepest identity and value consist in the capacity for an exchange of love, presence, and communion with another.

The second awakening occurs in the encounter with deeper sources of anguish within the self. Faced with their limits in fatigue, impatience, and anger, assistants report that they are led to confrontations with their inner pain and darkness. As Jean Vanier has remarked, "People may come to our communities because they want to serve the poor, but they will only stay once they have discovered that they themselves are the poor."[33] In order to become full members of a community, assistants must make a passage from seeing themselves solely as caregivers to recognizing that they themselves are weak, broken, and in need of care and love: a passage of humility.

The third awakening is an experience of peace and self-acceptance, because of a radical acceptance by the other that frees the assistants from their pretense of self-sufficiency and autonomy and allows them to be more fully who they are. According to Michael Hryniuk, "This third movement—has been maintained—is one of the great mysteries at the heart of [the] L'Arche experience."[34] It involves a change from the "false self" toward a new identification with the original "true self," an identification made possible through the unique experience of vulnerability and mutuality with persons with disabilities.

THE RELATIONSHIP AT THE CENTER OF L'ARCHE

Although there are few testimonies of the core members,[35] it becomes evident from the accounts of assistants that at L'Arche the person living with a disability is an active agent in the community, a subject, and not an object of care. Salenson says: "*The consequence of this is that it is not the person with disabilities that is in the centre of L'Arche, but the relationship between the person with disabilities and other community members. Everyone has the possibility of being welcomed into L'Arche, as they are along with all their weaknesses and their fragility.*"[36]

At the crux of L'Arche is not the person with a disability but rather the relationship. This nuance is essential. "It is because of the relationship that each person, in his life shared with people with disabilities, is called to face again his own humanity, a humanity likewise shaped by the experience of weakness, suffering, woundedness and fragility."[37] The core members with disabilities, those who are weak and vulnerable, are the healers who teach the assistants by helping them to discover their own vulnerability, to live at the level of the heart. As Therese Vanier, the sister of Jean Vanier who spent a large part of her life at L'Arche in England wrote, "For me, the poor and the weak are all those who live primarily, or it may seem entirely, at the level of their hearts. Their needs and vulnerability is [*sic*] very great. They have evangelized me in revealing the truth of me. . . . L'Arche . . . is a place where we recognize our common humanity, discover we share the same deep seated needs as those we care for."[38] *From the centrality of relationships involving mutual vulnerability*, several practical consequences arise in the organization of L'Arche, including the need for communities to remain small, to allow each member to know one another by name.[39] The everyday life of each community involves a routine that allows for time to relax, to share, to care for one another, and to celebrate. It is a simple lifestyle: it implies a distinct conception of time from the predominant approach to time in Western culture.[40] L'Arche requires one to slow down, to be patient, to be disposed to take two hours to eat a meal or to bathe a body not easily "handled."[41]

From this perspective, "giving thanks" (for being together, for moving from loneliness to togetherness, for being alive) and celebrating (our creatureliness as human beings) play important roles.[42] Celebrations are at the heart of L'Arche: whether anniversaries, arrivals, departures, or visitors, any occasion is counted as worthy of celebrating with joy. This is especially important for those who grew up with the sense that they were disappointments to their parents: celebration reveals to them the joy of being together; it creates unity in the community and flows forth from the union of hearts and mutual trust.[43] Hence, "food is important, and it should be good."[44] Meals are times of communion, sharing, laughter, and relaxation: "A group that laughs is a group that is relaxed. And when people are relaxed, they can begin to grow together."[45]

Sharing meals, celebrating, traveling, and laughing together are sources of presence and communion. "*To be with*" is the crux of the pedagogy of L'Arche, according to which "*To love someone does not mean first of all to do things for that person. It means helping her to discover her own beauty, uniqueness, the light hidden in her heart and the meaning of her life, helping her to discover that she is loved as she is, with her broken body and her limited intellectual capacities, with her wounds and her anguishes.* Through love, a new hope is communicated to the person and thus the desire to live and to grow."[46]

L'ARCHE AS A COMMUNITY OF FAITH

Mutuality, as a key component of the experience lived in L'Arche, has a close link with the Christian faith and the Judeo-Christian tradition. In it, fundamental characteristics of the Christian Revelation can be detected: "Life in community must be orientated towards the Kingdom, not simply by enabling people living with disabilities to overcome their disability or to succeed in their daily lives, but also by opening the door of personal transformation to everyone, so that they might once more be able to see, to hear, to speak out and walk on."[47]

As Salenson writes: "L'Arche does not choose a secular approach in addressing this fact of religious diversity: L'Arche is clear that it includes in its self-description, and moreover claims it as core of its identity, a religious dimension."[48] *It is a faith community*: "People with learning disabilities are recognized in L'Arche as a gift of God for the world and as being blessed by God. They have gifts and vocations that are necessary for others and are vital for God's project for the Church and the world." L'Arche is an "Easter experience"; it is part of the Pascal mystery in the spirit of the Second Vatican Council.[49]

This experience requires faith: "Faith that new life will be born from my own woundedness, and that it is a promise of fecundity for me and for others. Each one is invited, in a very concrete way, to give their consent. Faith in what? Faith in the Paschal mystery lived out in a concrete way, regardless of one's religious membership or non-membership."[50]

The Christian nature of L'Arche does not discriminate as to the religious affiliations of its members. On the contrary, the experience of living together at L'Arche generates unity, independent from religious adherences: "*There is a profound unity between people living with a disability and people living without a named disability: they are united in their experience of vulnerability as a source of life.*"[51]

THE MUTUAL WASHING OF THE FEET

A paradigm for the experience of L'Arche as an encounter is manifest in the washing of the feet, a ritual of the Catholic Church, which has traditionally been practiced on Holy Thursday when the priest washes the feet of a select group of twelve people representing the Apostles.[52]

The ritual of the mutual washing of feet is often practiced during celebrations in the communities of L'Arche. Since the early 1970s,[53] when it began among small groups of community members, and up to its being enacted among groups of thousands, the ritual has always been at the center of the retreats given by Jean Vanier.[54]

This symbolic gesture, which Jesus indicated we must do for one another, expresses many values: tenderness, service, communion, mutual forgiveness, togetherness, and oneness, in addition to the centrality of the body as the Temple of God, which, as such, has to be cared for and honored. By focusing on the feet, the parts of the body that are the least presentable and the weakest, Jesus communicates, "Be attentive to the littlest, to the weakest, to the poorest, to those who are the most broken: for I am living there."[55]

L'ARCHE AS A SIGN

The experience of Jean Vanier was that of an encounter: "Hidden in those who are powerless is a mysterious power: they attract and awaken the heart. . . . We were happy to be together. . . . We were beginning to discover that people with mental handicaps are not first of all 'problems' or sources of death: if we welcome them just as they are, if we communicate with them, then they become truly a source of life that awakens our hearts and calls us to community life."[56] Accordinging to this experience, "For people with handicaps, even more important than 'normalization' is their growth in love, openness, service, and holiness, *which is the ultimate purpose of each human person.* This growth in love does not exclude in any way doing all we can to help each person to acquire knowledge and independence or be well integrated into the life of society and of the Church. In fact, it emphasizes their importance."[57]

Moreover, Vanier continues: "Maybe normalization does not sufficiently consider the deepest needs of persons with handicaps and the special gifts they give to society. Their affectivity is rich, spontaneous and true; they are constant reminders of the values of the heart in a society that tends to exalt competence and efficiency and forget love. *The cry for community from people with handicaps constantly reminds us that we all need community.*"[58]

Relating this understanding of persons with disabilities to the poor is easy: within L'Arche and Jean Vanier's writings, vulnerability encompasses persons with disabilities and handicaps, weakness and poverty, otherness and strangeness.[59] Jean Vanier writes:

I saw the person before I saw his or her poverty. And I realized that a person who is hungry, abandoned or in need is first of all a heart who needs to find another heart; someone who will listen, understand and love. *People who are poor and discouraged need to hear someone say to them "I love you. I have confidence in you. You are beautiful. You can give life to others." . . .* The poor do not need to hear a lot of words, not even pious words. They may need people who will do things for them. Above all, they need friendship: friends who love them and are willing to do things with them. This will help them grow and develop both humanly and spiritually.[60]

Each person with a mental handicap has a message to bring to the Church and to the world. He or she is essentially a heart that loves, a heart that calls us to communion and to community. *In this way people with mental handicaps are prophetic,* and, like prophets, they disturb. They call us to change and let ourselves be transformed; they invite us to become more deeply human, more loving; they invite us to enter into communion and community, instead of throwing ourselves into work, hyperactivity and seeking success, wealth and reputation.[61]

Foundational to this perspective is a vision of the human person, a true anthropology of L'Arche. As Vanier writes: "We have a treasury in L'Arche. People with mental handicaps reveal important elements of our human nature that are often hidden in people who have developed their intellectual and manual capacities. We will have to deepen, explain and reflect on these elements to show what it means to grow and develop as a human being, and what we need in order to live and deepen our humanity."[62]

Thus L'Arche is a place where the good news is announced to the poor and by the poor. L'Arche is not a solution to problems but rather a sign. Vanier writes: "*L'Arche is a sign* that love is possible, that the weak, *whatever their weakness,* have gifts and a message to give. *L'Arche is a sign that faith and competence can embrace and work together for the human and spiritual growth and development of each person.* It is a sign that institutions can become communities when people work together in a spirit of love and unity."[63]

NEW CHALLENGES

The origin of L'Arche is deeply rooted in a specific era, the 1960s, in which the idea of community exploded; the needs in the field of intellectual disabilities were enormous, and any new solution was welcomed by the public administration. The Church, after the Second Vatican Council, was rediscovering the centrality of the Gospel. Jean Vanier himself remarked, "L'Arche foundations of that era were the fruits of a changing world and of a Church seeking new ways of living and announcing the good news."[64]

Since then, the world has experienced dramatic changes. Each of the three pillars that help to explain L'Arche's foundation are in crisis in Western societies: individualism is overcoming community life; the medicalization and bureaucratization of the approach to mental disabilities have increased; and the process of secularization has marginalized religion and spiritual life.

These changes generated important consequences for L'Arche. The medical approach to disabilities requires more and more trained assistants, and labor policies and ethical concerns prevent people from undertaking voluntary commitments for life. Long-term committed assistants are today a minority, and most assistants live in a community only for one or two years. New live-in assistants are usually young people, often fulfilling their civil service obligations, and with little experience of family life and religious faith. There is an increase in the number of married assistants living with their families and participating in community life only according to their work schedules. On the other hand, the needs of disabled people have also changed. Their spiritual needs and personal aspirations have evolved. Some of them would prefer more independent lives in small studios. In many ways, the idea of a network is replacing that of community. Bureaucracy, regulations, and the medicalization of care undermine the original intuition of the need to share and celebrate life together.

The challenge for L'Arche is to maintain its identity in this changing world. If at the center of L'Arche there remains a vision of the human person as needing authentic, tender, and faithful relationships, which can bring broken persons to life; if the healing process involves the experience of *being with someone*, the experience of renewal, each time, of the Pascal mystery, who will be the healers of the present day? How can this process, which takes many years and millions of gestures of love, develop in twenty-first-century, high-speed societies shaped by the "technocratic paradigm"?[65] Both aspects of L'Arche, as a community of life and as a community of faith, are in question.[66]

The more recent documents of L'Arche testify to the difficulty of remaining faithful to the original vision while searching for a new approach that would integrate the organization's founding identity with contemporary developments of Western society. In order to fulfill its mission, L'Arche has to reshape its identity: to accept a new, evolving vision of community and to continue fostering the spiritual life in a secularized society.

Nevertheless, I believe that the task of L'Arche is still far from being accomplished and that it has an important role to play in our century, in which fears, divisions, separations, fences, and walls are growing, as is the distance between abstract proclamations and concrete practices of human dignity.

L'Arche offers an important contribution to the current debate on integral human development by providing a paradigm of the human experience of dignity and growth.

In its *"petitesse,"* L'Arche is a sign that the divisions among people may be overcome, that unity and peace are possible, a sign that places can exist in which every human person is allowed to flourish and grow, in which everyone is embraced and loved in his or her uniqueness.

NOTES

I wish to express my gratitude to all the members of La Ferme and L'Arche who welcomed me countless times in Trosly-Breuil. A special thought is for Jean Vanier, for his gentle and deeply loved life. I am profoundly grateful for his friendship and for his call to the whole world to become human.

1. Jean Vanier, prepared remarks, Templeton Prize Ceremony, St. Martin-in-the-Fields, London, May 18, 2015, http://www.templetonprize.org/pdfs/2015/20150518-Vanier-Templeton-Prize-ceremony-talk.pdf. The emphases here and in the quotations throughout the chapter are mine.

2. L'Arche International, *Annual Report, 2015–2016* (Paris: L'Arche International, 2016), http://www.larche.org:8080/en_US/annual-report.

3. See Hans S. Reinders, "Human Vulnerability: A Conversation at L'Arche," in *The Paradox of Disability: Responses to Jean Vanier and L'Arche Communities from Theology and the Sciences*, ed. Hans S. Reinders (Grand Rapids, MI: William B. Eerdmans, 2010), 3.

4. "Normative" in the sense that they must be followed by all communities intending to join or to remain members of the International Federation of L'Arche.

5. "Identity, Mission, and Charter," L'Arche USA, https://www.larcheusa.org/who-we-are/charter/. See also the "Constitution of the International Federation of L'Arche Communities" (Atlanta: L'Arche International, June 6, 2012), article 5, para. 1, http://inter.larche.org/f/nf3960ai/di102constitutionen.pdf: "L'Arche, founded by Jean Vanier, is an organization of people with and without intellectual disabilities sharing life together in Communities based on mutual relationships and trust in God. The mission of L'Arche is to reveal the value of each person and to work towards a more human society."

6. See "Identity, Mission, and Charter," L'Arche USA, and "Creating a World Where Everyone Belongs," L'Arche Canada, http://www.larche.ca/en/members/vision_future/larche_charter/. According to most persons I interviewed with L'Arche, the charter needs to be revised and is presently in the process of revision. See also the "International Federation of L'Arche Mandate for 2012–2017," L'Arche International, Atlanta, GA, June 2012, http://www.larchecommons.ca/f/nf3689ca/international_mandate_201217.pdf. The mandate includes proposition 4.4: "Discern how the Charter continues to be life-giving for L'Arche today, and revise it if necessary." Additionally, "Taking Responsibility Together! Mandate for the Federation 2017–2022" lists the revision of the charter among the organization's priorities (Belfast: L'Arche International, Federation Assembly, June 2017), https://www.larche.org/documents/10181/818363/DI-207-International-Federation-Mandate-2017-22-EN/a1263cf5-2913-4f54-a99a-3e5edd4aa465.

7. An example of this change of vision is the move from the centrality of the person with intellectual disabilities toward the centrality of the person in general, that of each person and of mutual relationships. According to the charter: "The aim of L'Arche is to create communities which welcome people with a mental handicap. In this way, L'Arche seeks to respond to the distress

of those who are too often rejected, and to give them a valid place in society." The more recent "Identity and Mission Statement" states that the mission of L'Arche is to "Make known the gifts of people with intellectual disabilities, revealed through mutually transforming relationships. Foster an environment in community that responds to the changing needs of our members, while being faithful to the core values of our founding story. Engage in our diverse cultures, working together toward a more human society." This perspective is reflected in the *Constitution of the International Federation*, according to which "The mission of L'Arche is to reveal the value of each person and to work towards a more human society." See article 5, para. 1.

8. "Identity, Mission, and Charter," L'Arche USA.

9. Ibid.

10. Ibid.

11. Ibid.

12. Ibid.

13. Ibid.

14. Ibid.

15. See L'Arche Canada, *L'Arche House Leader Role Guide*, February 24, 2013, http://www.larchecommons.ca/f/nf3801ca/hl_role_guide__bom_april .pdf.

16. See Michael Hryniuk, *Theology, Disability, and Spiritual Transformation: Learning from the Communities of L'Arche* (Amherst, MA: Cambria, 2010), 91 ss.

17. Ibid., 92.

18. On Vanier's experience and vision of L'Arche, see especially Jean Vanier, *An Ark for the Poor: The Story of L'Arche* (Toronto: Novalis, 1995), and, more recently, Jean Vanier, *The Heart of L'Arche: A Spirituality for Everyday Life* (Toronto: Novalis, 2013). There is a vast literature, published and unpublished, on L'Arche. As a specialized documentation center or a central library does not exist, it is not always easy to find. I worked at the small library of La Ferme in Trosly. For the testimonies of the protagonists of the first years of L'Arche see Jean Vanier, *The Challenge of L'Arche* (London: Darton, Longman, and Todd, 1982); Bill Clarke, *Enough Room for Joy: The Early Days of L'Arche* (Toronto: Novalis, 2006); and Alain Saint-Macary, *Mes premières années à L'Arche, "Je ne pensais pas qu'un endroit pareil puisse exister"* (Bruges, France: Aquiprint, 2015). See also Sue Mosteller, *A Place to Hold My Shaky Heart: Reflections from Life in Community* (New York: Crossroad, 1998); Christella Buser, *Flowers from the Ark: True Stories from the Homes of L'Arche* (New York: Paulist Press, 1996); Geoffrey Rigby, Stephen Rigby, and David Treanor, *My Home in L'Arche: Stories from L'Arche Communities in Australia* (Garden Suburb, NSW: Hunter Friends

of L'Arche Inc., 2014); Bertrand Ledrappier, *Le coeur autrement: L'arche de Jean Vanier, témoignage d'un responsable de foyer* (Longué-Jumelles: Arsis, 2007); Antoinette Maurice, *Cette richesse qui vient du pauvre* (Trosly-Breuil, France, n.d.); and K. Spink, *Tu danses avec moi?* (Association Jean Vanier, 2016). A special testimony is that of Henri J. M. Nouwen, *Adam: God's Beloved* (Maryknoll, NY: Orbis Book, 1997), and Nouwen, *The Inner Voice of Love: A Journey through Anguish to Freedom* (New York: Doubleday, 1996).

19. Christopher Newell, "On the Importance of Suffering: The Paradoxes of Disability," in Reinders, *The Paradox of Disability*, 174.

20. The story of the founding of L'Arche, as well as the early life and the personality of Jean Vanier, has been well illustrated by Kathryn Spink in *The Miracle, the Message, the Story: Jean Vanier and L'Arche* (London: Darton, Longman, and Todd, 2006), and Anne-Sophie Constant, *Jean Vanier: Portrait d'un homme libre* (Paris: Albin Michel, 2014). See also the testimony of Jean Vanier, presented in many of his books, among them Jean Vanier, *Our Life Together: A Memoir in Letters* (Toronto: Harper Collins, 2007).

21. Reflections of Jean Vanier, quoted in L'Arche International, *50 Years of Shared Life*, February 24, 2014, 7–9, https://issuu.com/larcheinternationale/docs/hs_arche.

22. Jean Vanier, quoted in Spink, *The Miracle, the Message, the Story*, 63.

23. Vanier, *The Heart of L'Arche*.

24. Christian Salenson, *L'Arche: A Unique and Multiple Spirituality* (Paris: L'Arche en France, 2009). A more complete version has been published in French: Salenson, *Bouleversante fragilité: L'Arche à l'épreuve du handicap* (Bruyères-le-Châtel: Nouvelle Cité, 2016).

25. Salenson, *L'Arche: A Unique and Multiple Spirituality*, 18.

26. On vulnerability as an opportunity to discover our common humanity, see Clemens Sedmak, "Human Dignity, Interiority, and Poverty," in *Understanding Human Dignity*, ed. Christopher McCrudden (Oxford: Oxford University Press, 2013), 567–68, in which the author refers to the L'Arche experience.

27. See Stanley Hauerwas, "Seeing Peace: L'Arche as a Peace Movement," in Reinders, *The Paradox of Disability*, 121.

28. Salenson, *L'Arche: A Unique and Multiple Spirituality*, 96.

29. On this process of transformation among the assistants at L'Arche, see Pamela Cushing, "Shaping the Moral Imagination of Caregivers: Disability, Difference, and Inequality in L'Arche," (PhD diss., McMaster University, Hamilton, Ont., 2003), quoted by Pamela Cushing in "Disability Attitudes, Cultural Conditions, and the Moral Imagination," in Reinders, *The Paradox of Disability*, 85.

30. Salenson, *L'Arche: A Unique and Multiple Spirituality*, 24.

31. Ibid., 32.

32. Hryniuk, *Theology, Disability, and Spiritual Transformation*, 123.

33. Jean Vanier, *From Brokenness to Community* (New York: Paulist Press, 1992), 20.

34. Hryniuk, *Theology, Disability, and Spiritual Transformation*, 141.

35. A collection of testimonies (*Source de vie*, Mesnil Saint Loup: Editions du livre ouvert) has been launched by Jean Vanier, but only a few books have been published. Among them are Ange Pinsard, *On ne m'a jamais dit pourquoi* (Livre Ouvert, 2000); René Leroy, *Moi, tout seul, pas capable* (Livre Ouvert, 2005); Jean-Pierre Crépieux, *Je n'ai pas peur de devenir vieux* (Livre Ouvert, 2009).

36. Salenson, *L'Arche: A Unique and Multiple Spirituality*, 60.

37. Ibid., 32.

38. Quoted by Hryniuk, *Theology, Disability, and Spiritual Transformation*, 128.

39. "Littleness" or "smallness" ("*petitesse*" in French), the word Jean Vanier often uses to describe L'Arche, is the very same word he uses when he speaks of Jesus. In a personal conversation, he quoted the work of Ernst F. Schumacher in *Small Is Beautiful: Economics As If People Mattered* (London: Blond and Briggs, 1973).

40. Hans S. Reinders, "Watch the Lilies of the Field: Theological Reflections on Profound Disability and Time," in Reinders, *The Paradox of Disability*, 154.

41. On patience ("which turns out to be but another name for peace") as an element at the heart of L'Arche, see Stanley Hauerwas, "Seeing Peace," 120.

42. Hans S. Reinders. "Human Vulnerability: A Conversation at L'Arche," in Reinders, *The Paradox of Disability*, 14.

43. Jean Vanier, *Our Journey Home: Rediscovering a Common Humanity beyond Our Differences* (Toronto: Novalis, 1997), 199.

44. Jean Vanier, *Be Not Afraid* (Toronto: Griffin House, 1975), 82–83.

45. Ibid.

46. Jean Vanier, *The Scandal of Service: Jesus Washes Our Feet* (Toronto: Novalis, 1996), 5, reproduced in Jean Vanier, *Essential Writings*, ed. C. Whitney-Brown (London: Darton, Longman, and Todd, 2008), 104.

47. Salenson, *L'Arche: A Unique and Multiple Spirituality*, 23.

48. Ibid., 26.

49. Vatican Council II, Pastoral Constitution on the Church in the Modern World *Gaudium et spes*, which affirms: "We must hold that, in a manner known to God, through the Holy Spirit, all humankind is associated to the Paschal mystery." Vatican website, December 7, 1965, http://www.vatican.va /archive/hist_councils/ii_vatican_council/documents/vat-ii_const_19651207 _gaudium-et-spes_en.html, secs. 22.

50. Salenson, *L'Arche: A Unique and Multiple Spirituality*, 35.

51. Ibid., 38.

52. See Corinne Egasse, *Le lavement de pieds: Recherches sur une pratique négligée* (Geneva: Labor et Fides, 2015).

53. In a conversation with the author on April 8, 2016 in Trosly, Jean Vanier explained that the washing of the feet was introduced as an ecumenical gesture in the early 1970s during an ecumenical meeting in Liverpool involving Catholics and Anglicans. See also Jean Vanier, *The Scandal of Service: Jesus Washes Our Feet* (Toronto: Novalis, 1998).

54. See the testimony of Emmanuel Carrère recounting his experience of Holy Thursday in Trosly: Emmanuel Carrère, *Le Royaume* (Paris: Gallimard, 2014).

55. Jean Vanier, "On the Meaning of the Washing of the Feet," address to the bishops of the Lambeth Conference of the Anglican Communion, London, UK, July 30, 1998, https://zenit.org/articles/jean-vanier-on-the-meaning -of-the-washing-of-feet/.

56. Vanier, *Ark for the Poor*, 26.

57. Ibid., 32.

58. Ibid., 60.

59. Benjamin S. Wall, *Welcome as a Way of Life: A Practical Theology of Jean Vanier* (Eugene, OR: Cascade Books, 2016), 52.

60. Vanier, *Ark for the Poor*, 57.

61. Ibid., 112.

62. Ibid., 101–102.

63. Ibid., 115. On L'Arche as a sign, see Stanley Hauerwas and Jean Vanier, *Living Gently in a Violent World: The Prophetic Witness of Weakness* (Downers Grove, IL: Intervarsity Press, 2008).

64. Vanier, *Ark for the Poor*, 48.

65. In this sense, we could quote the words of Pope Francis regarding the ecological culture: "There needs to be a distinctive way of looking at things, a way of thinking, policies, an educational programme, a lifestyle and a spirituality which together generate resistance to the assault of the technocratic paradigm." See Pope Francis, *Laudato si'*, Vatican website, May 24, 2015, http:// w2.vatican.va/content/francesco/en/encyclicals/documents/papa-francesco _20150524_enciclica-laudato-si.html, sec. 111. L'Arche is integrally invested in this struggle to resist the technocratic paradigm.

66. Personal conversation with Christine McGrievy, leader of the L'Arche community in Trosly, and with Ben Nolan, leader of the L'Arche community in Cuise-la-Motte, France, April 7, 2016.

SIXTEEN

Increasing the Efficiency of Outcomes through Cooperation and Initiative

An Integral Economics Approach to Randomized Field Experiments

Maria Sophia Aguirre and Martha Cruz-Zuniga

EVALUATING A HOLISTIC NUTRITIONAL INTERVENTION

Achieving sustainable development encompasses more than economic processes; it also includes social and political processes. The interaction among these processes influences each in ways that hinder or facilitate the achievement of sustainable development. At the center of these dynamics is the human person, who, by the way he or she relates to others, promotes or jeopardizes the achievement of integral human development, a development aligned with the dignity of the human person. How people relate is not value-neutral. Identifying those effective channels of relations, behavior, or habits that unleash integral human development requires the acknowledgment of an encounter, proactive participation, which generates an empowering presence. Using an integral economic approach, in this chapter we seek to enact dignity in the design and implementation of a development intervention in Guatemala.

Asociación Puente (AP), a Guatemalan nonprofit organization, seeks to reduce extreme poverty and prevent malnutrition through the development of skills by women living in extremely poor rural communities. Recognizing the dignity of every person, its development program *Aprendamos Juntas* (AJ) brings about community and societal change by working to improve the lives of women and their families. AJ's intervention targets five axes: food security and nutrition, health, education, entrepreneurship, and community agency. This program was implemented by AP between 2011 and 2014 in six communities of Santa María Cahabón in Alta Verapaz, Guatemala—communities where 78.8 percent of the inhabitants live in extreme poverty and a rate of 51.1 percent stunted growth among schoolchildren indicates the prevalence of malnutrition.[1]

Using an integral approach, we evaluated AJ's intervention in 2015.[2] The outcomes of this evaluation indicated that there was significant improvement in the lives of AJ's participants and their families on all five axes. The outcomes also indicated areas in which greater efficiency could be achieved, especially in the food and nutrition and entrepreneurial components of the program. Specifically, the intervention marginalized husbands from home garden production,[3] which generated hostility among them toward their wives' independent activities to the extent that their wives faced harassment.[4] AJ also prohibited the commercialization of vegetables grown with seeds they provided, requiring recipients to grow vegetables only for household consumption. Women in the treatment villages saw this restriction as a loss of potential income and missed opportunities for food diversification. In fact, women who sold part of the garden's production in defiance of AJ's policy achieved better nutritional outcomes than those who abided by AJ's regulations. With the increase in household income and liquidity, women could introduce a greater variety of foods into their families' diets without compromising their nutritional health. However, because AJ did not support collaboration among entrepreneurial and agricultural trainers or among trainers and the women growing the gardens, commercialization of the garden produce, when it took place, was not as efficient as it could have been.

Based on the results of our evaluation, we ran a lab field experiment designed as a randomized framed staged field experiment (RFSF) to test a solution for these missed opportunities. The experiment included 234 women, their respective husbands, and four trainers, a total of 471 subjects. Our goal was to explore the impact of introducing proactive participatory instruments (PPIs) on the outcomes of economic decisions—specifically, household decisions to produce, consume, and commercialize produce from a home garden.

The methodology and outcomes of the RFSF recognize the dignity of each person and seek to overcome marginalization. The PPI tested in the experiment facilitated the opportunity for participatory decision-making between husband and wife and between couples and agricultural and entrepreneurship trainers. The results indicate that participatory solutions generate more efficient outcomes than do nonparticipatory ones. Incentives reduced husbands' antagonism, elicited in them a supportive disposition toward their wives' earning income, increased the consumption of home garden production for nutritional purposes, and reduced the women's burden in garden maintenance. They also elicited other family members' collaboration. This chapter describes in detail our methodology and findings.

ENGAGING THE HOUSEHOLD TO SOLVE MALNUTRITION

The theory of change behind the intervention design began with the identification of a specific population's real need: to increase AJ's efficiency in the reduction of malnutrition and to eliminate the marginalization caused by some aspects of AJ's intervention design. The instrument used to meet these needs was the introduction of proactive participation opportunities for couples and for trainers in the design of AJ's intervention. Immediate as well as long-term impacts were expected as a consequence of these modifications. Specifically, we expected both efficiency gains in the production and management of home gardens and the reduction of malnutrition in households. We also expected a change in behavior that would improve institutional factors surrounding AJ's intervention, such as the substitution of proactive participatory behavior in place of marginalization. These changes would contribute to sustainable development.

Literature on home gardens, microsavings, and microcredit provides useful insights into this experiment design. Research on home gardens indicates they increase consumption of micronutrient-rich foods, which alleviates the harm caused by a lack of variety in food intake.[5] It also suggests that planting gardens is the most efficient way to decrease malnutrition[6] and that they are effective in increasing food security among rural families.[7] Recent research has identified the characteristics of a successful farmer-to-farmer approach through home gardens: community selection of farmers' trainers, a simultaneous focus on techniques and community development, and mutual learning among farmers. Instead of one-directional training, empirical evidence shows that a mutual training approach increases knowledge, yields, and agricultural sustainability.[8] New studies further suggest that although women in developing countries typically identify themselves as housewives, the participation of women in the agriculture sector increases its income and productivity.[9] Empirical evidence provides support for home gardens as an effective means for providing food security and suggests that a household and community participatory approach to implementation improves outcomes significantly.

Social network research highlights the relevance of relations for understanding people's health outcomes.[10] In so doing, researchers have shifted the focus from the individual to his or her relationship with others. These studies report that, in many developing countries, women's social networks influence members' decisions.[11] However, husbands are rarely included as part of the relational networks in these studies. Valente (2015) highlights the positive effects on health of participation among relatives and within households and communities. Others show how participation and a richer community life assist people in achieving more efficient economic outcomes.[12] But these studies often fail to include husband and wife relationships in their participatory approach. The RFSF experiment presented here seeks to complement the participation and networks literature. It does so by exploring the impact of introducing a participatory approach among spouses on behaviors that affect economic decisions.

PARTICIPATION AS INCENTIVE IN
RANDOMIZED FIELD EXPERIMENTS

We used Aguirre's integral approach to economic development to design the RFSF experiment.[13] At the core of this methodology is the person's social dimension, which he or she maximizes in the economic decision-making process. The person acts not as a self–utility maximizer but as a social person. This approach accounts for interpersonal-relational dimensions of economic actions, as the way people interact can support or jeopardize sustainable development. Agents can be positive or negative agents of change. Therefore, the integral approach focuses on the direct beneficiaries of interventions and their interpersonal relationships, and it seeks to identify effective channels of relationships that make economic development sustainable.

When evaluating an intervention, this approach seeks measurement beyond the direct or immediate impact (e.g., participants' knowledge and use of home gardens) by expanding the definition of success to include impact on the quality of life of its beneficiaries, their families, and their communities. This approach requires measuring changes in the way of life and actions of those benefitting from a program. This way of life should reflect the dignity all human beings possess as well as how they live out their social and civic responsibilities. Thus primacy is given to "action" when measuring. To achieve this, the integral approach uses four tools: behavioral and experimental economics, survey design, market research techniques modified to allow a rigorous quantitative analysis, and econometrics. In designing randomized field experiments, this approach introduces PPIs to encourage changes in behavior that improve outcomes.

In the decision-making process the integral approach offers a more complex understanding of maximization than of self-utility. Economic agents are seen as persons who are social by nature and maximize as such.[14] This expansion in the maximization process for the design of RFSF experiments means that we do not rely solely on monetized incentives to stimulate behavioral change.[15] Instead, drawing on the work of Edgar Schein and other organizational sociologists and psychologists, the incentive provided in this case is the opportunity for spouses and trainers to engage in home gardening in a participatory cooperative manner.[16]

Within this framework, as in standard experimental design, subjects are motivated by their desire to better their lives and those of their families, but they do not receive monetary compensation as incentives or rewards for participating. Instead, instruments are generated by providing participatory alternatives that seek to create opportunities for spouses to make joint decisions and act according to those decisions. This method applies to the home garden production, consumption, and commercialization and to engagement with trainers.

Design of the RFSF takes the form of a framed stage experiment, as proposed by John List, but our experiment is conducted in the actual environment in which the subjects live—a more "real" environment than is used in the typical framed experiment. Seven stages were added, each composed of six steps.[17] Through the stages, the experiment moved participants from passive nonparticipatory positions to participatory roles in which they changed their mindsets and actions to maximize outcomes in a way that improved their lives as spouses and as family members. Each stage placed participants in situations they regularly faced in home gardens; these situations highlighted inefficiencies generated by their lack of participation. By means of a 360 methodology, simulated by introducing at each stage a different type of role-playing (in this case that of a wife, husband, and trainer), subjects were able to consider situations from the perspectives of different actors. As the stages progressed, a more complex participatory behavioral option was presented. The steps included at each stage moved from passive to proactive behavior, allowing participants to develop an understanding of personal responsibility and its consequences for action. Figure 16.1 presents a diagram of the framed stage experimental design.

Framed experiments can raise concerns about outcomes, because part of the treatment group may react to incentives in a way that leads to biased results. Bias could be due to self-selection problems or to awareness of the artificial setup.[18] Framed randomized field experiments and role-playing techniques mitigate these concerns. The former tackles both of these problems because the experiment occurs in the subjects' natural environment. This provides randomization and realism.[19] Role-playing addresses the risk of biased behavioral outcomes by requiring subjects to engage in hypothetical situations and act as they would if they were to experience the situations in real life. This method captures

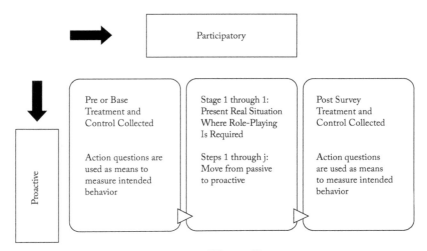

FIGURE 16.1. Framed Stage Experimental Design Diagram

subjects' psychological processes while generating acceptable levels of their involvement.[20] Although role-playing captures intended, not actual, behavior, it reveals whether instruments, in this case participatory behavior, contributes to efficiency gains. It does so by revealing the value participants give to PPIs in modifying (or not) their intended behavior.[21]

Our experiment was conducted in the surrounding communities of Santa María Cahabón, where the beneficiaries and their families lived and grew home gardens. It was conducted at the meeting place where the communities typically gather on Sundays for religious services, family gatherings, or community meetings. Since the stage framed experiment was conducted in the subjects' natural living environment, it provides different parameter estimates than those obtained from laboratory and artificially run experiments. Additionally, the control and treatment groups were randomized, thereby eliminating any self-selection bias. Thus the potential biases of framed field experiments were reduced, if not overcome.

This methodology offers two additional benefits: it provides a tool for rigorously testing recommendations in the context of impact evaluation before scaling up implementation, and it significantly decreases costs while increasing efficiency by avoiding ineffective large-scale randomized field experiments. There have been numerous randomized experiments requiring large sums of money that have found that the solutions tested were ineffective.[22] Our approach, without compromising effectiveness or methodological rigor, provided a less financially burdensome means to test potential solutions to problems encountered in impact evaluations.

EXPERIMENTAL DESIGN SPECIFICS

The randomized sample for this experiment was obtained from subjects within AJ's treatment groups: women who participated in and completed the intervention, their husbands, and their agricultural and entrepreneurial trainers. Randomization was carried out at the level of *aldeas* (small groups of houses) within each community. These *aldeas* were far from each other and difficult to access, so the risk of contamination was low. As previously mentioned, the sample included 121 women, their respective husbands, and four trainers, a total of 245 persons. Those not selected for the treatment group served as a control group—a total of 113 women and their husbands (226).

The frame addressed a real situation faced by couples and trainers—although vegetable gardens helped women meet their families' basic nutritional needs, the women desired to sell part of their produce to obtain cash to further diversify their household's food consumption while generating extra income or savings. AJ policies forbid this, and trainers were unwilling to assist the women with commercialization. AJ did not encourage cooperation between spouses, which added to tension in households.

The narrative of this staged experiment began with the presentation of the scenario just described. Gradually, this narrative introduced subjects to the possibility that AJ would allow the sale of garden produce without compromising nutritional outcomes. It also engaged the assistance of husbands and trainers in the decisions of production, consumption, and commercialization in a manner that increased the efficiency of the production of home gardens while eliciting participation among all parties involved.

The experiment lasted 45–60 minutes. Through the six consecutive steps in each of the seven stages, subjects were gradually moved from passive to proactive and participatory courses of action. Passivity for the women involved not selling products of the vegetable gardens, continuing to marginalize their husbands, and suffering continued hostility from them. On the opposite end, the most proactive behavior entailed including husbands in all matters related to the gardens and the commercialization of produce. Proactive behavior also involved couples' engaging the assistance of AJ's agriculture and entrepreneurial trainers to discuss production, consumption, and commercialization strategies. Passivity for trainers meant abiding by AJ's "no sales" rule even though they were aware of the opportunities missed. Proactive and participatory behavior meant taking initiative by proposing a policy change to AJ. In accordance with the modified 360 methodology, as subjects moved through the scenarios at each stage, they were asked to role-play, sometimes as wives, sometimes as husbands, and sometimes as trainers. This allowed them to experience the situation from all perspectives. The degree of participation grew in complexity from one stage to the next. Each stage led couples to work more closely together and to make decisions in a more participatory manner than before.

We predicted that, following the intervention, spouses would desire to make economic decisions together, and, as a consequence, they would be more efficient in the production and commercialization of vegetables while the hostility that had been provoked by the wives' engagement in production would reduce. Similarly, we predicted that AJ trainers would be more proactive and participatory in their work.

DATA COLLECTION

The experiment was run in the summer of 2014, less than three months after the collection of data was completed. We collected baseline, pre- and post-experiment data from the treatment group and baseline data from the control group. Given that the lab field experiment was designed as a framed field experiment and its duration was short, no change would be expected in the control group's behavior. Therefore, we did not collect post data from them. The pre and post data from the treatment group was collected immediately before and after the experiment was run.

Table 16.1 summarizes the baseline social characteristics of the treatment and control groups. The two groups are statistically comparable.

TABLE 16.1. Baseline Social Characteristics of Treatment and Control Groups (Average Values)

	Women Treatment/Control n = 121/113	Men Treatment/Control n = 121/113
Ethnic Group	Indigenous/same	Indigenous/same
Age	33/33	39/37
	(8)	(12)
Marital Status	Married (80%)/same	Married (80%)/same
	Unions (20%)/same	Unions (20%)/same
Number of Children	5/5	4/4
	(3)	(3)
Occupation	Agriculture/same	Agriculture/same
Education Achieved	Less than primary/same	Primary/same
Monthly Level of Income	Q400–500/same	Q600–700/same
	(Q400)	(Q500)
Religion	Catholic/same	Catholic/same

Note: Standard deviations are reported in parentheses. All tests for difference of means or proportions were not statistically significant.

The population served by this program is of indigenous origin, and both men and women are in their thirties and typically are married. On average, the number of children reported in the treatment group (five) is higher than that of the control group (four), but the difference is not statistically significant. The reported income places both men and women in extreme poverty; on average, their occupation is agriculture. On average, the women had not completed a primary education, while the men had. Finally, Catholicism is their prevailing religion.

Survey questions designed to evaluate the AJ program allowed us to measure the behavior and attitudes of both spouses regarding home garden work and the use of produce, as well as their use of any income generated from the vegetable garden. Unless otherwise indicated, all responses were binary (YES = 1, NO = 0), collected from women and their husbands as appropriate. Baseline proportions for the behavioral measures are reported in table 16.2.

Both spouses had a clear preference for saving on their own (women = 64 percent, men = 68 percent). A significantly higher proportion of women reported holding savings together with their husbands

TABLE 16.2. Variables Used to Measure Behavioral Change
(Proportions of Those Agreeing)

	Women Baseline n = 121/113		Men Baseline n = 121/113	
YES/NO responses	Treatment	Control	Treatment	Control
I would prefer to have my own savings	64	64	68	68
I save together with my wife/husband	39	38	2	2
We save and decide together			0	0
The business is selling home garden's produce	62	61		
I encourage my wife to expand her business			32	32
I sow alone			42	42
I sow with the help of my children	52	53	28	28
I work with my wife in the home garden			33	34
We use the home garden's harvest only to feed family	49	49		
We use the home garden's harvest to sell it	51	50		
We share the home garden's harvest with people in my community	43	43		
I run my business alone			38	38
I run the business with my wife/husband	48	48	72	72
I run the business with my children			31	31

Note: Both treatment and control groups were randomly assigned from the pool of treated subjects. All tests for difference of proportions were not statistically significant.

(women = 38, men = 2), although husbands were not willing to share decisions about the use of savings with their wives. Some 62 percent of women indicated that they had some type of business, while only 32 percent of men reported a willingness to encourage their wives to expand the business. Overall, women tended to be more participatory than their spouses when carrying out work in households and in their community. Regarding the use of produce for business purposes, women reported a 50/50 percent split. Some used produce only for household consumption, while others commercialized a portion of the harvest. Regarding the participation of family members in the husband's business, 72 percent of the husbands reported running their agricultural businesses with their wives, while 38 percent reported running them alone. Some 31 percent of men reported that their children also helped them with their work. The treatment and control groups were found to be comparable at baseline not only because of their similarity in social characteristics but also because they reported similar behavior and/or attitudes.

ESTIMATIONS AND RESULTS

Table 16.3 presents the proportions for the pre- and post-survey outcomes, along with corresponding base and control values, for each of the variables used to measure intended behavioral change. It also indicates the level of significance for the difference of proportions test. All outcomes are consistent with the expected changes in intended behavior. This suggests that subjects responded positively to the PPIs. After the experiment, both spouses were more willing to save together rather than alone or with other parties. They were also more willing to work together in their respective businesses. In addition, husbands' responses indicated a reduction in hostility toward their wives' business engagement. Specifically, they were not only willing to assist their wives with their home gardens but were also supportive of their expanding their own businesses. Furthermore, this increasing participatory behavior spilled over to other members of their households (they were engaging their children in the home gardens even more than before) and to the husbands' work in agriculture (the involvement of both wives and children in the husbands' work increased).

The analysis of the experiment's impact on the intended behavioral change can also be evaluated by means of a difference-in-difference methodology. For each intended change in behavior, equation 1 was estimated:

$$\textit{Post-Pre}_{ij} = \beta_0 + \beta_1 \Delta \textit{ Index}_i + \beta \textit{ Demographics}_i + v_j + \varepsilon_{ij}, \qquad (1)$$

where *Post-Pre* was the variable of interest, defined as the difference between responses on the post-experiment survey and the pre-experiment surveys. Δ *Index* is the change in the last versus the first stage estimated participatory index. Finally, the *Demographics* vector included age, level of education, marital status (1 = marriage or permanent union,

TABLE 16.3. Intended Behavior Change (Proportions)

	Women n = 121/113				Men n = 121/113			
	Control	Based	Pre	Post	Control	Based	Pre	Post
I would prefer to have my own savings	64	64	64	0*	68	68	68	14*
I save together with my wife/husband	39	38	38	76*	2	2	0	70*
We save and decide together					0	0	0	2.4*
The business is selling home garden's produce	62	61	61	100*				
I encourage my wife to expand her business					32	32	30	59*
I sow alone					42	42	42	0*
I sow with the help of my children	52	53	53	100*	28	28	28	100*
I work with my wife in the home garden					33	34	34	44*
We use the home garden's harvest only to feed family	49	49	49	0*				
We use the home garden's harvest to sell it	51	50	50	100*				
We share the home garden's harvest with people in my community	43	43	50	100*				
I run my business alone					38	38	38	0*
I run the business with my wife/husband	48	48	49	100*	72	72	72	100*
I run the business with my children					31	31	31	100*

Note: Both treatment and control groups were randomly assigned from the pool of treated subjects.

Note: Baseline values correspond to the reported behavior after AJ was implemented.

Note: All tests for difference of proportions were not statistically significant.

* Significant at the 1% level.

0 = other), house materials (1 being brick and 8 being wood and hay, so as the numbers increased, the quality of the materials used for home construction deteriorated), access to electricity (1 = yes, 0 = no), religion (1 = Catholic, 0 other), number of children, and numbers of persons living in the homes. Since 100 percent of the population is indigenous, race was not included among the demographic characteristics. v_j captures the fixed effect introduced for the *aldeas*.

The first difference comes from the change between the post-experiment survey responses and the pre-experiment survey responses (dependent variable). The second change comes from the change in the participatory index (Index). The latter consists in a weighted index that measures the change in intended participatory behavior as a result of the experiment. To construct it, the following steps were followed. First, each step in a given stage was assigned the value of 1 or −1 to capture, respectively, a proactive (participatory) or passive (not participatory) response. Second, each of these values was transformed exponentially. The justification for this mathematical transformation was that the participatory instrument, since it was repeated at each stage, generated a cumulative effect in the subjects. Thus, after several repetitions, it was expected to generate a change of intended behavior that would last (a habit). Therefore, once the subject changed his or her intended behavior (made decisions regarding the home garden production, allocation, etc., in a participatory manner), the remaining stages should report the same or minor changes in the participatory index value. In the third step, the transformed exponential values were multiplied by a cumulative weight, which ranged from 0 to 2 for each stage. The number 2 was assigned to the best proactive and participatory decision at each stage. All other steps received a weight of between 0 and 1. The calculated multiple was then multiplied by the actual response of the subject on each of the steps of a given stage. Finally, we summed the results. The larger the estimated sum index, the more proactive and participatory was the intended behavior of the subject.

For the experiment to be effective, the change in the participatory index should be significant in determining the reported intended behavioral change. Its distribution should follow an exponential form, as this would capture the cumulative nature of the learning process. In addition, if the incentive was effective, once the subjects changed from passive to proactive intended behavior, this latter behavior should be sustained for

TABLE 16.4. Change in Participatory Index

n = 121	Index Stage 1	Index Stage 2	Index Stage 3	Index Stage 4	Index Stage 5	Index Stage 6
Mean	3.68	7.03	10.29	11.56	11.66	11.68
Std. Dev.	4.85	4.97	4.94	4.42	4.27	1.56
Percentage Change		91	46	12	0.09	0.00
Test for Difference of Two Means						
p-value (2 = 1)		0.00				
p-value (3 = 2)			0.00			
p-value (4 = 3)				0.00		
p-value (5 = 4)					0.02	
p-value (5 = 6)						0.20

the remainder of the experiment. Table 16.4 presents the participatory index mean for each stage of the experiment, the percentage change between each pair of consecutive stages, and the test for the difference of means. The index changed at a decreasing rate as it moved from stage 1 to 6. After stage 4, the change was not statistically significant, indicating the stability of the change of intended behavior.

Figure 16.2 displays the cumulative distribution of the participatory index change. The values of the change in the index range from −1.27 to 12.21. The negative range reflects the 8.1 percent of the subjects in whom the experiment did not generate the expected behavior change. The positive change in behavior was registered in 91.9 percent of the subjects.

Finally, table 16.5 presents equation 1 estimates for the most relevant variables included in table 16.2.[23] In all cases the results indicate a significant response to PPI on the part of both spouses, as captured by the change in the participatory index coefficient. This more cooperative behavior between spouses, in turn, affects behavioral outcomes and/or attitudes toward savings management (women are now willing to save together with their husbands), husbands' support for their wives running businesses, for home gardening work, and for commercialization of some of the garden produce. For the most part, the estimation outcomes indicate that the effectiveness of the participatory instrument is independent of the subject's personal characteristics.

TABLE 16.5. Regression Estimations

Variable	Saving with Husband		Encourage Wife to Expand Business		Sell Produce from Vegetable Garden		Work with Wife in Garden	
	Coefficient	Std. Error	Coefficient	Std. Error	Coefficient	Std. Error	Coefficient	Std. Error
Intercept	2.41*	1.08	.50	0.73	1.02	0.68	-0.06	0.95
Δ Index	3.04*	0.06	4.02*	0.03	6.02*	0.03	4.01*	0.04
Married	0.28	0.51	0.39	0.27	0.30	0.31	0.24	0.28
Woman's Age	0.04***	0.02	0.00	0.02	0.04	0.01	0.01	0.02
Primary Educational Level	0.59	0.59	0.16	0.29	0.15	0.40	-0.28	0.34
Level of Income	0.05	0.14	0.03	0.06	-0.04	0.05	-0.02	0.06
Catholic	-3.43*	1.26	-0.88	0.63	-1.81	0.63	-1.69	0.84
Number of Children	0.22*	0.11	0.05	0.07	-0.09	0.05	-0.06	0.08
Electricity	0.46	0.57	0.51**	0.26	0.16	0.27	0.63	0.39
House Material = Bamboo & Cane	-0.06	0.61	0.09	0.26	0.14	0.15	-0.11	0.32
Number of People Living in the House	-0.14***	0.08	-0.05	0.05	-0.06	0.05	-0.01	0.06
R²	43		32		57		38	
N	387		387		387		387	

Note: $Post\text{-}Pre_{ij} = \beta_0 + \beta_1 \Delta Index_i + {}_j + \beta\ Demographics_i + v_j + \varepsilon_{ij}$

Note: OLS estimates reported.

*** Significant at 1% level, ** significant at 5% level, and * significant at the 10% level.

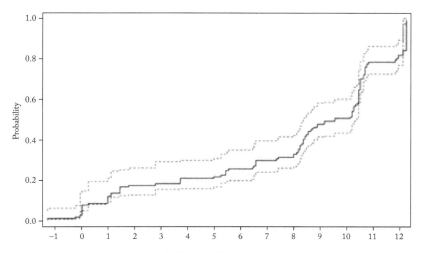

FIGURE 16.2. Participatory Index's Change Cumulative Distribution

The outcomes of the experiment helped identify relational channels—encounters—that can improve the socioeconomic and nutritional outcomes *Aprendamos Juntas* is intending to achieve through the intervention. Thus modifications were made to the original intervention design so as to allow for and foster proactive participatory opportunities between spouses, between them and other family members, and between couples and trainers. Specifically, now spouses are encouraged to work together in the garden, and both agricultural and entrepreneurship trainers coordinate efforts to assist couples in the design, management, and commercialization of the home gardens. In doing so, the marginalization and antagonism encountered during the evaluation of *Aprendamos Juntas* are overcome, while more efficient outcomes can be achieved.

IS PARTICIPATION RELEVANT TO EFFECTIVE INTERVENTIONS?

In this chapter we have proposed an integral approach to experimental design as a way to highlight the relevance of acknowledging a person's dignity. At the core of the methodology is the recognition of something we all experience—we exist, live, and act together with others. Consequently, we maximize in the decision-making process not as self–utility maximizers but as social persons. Thus marginalizing "others" is harmful to all parties in this context, as it generates negative effects. Instead, in the experiment we sought to identify effective channels of relationships to improve outcomes. It acknowledged the interpersonal-relational dimension of economic actions by introducing an opportunity for spouses to participate—to cooperate—in the home garden decision-making process as an instrument to influence behavior and attitudes. In doing so, it overcame the bias introduced by monetary incentives while providing insight into how the interpersonal dimension of any economic activity—more specifically, participation understood as proactive cooperation—can be a path to finding solutions to problems encountered in the economy.

Finally, the results of the experiment suggest such a tool could be a useful means of testing recommendations before large-scale experiments are implemented. While the technical rigor proper to experiments is maintained, there are significant cost savings. At the time of this publication, the modifications indicated by the outcomes of this experiment are being implemented.

Using an integral approach to the design of the experiment helps highlight the role of dignity as part of the conceptualization, methodology, and intervention design. It also highlights the role of dignity as an outcome. By recognizing the relational dimension of the economic agent, we identify opportunities for proactive participation, for collaboration, in the design and implementation of the home gardens. These include opportunities for participation in nutritional as well as other nonmaterial outcomes. The maintenance and management decisions related to home gardens are now shared by the whole family, and trainers, through their coordinated work, help couples increase their home garden productivity. At the same time, behavioral and attitudinal changes on the part of husbands and trainers, generated by introducing PPIs, diminish the harassment women experienced from their husbands while encouraging more collaborative behavior among family members.

NOTES

1. Estimations based on baseline data collected. A nationwide malnutrition study reported a 69.3 percent malnutrition rate among indigenous

children living in rural areas. See Susan M. Richter, Jef L. Leroy, Deanna Olney, Esteban Quiñones, and Marie Ruel, *Strengthening and Evaluating the Preventing Malnutrition in Children under 2 Approach in Guatemala: Report of the Enrollment Survey* (Guatemala: Food and Nutrition Medical Assistance [FANTA], 2013).

2. Sophia Maria Aguirre and Martha Cruz-Zuniga, "An Impact Evaluation of Aprendamos Juntas in Guatemala: An Integral Approach," *IEDP Report No. 3*, School of Business and Economics, Catholic University of America, Washington DC, 2015.

3. Home gardens are a time-tested local strategy that has been adopted and practiced by local communities with limited resources. For a review of the literature on the benefits and limitations of home gardens, see Dilrukshi Hashini Galhena, Russell Freed, and Karim M Maredia, "Home Gardens: A Promising Approach to Enhance Household Food Security and Wellbeing," *Agriculture & Food Security* 2, no. 8 (2013): 1–13.

4. This type of reaction on the part of marginalized husbands has been found in previous studies. See, for example, Hanstad T. Mitchell, "Small Home Garden Plots and Sustainable Livelihoods for the Poor," Livelihood Support Programme (LSP) Working Paper 11, Food and Agriculture Association, United Nations, March 2004, and Galhena et al., "Home Gardens."

5. Kraisid Tontisirin, Guy Nantel, and Lalita Bhattacharjee, "Food-Based Strategies to Meet the Challenges of Micronutrient Malnutrition in the Developing World," *The Proceedings of the Nutrition Society* 61, no. 2 (2002): 243–50; Olaf Müller and Michael Krawinkel, "Malnutrition and Health in Developing Countries," *Canadian Medical Association Journal* 173, no. 3 (2005): 279–86; and Heriberto E. Cuanalo de la Cerda and Rogelio R. Guerra Mukul, "Homegarden Production and Productivity in a Mayan Community of Yucatan," *Human Ecology* 36, no. 3 (2008): 423–33.

6. Peter R. Berti, Julia Krasevec, and Sian FitzGerald, "A Review of the Effectiveness of Agriculture Interventions in Improving Nutrition Outcomes," *Public Health Nutrition* 7, no. 5 (2004): 599–609; and C. Johnson-Welch, B. Alemu, T. P. Msaki, M. Sengendo, H. Kigutha, and A. Wolff, "Improving Household Food Security: Institutions, Gender and Integrated Approaches," paper prepared for the Broadening Access and Strengthening Input Market Systems (BASIS) Collaborative Research Support Project (CRSP), 2000, downloaded from http://www.hubrural.org/IMG/pdf/basissem9911_panel3c.pdf, March 26, 2020.

7. K. Khammounheuang, P. Saleumsy, L. Kirjavainen, B. K. Nandi, P. Mahlberg Dyg, and L. Bhattacharjee, "Sustainable Livelihoods for Human Security in Lao PDR: Home Gardens for Food Security, Rural Livelihoods,

and Nutritional Well-Being," *Regional Development Dialogue* 25, no. 2 (2004): 203–28, and Mieke Faber, Michael A. S. Phungula, Sonja L. Venter, Muhammad A. Dhansay, and A. J. Spinnler Benade, "Home Gardens Focusing on the Production of Yellow and Dark-Green Leafy Vegetables Increase the Serum Retinol Concentrations of 2-5-Y-Old Children in South Africa," *American Journal of Clinical Nutrition* 76, no. 5 (2002): 1048–54.

8. Maria E. Fernandez-Gimenez, "The Role of Mongolian Nomadic Pastoralists' Ecological Knowledge in Rangeland Management," *Ecological Applications* 10, no. 5 (2000): 1318–26; K. Wellard, J. Rafanomezana, M. Nyirenda, M. Okotel, and V. Subbey, "A Review of Community Extension Approaches to Innovation for Improved Livelihoods in Ghana, Uganda and Malawi," *Journal of Agricultural Education and Extension* 19, no. 1 (2013): 21–35.

9. Alan De Brauw and Scott Rozelle, "Reconciling the Returns to Education in Off-Farm Wage Employment in Rural China," *Review of Development Economics* 12, no. 1 (2008): 57–71; Constantina Safiliou-Rotschild, Eleni Dimopoulou, Raina Lagiogianni, and Spyrithoula Sotiropoulou, "Trends of Agricultural Feminisation in Kastoria, Greece," *Journal of Comparative Family Studies* 38, no. 3 (2007); and Ardey Codjoe and Samuel Nii, "Population and Food Crop Production in Male- and Female-Headed Households in Ghana," *International Journal of Development* 9, no. 1 (2010): 68–85.

10. Thomas W. Valente, *Social Networks and Health: Models, Methods, and Application* (Oxford: Oxford University Press, 2010); Thomas Valente, "Social Networks and Health Behavior," in *Health Behavior: Theory, Research, and Practice*, ed. Karen Glanz, Barbara K. Rimer, and K. Viswanath (San Francisco: Jossey-Bass, 2015).

11. Stephen P. Borgatti, Martin G. Everett, and Jeffrey C. Johnson, *Analyzing Social Networks* (London: Sage Publications, 2013); Valente, *Social Networks*; and W. Ricard Scott, *Institutions and Organizations: Ideas and Interests* (London: Sage Publications, 2008).

12. See, among others, George Akerlof and Janet Yellen, *Gang Behavior, Law Enforcement, and Community Values* (Washington DC: Brookings Institution Press, 1994); Esther Duflo and Emmanuel Saez, "The Role of Information and Social Interactions in Retirement Plan Decisions: Evidence from a Randomized Experiment," *Quarterly Journal of Economics* 118, no. 2 (2002): 815–42; and Thomas Valente, "Social Networks and Health Behavior," in *Health Behavior: Theory, Research, and Practice*, ed. Karen Glanz, Barbara K. Rimer, and K. Viswanath (San Francisco: Jossey-Bass, 2015).

13. Sophia Maria Aguirre, "Achieving Sustainable Development: An Integral Approach to an Economics Perspective," in *The Ethics of Sustainable*

Development, ed. Luis G. Franceschi (Nairobi: Strathmore University Press, 2011), and Sophia Maria Aguirre, "An Integral Approach to an Economic Perspective: The Case of Measuring Impact," *Journal of Markets and Morality* 16, no. 1 (2013): 53–67.

14. Jerald Greenberg and Don E. Eskew, "The Role of Role Playing in Organizational Research," *Journal of Management* 19, no. 1 (1993): 221–41.

15. For a review of the literature on the shortcomings and distortions generated by monetary incentives, see Samuel Bowles and Sandra Polania-Reyes, "Economic Incentives and Social Preferences: Substitutes or Complements?," *Journal of Economic Literature* 50, no. 2 (2012): 368–425, and Viviana A. Zelizer, *The Social Meaning of Money: Pin Money, Paychecks, Poor Relief, and Other Currencies* (Princeton, NJ: Princeton University Press, 1996).

16. Edgar Schein, *Process Consultation Revised* (Englewood Cliffs, NJ: Prentice Hall, 1999); Edgar Schein, *Helping: How to Offer, Give, and Receive Help* (San Francisco, CA: Barrett-Koehler, 2009); Edgar Schein, *Organizational Culture and Leadership* (San Francisco: Jossey-Bass, 2010); and Rahul Oka, "Coping with the Refugee Wait: The Role of Consumption, Normalcy, and Dignity in Refugee Lives at Kakuma, Kenya," *American Anthropologist* 116, no. 1 (2015): 1–15.

17. John A. List, "Field Experiments: A Bridge between Lab and Naturally Occurring Data," *The B.E. Journal of Economic Analysis and Policy* 6, no. 2 (2006); and John A. List, "The Behavioralist Meets the Market: Measuring Social Preferences and Reputation Effects in Actual Transactions," *Journal of Political Economy* 114, no. 1 (2006): 1–37.

18. Omar Al-Ubaydli and John A. List, "On the Generalizability of Experimental Results in Economics," in *Methods of Modern Experimental Economics*, ed. G. Frechette and A. Schotter (Oxford: Oxford University Press, 2013).

19. John A. List, "Why Economists Should Conduct Field Experiments and 14 Tips for Pulling One Off," *Journal of Economic Perspectives* 25, no. 3 (2011): 3–16.

20. Sina Fichtel, *"What Is Beautiful Is Good": Impact of Employee Attractiveness on Market Success* (Munich: FGM-Verl, 2009), and John Derek Greenwood, "Role-Playing as an Experimental Strategy in Social Psychology," *European Journal of Social Psychology* 13, no. 1 (2006): 235–54.

21. Greenberg and Eskew, "The Role of Role Playing."

22. See, for example the study by Esther Duflo, Pascaline Dupas, and Michael Kremer, "Education, HIV, and Early Fertility: Experimental Evidence from Kenya," *American Economic Review* 105, no. 9 (2015): 2757–97.

23. All other estimations are available upon request.

CONTRIBUTORS

Paolo G. Carozza (editor) is professor of law and concurrent professor of political science in addition to serving as director for the Kellogg Institute for International Studies at the University of Notre Dame.

Clemens Sedmak (editor) is professor of social ethics at the Keough School of Global Affairs and concurrent professor at the Center for Social Concerns, University of Notre Dame.

Maria Sophia Aguirre is ordinary professor of economics in the Department of Economics at the Catholic University of America.

Simona Beretta is professor of international economics at the Università Cattolica del Sacro Cuore in Milan, Italy.

Matt Bloom is associate professor of management and principal investigator for the Wellbeing at Work Project at the University of Notre Dame.

Catherine E. Bolten is associate professor of anthropology and peace studies at the University of Notre Dame.

Luigino Bruni is professor of political economy at the Libera Università Maria SS. Assunta (LUMSA) in Rome, Italy.

Dominic Burbidge is research director at the University of Oxford and director of the Canterbury Institute.

Martha Cruz-Zuniga is associate clinical professor in the Department of Economics at the Catholic University of America.

Séverine Deneulin is associate professor of international development at the University of Bath and an affiliate scholar of the Laudato Si' Research Institute, Campion Hall, University of Oxford.

Robert A. Dowd, C.S.C., is associate professor of political science and concurrent associate professor at the Keough School of Global Affairs in addition to serving as director of the Ford Family Program in Human Development Studies and Solidarity at the University of Notre Dame.

Tania Groppi is professor of public law at the University of Siena in Siena, Italy.

Deirdre Guthrie is research advisor and translator for the Wellbeing Project based in Paris, France; owner of Spore Studios Consulting; and director of Wellbeing Programs at Fernwood Botanical Gardens.

Elizabeth Hlabse is a research project manager at the Kellogg Institute for International Studies, University of Notre Dame.

Travis J. Lybbert is professor of agricultural and resource economics at the University of California, Davis.

Paul Perrin is director of monitoring and evaluation at the Notre Dame Initiative for Global Development and concurrent associate professor of the practice at the Keough School of Global Affairs, University of Notre Dame.

Giada Ragone is a junior research fellow in constitutional law at the Università degli Studi di Milano in Milan, Italy.

Steve Reifenberg is associate professor of the practice of international development and co-director of the Integration Lab at the Keough School of Global Affairs, University of Notre Dame.

The Reverend Monsignor Martin Schlag is the Alan W. Moss Endowed Chair for Catholic Social Thought, professor of Catholic studies and ethics and business law, and director of the John A. Ryan Institute at the University of St. Thomas, St. Paul and Minneapolis, Minnesota.

Ilaria Schnyder von Wartensee is research assistant professor with the Ford Family Program in Human Development Studies and Solidarity at the University of Notre Dame.

Lorenza Violini is professor of constitutional law at the Università degli Studi di Milano in Milan, Italy.

Bruce Wydick is professor of economics at Westmont College near Santa Barbara, California, and at the University of San Francisco in addition to acting as distinguished research affiliate of the Kellogg Institute, University of Notre Dame.

INDEX

accompaniment
  and CES, 21, 247–48, 249, 250
  and community health worker
    (CHW) model, 248
  in international organizational prac-
    tice, 249, 259n.11
  as key concept, 8, 12, 13, 17
  relationship to dignity, 7, 12, 13, 17,
    20–21, 247, 248–49, 251–53, 254,
    257–58, 281–82
  relationship to human development,
    247
  role of empathy in, 21, 247, 251, 252,
    257, 285
  role of listening in, 21, 247, 251, 252,
    257
  role of mutuality in, 251, 252, 257
ActionAid's Mission Statement, 165
Action Contre la Faim, "About Us"
  Statement, 165
Acumen, 134n.3
Adorno, Theodor
  "Education after Auschwitz," 1–2
  on efficiency, 1–2
  on the manipulative character, 1–2
adverse circumstances, dignity under,
  15, 34, 40–42
Afghanistan, Donini report, 174
African, Caribbean and Pacific (ACP)
  development countries, 235
Agamben, Giorgio, 274–75

agape (Christian love), 208
agency
  and capability approach, 48, 49, 52,
    58n.13
  Catholic vs. Protestant women
    regarding, 18, 145, 146–47,
    149–56
  as component of hope, 140, 141, 142,
    143, 155
  definitions of, 48, 51, 109
  of economic agents, 321
  and efficiency, 1–2
  and freedom, 48, 49, 61, 64–67
  "how" dimension, 10–11, 72–73
  inner drivers of human decisions/
    choices, 61, 63–64
  as intersubjective, 15, 51–53
  in Judeo-Christianity, 143–47
  Pereira on, 51–52
  and relationality, 51–53
  relationship to authenticity, 108–9
  relationship to beauty, 74
  relationship to development, 64–67,
    72, 75
  relationship to dignity, 15, 34–35, 47,
    53, 108–9, 140, 143, 144, 200
  relationship to God's will, 142, 143,
    144, 145, 147, 158n.27
  relationship to love, 74
  relationship to passivity, 16, 88–89,
    91, 93–96

political conditions, 83–85, 92
public participation in, 84
Siaya County, 83, 84, 85
Taita Taveta, 84–85
Knight, Kelvin, 94
Kretzmer, David, 231
Kundera, Milan, on memory, 39

Lamberty, Kim, 249
Lancet Commission for Health Profes-
    sions Education, 260n.20
L'Arche, 11, 12, 15
    celebrations at, 306
    "Charter of the Communities of
        L'Arche", 298–99, 312nn.6, 7
    and common humanity, 299,
        305–6
    as community of faith, 22, 307, 309,
        310–11
    "Constitution of the International
        Federal of L'Arche Communities",
        312nn.5, 7
    core member-assistant relationship as
        center of, 305–6
    core values of, 298–301
    and dignity, 298
    as experience of encounter, 302–5,
        308
    as experience of transformation,
        303–5
    human development and community
        in, 298
    "Identity and Mission Statement",
        298, 312n.7
    literature on, 313n.18
    as mystery, 300–301
    new challenges to, 310–11
    and patience, 306
    ritual of the mutual washing of feet
        at, 307–8, 316n.53
    as sign, 308–9, 311
    and spiritual life, 300, 311

Vanier as founder, 22, 108, 298
and vulnerability, 303, 305, 306, 307,
    308–9
Lecouteux, Guilhem, 79n.29
legal discourse on human dignity, 20,
    229–30, 231–32
Lévi-Strauss, Claude, on cooking, 33
liberation theology, 21, 142, 147, 249
Lisbon Treaty, 231
listening, 7, 8, 40, 55, 56–57, 84
    as changing the listener, 89, 94–96
    deep listening, 21, 247, 251, 252,
        257
    and passivity, 9, 16, 89, 91
    relationship to leadership, 85
List, John, 322
local knowledge, 8–9
Locke, John, 224n.1
Lomé I Convention, 235
longitudinal studies, 132–33
love, 73–75, 81n.44
    for God, 34, 145, 156
    of neighbor, 34, 145, 156
Luke 1:37, 143
Lutheran World Relief
    and accompaniment, 249
    Vision Statement, 167
Luther, Martin, 208

M&E. See monitoring and evaluation
MacFarlane-Barrow, Magnus, 29–30,
    36–37, 42
MacIntyre, Alasdair, 193
Macklin, Ruth, on dignity, 170
Mainardi, Diogo, 38
Malawi, Mary's Meals, 29–30, 36, 42
Mann, Jonathan, on dignity, 170
Margalit, Avishai
    on blindness to the human aspect, 2
    on humiliation and violations of
        human dignity, 5
Maritain, Jacques, 231–32

CPSIA information can be obtained
at www.ICGtesting.com
Printed in the USA
LVHW081303261020
669841LV00007B/77